MW00460431

"We act in these matters in the right, as a matter of high principle. We act out of the integrity and conviction of our most deep-founded beliefs. If we permit ourselves to be tempted by narrow self-interest and vain ambition, if we barter our beliefs for short-term advantage, who will listen when we claim to speak for conscience, and who will contend that our words deserve to be heeded? We must speak out on major world issues, courageously, openly and honestly, and in blunt terms of right and wrong. If we yield to blandishments or threats, if we compromise when no honorable compromise is possible, our influence will be sadly diminished and our prestige woefully prejudiced and weakened. Let us not deny our ideals or sacrifice our right to stand as the champions of the poor, the ignorant, the oppressed everywhere. The acts by which we live and the attitudes by which we act must be clear beyond question. Principles alone can endow our deeds with force and meaning. Let us be true to what we believe, that our beliefs may serve and honor us."
- Emperor Haile Selassie I

Seventy Years Accomplished

The Second Coming

Written By

Omar TobiJah

All inquiries should be forwarded to:
Divine Child Publications
PO Box 2934
Norcross, Ga 30091
(404) 855-6791
www.divinechildpublications.com

ISBN: 978-0-9793619-1-3

Library of Congress Catalog Card No. 2008907670

"In the first year of his reign I Daniel understood by books the number of the years, whereof the word of the Lord came to Jeremiah the prophet, that he would accomplish seventy years in the desolations of Jerusalem" (Daniel 9:2).

Illustrations

Frontispiece Emperor Haile Selassie I ii

Kenton Helem 29

Omar TobiJah. 100

Troy Prince 134

Primus St. Croix 214, 300

Contents

Introduction 1
By: Primus St. Croix

Providence... 6
By: Kenton Helem

Seventy Years Accomplished in Babylon................................ 45
By: Omar TobiJah

For it is Written 123
By: Troy Prince

The Letters of Primus Saint Croix 143
By: Primus St. Croix

Conclusion 353
By: Primus St. Croix

Bibliography 356

Introduction

Faith comes from the heart. It is a personal conviction and drive that motivates a person to replicate their higher self in all activities. Good and evil therefore cannot abide simultaneously; the servants of sin do not practice righteousness and those who are pious abhor iniquity. No one can serve two masters. Therefore let your yes mean yes and your no mean no; be true to your word. If you have devoted yourself to following God then you must abdicate from all wrongdoings. Why do the things that you are ashamed of? The wages of sin is death but the gift of God is life eternal through Christ.

When the heathen said to turn stone into bread,[1] this means to observe a new sabbath because the devil is attempting to change time and law. Jesus said that man shall not live by bread alone but by every word of the Lord. God's Prophet commanded the people to praise the Almighty on the seventh day; this signifies worshipping the true God Emperor Haile Sellassie The First. There are many who have been deceived into worshipping on the wrong day, the new sabbath, which is the first day of the week. This means that the people have been led astray from knowing and accepting the living God of Ethiopia: His Imperial Majesty Emperor Haile Sellassie The First, who proved to be the Almighty Power of the Trinity when he established his theocratic government upon the Throne of David. If we do not accept this gospel then we are not keeping God's commandments holy by observing the

---

[1] Matthew 4:3

Sabbath day. In Mark 12:29-30 it says, "Jesus answered, The first of all the commandments is Hear, O Israel; The Lord our God is one Lord: And you shall love the Lord your God with all your heart, and with all your soul, and with all your mind, and with all your strength; this is the first command-ment." To worship on the first day is sin when God said to praise him on the seventh day; this means that it is sin not to believe in Emperor Haile Sellassie The First when God was manifest in the flesh.[2] The pope is cursing the people with his dogma but Christ and his disciples have rest (salvation) because they know who God is. It said in Romans 6:23 that the wages of sin is death. Therefore the people who practice a false religion are separate from God, they are spiritually dead but salvation comes from Christ to the glory of God Emperor Haile Sellassie The First. Israel has to keep the law according to the commandments of the Lord. The earth is defiled because they do not observe the law but the spiritual sense will hold Israel and give them hope. Haile Sellassie The First reigned with the titles King of Kings and Lord of Lords so that the world would take notice and praise him. Nothing can be done to erase this history even if certain people seek to destroy the truth. On November 2, 1930, in Ethiopia, the Lord established his kingdom on earth. People often think that the Bible is referring to ancient times but the scrip-tures are centered on God Emperor Haile Sellassie The First.

We have evidence of the Lord's presence therefore nothing can refute this gospel. Jesus said that if we were of God then we would praise Haile Sellassie The First (John 8:42-47). Why is this so hard for some people to understand? It is because they have crucified (rejected) Jesus, for Christ kept us in the name of his Father.[3] The Messiah did not talk about himself but the Lord of hosts who sent him.[4] If we do not accept the testimony of Christ then we are follow-ing satan. The pope, who has the berth of ungodliness, has chosen to fight God by creating a culture of miseducation and paganism so that he can lead the world astray. His Majesty has always encouraged us to read and study the Bible so that we may understand the truth. Now who can say that Haile Sellassie The First is not God? He has fulfilled the prophecy so why would you not believe the manifestation of righteousness? It is because you are of the devil and the lusts of your father you will do. The pope will not praise Haile Sellassie The First because he is a deceiver and abode not in the truth because his church

---

[2] 1 Timothy 3:16
[3] John 17:6
[4] Hebrews 5:5

would fall if he accepted the true Christ. He has made up his own doctrine which is not according to the teachings of the Bible. The vatican is the leader of all spiritual wickedness: MYSTERY, BABYLON THE GREAT, THE MOTHER OF HARLOTS AND ABOMINATIONS OF THE EARTH (Revelation 17:4-18). "Jesus answered, If I honor myself, my honor is nothing: it is my Father who honors me; of whom you say, that he is your God. Yet you have not known him; but I know him: and if I should say, I know him not, I shall be a liar like unto you: but I know him, and keep his sayings" (John 8:54-55). In this the children of God are revealed along with the children of the devil. Whosoever denies Emperor Haile Sellassie The First, is not of God (1 John 3:10). By accepting the testimony of God's Prophet we can see God in the flesh; thus curing the blind. He that believes not has made the Lord into a liar because he believes not the record that God established in Ethiopia (1 John 5:10). All who do not accept His Majesty are lost and all unrighteousness is death. Whoever believes in Emperor Haile Sellassie The First does not sin, but keeps himself away from corrupt philosophies so that he is not led astray. We are of God because we follow his Word and the whole world lies in wickedness for they are contrary to the promises. We know that the Son of God is come, and he has given us an understanding, so that we may know that Emperor Haile Sellassie The First is the Almighty. This is the true God and these are the eternal edicts of the Lord's kingdom (1 John 5:17-21).

False prophets will preach that Haile Sellassie The First is not the Almighty but Christ has testified that he is the living God. They speak against His Majesty and promise salvation when they themselves are not saved. Through dishonest exhortations they allure and deceive but those who praise Haile Sellassie The First can overcome their treachery. After God established his kingdom on November 2, 1930, if we are to turn away from him then we will not escape condemnation. The commandments of God are not a burden; by believing in Haile Sellassie The First we inherit salvation. Do not take the name of the Lord in vain because you will not be found guiltless. Haile Sellassie The First is the light and strength for all humanity, who can fail in him? Our enemies are easily overcome, even if an army should encamp against us, we shall not fear; we will be confident in war. Our desire is to dwell in the house of the Lord because in the time of trouble we shall escape. God shall stand with us and our heads shall be lifted up above our enemies. Therefore we will praise Emperor Haile Sellassie The First. We will sing unto him openly. Have mercy on us O Lord and answer us when we call (Psalm 27). The Bible said if you seek then you shall find, therefore search for the Lord.[5] God is the great King of the earth, Governor of the nations, among Israel he is found. Jesus Christ exalted HIM Haile Sellassie The First and we bear witnesses of the gospel. Those who accept the doctrine of Christ are the children of Israel and worthy of forgiveness. The gentiles shall be confused and ashamed at the testimony of the Lord's Prophet. Emperor Haile Sellassie The First completed his work and what he has done shall stand forever; there is only one Savior, the one God. He speaks of righteousness and does what is right. Gather yourselves and worship the Most High Haile Sellassie The First. They have no knowledge who neglect the Emperor. Who is the King of Kings and Lord of Lords? Look to him and be saved all ye ends of the earth, for His Majesty is God, and there is none else.

And it shall come to pass that in the place where it was said, you are not Israel there shall they be called the children of the living God. "For I am not ashamed of the gospel of Christ: for it is the power of God unto salvation to everyone that believes, to the Jew first, and also to the Greek. For therein is the righteousness of God revealed from faith to faith: as it is written, the just shall live by faith. For the wrath of God is revealed from heaven against all ungodliness and unrighteousness of men, who hold the truth in vain. Because that which may be known of God is manifest in them; for God has showed it unto them. For the invisible things of him from the creation of the world are clearly seen, being understood by the things that are made, even his eternal power and Godhead, so that they are without excuse" (Romans 1:16-20). Therefore seeing we have this ministry, we faint not; but have renounced idolatry, never again to handle the word of God deceitfully. For God who commanded the light to shine over darkness, has blessed our hearts, to preach true knowledge unto all men (2 Corinthians 4). We are now knit together in love unto all riches of the full assurance of understanding, to the acknowledgement of the mystery of God, the Father of Jesus Christ. In Haile Sellassie The First are hid all the treasures of wisdom and knowledge. And this I say, lest any man should beguile you with a foreign philosophy. For though I be absent in the flesh, yet am I with you in the spirit, joying and beholding your faith and order in Christ. As you have therefore received Jesus Christ the Lord, so walk in him. Built up and established in the faith, as you have been taught, abounding therein with thanksgiving (Colossians 2:2-7). Let the peace of God rule in your hearts, to the which also you are called in one body, one gospel, and be thankful. Let the word of Christ dwell in you richly in all wisdom and teachings, admonishing

---

[5] Deuteronomy 4:29

one another in psalms and hymns and spiritual songs, singing with grace in your hearts to His Majesty. And whatsoever you do in word or deed, do all in the name of the Lord Jesus, giving thanks to Emperor Haile Sellassie The First, the Eternal Father of Christ (Colossians 3:15-17).

Providence

"Brethren, be not children in understanding: howbeit in malice be ye children, but in understanding be men" (1 Corinthians 14:20).

Greetings in the name of the King of Kings and Lord of Lords, Emperor Haile Selassie The First. I am delighted that we can share in the wisdom and blessings of the Bible. We all must search for the truth, because it is only the truth that can set us free. His Imperial Majesty said, "Any who may wish to profit himself alone from the knowledge given him, rather than serve others through the knowledge he has gained from learning, is betraying knowledge and rendering it worthless."[1] Therefore it is important to teach those who are willing to learn and to create a platform for those who want to know God to be able to inherit the promises.

It is evident that the masses do not understand the message conveyed in the holy scriptures. The sacred books teach us that God is our salvation, our hope of a better world, our Redeemer, the Holy One, the Lord of hosts, Jehovah, Allah, Vishnu, Krishna, Yahweh, the All-seeing, All-knowing, Almighty; but these are all epithets, they are referring to the Supreme Being who created the universe. It is only when you acknowledge the person whom these titles belong to, that you can then understand the scriptures.

---

[1] The Selected Speeches of His Imperial Majesty Haile Selassie I, page 46

Zechariah 14:9 said, "The Lord shall be King over all the earth, in that day there shall be One Lord and his name One." The One Power of the Trinity - Emperor Haile Selassie The First, He carries the hopes and aspirations of the downtrodden to overthrow the evil system which oppresses humanity. Scholars remember RasTafari as an immortal historical figure whose wise counsel could have prevented World War II from occurring if the League of Nations would have only given heed to His prophetic instructions when He declared, "In December, 1935, the Council made it quite clear that its feelings were in harmony with those of hundreds of millions of people who, in all parts of the world, had protested against the proposal to dismember Ethiopia. It was constantly repeated that this was not merely a conflict between the Italian Government and the League of Nations, and that is why I personally refused all proposals to my personal advantage made to me by the Italian Government, if only I would betray my people and the Covenant of the League of Nations. I was defending the cause of all small people who are threatened with aggression."[2] An indefatigable worker, He initiated Ethiopia's first written Constitution, modernized His country and is the pillar of its unity, He also was an outstanding international statesman and the leading figure in the preservation of peace in Africa; being the founding Father of the Organization of African Unity. But His Imperial Majesty was more than just the Father of modern Africa, He also guided and steered the european powers into adopting better diplomatic policies by challenging them to follow the principles of collective security and international morality. He compelled the United Nations to fight poverty, colonialism, disease, and racism. Haile Selassie The First called for the surcease of the arms race and for those funds to be reallocated towards education. He told the world leaders that there is no justification for war. He exhorted the rich countries to assume the responsibility of helping the poor countries to develop; by stating, "The perpetuation of the status quo will not, in the long run, serve even the narrow interest of the few, and it will inevitably prove disastrous to the world economic situation. It is, therefore, to be ardently hoped that the governments of the economically advanced countries will rise to this challenge and join in a concerted effort to alleviate the world's economic ills which are but the root and cause of many other international problems."[3] There is no end to the good works which RasTafari has accomplished both politically and spiritually. He was given the title "Defender

---

[2] Ibid, page 312
[3] Ibid, page 159

of the Faith" for His efforts in uniting the different Christian denominations and further demonstrated true piety by not rendering evil for evil after Italy sought to commit genocide in Ethiopia. The Italians systematically annihilated as many lives as they could through the use of mustard gas, which is an outlawed agent. Men, women, and children were all brutally murdered in hellacious proportions, even the priests and clergymen of the church were not spared, buildings were burnt and artifacts were looted in an effort to erase the entire Ethiopian civilization. Haile Selassie The First was the only one who could safeguard Ethiopia's independence under those circumstances. Italy had the biggest and most modern military at that time whereas the Ethiopians were fighting with outdated machinery and were severely outgunned. These were not the same conditions as the Battle of Adowa, neither was a force of this magnitude ever inflicted upon the Ethiopians before, including the successful British campaign in 1868 against Emperor Tewodros II and Ahmed Gran's brutal crusade in the 16th Century. His Imperial Majesty defeated Mussolini by attaining international support and upon returning to His throne, He forgave the Italian people because He knew that they were the victims of fascist disinformation, He told them that they could stay in Ethiopia if they would help Him to rebuild, and instructed His people not to harm them. Haile Selassie The First was called the conscience of the world because He always did the right thing. The League of Nations had to be discarded due to their incompetency in abandoning The Emperor during this campaign. They mocked and jeered Him when He called for collective security in Geneva but in the end it was Mussolini who was put to shame and overthrown. They called Him a coward for going into exile but in the end He demonstrated how the ink from a scholar is worth more than the blood of a martyr. His speeches are eternal documents that give the best advice on how to avoid conflict and solve the problems of the world. Deuteronomy 4:32-35 says, "For ask now of the days that are past, which were before thee, since the day that God created man upon the earth, and ask from the one side of heaven unto the other, whether there has been any such thing as this great thing is, or hath been heard like it? Did ever people hear the voice of God speaking out of the midst of the fire, as you have heard and live? Or has God assayed to go and take him a nation from the midst of another nation, by temptations, by signs, and by wonders, and by war, and by a mighty hand, and by a stretched out arm, and by great terrors, according to all that the LORD your God did for you in Egypt (oppression) before your eyes? Unto you it was shown, so that you will know that the LORD he is God; there is none else beside him." The signs from heaven are those from the

King of Kings and Lord of Lords, since the beginning of time there has never been anyone who reigned on earth with those titles except for Emperor Haile Selassie The First. This was done so that you will know that He alone is God, He is the first and the last person that will ever bear the name of the Most High. His Imperial Majesty set a perfect example to follow in all aspects; there is no one who can be compared to him.

It is a fact that Emperor Haile Selassie The First is the Almighty God. Those who say He is not, do so because they are either lost on the mysteries of the Bible or they don't know the history of His Imperial Majesty. The Bible teaches us that God is the Savior of the world, therefore the blessings are upon those who can understand the parables: "Great is the mystery of godliness: God was manifested in the flesh, justified in the Spirit, seen of angels, preached unto the Gentiles, believed on in the world, received up into glory" (1 Timothy 3:16). The scriptures teaches us that God physically appeared on earth in the form of a man, we now must wholeheartedly accept this fulfillment. Psalm 87 said the Highest Himself was born in Ethiopia (Zion): this would be Emperor Haile Selassie The First, the wisest and most faithful Ruler of all time. His Imperial Majesty said, "Global peace and security can only be permanently secured if all people of the world pool their resources towards the complete eradication of man's common enemies - ignorance, hunger, and disease."[4] If we would follow the instructions of Emperor Haile Selassie The First then salvation would be achieved in real terms. Isaiah 9:6-7 said, "For unto us a child is born and unto us a son is given, and the government shall be upon his shoulder and his name shall be called Wonderful Counselor, The Mighty God, the Eternal Father, the Prince of Peace." Study these scriptures honestly, these verses are clearly talking about the Eternal Father making His presence known before humanity; it is not referring to Jesus Christ the Son. November 2, 1930, is the day the prophecy of God was revealed. RasTafari was crowned King of Kings and Lord of Lords, Light of the World, Lion of Judah, these are all apocalyptic titles that the Bible illustrates can only be fulfilled by God. This makes the Coronation of Haile Selassie The First, the Sabbath, for this is the Holy Day, the day which the Lord revealed Himself on earth. According to the books of Moses: God spoke to His Prophet in the Mount called Zion, on the Sabbath day; this was to be a sign throughout the world that God is real (Deuteronomy 4:32-35). Hebrew 4:4 said that God spoke in a certain place on the seventh day. Hebrew 12:18-23 conveys that we shall be gathered before God in Mount

---

[4] Ibid, page 499

Zion; this is Ethiopia, the first civilization on earth and the bearers of the Ark of the Covenant. Ethiopia has the oldest and purest religious tradition, the Bible comes from there. Her heritage is envied by the nations which is why fascist Italy was aroused to attack Ethiopia so that they could erase the true history and proclaim the pope to be the vicar of Christ; but God would not let evil triumph.

Study the Bible with an open mind, he who has ears to hear let him hear. Look at the works of His Imperial Majesty objectively and judge for yourself; everything illustrates that He is the Almighty Father. "The LORD is a great God, and a great King above all gods" (Psalm 95:3). Consider how all the religions of the world believe in an invisible god, or paintings and graven images but Jeremiah 10:1-10 exhorts us not to trust in idols, things made with man's hands. We are to trust in the living God, for salvation cannot come through pagan practices. Isaiah 42:8 said that God will not give His glory to graven images. Therefore the paintings and the images that they portray to be Jesus are all fake. Learn about Haile Selassie The First, read all His books and speeches, research the true history and you will see that He is the Most High; because God is invisible only to those who do not believe in Him, He is clearly seen if we accepted the truth. "By faith Enoch was translated that he should not see death; and was not found, because God had translated him: for before his translation he had this testimony, that he pleased God. But without faith it is impossible to please him: for he that comes to God must believe that he is, and that he is a rewarder of them that diligently seek him. By faith he forsook Egypt, not fearing the wrath of the king: for he endured, as seeing him who is invisible" (Hebrew 11:5, 6, 27). The Prophet was able to see God because he had the true faith, not according to the common misinterpretations found throughout the world. The idea that the Lord is invisible is false, only associated with those who are not of God. The message of the Bible says that the Lord is visible to those who believe in Him. "Behold, what manner of love the Father has bestowed on us, that we should be called the sons of God: therefore the world knows us not, because it knew him not. Beloved, now are we the sons of God, and it does not yet appear what we shall be: but we know that, when he shall appear, we shall be like him; for we shall see him as he is. And every man that has this hope in him purifies himself, even as he is pure" (1 John 3:1-3). The sons of God are those who know God, this is the true meaning of Christianity. When the Lord appears, those who will obtain salvation shall accept Him. The prophecy clearly states that God will show His face on earth, the only reason that people cannot see God is because they do not believe in

Haile Selassie The First. "Blessed are the pure in heart: for they shall see God" (Matthew 5:8). It is necessary for people to know the Lord because the idea of God being an invisible supernatural nebulous provides no tangible solutions for the problems plaguing the earth. The Lord knows this better than anyone else, which is why He manifested himself in the flesh to teach people how to create a better world. His Imperial Majesty is the Supreme Being, from Him alone comes Providence, He is the Law of righteousness. It is a contradiction to say that God is the exemplar of all that is good as well as an invisible omnipresent spirit found everywhere. If God was found in all things, He would not have to reveal Himself to mankind. Why would He have to show Himself to the world, if He was already divulged in us? But the Bible cautions us to be aware that the Almighty will appear on earth and set up His Kingdom. "Oh that my words were now written! Oh that they were printed in a book! That they were graven with an iron pen and lead in the rock forever! For I know that my redeemer lives, and that he shall stand at the latter day on the earth: And though after my skin worms destroy this body, yet in my flesh shall I see God: Whom I shall see for myself, and my eyes shall behold, and not another; though my reins be consumed within me" (Job 19:23-27). The promise is for us to see God; this means that you cannot find the Lord in all of nature. God is a specific vessel, He is not found in all things. From God you will learn how to better yourself and how to make the world a better place, that is why He is called the Savior. We cannot learn how to solve the problems of injustice and war from the wind, trees, or animals. If the Lord was in everyone then God would not have to come and save us; because we would already have Him. If God was in everything, then you could not condemn the evil that people do; without also condemning God. The concept of the Lord being in all things, would make it so that you can look to all things for the Lord. There would be no definition of righteousness because everything is God. A murderer would be just the same as a saint because the Lord is in everyone, that would mean that anything goes. People would be free to interpret good and evil according to whatever that wanted it to be because God is everything.

"Then said I, Woe is me! For I am undone; because I am a man of unclean lips, and I dwell in the middle of a people of unclean lips: for my eyes have seen the King, the LORD of hosts" (Isaiah 6:5). If we say that we have seen the King, the LORD of hosts and His name is Emperor Haile Selassie The First, then woe is me, for the people would label us as men of unclean lips. They say that we are liars although everything we proclaim is written in the Bible. Rather than adhering to the message of the Bible they blindly follow worldly ministers who have not the truth in them. They also say that they can feel God which would make the revelation of the Lord not according to knowledge but emotions. Why was the Bible written if God communicates with us telepathically? The descriptions of the Lord were outlined for us to identify Him because God does not operate by supernatural means. "Then Paul stood in the middle of Mars hill, and said, You men of Athens, I perceive that in all things you are too superstitious. For as I passed by, and beheld your devotions, I found an altar with this inscription, TO THE UNKNOWN GOD. Whom therefore you ignorantly worship, him declare I unto you. God that made the world and all things therein, seeing that he is Lord of heaven and earth, dwells not in temples made with hands; Neither is worshipped with men's hands, as though he needed any thing, seeing he gives to all life, and breath, and all things; And has made of one blood all nations of men for to dwell on all the face of the earth, and has determined the times before appointed, and the bounds of their habitation; That they should seek the Lord, if haply they mighty feel after him, and find him, though he be not far from everyone of us: For in him we live, and move, and have our being; as certain also of your own poets have said, For we are also his offspring. For as much then as we are the offspring of God, we ought not to think that the Godhead is like to gold, or silver, or stone, graven by art and man's device. And the times of this ignorance God winked at; but now commands all men everywhere to repent" (Acts 17:22-30). When the Lord shall appear, the message of the Bible takes on a greater meaning. It is only then that you can truly understand the parables. Humanity made up their own interpretation of what they wanted God to be and what they thought the scriptures meant because they could not see God. But after the Lord has manifested Himself before the entire world, we would then have to repent from these false and incorrect doctrines. This understanding only comes through Haile Selassie The First, He fits all the descriptions of God in the scriptures as well as based upon His personal character.

If people think that His Imperial Majesty is not the Almighty because He behaved in a normal manner then their rationale is wanting. God does not use magic because witchcraft is of the devil. When the Lord appears on earth He will follow the honest approach to life; the law of righteousness could only be established based upon these precepts. Genesis 1:26-27 tells us that God created man in His own image and likeness. It is perplexing how many different religious traditions have misinterpreted God to be an invisible spirit yet the Bible, Torah, Quran, Bhagavad Gita, and many other inspired scriptures have clearly foretold that God is a monarch who will manifest Himself on earth.

"Sing praises to God, sing praises: sing praises unto our King, sing praises. For God is the King of all the earth: sing ye praises with understanding. God reigns over the heathen: God sits upon the throne of his holiness" (Psalm 47:6-8). What will we then say, that the scriptures are false? The problem is that we have been programmed to believe in mythology and superstition. Therefore when God comes in human form and lives naturally, this seems unusual. The laws of nature were established by God; it only makes sense if the Lord was perfect for Him to follow the laws that He set up at the beginning of the world. That is why Paul said God has chosen the foolish things of the world to confound the wise (1 Corinthians 1:27). Christ doctrine is reality, simple yet sublime, man cannot comprehend it because they misinterpret it as being supernatural (Acts 17:22-31). If you should conduct a survey of all the religions and their doctrines you will find that they all adhere to pagan principles because they either think that God is an invisible nebulous or they believe in superstition. Both of these tenants are counterfactual but how many of us are brave and wise enough to question these ideas? Did the Bible or any of the great books confirm pagan dogmas? The answer is no. We have been taught from childhood by misguided spiritual guides that heaven is in the sky or that you have to physically die before you see God. However, the holy scriptures do not comply with their doctrine. The Bible said that Jesus is the way and the truth, the teacher of God's law, therefore we should believe Christ when he said, "Swear not at all; neither by heaven: for it is God's throne" (Matthew 5:34). The Bible said that Jehovah will establish His throne in Zion, "Thy kingdom come thy will be done on earth as it is in Heaven" (Matthew 6:10). We therefore are supposed to be looking for God on earth, not in the sky or after we physically die. The scriptures said that God will be manifested on earth and when we accept Him then we will be in heaven for we will know the truth. Religious leaders have been misleading the multitudes and interpreting the scriptures falsely and it is not hard to understand their motives. There are certain high officials who use religion as a means to pacify, brainwash, and control the masses. The vatican is behind this farce, they have went to war in the past against people of different faiths with the intentions of killing those who do not follow their views, unleashing a scourge of darkness on earth. Rome has gained their high position in the world by the most barbaric and cretinous methods; then they have the audacity to call the pontiff "lord god the pope." But God will fight for His people (everyone seeking to live in peace and harmony) and the truth will be established. The Lord fought for us by appearing on earth and establishing righteous principles for all of humanity to emulate. The vatican and their followers (who are of diverse traditions, countries, races, and governments) are against the Bible and actively prevent people from learning the truth about God. That is why they created an idol and proclaimed it to be Jesus. Since Christ has the true testimony of God and the scriptures said that only the Son has seen the Father, and he will reveal him unto his disciples (John 6:45-47, John 15:14-15, John 17:6-8), then it is clear that Rome would only want to bury this prophecy in a graven image because they are of the devil. The Bible said do not make idols (Exodus 20:4), how do you oppose the law of God and then portray yourself to be a Christian; that is deception. The vatican is the harlot that has caused many to stray from the true message of the Bible (Revelation 17:1-6). In the year 2000 a preacher named Primus Saint Croix was arrested for publicly denouncing the doctrine and idols of the Roman Catholic Church. "Now is the judgment of this world: now shall the prince of this world be cast out" (John 12:31). The news reporters stated that Primus testified to the authorities (Frank DeRosa, spokesman for the Catholic Diocese of Brooklyn, NYC Mayor Rudolph Giuliani, the DEA and a private team called the Bias Unit sent directly by the vatican) that Haile Selassie The First is the true and living God. He told them that the pope is the devil who has been misleading the world. Primus warned them that if the world leaders do not follow the principles of His Imperial Majesty then injustice will never end and everyone will suffer. These sayings hold significant weight for those who know the true history of Haile Selassie The First because it is a factual claim to state that His policies will save the world. Primus Saint Croix understood the importance of getting the people to follow RasTafari for He is the only source of salvation; the pope is intent upon oppressing and misleading the world. The testimony which Primus taught us is that Haile Selassie The First is the God and Father of Jesus Christ; these are the true sayings of the Lord. It is written in 2 Peter 1:20-21 that, "No prophecy of the scripture is of any private interpretation, for the prophecy came not in old times by the will of man: but holy men of God spoke as they were moved by the Holy Ghost," therefore we must accept the revelation of the King of Kings and Lord of Lords which took place on November 2, 1930 in Ethiopia, not in antiquity. A little leaven, leaveneth the whole bread; the vatican said Jesus came thousands of years ago, but this theory does not correlate with the message of Christ or the scriptures. How could Jesus show us God thousands of years ago when the only record of the King of Kings and Lord of Lords took place on November 2, 1930? Satan is a liar, you cannot trust the pope. The Bible was written afore time for our learning; the scriptures are not recording the past, they are parables foretelling what is to come.

Yet the vatican teaches the opposite that the Bible is a history book, recording ancient supernatural events; they deliberately misinterpret the scriptures
so that people do not know the true meaning. The testimony of Christ is that
God comes in the flesh or more frankly in human form (John 3:31-34). Many
people have rejected the fact that Emperor Haile Selassie The First is God, not
because He was unrighteous or His philosophy not paramount above all the
other sages and world leaders, but simply because they have not been conditioned to accept the truth. It is a foreign concept to many for God to appear on
earth and live according to the same laws of nature which He established at the
beginning of the universe. But it is time to remove the veil which the devil has
set up that keeps the world blind to their own salvation. The true revelation has
been made known and there are those who behold the Lord in His full glory
and majesty.

It is important that we understand, not only through prophecy but also by
history and experience, that God is the Savior of humanity. For us who have
taken the time to study, we know that there is no one even remotely equal with
Emperor Haile Selassie The First; He is more than worthy to bear the titles
King of Kings and Lord of Lords. His Imperial Majesty said, "The major challenges confronting the world today are two: the preservation of peace and the
betterment of the living conditions of that half of the world which is poor. These
are, of course, mutually interdependent. Without peace, it is futile to talk of
improving man's lot; and without such improvement, the task of guaranteeing
peace is rendered many-fold more difficult."[5] The Bible is a book of prophecy;
it contains the foretelling of God revealing himself on earth to save mankind;
in Psalm 67:1-3 it says, "God be merciful unto us and bless us, And cause your
face to shine upon us, Selah. That your ways may be known on earth, Your salvation among all nations. Let the people praise you, O God; Let all the people
praise you." This means that the only way for the Lord to save the nations is
for Him to shine His face upon us and make His ways known on earth. Haile
Selassie The First stood for justice and equality; He advocated for the rights
of all men to the governing bodies of the world and instructed them to adopt
more humane principles so that peace would finally reign upon earth. But they
refused to listen and as a result the world is still faced with dire calamities.
Romans 1:19-21 said, "For the wrath of God is revealed from heaven against all
ungodliness and unrighteousness of men, who hold the truth in unrighteousness; Because that which may be known of God is manifest in them; for God

---

[5] Ibid, page 167

has showed it to them. For the invisible things of him from the creation of the world are clearly seen, being understood by the things that are made, even his eternal power and Godhead; so that they are without excuse: Because that, when they knew God, they glorified him not as God, neither were thankful; but became vain in their imaginations, and their foolish heart was darkened. Professing themselves to be wise, they became fools, And changed the glory of the incorruptible God into an image made like to corruptible man, and to birds, and four footed beasts, and creeping things. Wherefore God also gave them up to uncleanness through the lusts of their own hearts, to dishonor their own bodies between themselves: Who changed the truth of God into a lie, and worshipped and served the creature more than the Creator, who is blessed forever. Amen." The Bible tells us that God is not invisible, He is clearly seen by those who understand, therefore the people are without excuse for not accepting Haile Selassie The First. The reason they glorified Him not as God is because they misinterpret the Lord to be a supernatural phantasm. They expected Him to walk on clouds, rain fire from the sky, live forever in the flesh, and communicate with us through telepathic means. But the Bible is directing us towards a tangible solution to the problems that we are faced with; not a comic book redemption. It is up to us to follow the perfect example that has been set by Emperor Haile Selassie The First. Just as with the League of Nations, they were given an opportunity to avoid the disasters of World War II but they choose not to because they thought they could get away with evil. His Imperial Majesty said, "Do the people of the world not yet realize that by fighting on until the bitter end I am not only performing my sacred duty to my people but standing guard in the last citadel of collective security? Are they too blind to see that I have my responsibilities to the whole of humanity to face? I must still hold on until my tardy allies appear. And if they never come, then I say prophetically and without bitterness the west will perish."[6] The europeans colonized the entire planet except for Ethiopia, this was the last independent country. If the Italians were successful in their campaign, they would have destroyed the Ark of the Covenant, which signifies that there would be no hope for humanity. When people pray to God, they ask Him to help them in their time of need and there never was a greater threat to global security than under the circumstances in which Emperor Haile Selassie The First arose to defend the cause of all people who are threatened with aggression. If we refuse

---

[6] New York Times, April 30, 1936

to accept His Imperial Majesty, than just as with the League of Nations, we would only be inciting our own demise.

"Thus will I magnify myself, and sanctify myself; and I will be known in the eyes of many nations, and they shall know that I am the LORD" (Ezekiel 38:23). When God Emperor Haile Selassie The First appeared on earth, there was many people who thought that He was a regular person because to them the Lord by definition is supernatural. They thought that He who created the stars, the wind, water, and all life should perform magic tricks and defy logic. Because His Imperial Majesty did not perform any supernatural miracles, He therefore could not be God. But to this Emperor Haile Selassie The First said, "The Lord, who is above all creations, although possessing the power to order everything according to His will, has nevertheless wished to establish the rule of law and to subject it to all creation."[7] This means that God can do anything but He will not do everything. He created the laws of nature, the law of gravity, the law of matter, the law of entropy, the laws of reproduction, etc.; how can the Lord be defined as a perfect ruler without flaw if He does not follow His own tenants? God does not have to deviate from His operation to prove who He is. Therefore Emperor Haile Selassie The First accomplished everything through natural means because this is the perfect example. God was correct from the beginning so therefore He would not have to change anything regarding how things work when He reveals Himself to mankind. Furthermore to also believe that God can break his own commandments would leave the door open for the Lord to be a rapist or a murderer because He could deviate from being good as He could do anything, there would be no boundaries or standards for His actions. But God has established certain rules for Himself and everyone else, for which He chiefly adheres to all of His precepts because that would be the only way for Him to be justified as being perfect. The Lord is righteous therefore He must adhere to His principles; with God all things are possible within the confines of the law, for it is impossible for him to lie and go against his own order. "Archbishop Kyrillos, with his hand upon the Holy Bible, poses a series of questions to the Emperor to which the latter replies in the affirmative, swearing that he will fulfill his duties as ruler. Are you willing to defend the permanent laws established by the Orthodox Church of Alexandria which, from the time of the Holy Kings, Abraha and Asbaha, have been in existence and in force? Do you pledge that during your reign you will handle the populace with justice, kindness and integrity? ***Will Your Majesty***

---

[7] The Selected Speeches of His Imperial Majesty Haile Selassie I, page 388

be under the obligations of the laws that Your Majesty established, and will you protect your Empire and people in accordance with the codes of law you will have established? With his hand on the Holy Bible, His Imperial Majesty pledges his word of honor that he will be the righteous monarch demanded of himself, kisses the Bible with a strikingly obvious gesture of sincerity and solemnity, and then affixes his signature to a book in which is recorded all the words of the oath. Then the Emperor sits back on his throne."[8]

The promise of the Bible is that we shall see God. The Lord will teach us the true definition of all that is good and establish the principles necessary for our survival and development; this was fulfilled by Haile Selassie The First. His Imperial Majesty said, "As the price of honesty will be paid to the blessed sons of God so shall We lead Our people gradually to honest gain and prosperity. Honesty means not to oppress anybody and deny him his deserved share. It does not mean being irresponsible or conceited and dictatorial. We, on Our part, will never cease to eliminate conceitedness, oppression, subversion, and corruption in order to maintain peace and national security."[9] Therefore while the concept of God being a supernatural invisible nebulous sounds appealing because it is popular, the end result of this idea is completely unprofitable. Humanity needs a Wise Counselor, somebody who will lead by example and teach us how to live righteously, a Prime Mover. These qualities have been exemplified by Emperor Haile Selassie The First. His Imperial Majesty said, "Leaders are people who raise the standard by which they judge themselves - and by which they are willing to be judged. The goal chosen, the objective selected, the requirements imposed, are not merely for their followers alone."[10] The Almighty would therefore have to follow His own tenants; whereas the supernatural is an unreal concept for which we have no evidence of its existence. The laws of nature were created by God, therefore He must adhere to them. November 2, 1930, is the fulfillment of prophecy, when Haile Selassie The First was crowned with the titles of God (1 John 3:1-3); anyone can research these events and prove its validity. "This is the day which the LORD has made, we will rejoice in it and be glad" (Psalm 118:24). True faith does not rest in superstition because faith is the substance of things hoped for, the evidence of things not seen (Hebrews 11:1-6). God made man in His image (Genesis 1:26-27), therefore it is absurd to think that God cannot appear on

---

[8] Talbot, David Abner, The Silver Jubilee, page 27
[9] The Selected Speeches of His Imperial Majesty Haile Selassie I, page 393
[10] Ibid, page 14

earth. All of the religious prophecies found in all sacred texts indicate that the Lord will manifest Himself before the nations. The most logical way to validate the existence of God is through proof of His existence and November 2, 1930 is the means by which He has chosen to prove His divinity. The concept of the supernatural prevents people from accepting the revelation because they are looking for something to transpire that will never occur. Exodus 20 warned us not to worship idolatry, for the Lord is a jealous God. It is for this reason the preacher Primus Saint Croix broke the graven images in the year 2000 (Deuteronomy 12:1-4), in the heart of New York City, where all kindreds and nationalities live because the whole world needs to know that His Imperial Majesty is the Almighty. "And it shall come to pass in that day, that Tyre shall be forgotten seventy years, according to the days of one king: after the end of seventy years shall Tyre sing as a harlot. Take a harp, go about the city, thou harlot that hast been forgotten; make sweet melody, sing many songs, that thou may be remembered. And it shall come to pass after the end of seventy years, that the LORD will visit Tyre, and she shall turn to her hire, and shall commit fornication with all the kingdoms of the world upon the face of the earth. And her merchandise and her hire shall be holiness to the LORD: it shall not be treasured nor laid up; for her merchandise shall be for them that dwell before the LORD, to eat sufficiently, and for durable clothing" (Isaiah 23:15-18). The religious world has the incorrect interpretation of the scriptures therefore they have been stripped of their spiritual inheritance. The time has arrived for the true principles of righteousness to be established because God has sent forth His Son to give us the proper understanding of the scriptures.

We must honor the man who opened the door and made it possible for us to understand the mysteries of godliness in the brightness of a pure light. This man, Primus Saint Croix, was arrested in the year 2000, seventy years after His Imperial Majesty's Coronation, for denouncing the falsehood of the vatican authority (babylon the harlot rome). He broke the idols of the beast to demonstrate to the world that wickedness must be destroyed (Deuteronomy 12:1-5). Primus told the people of New York City (where all kindreds and tongues are present) to put their trust in Haile Selassie The First, the only true and just God, and to renounce their false teachings (Jeremiah 10:1-14). "What say I then? that the idol is anything, or that which is offered in sacrifice to idols is anything? But I say, that the things which the Gentiles sacrifice, they sacrifice to devils, and not to God: and I would not that ye should have fellowship with devils. Ye cannot drink the cup of the Lord, and the cup of devils: ye cannot be partakers of the Lord's table, and of the table of devils" (1 Corinthians

10:19-21). The Bible warns us that Satan is a liar and he comes to deceive the world through idolatry and graven images (Revelation 12:9-17). But RasTafari loves us so He rose up a Prophet to save humanity by exposing that man of perdition, the pope, whose entire dogma is false (2 Thessalonians 2:1-10), and to declare to the people that Emperor Haile Selassie The First is the God of the Bible (1 John 5:20-21). John 3:16 said, "For God so loved the world he sent his only begotten son, that whosoever believeth in him shall not perish but have everlasting life." This eternal life does not mean to never physically die; it is referring to knowing who is the living God and following His messenger (John 17:2-3).

The prophecy of the seventy years is referring to the period from November 2, 1930, to the year 2000 when Primus Saint Croix blew the trumpet. Concerning this sign Jeremiah 29:10 says, "For thus saith the LORD, that after seventy years be accomplished at Babylon I will perform my good word toward you, in causing you to return to this place. For I know the thoughts I have toward you, saith the LORD, thoughts of peace, and not of evil, to give you an expected end." God The Father appearing on earth already demonstrates that the truth has been made manifest but the only one who would be able to explain this revelation properly is the Prophet Jesus Christ. The destruction of graven images signifies the abolishment of false religious principles; this is the sign of the coming of the Messiah. Primus Saint Croix preached the lawful message of Haile Selassie The First because he accepted God and the Bible as it is, without adding his own beliefs into the testimony. Deuteronomy 18:15-18 says that God put His word into the mouth of Christ to "Proclaim the acceptable year of the LORD and the day of vengeance of our God (November 2, 1930); to comfort all that mourn" (Isaiah 61:1-2). This is how Haile Selassie The First of Zion, the Holy One of Israel, visited us again in these perilous times; He sent forth His Prophet whose glorious gospel is the image of God because only Christ preached the correct doctrine of His Imperial Majesty. Primus knew the true Word because he did as the scriptures told him to do; it is now up to us all to follow in the footsteps of the Prophet. This does not mean to take a hammer and to break statues that are in front of churches, we must deny all inaccurate principles which prevent us from adhering to the instructions of Emperor Haile Selassie The First. His Imperial Majesty taught us the precise path towards liberation; all we have to do is follow His principles. "God hath spoken once, twice have I heard this; that power belongs unto God" (Psalm 62:11). God has spoken once means that the Almighty was manifest in the flesh, Haile Selassie The First was a perfect ruler who reigned as King of Kings and Lord of Lords; there is no one else for us to look to for our salvation. November 2, 1930, in Ethiopia is the only historical record of a government being established on earth with the titles of the Most High. Twice have I heard this means that after seventy years Primus Saint Croix, the Prophet of God, preached that His Imperial Majesty must be worshipped and emulated because He is the only genuine liberator of mankind. Primus invoked the name of Emperor Haile Selassie The First and put us in remembrance of Him because power belongs unto God, only He can save the world. "To fulfill the word of the LORD by the mouth of Jeremiah, until the land had enjoyed her Sabbaths: for as long as she lay desolate she kept Sabbath, to fulfill three-score and ten years" (2 Chronicles 36:21). The coming of God and Christ according to the seventy year prophecy is also foretold in Exodus 4:8-9, "And it shall come to pass, if they will not believe thee, neither hearken to the voice of the first sign, that they will believe the voice of the latter sign. And it shall come to pass, if they will not believe also these two signs, neither hearken unto thy voice, that thou shalt take of the water of the river, and pour it upon the dry land: and the water which thou takest out of the river shall become blood upon the dry land." These two immutable things are the Father who was revealed on November 2, 1930, in Ethiopia, and his Son who was affirmed in the year 2000; we must accept His Majesty and His messenger, on this parable the entire prophecy rests.

Being able to identify who God is and who His Prophet is, will allow us to analyze the Bible from the correct point of view and interpret the scriptures properly. Those who are unable to accept the fulfillment of the revelation due to their own unbelief, are left in the dark to make precarious assumptions and invalid interpretations of the scriptures. One of the most common distortions of the Bible is the theory which says that Jesus is God. This idea originated from people who do not know who Christ is, they formulated a doctrine based upon verses that are taken out of context which if placed within the framework of the entire prophecy would contradict itself because it is false. Now there are some scriptures where Jesus is referenced with the characteristics of God but this association is based upon him being the representative of the LORD. Ephesians 3:9 and Colossians 1:16 says that God created all things by Jesus Christ, then in Genesis 1:26 it states, "God said, Let us make man in our image." This does not mean that both God and Christ are the Almighty because in Deuteronomy 6:4 it says, "Hear, O Israel: The LORD our God is one LORD." It is not a coherent postulate to think that two different people are the same entity. If two separate individuals, the Father and the Son, are both referenced as "creating" man (let "us" make man in our image), then this is not describing the physical conception of the universe. The gospel of Christ is the true message of salvation; he properly explained how Haile Selassie The First is the Almighty, according to the scriptures. We are made in the image of God when we accept the Messiah's testimony concerning the King of Glory. You will be a "man" when you submit unto the LORD and accept his ordinances; the people have left their natural use for that which is unseemly by neglecting the Creator. Christ beckoned us all to be one with God as he and his Father are one (John 17:21-22); this means to accept the divinity of Haile Selassie The First. Jesus being one with God does not mean that they are equal because he later stated that the Father is greater than he is (John 14:28). The power which Christ possessed, he gave unto his disciples; which is the Word. In John 1:14 it says, "And the Word was made flesh, and dwelt among us, and we beheld his glory, the glory of the only begotten of the Father, full of grace and truth;" this is the message of salvation. Christ said that the Word which you hear is not his but the Father's which sent him (John 14:24) also in Deuteronomy 18:18-19 it says that God put His Word into the mouth of His Prophet Jesus. Therefore when you read that the Word is God in John 1:1, Christ bearing this message also is representative of God's presence because his purpose is to glorify the Almighty. Jesus carrying the Word does not mean that he is God because that would contradict the entire prophecy; Jesus further stated in John 7:16-18 that if you knew the doctrine then you would know that the Word is pertaining to the Father and not Christ. The depiction is that of the LORD giving His message to the Prophet, not of Christ being God and preaching about himself. In Hebrews 5:5 it says that Jesus did not speak about himself because the Word appertains to the Father not the Son; God and Christ are two separate individuals. Jesus is the messenger of the LORD, the Word was put in him to preach the message of salvation unto the masses that Emperor Haile Selassie The First is the Almighty. Therefore in Revelation 17:14, Revelation 1:8, Hebrews 1:8, etc., it describes the oneness of Christ with God which does not mean that Jesus is the Father. Christ is the express image of the LORD, which denotes that only through him can you get the true knowledge of God. Jesus is depicted with the attributes of the Almighty only in the sense that he is the mediator between God and man, in order to know the Father you must go through the Son. This is the Kingdom of Zion, Christ did not preach of another administration other than that of Emperor Haile Selassie The First, therefore his portrayal should be of that which he represents and died for. There is no other way to understand the relationship between the Father and the Son; the only way that the Bible will make sense is if you know the actual people whom the scriptures are referring to.

Now lets see who the apostles of Christ are, remember "Many will say to me in that day, Lord, Lord have we not prophesied in thy name? and in thy name have cast out devils? and in thy name done many wonderful works? And then will I profess unto them I never knew you: depart from me ye that work iniquity" (Matthew 7:22-23). Therefore be not dismayed when they say, "Selassie is not God, he is dead and gone, nobody can see God," for surely the Bible said, "Not that any man hath seen the Father, save he which is of God, he hath seen the Father" (John 6:46). The promises of God are reserved in Christ the messenger for those to whom it was prepared for. "After these things the Lord appointed other seventy also, and sent them two and two before his face into every city and place, whither he himself would come. Therefore said he unto them, The harvest truly is great, but the laborers are few: pray ye therefore the Lord of the harvest, that he would send forth laborers into his harvest" (Luke 10:1-2). Despite all the slander surrounding the gospel there are people who will accept the message of Jesus and receive the blessings in knowing the Father and the Son. Matthew 12:44-45 says, "Jesus cried and said, he that believeth on me, believeth not on me, but on him that sent me. And he that seeth me seeth him that sent me." The mission of Christ, as conveyed in the Bible, is to testify to the world - who God is. Many religious fanatics will say, "Jesus was referring to himself as being God" because he said, "He that seeth me seeth him that sent me." However, in John 12:49 it said, "For I have not spoken of myself: but the Father which sent me, he gave me a commandment, what I should say, and what I should speak." Now speaking boldly (according to the revelation for which I am a debtor) the doctrine of Jesus Christ is that Emperor Haile Selassie The First is the Almighty God manifest in the flesh, justified in the Spirit (which means that His veneration is justified in the Bible). John 3:32 said, "And what he had seen and heard, that he testifieth; and no man receiveth his testimony. He that hath received his testimony had set to his seal that God is true" (not an invisible nebulous floating in the air).

The Bhagavad Gita said, "No one can understand how Krsnha the Supreme LORD comes to earth in physical form and executed common activities as an ordinary human being."[11] The Bible calls this the mystery of God that has been hidden from the wise and prudent. "The LORD will lay bare his holy arm in the sight of all the nations, and all the ends of the earth will see the salvation of our God" (Isaiah 52:10). Again there are some who misinterpret these verses to mean that Jesus is God but the Bible said not to add or take away from the Word (Proverbs 30:5-6). The scriptures have stated that God and his Son

---

[11] The Bhagavad-Gita 10:2

are two different people united in the same Spirit which is the gospel. In John 6:63, Jesus said, "The words I speak unto you, they are spirit and they are life." Proverbs 30:4 asked, "Who hath ascended up into heaven, or descended? Who hath gathered the wind in his fists? who hath bound the waters in a garment? who hath established all the ends of the earth? what is his name (Haile Selassie The First) and what is his son's name (Primus Saint Croix), if thou canst tell?"

"The LORD has made his salvation known and revealed his righteousness to the nations" (Psalm 98:2). This was fulfilled on Sunday, November 2, 1930, when RasTafari Mekonnen, who was the Crown Prince and Regent of Ethiopia, ascended the ancient throne of the Solomonic dynasty according to the Ethiopian Orthodox Tewahedo tradition and was crowned as Emperor Haile Selassie The First. Keep in mind that Ethiopia is the oldest Christian nation on earth; she has the original version of the Bible. Psalm 68:31-32 says, "Princes shall come out of Egypt, Ethiopia shall soon stretch forth her hands unto God. Sing unto God, ye kingdoms of the earth; O sing praises unto the Lord; Selah." At the Coronation representatives from around the world were present when His Imperial Majesty was crowned King of Kings and Lord of Lords, Elect of God, Light of the World, Conquering Lion of the Tribe of Judah. Psalm 48 said, "Great is the LORD and greatly to be praised in the city of our God, in the mountain of his holiness. Beautiful for situation the joy of the whole earth is mount Zion, on the sides of the north, the city of the great King. God is known in her palaces for a refuge. For, lo, the kings (the representatives from various nations such as France, England, America, Germany, and Italy) were assembled, they passed by together. They saw it, and so they marveled; they were troubled and hasted away." His Holiness Abuna Kyrillos, the Archbishop, exhorted the people to be loyal and obedient to the Emperor, the Elect of God; by saying, "Ye princes and ministers; ye nobles and chiefs of the army; ye soldiers and people of Ethiopia; ye doctors and chiefs of the clergy; ye professors and priests; look ye upon the Emperor, Haile Selassie The First, descended from the dynasty of Menelik I, who was born of Solomon and of the Queen of Sheba, a dynasty perpetuated without interruption from that time to King Sahla Selassie and to our time."[12] Psalm 24 asks us, who is this King of Glory; the LORD strong and mighty, He is the King of Glory.

After RasTafari proclaimed that He is the Almighty God,[13] the vatican city, also known as the dragon, decided to break her agreement with the League of Nations and invade Ethiopia. Mussolini promised the pope that he would

---

[12] Talbot, David Abner, Haile Selassie I Silver Jubilee, page 26
[13] Isaiah 43:8-13

dethrone Haile Selassie The First and conquer the last remaining indigenous country on earth. The members of the League (which mainly consisted of racist european powers) abandoned Ethiopia to the fate of Mussolini who led an invasion of over 500,000 foot soldiers, 800 tanks, 600 warplanes, 6,000 modern machine guns, and tons of ammunition.[14] The Ethiopian Army was gravely out gunned in this combat for they had a small amount of outdated artillery left over from the Battle of Adowa in 1896; along with 3 tanks, and 3 aircrafts at their disposal. When His Imperial Majesty went to Geneva to request for the right to purchase arms they mocked and jeered Him as He delivered His speech. The Light of the World asked the representatives of the nations for assistance in stopping the common enemy of all humanity (which was Mussolini and Hitler who both were under the command of the vatican).[15] But the League did nothing because they also worked for the devil. Psalm 82 said, "God standeth in the congregation of the mighty, he judgeth among the gods. How long will ye judge unjustly, and accept the persons of the wicked? Selah. Defend the poor and fatherless: do justice to the afflicted and needy." His Imperial Majesty told them, "It is us (Ethiopia) today. It will be you tomorrow;"[16] and sure enough that is what happened. The Italian forces were defeated with the help of Britain and Mussolini was butchered and dragged in the streets of Italy by his own people. Hitler demolished most of Europe before he killed himself like a coward. America stepped in at the end to defeat Japan and thus became the new world power. But currently we see the reincarnation of Mussolini, Hitler, and Tojo in various world leader's policies and relations. This goes to show that we are in a perpetual cycle of death and oppression; for the ways of man are corrupt. The Bible said that God is our salvation; Haile Selassie The First taught us how to stop tyranny and injustice. He educated the world leaders on better principles and philosophies but they did not take heed. It was RasTafari who said, "Until the philosophy which holds one race superior and the other inferior, is finally and permanently discredited and abandoned [...] until the color of a man's skin is of no more significance than the color of his eyes, that until the basic human rights are equally guaranteed to all without regards to race, that until that day, the dream of lasting peace and world citizenship, the rule of international morality will remain in but a fleeting illusion, to be pursued but never attained."[17] There are no adequate

---

[14] De Bono, Emilio, La Preparazione E Le Prime Operazioni, pages 175-177

[15] Cornwell, John, Hitler's Pope: The Secret History of Piux XII

[16] Time Magazine, The Lion is Freed, September 8, 1975

[17] The Selected Speeches of His Imperial Majesty Haile Selassie I, page 374

words to describe the importance in following Haile Selassie The First for He is God and there is no one else. The Selected Speeches of His Imperial Majesty is a book everyone must have because in it are all the answers to the current problems crippling the world.

We are grateful for the opportunity to share with you the testimony of our Lord Jesus Christ. Only the Creator, who is in heaven, knows how deeply gratified we are to be given this opportunity to express our ideas and ideals. We know that if it is God's will then these words will motivate people to follow Emperor Haile Selassie The First and if this is done with pure intentions then we will be able to change the world for the better. Brothers and sisters, it is without question that unity, faith, and love is the divine will of God our Father; for it is written in Psalm 133, "Behold, how good and how pleasant it is for brethren to dwell together in unity." It is good when people are able to put aside their petty differences and gather in harmony to meet one end, which is justice and peace for all of mankind. This, I must say is a sign of true faith.

Today, it is no longer a question of asking for unity, but rather it is a requirement for our survival as a whole. Let us all, no matter who we are or where we are from, whether European, Asian, or African, strive with all our heart to fulfill the love and faith of God; which Christ has taught us. For those who claim to be followers of Jesus and his Father, this task should not be very difficult. Christ said that if we believe in him, we would believe in the Father who sent him (John 12:44). It is also written in 1 John 5:9, "If we receive the witness of men, the witness of God is greater, for this is the witness of God which he has testified of his Son." Haile Selassie The First fulfilled this by stating, "When Jesus Christ was born from the Virgin Mary, from that time on he lived an exemplary life, a life which men everywhere must emulate. This life and the faith that he taught us assures us of salvation, assures us also of harmony and good life upon earth. Because of the exemplary character of the life of Jesus Christ it is necessary that all men do their maximum in their human efforts to see to it that they approximate as much as they can the good example that has been set by him."[18] Let us therefore, as God fearing people, honor this sincere testimony, that His Imperial Majesty Emperor Haile Selassie The First, has given about Jesus Christ. For it is written, in 1 John 5:10, "He that believes on the Son of God has the witness in himself: he that believes not God has made him a liar; because he believes not the record that God gave of his Son." His Imperial Majesty has given us counsel that the only way to have salvation is through

---

[18] Dawes, Mark, Jamaica Gleaner, December 16, 2003

Christ, everyone no matter what religion or tradition they profess must take heed unto this; if we are to be saved.

Today, all over the world, we are plagued with difficult problems including poverty, racism, injustice, wars, and diseases. These things should not be so if the religions of the world were living up to their responsibilities as spiritual guides. The purpose of any religion is to lead people to a better life. Martin Luther King Jr. said, "A religion true to its nature must also be concerned about man's social conditions [...] Any religion that professes to be concerned with the souls of men and is not concerned with the slums that damn them, the economic conditions that strangle them, and the social conditions that cripple them is a dry-as-dust religion." Let us now, with that understanding, examine if the religions of this world are following God or Beelzebub. When you look at the Middle East: Palestine and Israel seem to be involved in a perpetual conflict. What is the cause of this tragic and sad dilemma? Why is it that these two people, supposably in the "Holy Land," are unable to resolve their differences? How active is the ecclesiastical community in seeking solutions to this conflict? Faith requires holiness and charity, love and mercy, patience and temperance, caring and peace; this is the true faith of God. But the Jews and the Muslims are fighting because one believes that his religion or tradition is better than the other, that one is holier than the other, and therefore entitled to deprive the other of their basic human rights. They fight over who is the rightful owner of the land; they believe that one is superior to the other. Is this the calling of their religion or the righteous example of pious people? The nations of the world cannot choose to ignore this conflict. His Imperial Majesty severed ties with the Zionists due to their aggressive and lawless agenda, "In accordance with its consistent position against the annexation of territories, Ethiopia did everything it could in order to bring about an Israeli withdrawal from the territories of Egypt, Jordan, and Syria that it conquered in 1967 [...] Ethiopia's position has remained consistent: As long as Israel remains in these territories, there is no chance for peace in the Middle East [...] Since Israel has not withdrawn from the conquered territories, Ethiopia has decided to cut off diplomatic relations with it, and that is how it will be until Israel withdraws." The announcement was accompanied by a demand that all Israelis leave Ethiopia immediately; and within a week all the Israelis had left with their families.[19] But America has chosen to defend Israel in the face of numerous violations of international laws and morality committed by the Jews. The American media, politicians, and religious leaders (the pope) have all confirmed

---

[19] Erlich, Haggai, Alliance and Alienation, page 254

their partial judgment by supporting military assistance for Israel and condemning Palestinian resistance. Haile Selassie The First said, "By the word neutral, we do not, of course, mean that abstention from political activity which has been for so long the hallmark of a Switzerland. We can no more refrain from political activity in the year 1961 than man today can voluntarily refrain from partaking of the radioactive fall-out which will be bestowed upon him should a nuclear holocaust erupt on this globe. Nor does neutrality mean that without taking sides, we content ourselves with urging that the powers most intimately concerned negotiate in good faith to the solution of the issues in dispute between them; we have passed the point where prayerful pleading serves any purpose other than to debase those who thereby abdicate any responsibilities or power to influence events."[20] To be neutral is to be impartial, impartial to judge actions and policies objectively, as we see them either contributing or else detracting from the resolution of the worlds problems, the preservation of peace and the improvement of the general level of man's living conditions. Thus, we may find ourselves now opposing, now supporting; now voting, now vetoing; against the East or the West. It is the policies themselves that we must measure and not the source or sponsor, this determines the position of one who is truly fit for leadership; this, we maintain, is the essence of nonalignment. Those who would righteously denounce one side on every issue while preserving praise for the other despite wrongdoings cannot claim to practice good governance or to be followers of God. Nor can those whose policies and decision making is determined beforetime in lieu of the facts and the ramifications of the subject, but whose judgment is perverted by greed and monetary gain, be called upon to lead or offer any assistance in political or spiritual affairs.

Brothers and sisters, all of you have a stake in the preservation of our world. Let us therefore be honest in judgment by condemning war, injustice, and false principals. This is what Haile Selassie The First would be working on today, He would be counseling the world leaders to adopt a higher quality of governance. We can examine what His Imperial Majesty said when He quoted President Sarvapalli Radhakrishnan, "In the mystic tradition of the different religions we have a remarkable unity of spirit. Whatever religions they may profess they are spiritual kinsmen. While the different religions in their historic forms bind us to limited groups and militate against the development of loyalty to the world community, the mystics have always stood for the fellowship of humanity."[21]

---

[20] The Selected Speeches of His Imperial Majesty Haile Selassie I, page 168
[21] Ibid, page 132

We all should meditate fervently on the words that Emperor Haile Selassie The First has left with us. I am sure that the result of His guidance, if we put His policies into effect, will induce peace on earth because the true purpose of our religion does not lead to war and bigotry.

We all have sinned and fallen short of the glory of God, let us therefore repent from our crooked ways and seek to know the things that are proper in the sight of our Creator, that we may be able to provide righteous judgment when necessary. Daniel 1:22 says, "And judgment was given to the saints of the Most High and the time came that the saints possessed the kingdom." Let us therefore strive to become acceptable to God so that the promises of our faith may become fulfilled in us who believe the testimony of the scriptures. Blessed be Jah RasTafari Mekonnen Woldemikael.

The Bible teaches us that God is the Savior of the world and it exhorts us to trust in the power of His deliverance: "For the grace of God that brings salvation has appeared to all men" (Titus 2:11). Parallel to none Emperor Haile Selassie The First is the Most High. He was awarded the most excellent laurels and degrees including, Doctor of Law, Doctor of Philosophy, Doctor of Letters, Doctor of Civil Law. The world recognized the wisdom of His principles therefore it becomes even more irrefutable for us not to follow Him. We all hope for peace and prosperity, this foundation His Imperial Majesty has laid not in words only but by example. For this reason everyone who calls themselves followers of RasTafari, should sanctify and hallow the Sabbath Day, which is November 2, 1930, this is the memorial and glory of God. Ezekiel 38:23 states, "Thus will I magnify myself, and sanctify myself; and I will be known in the eyes of many nations, and they shall know that I am the LORD." Exodus 20:8 said, "Remember the Sabbath Day to keep it holy." On November 2, 1930, His

Imperial Majesty glorified the law and made it a living covenant for all of humanity; that is the day which the Bible said you must remember. Isaiah 42:21 said, "The LORD is well pleased for his righteousness' sake; he will magnify the law, and make it honorable." Therefore everyone who knows that Haile Selassie The First is God, should honor Him according to His works and righteousness and not according to their own tradition and ways, for although God is manifested in the flesh, He is not like you; for His ways are above that of man. Malachi 1:6 says, "A son honoureth his father, and a servant his master: if I then be a father, where is my honor? and if I be a master, where is my fear? saith the LORD of hosts unto you, O priests, that despise my name. And you say, wherein have we despised thy name?" This happens when we say that Haile Selassie The First is God, but don't follow His pattern and principles. For example, His Imperial Majesty was the Ethiopian head of state therefore it would be a mockery to say that you follow Him yet you don't participate in politics. Haile Selassie The First was a politician, His daily activities consisted of governing His country, tracking world events, and reaching out to the leaders to offer solutions to problems. How can anyone logically say that they follow His Imperial Majesty but they are not into politics? That would be like me saying that Pele is my hero but I hate football. Why would you look up to someone yet rebuke everything that they was about; do you admire their looks or their deeds? When we put our tradition and self made doctrine above the purpose and will of RasTafari then we are taking His name in vain.

According to the Bible, it is Jesus Christ alone who honors God the Father in Spirit and Truth. Therefore, we must be like Emperor Haile Selassie The First by adopting His principles, lifestyle, and traditions; if we are Christians, if we are Rastafarians. Do not follow the ways of men, for in them you will find no salvation. His Imperial Majesty commanded us to read and study the Bible. If we accepted the message of the scriptures with a clear conscience then we would understand that Jesus did not come thousands of years ago like the vatican says. The Christ that Haile Selassie The First commanded us to follow is not the false doctrine of the pope but the authentic Christ who enabled us to see God; which cured the blind through knowledge not necromancy. This was fulfilled when Primus Saint Croix preached the gospel, those who are truly seeking to follow the Emperor will accept this testimony.

Qedamawi Haile Selassie means: The First Power of the Trinity. His name in Ethiopic translates as Qedamawi for First, Haile means Power, and Selassie is Trinity. According to the Bible, the Trinity does not include Jesus Christ; but the pope says that it does. 1 John 5:7 says, "For there are three that bear record in heaven, the Father, the Word, and the Holy Ghost: and these three are one." This is the only reference in the scriptures of three attributes agreeing in one to describe the Lord (take careful note that it did not say that the father, the son, and the spirit are the trinity). The Father is the Creator, the Supreme Guide and Light on earth. The Word is the Bible or prophecy of God (for which Christ is a messenger {Ezekiel 3:1-4}). The Holy Ghost is the revelation of God. On November 2, 1930, the Glory of God was divulged when Emperor Haile Selassie The First was crowned King of Kings and Lord of Lords. The Bible teaches us that God the Father and his Son Jesus Christ are two different people (John 8:17-18). Jesus carries the Word of God for he spoke of his Father, he did not preach about himself (John 12:49). The only reference in the Bible to the Father, Son, and Spirit is found in Matthew 28:19 and it says to teach all nations about these three entities; which means that they are not all the same.

Jesus Christ is referenced in 1 John 5:8, "And there are three that bear witness in the earth, the spirit, and the water, and the blood: and these three agree in one." The spirit is the letter or prophecy of God. The water is the testimony and the blood is salvation through the gospel. This demonstrates how God rose up Christ and put His Word into the mouth of the Prophet (Jeremiah 1:9). Christ in turn preached the true message of God. Jesus is the express image of the Lord because he followed the Bible according to its true definition; he did not make up his own doctrine. For example, if I read the speeches of Mahatma Gandhi and followed his tenants; then his spirit would be in me but that does not turn me into Gandhi. I would be in his image because I follow his ways but me and him are two different people. God and Christ work the same way; which is always according to logic and reason. Primus Saint Croix is the Prophet of God, he was found worthy to open the book for he has the correct interpretation of the scriptures (the Word) and his name means: The First Saint of the Cross. Primus means The First, Saint is a messenger, and Croix means Cross. This illustrates how Jesus Christ has come in a new name as it is written in Revelation 3:12; he is the first begotten of the dead (the ignorant).

"Tell ye, and bring them near; yea, let them take counsel together: who has declared this from ancient time? who has told it from that time? have not I the LORD? and there is no God else beside me; a just God and a Savior; there is none beside me. Look unto me, and be ye saved, all the ends of the earth: for I am God, and there is none else. I have sworn by myself, the word is gone out of my mouth in righteousness, and shall not return, That unto me every knee shall bow, every tongue shall swear" (Isaiah 45:21-23). The name God by itself does not translate into you knowing who the Most High is; it simply means that you can articulate a lexeme. To say that you know God means a lot more than merely yelling out Jehovah, Allah, Lord, or Yahweh. You must be able to show who God is, as promised by Jesus. Remember the Bible said God made man in His own image and again it said God was manifest in the flesh. So if we deny this Biblical truth, then we doubt the power of God. Through studying the works and teachings of Haile Selassie The First it is conclusive that the Bible is correct in admonishing the King of Kings and Lord of Lords as the Savior because His Imperial Majesty has completely lived up to this admonition. Haile Selassie The First said, "Once a person has decided upon his life work and is assured that in doing the work for which he is best endowed and equipped, he is filling a vital need, what he then needs, is faith and integrity, compiled with a courageous spirit so that no longer preferring himself to the fulfillment of his task, he may address himself to the problems he must solve in order to be effective."[22] His instructions give the layout on how to better ourselves and the world.

The name Jesus Christ is likewise a title which means the messenger of God or the teacher of God's Word. To know the Prophet invokes much more than simple catch phrases and empty rhetoric. It is imperative that you know the person and are able to prove who is the Son of God; this must be done according to the prophecies of the Bible. Anyone can say that they are Christ but only one person will fulfill what has been written of him and that would be the actual Messiah. This saving grace cannot be validated through ancient paintings, statues, or graven images. As God is known by His deeds, so will Christ also be known by his actions; idolatry is the work of the devil therefore we should not be looking for the Son of God in ancient relics that cannot save anyone. The clearest illustration of the true messenger of God will be found in the wisdom of his gospel. The Bible describes Jesus Christ as a Prophet of God; "And when he was come into Jerusalem, all the city was moved saying, Who is this? And the multitude said, This is Jesus the prophet of Nazareth of Galilee" (Matthew 21:10-11). Those who are sincerely seeking the knowledge of the Lord will inherit everlasting life. Christ said, "This is life eternal, that they might know thee the only true God, and Jesus Christ, whom thou hast sent" (John 17:3). Therefore the promise of the Bible is for us to know God and His messenger. Christ understood the mystery of the religious texts such as the Bible, Quran, and Bhagavad Gita; he was able to declare God unto the world by referencing these books. John 17:6 states, "I have manifested thy name unto

---

[22] The Wisdom of Rastafari, page 13

the men which thou gavest me out of the world: thine they were, and thou gavest them me; and they have kept thy word."

On November 2, 1930, His Imperial Majesty Emperor Haile Selassie The First, fulfilled the prophecies pertaining to God. He was crowned with the highest titles in the universe: King of Kings and Lord of Lords. In fact, He held over three dozen grandiloquent appellations including Supreme Arbiter of the Ebb and the Flow of the Tides. Upon His throne He taught the nations good principles and He governed his people with love and justice. Years later, the vatican tested Him (through Mussolini) and He overcame them, proving that He merited the claim of His epithet. While the world stood in awe of Him, amazed by His high moral standards, taken by His foresight and wisdom, motivated by His tremendous work ethic and resolve; they still did not believe that He was God. "And I saw a great white throne, and him that sat on it, from whose face the earth and the heaven fled away; and there was found no place for them" (Revelation 20:11). Therefore the Lord sent forth His Prophet, seventy years after the Coronation, to teach the people that His Imperial Majesty is the Almighty. If we do not put our trust in the Emperor then we will never inherit the promises of life, for it is written that He is the first and the last. On May 18, 2000, a Rastafarian preacher was arrested because he denounced the worshipping of graven images and testified to the authorities that Emperor Haile Selassie The First is the true and living God; whose principles and policies must be adhered to. This man, Primus Saint Croix, was warning the people of the impending doom that will follow if the world continues to deny the divinity of His Imperial Majesty. He explained how the religious texts were directing us to praise Haile Selassie The First. For this purpose we must declare that Primus Saint Croix is the very Christ because only Jesus can show us God in the Bible. "And the seventy returned again with joy, saying, Lord, even the devils are subject unto us through thy name. And he said unto them, I beheld Satan as lightning fall from heaven. Behold, I give unto you power to tread on serpents and scorpions, and over all the power of the enemy: and nothing shall by any means hurt you" (Luke 10:17-19).

As a man, Primus, is no different from anyone else. We all suffer from our own infirmities and must work towards correcting our errors. Only the Lord is perfect, that is why Jesus said, "Why do you call me good, there is none good except for one, that is God" (Mark 10:18). But Primus Saint Croix was perfect according to the scriptures for he was able to show us God manifest in the flesh and these are the descriptions of the Messiah. In Revelation 5, it says that no man was worthy to open the Bible except for Jesus Christ. That means that only he will interpret the scriptures correctly, he is the door into heaven; the only way to know the truth about God is through Christ. The Bible will only make sense through Jesus, other people will have an invalid supernatural interpretation of the scriptures. You will know that he is the Christ by his message; he taught us as one having authority (valid comprehension) and not as one of the scribes (worldly ministers who have no knowledge).[23]

Ask yourself does it make sense for a father and his son to be the same person; is that how God created the world? (If someones interpretation takes away from your gumption then you have been brainwashed. How can somebody's gospel save you if it defies logic and reason?) If you have a child, is your son the same person as you? No, he is not. According to the laws of nature that God established, it is impossible for a father to have a child and they somehow be the same entity. But this is the doctrine that the blind world follows. They believe that the father and son share the same soul; even though it is impossible for that to be true. The Bible describes Christ as the blessed youth of the Father, "For of a truth against your holy child Jesus, whom thou has anointed, both Herod, and Pontius Pilate, with the Gentiles, and the people of Israel, were gathered together, for to do whatsoever thy counsel determined before to be done. And now, Lord, behold their threatenings: and grant unto thy servants, that with all boldness they may speak thy word, By stretching forth thine hand to heal; and that signs and wonders may be done by the name of thy holy child Jesus" (Acts 4:27-30). There are many false interpretations of the scriptures that the world follows. Such as the literal interpretation of the Virgin Mary but a woman who has never been with a man cannot give birth. They want you to believe in the supernatural because you will never know God with that perspective. In Matthew 12:46-50 Christ tells you that his mother are those who do the will of God. The Bible describes a woman as a church (1 Corinthians 7) and Mary as the disciples of Jesus. The scriptures do not teach witchcraft, God is not the author of confusion! The Lord did not establish the world in a manner which would make a woman who never received the seed of a man able to give birth to a child. And likewise a father and his son cannot be the same entity. When you break the rules of nature, you are going against the order that the Lord established. That is the sign of the antichrist because God does not break His own rules; it is the devil who goes against the tenants of the Lord. But God is perfect and He instructed us to follow His laws.

---

[23] Mark 1:22

In Mark 1:15 it says, "The time is fulfilled, and the kingdom of God is at hand: repent and believe the gospel." This demonstrates how Jesus preached that Haile Selassie The First is the Almighty. John 5:19 says, "Verily, I say unto you, the Son can do nothing of himself but what he sees the Father do: for whatsoever he does, these the Son does likewise." God manifest Himself on earth first and then Jesus came after Him; that is why Christ said the kingdom is at hand because he followed what he seen the LORD accomplish. It is also natural law for the Father to come first and then the Son. Jesus was sent to teach what is acceptable, to admonish the world to put their trust in the King of Heaven Emperor Haile Selassie The First. Christ has declared what he has seen of his Father therefore God must be visible. In John 8:54-55 it says, "If I honor myself, my honor is nothing: it is my Father that honors me of whom you say that he is your God: Yet you have not known him, but I know him: and if I should say that I know him not I shall be a liar like unto you: but I know him and keep his sayings." The difference between Christ and the rest of the world is that Jesus was true to the Word of God. The Bible said that the Almighty is the King of Kings and Lord of Lords (Revelation 19:15-16). His Imperial Majesty was crowned with these titles on November 2, 1930. Jesus believed in the Word of God, as well as the fulfillment of the prophecy, whereas the world cannot make the correlation between Haile Selassie The First and the Bible; even though it said that the Lord will not give His glory to another (Isaiah 48:11-12). In Hebrews 11:27 it says, "By faith he forsook Egypt, not fearing the wrath of pharaoh: for he endured, as seeing him who is invisible." The only reason that God is invisible is because the world does not believe in His Imperial Majesty; but Jesus does, that is why he said, if I should say I know him not, I shall be a liar like you are (John 8:55). Christ is a preacher who did not speak about himself, he kept us in the name of his Father (John 17:12). In Hebrews 5:5 it says, "So also Christ glorified not himself to be made a high priest: but he that said unto him, Thou art my Son, today have I begotten thee."

"But wisdom is justified of all her children" (Luke 7:35). Now ask yourself if it is prudent to believe in a gospel that goes against the laws of God? How can superstition be correct, when a father and his son are not the same person? Or does it make more sense to use logic if we want the truth? Primus Saint Croix is the only one who can interpret the Bible correctly; he is the only one who can show you God. The rest of the world interprets the scriptures in a false supernatural manner. In Isaiah 40:5, it says that it is promised for you to see God; but the only way to know the Lord is through His Son. So if we know that Haile Selassie The First is God, then we also must identify His Prophet. He comes like a thief in the night but you will know him by his works, because his doctrine will be greater than all others. He will teach you with sound reason and knowledge so that you may gain the right understanding of the Bible which will not rob you of your intelligence. It is written that the truth will be manifested by Jesus Christ. Seek and you shall find, knock and it shall be opened. The Kingdom of God is at hand, repent and believe the gospel.

Do not worry if your family and friends are against your beliefs; they will do this if they have never tasted the new wine (2 Corinthians 4:1-4 indicates that the world has been deceived by the devil, therefore Christ has come preaching the new testament, which is a new understanding of the Bible). Matthew 10:37 says, "Anyone who loves his father or mother more than me, is not worthy of me, anyone who loves his son or daughter more than me is not worthy of me." This means that we must place God above everything because it will not profit us if we gain the whole world yet lose our souls. If you are able to understand that Emperor Haile Selassie The First is God, yet your family and friends disagree with you, then you must continue in the faith; for the validity of the Lord does not rest in the approval of men. If the entire world denies this gospel, it does not change the fact that His Imperial Majesty is God. The Gentiles (unbelievers) say that Haile Selassie The First is not God because they do not have the correct understanding of the Bible. The vatican has forced the interpretation founded at the Council of Nicaea upon the world despite the fact that the supernatural is a pagan concept and Jesus is not God. In doing so, the pope has denied the true identity of Christ and the only reason that Catholicism is a major world religion is because they brutally murdered and tortured those who did not accept their dogma. The Bible is prophetic; the scriptures foretold the coming of the Kingdom of God. Our forefathers were warned not to set up idols (their own false interpretation), but instead to study and wait for the revelation of the scriptures. Romans 15:3 said, "For whatsoever things were written aforetime were written for our learning, that we through patience and comfort of the scriptures might have hope." The key word here is hope; when a promise is made we expect to see it fulfilled. So where is the revelation of the Bible? In Isaiah 45:22 it says, "Turn to me and be saved, all you ends of the earth; for I am God, and there is no other." Are we to neglect Emperor Haile Selassie The First, even though He has the titles and the character of God, just because the pope and the other popular spiritual guides have not given their approval to worship Him? Do we need our family and friends to agree with the gospel in order for us to believe it? If this was the case then it would be clear that we put our trust in man and not in God. Luke 12:49-53 says, "I am come to send fire on the earth; and what will I, if it be already kindled? But I have a baptism to be baptized with; and how am I straitened till it be accomplished! Suppose ye that I am come to give peace on earth? I tell you No, but rather division: For from henceforth there shall be five in one house divided, three against two and two against three. The father shall be divided against the son, and the son against the father; the mother against the daughter and the daughter against the mother; the mother in law against her daughter in law and the daughter in law against her mother in law." The common Christian doctrine (adopted from the ecumenical councils) is composed of superstition, ancient mythology, romance, and idolatry, the very things the Bible warns us against (Exodus 20). The vatican teaches the people that their graven images are a depiction of Jesus Christ, which leads the people to put their trust in inanimate objects. Remember in Acts 17:29 it said, "For as much as we are the offspring of God, we ought not to think that the Godhead is like unto gold, or silver, or stone, graven by art and mans device." If God is represented by a statue, then we would never be able to accept the Lord when He comes in the flesh. This is precisely what Satan wants, because they know that only Jah can stop their evil intentions. Unfortunately Christendom follows the deception of the pope, they worship the pagan Jesus idol and think that this image is an actual depiction of how Christ looks; that is why they cannot comprehend that the prophecy has been fulfilled by Emperor Haile Selassie The First. Paul said, "For what if some did not believe? shall their unbelief make the faith of God without effect? God forbid: yea, let God be true, but every man a liar; as it is written, THAT THOU MIGHTEST BE JUSTIFIED IN THY SAYINGS, AND MIGHTEST OVERCOME WHEN THOU ART JUDGED" (Romans 3:3-4). Many religious people are conceded into thinking that they have the truth because they follow that which is common and popular. Many Christians believe that by making a simple rhetorical statement that Jesus is your Lord and Savior that this by itself is sufficient to gain entry into the Kingdom of God. Many believe that because they do some good deeds, like caring for the sick and helping the poor, that they are righteous. But the truth is that while doing moral deeds is good, that does not commend the righteousness of God. You must know who God is, you must follow His instructions, you must acknowledge that Emperor Haile Selassie The First is the Almighty. That is the promise, "And this I say, that the covenant, that was confirmed before of God in Christ, the law, which was four hundred and thirty years after, cannot disannul, that it should make the promise of none effect" (Galatians 3:17).

Follow me for a moment while we journey into the third degree of light: the law of God as mentioned in the Bible is what the religious world claims to follow. But reading the scrolls does not equate with comprehending its meaning. The law is the prophecy or shadow of things to come; the scriptures are a roadmap which leads you to the King of Glory. Our spiritual guides, the biblical scholars, were supposed to know these things; in fact many of them do, but for the love of money and power they follow the pope and his false doctrine. The Bible, even the Bhagavad Gita, have foretold that the Almighty will manifest Himself on earth as a man. That is why we were warned not to make idols representing God because the Lord will show the world who He is. But when He comes, if He does not look like the image that you see on your statues and paintings then you will not believe that He is God; even if He fulfills everything according to the prophecy. The ecumenical councils incorporated many pagan concepts into Christianity to make it more appealing, to pacify the masses, and to carry on ancient traditions. Yet idolatry is condemned by the Lord and this encompasses more than just graven images; this includes all false interpretations of the scriptures. The vatican has invoked their imagination about what they want God to look like and made it into an idol. Nothing they teach is justified in the scriptures, yet they claim to be the vicar of Christ on earth. If this is the case then when people go to the pope looking for the Lord, all they will find are the works of the devil. When you ask them about God and Jesus, instead of admitting that they don't know, they blaspheme the truth by directing people towards graven images. It is up to the people now to stop putting their trust in men and to seek the Lord wholeheartedly. If the Bible said that these things are wrong then we should not follow them, even if it is the pope who said that it is okay; remember that the devil is a deceiver. If we loved God then we would be able to accept His Word, as well as the fulfillment of prophecy. Paul said, "For that which I do I allow not: for what I would, that do I not; but what I hate, that do I. If then I do that which I would not, I consent unto the law that it is good. Now then it is no more I that do it, but sin that dwelleth in me" (Romans 7:15-17). Therefore, we must make sure that our righteousness complies with the laws of God. If we are following traditions that are forbidden by the Lord then we must repent from these practices. Your family and friends are not going to be able to save your soul if you do not accept Haile Selassie The First; you cannot expect God to accept you when you have broken His commandments. Ignorance of the law causes moral citizens to deny the Lord. If you are a naturally decent individual, that is great and you must stay that way but your values do not equate with knowing who God is; this requires faith. Romans 7:5-6 said that it is time for us to seek God in newness of spirit; this means that we must reexamine the Bible and our lives to determine if we have inherited the promises of salvation. Anyone who is sincere in this study will know that there is more to be attained and if more is required then we should not act as if we already have everything. They all are waiting for the second coming of Christ but refuse to listen to the reasoning on Haile Selassie The First. 1 John 3:4 says, "Everyone who sins breaks God's law, for sin is the transgression of the law;" therefore sin is a lack of understanding, the wrong interpretation. "For we know that the law is spiritual: but I am carnal, sold under sin" (Romans 7:14). To be carnal minded is to be spiritually ignorant. They have fallen short of the truth by not accepting the divinity of His Imperial Majesty. There is some good in them by keeping high morals but in order to be accepted by God, you must believe in Haile Selassie The First.

The council of Nicaea convened in 325 AD and established the doctrine that the Father and the Son are somehow the same person; thus turning Jesus into God. This was done to quell the escalating dissension within the Roman Empire caused by Arius and others surrounding the true nature of Christ. The Arians argued that the Father and the Son are not the same entity because during the material construction of the universe Christ was created after God. The council of Nicaea was successful in defeating Arianism but their arguments also was not fully correct because they incorporated pagan principles into their canon by claiming that the Lord and His Prophet are consubstantial. Arius was wrong because there is no way to confirm how God created the physical universe. The Bible is referring to spiritual events pertaining to the revelation of the King of Sion; the scriptures cannot be used to teach about ancient history because it is not recalling those matters. Therefore anyone will be disproven if they try to argue that the Bible is evoking archaic situations. The council condemned Arianism and burnt all the literature pertaining to their beliefs thus making their findings the dominant theory because it was the only opinion for people to study; but wiping out another ideology does not make yours valid. We know that Arius was wrong but the canon founded at Nicaea is also incorrect; the Bible said that no one understood the mysteries (Jeremiah 4:20-27). To state that two different people are the same entity defies logic and reason, if scriptures are used to support this position then they are being used improperly. God the Father and His Son Jesus could not both be God, Christ said, "He that speaks of himself seeks his own glory: but he that seeks the glory of him that sent him, the same is true and no unrighteousness is in him" (John 7:18). The Bible is against the notion that Jesus is God, that is why in the good book the only people that you read about who refer to Jesus as being God are his enemies (John 5:18, John 10:30-38, Luke 5:21-26). Those who follow Christ exhort him as being the Son of God which means that he is the Prophet (John 4:19 & 44, John 6:14, Luke 4:24, Luke 7:16). "Jesus answered them and said, My doctrine is not mine, but his that sent me. If any man will do his will, he shall know the doctrine, whether it be of God, or whether I speak of myself" (John 7:16-17). The ecumenical councils would have you to believe that Christ was talking about himself because they interpret Jesus to be God; despite this being contrary to his message. Just because the vatican has given their doctrine the moniker of cannon law does not mean that we can disregard what the Bible says. Christ said that he and his Father are one but this does not mean that they are the same entity because in John 17:21 it calls for us all to be one with God, just as Jesus and his Father are one. Therefore if Jesus is God because he is one with the Father, then that also means that I am God because I am one with the Father; but we know that is false. It has been extended to everyone to become one with the Father to illustrate that this description does not mean that Christ is God.

Haile Selassie The First gave a famous speech during the Conference of Oriental Churches on January 15, 1965, where He said, "May God who helped the 318 Fathers of the council of Nicea enlighten and help us all."[24] There would be some who take this statement to mean that He agrees with the gospel of the vatican but we know that interpretation is incorrect. Without taking this statement out of context we would know that His Imperial Majesty's entire speech is referring to unifying the churches and the purpose of this meeting was to bring together the different Christian denominations. That is why He said, "For centuries past our Orthodox Churches have been without contact. Perhaps that which still divides the two groups is a matter of some importance. Perhaps it is not. In any case, we live in a time when even political differences are discussed around the conference table and peaceful and amicable solutions sought by all. The Church can afford to do no less."[25] The council of Nicaea was a grand achievement for many reasons including gathering 318 bishops from around the world into forging an agreement, if others would follow this example by uniting there is no telling the incessant achievements that they could accomplish. His Imperial Majesty was working to get the churches to band together, just as they did in 325 AD, that is why He said may God help us in this

---

[24] The Selected Speeches of His Imperial Majesty Haile Selassie I, page 639
[25] Ibid, page 638

endeavor. It is an unbelievably difficult task to get people to unify even when it is in their best interest to do so but this is the task which Haile Selassie The First has advised us is the true calling of our faith. The Emperor said, "'Behold, how good and how pleasant it is for brethren to dwell together in unity' (Psalm 133:1). The Unity of the Church, as Your Holinesses well know it, is the will of God and ought to be an inspiring example to all men. It should always be a help and not a hinderance to the unity of men of different religions."[26] His Imperial Majesty was trying to get the different denominations to come together and find a resolution to their disputes. This demonstrates that He was asking for a new ecumenical council due to the present turmoils within Christendom; no one can accurately reference these events to state that He agrees with the Roman ideology founded at Nicaea. The world seems to have accepted the idea that the trinity is the Father, the Son, and the Holy Ghost although the scriptures do not reference them in this manner. Haile Selassie The First was working to gather everyone together so that they can discuss their differences in the faith thereby advocating for a change in canon. His Imperial Majesty was awarded the formal appellation of Defender of the Faith shortly after this Conference for His efforts in seeking to inspire people to accept the truth; because this was not accomplished at Nicaea.

We as RasTafarians, sons and daughters of the Almighty, cannot be resolved to Hail His Imperial Majesty without following the great example and mission that the Emperor instructed us to emulate. Everything about Haile Selassie The First awakens our higher conscious of thought and action, let us be diligent in His noble calling to achieve what we have been destined to fulfill which is to organize and centralize. This theme, while popular amongst all our RasTafarian brothers and sisters is wanting because the means towards manifesting this goal is either lost or circumvented. The only way that we as a people will be able to succeed is if we are united; our unity is our strength. Currently the various houses are divided based upon ideological differences and the only way to forge an effective collective movement is if these issues are resolved. Our King has said, "I believe that these are not confined to our times and that leaders must from time to time come together, face each other, and discus problems they share in common."[27] We cannot be myopic or cowardly in not taking on the larger and difficult challenges that will open the doors for us to take our rightful position in the world. Some think that His

---

[26] Ibid, page 635
[27] Ibid, page 153

Imperial Majesty is the Almighty, others say that He is Christ, and there are those who take Him for a great man. Since Haile Selassie The First is the tie which binds us all, we should be able to come together and study His words to forge an agreement. This is what the Emperor worked towards His whole life, including His undertakings at the League of Nations where He petitioned the need for collective security and His efforts at the forefront of the Pan-African movement when He established the OAU. The time has come for us to become real with ourselves and honest with God. If we are not able to put our ideas to the test to validate our positions then this could only mean that they are false, in addition to the fact that this indignant stance is in total opposition to what Haile Selassie The First has asked of us: "In addition, in this day and age, he must keep far from his mind the belief that he knows quite enough."[28] There have been many attempts to formulate one doctrine for all the various RasTafari houses to agree upon but up until now they have been unsuccessful. These endeavors have not been in vain and the fact that this task seems almost impossible to accomplish should only motivate us to redouble our efforts to-wards achieving this goal. His Imperial Majesty said, "It is well known that if a people has the firm determination to work, it can overcome any and all its dif-ficulties and problems. We have no problem which is insurmountable. Let us work in unity and diligence."[29] His instructions at the Conference of Oriental Churches hold a vast legality that we must apply to our current situation con-cerning the plight of the divergent RasTafarian sects. We should be united but this can only be achieved if there was a resolution upon one doctrine. Haile Selassie The First was active in getting people of different spiritual ideologies to come together and resolve their discord; how can we who say we follow Him not put His principles into action?

We are the beginning of a new generation and consciousness of thought. I believe that we are the living angels of God because it is the role of an angel to spread the message of the Lord. His Imperial Majesty said, "Had we been Christian people, had we been worthy of the name, peace would have reigned on all the face of the earth. We would have risen to the level of the immortal angels who always glorify the Eternal God, and the people of the world would no longer have remained divided into hostile camps."[30] I hope that the nations will adhere to the teachings of His Imperial Majesty because besides Him

---

[28] Ibid, page 77
[29] Ibid, page 95
[30] Haile Selassie I, Interview with Dr. Oswald Hoffman, December 25, 1968

there is no Savior. The Bible has clearly said that the King of Kings and Lord of Lords is God, He is the first and the last. Therefore we are waiting in vain if we are seeking for someone else to save us; Haile Selassie The First alone acquaints salvation. The world must acknowledge Him, God is not somebody that you can ignore; this is not a small issue. This is the greatest event in the history of the universe, everyone must praise RasTafari. If we all followed the righteous example of His Imperial Majesty then how much better would the world become in such a short period of time.

The Coronation of Haile Selassie The First marks the creation of the spiritual world, the world of understanding, intelligence, and love. The Bible is beckoning us to remember God and to follow the gospel of Jesus Christ. Historians remember His Imperial Majesty as a champion for human rights and world peace. His enemies had to make up lies about Him because they have no facts for which they can discredit Him with. After the fall of the League of Nations, the Emperor became one of the founding Fathers of the United Nations and He called this institution perhaps the last hope for the survival of mankind. History teaches us that Haile Selassie The First was the chief legislator who acknowledged the principles of collective security and international morality; these principles if followed on a broad scale will dramatically uplift humanity.

"Him that overcomes will I make a pillar in the temple of my God, and he shall go no more out: and I will write upon him the name of my God, and the name of the city of my God, which is new Jerusalem, which comes down out of heaven from my God: and I will write upon him my new name" (Revelation 3:12). Again, the words of Christ state that he will tell you what is the name of his God and he will tell you his new name. This shows you that Jesus is not God because he said that he will let the world know who his God is. Christ did not preach about himself and to further prove that point Jesus also stated that he will write his new name on him who overcomes. This demonstrates that the Father and the Son are two separate people with two different names. There should be no more confusion concerning this topic. The Father and the Son are not the same person; Haile Selassie The First is God and Primus Saint Croix is His Prophet.

There are those who ask "Would God praise Himself?" They want to know who did Haile Selassie The First pray to when He communed in church and why does He have the title Elect of God if He is God? The answers to these questions are simple yet sublime. First, telepathy is not a force which any man possess so no one can tell you what another person was thinking when they prayed; but we do know that God was manifest in the flesh to teach people what is acceptable, to show us what we must do in our lives. Therefore His Imperial Majesty was praying to demonstrate to the world that this is an acceptable act. In fact everything He did was done to demonstrate how we must conduct our lives; for God is the Law. Secondly, the Bible said, "When God made the promise to Abraham, since there is no one greater for him to swear by, he swore by himself." This means that when Haile Selassie The First says that He is praying to God, this does not take away from His divinity; His Imperial Majesty being the Elect of God means that He is God. Who else was He going to invoke; it is written that He has sworn by Himself. Not only did He crown Himself King of Kings and Lord of Lords, He also merited the claim by performing the works of God. Haile Selassie The First does not have to say verbatim that He is the Almighty, He told us to look to God because if you accepted the descriptions of Jah written throughout the Bible then you will know that He is God. The Most High will not teach us how He is the Almighty, that is why He has a Son, the Prophet was sent to explain that His Imperial Majesty is God; if there were those who did not comprehend it based off His most excellent work and character. The books of the Prophets say that God speaks to us through signs and wonders. On November 2, 1930, RasTafari Mekonnen ascended the Throne of David with the titles of God; never in human history has anyone else been crowned King of Kings and Lord of Lords. There were certain Ethiopian and Persian rulers who were designated as King of Kings; but no one besides His Imperial Majesty held the complete appellation of the Most High. On His Imperial Majesty's Coronation vesture are two crowns and two crosses which means King of Kings and Lord of Lords; it is important to note that the Emperor helped to design His garments because He was conveying a specific message on that day which only those with (spiritual) eyes will see. The Bible said that God showed signs in heaven; some people think that His signs are thunder and lightning in the sky. However, Matthew 5:34 said that Heaven is the Throne of God. Haile Selassie The First is the King of Tsion, Jesus Christ worshipped Him because He fulfilled the prophecy, if the world accepted the revelation then the promises of salvation would improve all of society. His Imperial Majesty led us by example not drivel, if we should follow His commandments then we shall inherit the Kingdom and manifest Heaven on earth. Blessed be Jah RasTafari.

Seventy Years Accomplished in Babylon

"And this gospel of the kingdom shall be preached in all the world for a witness unto all nations; and then shall the end come" (Matthew 24:14).

The Beginning

"In the beginning God created the heaven and the earth" (Genesis 1:1). This means that God was manifest in the flesh and Emperor Haile Sellassie I has fulfilled the prophecy. Genesis is the beginning of the Lord's theocratic reign on this planet; the Bible is referencing the spiritual creation, when God revealed himself before the eyes of all the nations. Matthew 6:10 confirms this by stating, *"Thy kingdom come. Thy will be done on earth, as it is in heaven."* On November 2, 1930 in Addis Ababa, Ras Tafari Makonnen proved to be the Most High when he was crowned: Emperor of Ethiopia, Haile Sellassie I, The First Power of the Holy Trinity, King of Kings, Lord of Lords, Conquering Lion of the Tribe of Judah, Light of the World. His Majesty was proclaiming his assumption to the Throne of David and making known his regnal name for which he shall govern under. In Revelation 19:11-16 it says that God will reveal himself to mankind with the epithet "King of Kings and Lord of Lords;" he also had a name written that no man knew but he himself. The world knew His Majesty as Ras Tafari before he ascended to the Imperial Throne of Ethiopia but on that

day he changed his name to Haile Sellassie I, thus fulfilling the prophecy of the coming of the Lord. There also has never been anyone else who has established a government on earth with the titles of the Almighty; he is the first and the last.[1] This is the evidence of God and there shall be no other sign given.

"And the earth was without form and void; and darkness was upon the face of the deep. And the Spirit of God moved upon the face of the waters" (Genesis 1:2). This scripture explains how after the Lord fulfilled the prophecy, the people did not believe that Haile Sellassie I was the Almighty. They did not put their trust in him but nevertheless the truth remains the same. In Romans 3:3-4, it says, *"For what if some did not believe? Shall their unbelief make the faith of God without effect? God forbid: yea, let God be true and every man a liar."* In 1930 Ras Tafari invited all the nations to be present at his Coronation and to witness this historic event. His Majesty went on to become one of the most celebrated and popular celebrities of the twentieth century. In an era where video recorders and cameras were present to capture these events, there is no excuse for being uninformed about Haile Sellassie I; but we witness this occurring. *"For my people is foolish, they have not known me; they are sottish children, and they are wise to do evil, but to do good they have no knowledge. I beheld the earth, and lo, it was without form, and void; and the heavens, and they had no light"* (Jeremiah 4:22-23). The world had no understanding regarding the truth about God until Christ preached his message; read Isaiah 24:1-6 and 1 John 5:19.

"And God said, Let there be light and there was light" (Genesis 1:3). The Lord would not leave himself without witness, that is why it is written in Job 33:14 that he has spoken once (in 1930), yet twice have we heard his voice (again in the year 2000), but man perceives it not. The people did not understand how Haile Sellassie I is God based upon his own works therefore he sent forth his Son (the prophet) to teach the people how His Majesty is in fact the Almighty. The testimony of Primus St. Croix is the sole means for salvation, that is why it is written that Christ is the door into heaven and those who do not enter through him are thieves and robbers.[2] Anyone who does not accept the gospel of the Son of God does not have the true interpretation of spiritual matters; this is what it means by the mediator between God and man, you must go through him in order to have the correct understanding. Christ said, *"For I say unto you, You shall not see me henceforth, till you shall say, Blessed is he that comes in the name of the LORD"* (Matthew 23:39). There was no one who had the proper

---

[1] Isaiah 44:6
[2] John 10:1-10

understanding of the parables therefore Primus was sent to explain how it is that Haile Sellassie I is the God of the Bible. In the year 2000, there was a cry heard throughout the land as idols were broken, this was a call for the world to renounce their false understanding of the scriptures. Primus St. Croix gave the definitive explanation of the mysteries but the only way to know the truth is if you first renounce your fictitious comprehension of spirituality. In John 8:12 it says, *"Then spoke Jesus again unto them saying, I am the light of the world: he that follows me shall not walk in darkness, but shall have the light of life."* The light which God sent forth is Jesus Christ, this was done to save humanity. Only through the Messiah will we be given the perfect interpretation which would allow us to see and know the Most High.[3] It is written that no one in heaven or earth could correctly comprehend the oracle; until Christ came along, that is why he is described as the true light which enlightens the whole world.

"And God saw the light, that it was good and God divided the light from the darkness" *(Genesis 1:4).* This shows the difference between those who follow Christ and those who deny the gospel. Under God's law we will have the correct understanding of the parables but through satan we will only be deceived. Therefore it is up to us to learn about Haile Sellassie I and adopt his principals, then we can learn the ways of life and prosper. The doctrines and pernicious policies which hold the world back have been denounced by His Majesty. By examining the Emperor's life we can attain the knowledge of what we must do to please God, this will usher in heaven on earth. But if we put our trust in man made philosophies and deny the divinity of Ras Tafari then we will never know God and we will be going against our own salvation. Acts 14:4 says, *"But the multitude of the city was divided: and part held with the Jews, and part with the apostles."* This explains the division between those who accept Christ (the apostles) and those who claim to follow God but deny the Word (the Jews). Haile Sellassie I is *The Law*, which means that he is the definition of everything that is right, those who are of the light will accept him and emulate his deeds. The children of the night are the people who are unable to comprehend the oracle, unable to believe in their Creator, unable to accept the divinity of the Emperor. His Majesty established *The Law* through his own disposition. Without God setting the example of what is right and wrong, the people would be left to interpret these matters on their own. There is no greater definition of righteousness because Haile Sellassie I was perfect in all things and what greater condemnation for those who reject him without a just cause.

---

[3] John 1:18

"And God called the light Day, and the darkness he called Night. And the evening and the morning were the first day" (Genesis 1:5). Remember that first the world was void and then came the light, which is the prophet Jesus Christ. Haile Sellassie I admonished the world to follow the Messiah because the people did not have the truth. But the masses have been misled to think that the Son of God is a supernatural figure who came in ancient Arabia or there are certain questions regarding the Rastafarian leaders who preached that Haile Sellassie I is God before Primus St. Croix delivered his message. They ask how come the previous Rastafarians are not Christ or was His Majesty referring to that mythological fable concerning the Jesus of antiquity? Both of these questions can be answered with the same premise, namely that darkness covered the earth before Christ. Jeremiah 4:20-28 explains that no one had the truth about God, therefore the people need to stop taking a position that they can preach before they have accepted the testimony of Jesus. The idea that Christ came thousands of years ago is contrary to the Bible because it is written that the Messiah will show us God.[4] It is not possible to preach that the kingdom of heaven in at hand before theocracy was established on earth in 1930. Haile Sellassie I is the only King of Kings and Lord of Lords therefore the Bible begins with him. The Rastafarians were correct in admonishing his divinity but they have failed in knowing the complete truth because they also think that Jesus came during ancient times and shame His Majesty when they call him the second coming of Christ. This would make Jesus a supernatural figure who lived in antiquity and has returned again as the Emperor of Ethiopia. These false doctrines demonstrate that the truth was not revealed until the true Messiah came; which is exactly what the Bible says. The Lord's will is for humanity to be saved, that is why he sent his prophet to give us the correct interpretation. *"Jesus answered, Are there not twelve hours in the day? If any man walk in the day, he stumbles not because he sees the light of this world. But if a man walk in the night, he stumbles, because there is no light in him" (John 11:9-10)*. Through Christ we can learn the truth about God and be saved, this is what it means by walking in the day but if we deny his message then we will never understand the scriptures; which is darkness.

To better understand how Haile Sellassie I is the Savior of the World, we must be aware of his life and mission. He was born on July 23, 1892 into the Royal House of David, the Ethiopian Solomonic Dynasty, who also bear the Ark of the Covenant. Early in his childhood he witnessed his proud and

---

[4] Ibid

independent nation successfully defend itself against Italian imperialism at the Battle of Adowa; His Majesty also had to defeat fascist aggression and safeguard his country's sovereignty during Mussolini's invasion. The Emperor was a family man, he married Itege Menen Asfaw Walatta Giyorgis, to whom he had six children by: Princess Tenagne Worq, Crown Prince Asfa Wossen, Princess Zannaba Worq, Princess Tsahai, Prince Makonnen, and Prince Sahle Selassie. He also had a daughter, Princess Romana Worq, from a previous marriage to Woizero Altayech. Empress Menen was married three times prior to her marriage to Haile Sellassie I; she had two children from her first husband, two from her second, but none from her third. The Emperor showed her great respect, and by his considerate treatment of his wife and his high moral standards he has set a fine example to his people. Even those who like him least can have no ground for criticism in his marital life.[5] His Majesty possessed the foresight in government to understand that in order for Ethiopia to maintain its sovereignty it was necessary to modernize his country, educate his people, establish ties with diverse nations, strengthen the military, develop the middle class, and establish a strong central administration who would seek justice and not personal gain. His Majesty's administration is widely criticized despite all of his policies being correct. He raised the standards of greatness and benefited not only his country but the entire global community by offering guidance to various nations on varied issues. It is a well known fact that Haile Sellassie I presented to the world body the instructions on what needed to be done in order to prevent World War II from occurring. President Lyndon Johnson had this to say about him, "He and his people have inspired us by their heroic example in time of war. And they have impressed us by the wisdom of their advice in time of peace. The most destructive war in human history might well have been prevented if the world had only listened--30 years ago--to the Emperor of Ethiopia. Mankind has seldom been offered so accurate a prophecy. And it has never paid a grimmer price for ignoring one of its prophets."[6] By examining how he overcame challenges we then can gain the knowledge on what we need to do to make the proper decisions in our lives. When His Majesty was killed in 1975, Ethiopia suffered greatly through a dramatically polarized shift in policy as Mengistu Haile Mariam became the head of state

---

[5] Princess Asfa Yilma, Haile Selassie: Emperor of Ethiopia, page 246
[6] Lyndon B. Johnson, Remarks of Welcome at the White House to Haile Selassie I, February 13, 1967

and proved to be the most corrupt, inept, and pernicious ruler that country has ever experienced. The world was also affected as there was no one to take his place as the Governor of nations whose earnest approach liberated millions and uplifted humanity as a whole. The fact that Haile Sellassie I is dead perplexes some regarding the validity of the Rastafarian claim towards his divinity but that can be easily answered if we adhere to what His Majesty told us. God's law dictates that death is a fundamental part of life, no one can live forever in the flesh; we therefore must leave behind a legacy of righteousness for the future generations to emulate, if we wish to be eternal. Haile Sellassie I said, "To free the human race from superstition and fear that originate from ignorance; to enable him to transcend the apparent obstacles of race and religion; and to help him recognize the blood-ties of the whole human race, Your Excellency has labored. To this generation, so tormented between modern knowledge and ancient faith, your scrupulous studies have pointed the way by which man may be saved from traditional superstition and modern skepticism."[7] We should no longer adhere to false supernatural myths such as the concept of a fountain of youth, or going back in time, or living forever in the flesh for this all derives from ignorance and superstition; God did not create the universe in that manner. No one can physically die and come back to life, or be reincarnated, these beliefs are all false and contrary to the laws of nature which the Lord established. Haile Sellassie I was the Most High before he appeared on earth in a bodily form and he is the same after the flesh passed away; he always was and always will be God. We cannot base the validity of his divinity upon fictional ideologies such as being physically immortal or mystical. The message of Christ is the renunciation of idolatry.

The Evidence of God

Emperor Haile Sellassie I is the Almighty God; the scriptures reveal that he is the Supreme Being. Blessed are all those who accept the Savior of humanity.

"Bring forth the blind people that have eyes, and the deaf that have ears. Let all the nations be gathered together, and let the people be assembled: who among them can declare this, and show us former things? Let them bring forth their witnesses, that they may be justified: or let them hear, and say, It is the truth. You are

---

[7] The Selected Speeches of His Imperial Majesty Haile Selassie I, page 133

my witnesses, saith the LORD, and my servant whom I have chosen: that you may know and believe me and understand that I am he: before me there was no God formed, neither shall there be after me. I, even I, am the LORD; and beside me there is no savior. I have declared, and I have saved, and I have showed, when there was no strange god among you: therefore you are my witnesses, saith the LORD, that I am God. Yea, before the day was I am he; and there is none that can deliver out of my hand: I will work, and who shall let it" (Isaiah 43:8-13). In this modern era, technology has advanced to the point where we are able to learn about any subject within a matter of minutes; in the information age, ignorance is a choice. There is no excuse for not being aware that for the first time in history a government has been established on earth under the titles "King of Kings and Lord of Lords." The Bible does not say that this occurrence can be simplified; the scriptures clearly say that God is the only one who will come in this name. It is written that he will make himself known, when there was no strange god among you; before him there was no God formed (meaning before him no one on earth ever held these titles), neither shall there be after him, besides him there is no savior, we are all witnesses (anyone can verify this information). This passage indicates that God is the first and the last person who will ever reign with the appellation of the Most High. There was previous rulers in Ethiopia, and around the world, who held the honor of being the King of Kings but no one, besides Haile Sellassie I, also was the Lord of Lords simultaneously. His Majesty has the designation as well as the character of the Almighty; there is no one else for us to look to; the prophecy has a perfect fulfillment.

"For ask now of the days that are past, which were before thee, since the day that God created man upon the earth, and ask from the one side of heaven unto the other, whether there has been any such thing as this great thing is, or hath been heard like it? Did ever people hear the voice of God speaking out of the midst of the fire, as thou has heard, and live" (Deuteronomy 4:32-33). On November 2, 1930, Haile Sellassie I established theocracy on earth when he was crowned as the Savior; he invited all nations to be present as he declared to the world that he is God. He did this by using symbolic biblical references when he presented himself as the one and only King of Kings and Lord of Lords, Conquering Lion of the Tribe of Judah.[8] His Majesty did not verbatim say that he is the Almighty because that would prove nothing, anyone can do that; instead he did something which the Bible describes that only God can do, which is to sit upon the Throne

---

[8] L.A. Times, February 9, 1993, page 3

of David with the titles of the Most High. Ras means Lord in Amharic[9] and as Regent Plenipotentiary of the Ethiopian Realm he was the "Ras be Ras," also known as "Raessi Reussan" or "Ras of Rases"[10] (Lord of Lords) for he held supreme authority even as Empress Zewditu was legally the head of state. His Majesty deposed the precarious and uncrowned Lij Iyasu for apostasy, then he defeated Negus Mikael in battle as he was seeking to avenge his son, he was also effectively indomitable to all the schemes of the Empress and the nobility to stifle his command. He was the most eminent of all the various leaders in Ethiopia and this appellation was issued to signify his position. It should be noted that there were other great dignitaries who have held the honor of being Ras of Rases such as Ras Alula; and there have been monarchs who bore the title of King of Kings like Menelik II. But when Haile Sellassie I rose to become the Negus Negast,[11] this marked the first time in history that anyone has ever held both the titles King of Kings and Lord of Lords in unison. All other references to this epithet are held by fictional and mythological figures but the government of Emperor Haile Sellassie I is a real and definitive moment in history that cannot be erased, modified, or denied.[12] There is no other event or personality comparable to the revelation of God. It would lead to our inevitable downfall if we neglect His Majesty because it is impossible for an impostor to carry the rank of the Almighty; it is written that the Lord will not give his glory to another.[13]

"*The LORD is well pleased for his righteousness sake; he will magnify the law, and make it honorable*" (Isaiah 42:21). The clearest sign to identify who the Bible is referring to will be found in the fulfillment of prophecy. It is written

---

[9] A.R. Elia, Opening Round, page 157

　Ethiopia fact file, www.bbc.com

　Yoga Journal, July/August 1983 Issue No. 51, page 18

　The Rise of a Movement, www.ghanaweb.com

　Haile Selassie, el polemico redentor de Sion, www.almamater.cu

[10] Sir Charles Fernand Rey, The Real Abyssinia, page 117

　The Vancouver Sun, September 7, 1935, page 2

　L.A. Times, February 9, 1993, World Report page 3

　Evening Post, Volume CXXI Issue 2, January 3, 1936, page 8

　New York Times, November 3, 1930, page 1

　Prince Ermias Sahle-Selassie discussion at the Library of Congress, December 9, 2010

[11] King of Kings

[12] Ecclesiastes 3:14

[13] Isaiah 42:8

that the Lord will magnify the law which means that he will follow and accomplish what is written of him. It is also repeated that he is a jealous God[14]
therefore no one should think that the promises can be carried out by a charlatan. This is important to understand when considering the claim of Emperor
Haile Sellassie I as the Almighty. It has been said that His Majesty's name is
not written in the Bible therefore the scriptures cannot be referring to him but
that is a very simple minded position. How hard would it be for anyone to say
that the oracle is talking about them if all that it took was for someone to be
named one of the titles written in the scriptures? Should we be looking for
Jesus among all the people who are named Jesus, if it was solely based upon
the name then they all would have to be proclaimed as the Messiah but that
is completely illogical; we must approach this from a more intellectual and
accurate standpoint. The descriptions of God are more detailed than just an
epithet therefore we will have to understand the entire prophecy if we expect
to know who he is. It is also written that he had a name which only he knew,[15]
this indicates that he will come under a new appellation that is not written in
the Bible. In Zechariah 14:9 it is written that his name is One, this is also a
symbolic reference not that his moniker is simply a numerical digit. Emperor
Haile Sellassie I magnified the law and made it honorable which means that he
fulfilled every aspect of the prophecy concerning the Almighty. His Majesty
has the character, the descriptions, and he carried out the works of God; everything we are looking for is found in him.

*"For he spake in a certain place of the seventh day on this wise, AND GOD
DID REST THE SEVENTH DAY FROM ALL HIS WORKS"* (Hebrews
4:4). When the Bible says that God rested on the seventh day this means
that the Lord established his kingdom on earth. There are certain key points
and principals that the scriptures are constantly referring to. When we understand that the Creator is the one and only King of Kings and Lord of
Lords then we can progress and unlock other parables through his prophet
(Matthew 22:37-40). First, we have to accept the fact that Emperor Haile
Sellassie I is the Almighty God and Father of Jesus Christ. Other denominations of church and state would debate and challenge His Majesty's divinity
but this goes back to the scripture about Light and Darkness - Heaven or
Hell. Without Haile Sellassie I there is no God because we would be left to
our imagination to decipher the Lord. To believe that Haile Sellassie I is the

---

[14] Exodus 34:14
[15] Revelation 19:12

Almighty is to keep the seventh day holy, we have evidence that God was manifested in the flesh. If we do not put our faith in His Majesty then we are worshipping on the wrong day; which means holding the wrong faith. There are people who call Haile Sellassie I a wicked man, a thief, a traitor, or an impostor. He is also called Christ by some, a prophet by others, a good man, or a great politician. But until we come to know that he is God the Almighty we will never be observing the Sabbath. Since 1930 there have been various theories to explain the character of His Majesty but the truth has been revealed only through his messenger Jesus Christ. Primus St. Croix sent a message to the world when he went on a campaign breaking idols in the year 2000. He said to worship Emperor Haile Sellassie I on the seventh day, which means to acknowledge that His Majesty is God the Father.

"The LORD our God made a covenant with us in Horeb. The LORD made not this covenant with our fathers, but with us, even us, who are all of us here alive this day. The LORD talked with you face to face in the mount out of the midst of the fire" (Deuteronomy 5:2-4). If we accept the law and the testimony of the Lord then we would hear his voice speaking to us out of the midst of the fire, we would meet him face to face and have solid evidence of his presence. Again this covenant is to know that Haile Sellassie I is the Creator, he made not this covenant with disbelievers but with the faithful. Now some would argue that if he is God, how could he be dead? It is true that he died in 1975 and he will never come back again, neither will anyone else who lived in antiquity. He lived and died by normal means and accomplished all of his feats through natural occurrences to teach people how to achieve their goals. It would be vain for him to perform supernatural miracles if the rest of the world does not possess this same ability because this would not help us to solve our problems. Being that the Almighty is the Savior, he would have to communicate with us in a manner that would allow us to implement his instructions and guidance; this is why it only makes sense for the revelation to be fulfilled through natural means. We have also read in John 6:63 that the flesh profits nothing, it is the Spirit that quickens; this indicates that Haile Sellassie I was God before he showed his face on earth in 1892 and he is the same after he passed away in 1975; we therefore should not get hung up on his body for it was always intended to be a temporary medium. The supernatural is a false and worthless concept; the universe follows the laws of nature which God established. His Majesty said, "The Lord, who is above all creations, although possessing the power to order everything according to His will, has nevertheless wished to establish the rule of law and subject it to all creation."[16] For example, there is only one way to have a child and that is when a man and a woman are in union. Scientists can take sperm and stimulate a woman's egg to produce a child but that also follows the biological command. But if you say that a woman can get pregnant from praying or from a spirit (apparition) then you are highly deceived. Haile Sellassie I showed the world the meaning of life and in doing so established international law and morality. From him we know that everyone will eventually die and that eternal life is based upon your legacy and the future generations following what you have left behind. When people reproduce their offspring carry similar character traits of their parents and family, this is the closest that anyone will come to reincarnation or physical immortality. Mankind was not created to live forever in the flesh or to literally die and come back to life. The supernatural is a false dogma established by satan to deceive the world into believing in impossible acts that will never come to pass. You will never be able to recognize the Lord at his coming if you have the wrong perception regarding the prophecy. His Majesty has showed us that the Lord can do anything but he will not do everything. We have to accept reality and believe in the laws of nature that God established at the beginning of the universe; that is the only way to understand the Bible.

"Thus will I magnify myself, and sanctify myself, and I will be known in the eyes of many nations, and they shall know that I am the LORD" (Ezekiel 38:23). Concerning the Almighty, the Bible is constantly referring to the fact that the Creator will reveal himself on earth. This prophecy was fulfilled on November 2, 1930 when Haile Sellassie I was crowned in Addis Ababa. False religions use spirituality as a means to enslave the world instead of offering the true interpretation which leads to a mental awakening. Superstition is a weapon of fear, by teaching people that the supernatural is real, this opens the doors of chaos. It is a subliminal message that takes root in the back of your conscious and grows to rot out your entire understanding of life. Belief in the supernatural only leads to the development of a completely backwards thought process, for example people think that it is possible for the spirit world to communicate with our dimension, they blame occurrences which they do not understand on ghosts, and they become susceptible to emasculating doctrines which all rely upon superstition to maintain their hold. This incorrect concept stems from the religious world's inability to interpret the scriptures properly. When people have the wrong outlook on life they will not be able to decipher righteousness

---

[16] The Selected Speeches of His Imperial Majesty Haile Selassie I, page 388

and salvation will always be distant. This is why it is so important for God to make himself known on earth. Haile Sellassie I rebuked the theory of superstition to teach us what life is all about, he said, "That education which ignores man's intrinsic nature, and neglects his intellect and reasoning power cannot be considered true education."[17] If we have the wrong understanding about how the universe operates and what is possible or impossible to take place on earth, then we will be looking for God to appear in a manner which he will not fulfill. That will then lead to us denying the Lord at his coming due to our own ignorance with accepting the natural and permanent operation of life.

"Oh that my words were now written! Oh that they were printed in a book! That they were graven with an iron pen and lead in the rock forever! For I know that my redeemer liveth, and that he shall stand at the latter day upon the earth: And though after my skin worms destroy this body, yet in my flesh shall I see God: Whom I shall see for myself, and mine eyes shall behold, and not another; though my reins be consumed within me" (Job 19:23-27). If we do not accept the prophecy that God will appear on earth as the great King of Kings and Lord of Lords then we have not the Word of Truth. The Bible is very clear on this fact in numerous different passages. But the false religions of the world have misused the good book because they have not the correct understanding of the prophecy. By invoking a superstitious element into the Word, this puts the believer into a state of subliminal fear. They are afraid of apparitions and believe that they can become the victim of supernatural circumstances but nothing of the sort could ever happen in real life. When the scriptures said to fear God,[18] this actually means to believe in Haile Sellassie I. We was not designed to be afraid and to live our lives terrified and pacified; this would prevent us from maximizing our potential and fulfilling our mission in life. God has not hindered our progress, it was satan who did that through a deceitful prose. The Lord did not advocate supernatural idolatry, it was the devil who taught that to mankind. The Bible has been used for evil, to subjugate nations, enslave people, and to provoke wars. But it is not the holy scriptures which are harmful, it is the user with bad intentions who has manipulated the Word to fit their wicked agenda. This tactic can be accomplished with just about any manuscript but we have been warned in 2 Corinthians 11:14-15 to be aware that the devil will use the Bible to corrupt the world.

---

[17] Ibid, page 34
[18] Deuteronomy 6:13

"Not that any man has seen the Father, save he which is of God, he has seen the Father" (John 6:46). According to the Bible, we are supposed to see and know God. From him we will gain the correct understanding and outlook on life. Haile Sellassie I said, "We have been a child, a boy, an adult, and finally an old man. Like everyone else. Our Lord the Creator made us like everyone else."[19] If His Majesty lived and died by natural means then we must understand that all the scriptures which appear to deviate from universal law are in fact allegories and the Bible itself says that it is written in parables.[20] No one can operate outside of the laws of nature for the Lord did not establish his creation under those auspices. Furthermore God will not have to break his own tenants, which he established at the beginning of the universe, to prove his divinity. He is perfect therefore it would only make sense for him to follow the edicts that he has subjected to everyone and everything. In Numbers 23:19 it says that God is not a man that he should lie, what he said shall he not do it; therefore the Almighty is true to his Word and adheres to his own principles. That is why Haile Sellassie I operated purely in a realistic and natural manner. He was manifest on earth under the only normal circumstances for which God invested people to live by; he was born as a baby and grew in age. His father, Ras Makonnen Woldemikael Gudessa, and mother, Weyziro Yeshimebet Ali Abajifar, came together in a natural union to have a child; there is no other way for God to appear on this planet that would make sense. The world has been deceived into taking the scriptures literal despite the fact that their interpretation and understanding lacks evidence and logic. Science and religion was always meant to operate side by side since the Lord created both of these subjects. But you will not be able to speak on these topics properly unless you follow Haile Sellassie I. The idea which says that you cannot see God is contrary to the scriptures as well as this is a demonic tactic used to prevent humanity from accepting the Lord at his coming. If the world does not know who is the true Savior then they would be left dependent upon other people who cannot offer salvation. When the security of mankind is left in the hands of people who lack proper moral guidance and disobey God, then the end result will always be injustice and corruption. Haile Sellassie I rebuked these evil leaders and addressed what must be done to care for those in need and eliminate strife. His Majesty said, "It is a truism that self-help, hard work and initiative are requisites for any nation's economic and social advancement. Yet it is equally true

---

[19] The Chicago Tribune, Interview by Oriani Fallaci, June 24, 1973
[20] Mark 4:13

that there still are outmoded international arrangements which seriously limit
the efforts of developing countries to develop their potential. So long as there
remain impediments to the free flow of international trade; so long as there is
no guaranteed price of primary goods at remunerative level without discrimination, the economic and social development of the developing nations will
remain seriously handicapped. It is in this connection that the economically
advanced nations can render valuable contributions. Such nations could, as
an instance, extend further bilateral or multilateral assistance and waive ob-
structing arrangements such as preferential tariffs as well as other protective
systems which, in the long run, prove a disservice to the economic and social
progress of developing nations."[21]

   *"Again he said, Therefore hear the word of the LORD; I saw the LORD sitting
upon his throne, and all the host of heaven standing on his right hand and on his
left"* (2 Chronicles 18:18). We must accept the message of the Bible with a clear
conscience. It is promised unto the faithful in Christ to see and know God. This
means to accept Emperor Haile Sellassie I as the Almighty God and Creator of
the universe. If we do not accept the Bible's great message of salvation that the
Lord will establish his kingdom on earth then we will be subject unto lies and
vanity. There are forces at work whose aim is to misinterpret the scriptures so
that they can corrupt the world; that is why it is very important that we follow
the correct teachings. Superstition leads people to believe in a false reality and
when your perception is distorted you become more prone to accepting a miserable existence. For example, those who think that ghosts are real, become
more susceptible to adhering to a dogma which calls for your submission to
the spirit world. When you have been indoctrinated to anticipate the afterlife,
this can easily lead to you neglecting your present human condition. We have
witnessed colonial powers subjugate many nations under these same pretenses
therefore no one should think that we have presented a hypothetical scenario.
The ramifications of adhering to the wrong principles are far reaching therefore it is necessary to have the correct outlook on life, which only comes from
knowing God. His Majesty said, "In our times, there are those expansionists
who by shedding blood, desire to achieve their ambition and by dismembering
themselves they are seen as tools for alien interests. Our people from Ethiopia
shed blood, to save them from disintegration."[22] Haile Sellassie I has advised
us to safeguard our dignity and honor against any attempt to deprive us of

---

[21] The Selected Speeches of His Imperial Majesty Haile Selassie I, page 158
[22] Ibid, page 426

our basic human rights; the only shame to this mandate is if we choose not to follow this all important principle. The devil has stripped people of their common sense, virtue, and salvation. They teach people to accept depravity and humiliation in the hopes of being rewarded when they die. This backwards philosophy has prospered in part due to their violent means of coercion as well as the people's ignorance of righteousness. It is important to be able to identify the forces which hold us back; the supernatural has no beneficial purpose or biblical foundation, it is a false interpretation.

"And I saw a great white throne, and him that sat on it, from whose face the earth and the heaven fled away; and there was found no place for them" (Revelation 20:11). You cannot know God if you do not see him. There is no alternate reality that can debunk this premise. The Lord is not a feeling which comes over you or a force inside of you. God is the Supreme Being and it is written that the people fled away from his face because they did not accept him. But there was found no place for them because Haile Sellassie I alone is the King of Kings and Lord of Lords. The Creator is ubiquitous and omniscient but no one should take this to mean that the supernatural is real. The gift of Christ is to know who God is but the knowledge concerning the operation of the universe, such as how the world was created, how God knows everything and is everywhere; these keynotes are preserved only in the Most High. No one can answer those questions except for God and he has not revealed this to mankind. The Lord has established the laws of nature to create order in the universe but many people still cannot correctly decipher what is reality. This is due to false religious teachers who preach pagan principles such as the supernatural. Humanity has been given a great enough task in putting into practice the teachings of Emperor Haile Sellassie I; which begs the question, why do we wish to be at peace in the afterlife if we do not strive to live in harmony with all of God's creation in our present earthly dimension? It seems as if we are putting the cart before the horse. His Majesty taught us to do good on earth and to live our lives to its maximum potential. Let us concentrate upon the real task at hand which is to make the world a better place instead of spending time on useless discussions regarding spurious paranormal activity and the hereafter. Our purpose, with being given the gift of life, is not to neglect our human condition but to live comfortably and peacefully in unison with all of mankind.

"And they shall see his face; and his name shall be in their foreheads" (Revelation 22:4). The entire purpose of God appearing on earth is to teach the world how to live properly. Therefore this event will not be a private occurrence where only a small number of people will see his face. This will be a grand occasion for

the entire world to take notice. Emperor Haile Sellassie I was one of the most popular celebrities of the twentieth century, he was the most photographed and the most bemedalled ruler in the world;[23] and he gained his recognition the good old fashioned way - by earning it. Even if you did not count his well deserved forty or so Ethiopian awards, he was still the world's most decorated human being based upon all of the honors he received from other nations. We are able to look up this information since he came during a time when the technology was advanced so that cameras could record his actions and his deeds could be permanently recorded in the annals of history. That which we preach is not a myth or a misrepresentation. The revelation has come to pass not in a supernatural manner when the Bible said that everyone will see God,[24] but according to a definitive design because everybody has the opportunity to learn about him. Everything we say about His Majesty can be verified through simple research as there is concrete evidence of his wonderful works; the truth is hidden in plain view. Haile Sellassie I should be taught in the schools and churches as being the true Savior of humanity because that is who he is. But the real intentions of these institutions have been made manifest as they reject the divinity of the Emperor. That is why it said that his throne is established for judgment.[25] If the churches were real churches they will worship His Majesty, if the schools were real schools then they would teach the children about the goodness of Haile Sellassie I, if the politicians were sincere rulers then they would follow his policies. But we find them all contrary to God because their agenda is to deceive and oppress humanity.

"His foundation is in the holy mountains. The LORD loves the gates of Zion more than all the dwellings of Jacob. Glorious things are spoken of thee, O city of God. Selah. I will make mention of Rahab and Babylon to them that know me: behold Philistia, and Tyre, with Ethiopia; this man was born there. And of Zion it shall be said, This and that man was born in her: and the highest himself shall establish her. The LORD shall count, when he writes up the people, that this man was born there. Selah. As well as the singers and the players on instruments shall be there; all my springs are in thee" (Psalm 87). On top of the Bible being adamant about the fact that we shall see God, it further lists his descriptions when it said "Ethiopia; this man was born there." The text is referring to the highest himself. If we list all of the definitions of God, we will find that every single characterization of

---

[23] Boca Raton News, June 18, 1972, page 2B

[24] Isaiah 52:10

[25] Psalm 9:7

the Creator is pointing us to Emperor Haile Sellassie I. The Bible said that the Almighty is the first and the last, King of King and Lord of Lords, Conquering Lion of the Tribe of Judah, the root of David, Governor of the nations, he sits upon the rainbow circle throne (green, yellow, and red), his name is One. It would raise reasonable doubts if His Majesty only fulfilled some of the prophecy but the entire book correlates with him. The only thing that he did not do was perform supernatural acts because sorcery and witchcraft is not of God. Anyone who states that Haile Sellassie I is not written in the Bible does not understand what they are reading and denies the gospel of Christ.

"And without controversy great is the mystery of godliness: God was manifest in the flesh, justified in the spirit, seen of angels, preached unto the Gentiles, believed on in the world, received up into glory" (1 Timothy 3:16). The concept of prayer is a necessary edict for all of humanity to uphold but it is more important to know who we are praying to. The times of ignorance are behind us, the Almighty has appeared on earth to instruct humanity in righteousness. The scriptures indicate that Haile Sellassie I is God incarnate to whom we all must worship. Jesus Christ prayed to his Father and he instructed us to do the same.[26] We now must recognize who is the Almighty and give him his proper respect and honor; for the kingdom of heaven is at hand. It would therefore only makes sense for His Majesty to pray as an example for us to follow. Everything he did was to instruct humanity in the proper order; this would include him living by natural means, his diet, exercise, work ethic, academic study, military action, and even his death. Only if we analyze the Emperor's actions through the perspective of acknowledging his divinity and understanding that he appeared on earth to teach us how to live, would we then be able to properly explain the mystery of God without denying the good works of Haile Sellassie I. There is no contradiction between anything that His Majesty did and what we read in the Bible but the wrong interpretation will yield confusion. They imagine God to appear in a supernatural format, so when the Emperor rebuked this pagan concept, those who never accepted his counsel were not able to recognize the revelation. Nobody knows what Haile Sellassie I was thinking when he prayed but we do know that this act, along with everything else he did, was done to set the example of righteousness for all of mankind to follow. It further states that when God could swear by no one greater, he swore by himself.[27] This should further explain why His Majesty was the "Elect of God," why he always stated

---

[26] John 17
[27] Hebrews 6:13

that he was a "follower of God," and why he "prayed to God." It is also important to keep in mind that it is not uncommon for speakers to refer to themselves in the third person which does not mean that they are mentioning another person; this only creates distance and indicates that the topic is not open for discussion.

"And the LORD shall be king over all the earth: in that day shall there be one LORD, and his name one" (Zechariah 14:9). Haile Sellassie I was a member of the Ethiopian Orthodox Tewahedo Church and was crowned on November 2, 1930, in the cathedral of St. George in Addis Ababa. This grand procession followed traditional ancient Hebraic-Christian customs which esteem the Emperor of Ethiopia as the indubitable head of both church and state. More than 700 guests and officials from all around the world were present at his historic coronation. The foreign envoys bowed to His Majesty and wished him a successful reign. Being a pious and righteous leader, Haile Sellassie I epitomized the character of the virtuous. He gave us proper guidance in instructing all of mankind to follow Jesus Christ because it is written in John 8:18 that the Father will testify of his Son. He also prayed in church to lead by example reinforcing beneficial practices. Everything he did was to teach the world what is acceptable; this is the entire purpose of God revealing himself on earth. This is also why His Majesty petitioned for the independence of the Ethiopian bishops from Egypt's Holy Synod in 1942 and 1945. His appeals led the Coptic Primate to permit the Tewahedo Church to be autocephalous in 1948. The Ethiopians were subjected to a servile administration that lasted for over eight centuries until Haile Sellassie I was able to make his country's parish independent. Under the regulations of the Oeucumenical Council of 325 AD only the mother church, in this case being the Alexandrian Cathedral, had the right to elect bishops. This arrangement prescribed an Egyptian Abuna to preside over the Tewahedo congregation whose language and culture they never expressed any particular interest in regarding. A conflict of nationalism was evident and this problem came to a head during the fascist occupation when Pope Kyrillos sided with the invaders and said that the Italians were a blessing to Ethiopia. After His Majesty returned to his country in 1941, Ethiopian Episcopacy with unmitigated rights and prerogatives was pursued as the Nicene canon could no longer be honored due to the Coptic's betrayal.[28] Haile Sellassie I was able to separate from the See of Mark and nullify the traditional Christian doctrine because there is a difference between what Christ stood for and what those who

---

[28] Talbot, David Abner, *Contemporary Ethiopia*, page 189

say they follow Jesus stand for. The Emperor regarded spiritual affairs equally as important with political matters therefore he would not make a decision outweighing one over the other if either standpoint were absolute, "We believe that the spiritual and moral welfare of Our people is as important as their material well-being."[29] In other words, if the gospel of the Church was correct then their secular shortcomings would not have led him to reject their authority. His Imperial Majesty was a great leader, if the principles of Christendom were true then he would have accepted these tenants for his people and never pursued becoming autocephalous. Yet the Ethiopian Orthodox Church had petitioned for autonomy for several centuries[30] due to the problems in administration found between what men do and what the Bible decrees. It is also written in Revelation chapters 2 and 3 that the churches have defects therefore God will reveal himself on earth and make all things new.[31] If their interpretation was already factual there would be no need for correction, renewal, or a separation. It is fundamental that we accept the real message of the scriptures which affirms that the world has the wrong spiritual interpretation. Only when you know that Emperor Haile Sellassie I is God are the promises of salvation revealed unto you.

"For unto us a child is born, unto us a son is given: and the government shall be upon his shoulder: and his name shall be called Wonderful, Counselor, The Mighty God, The Everlasting Father, The Prince of Peace. Of the increase of his government and peace there shall be no end, upon the throne of David, and upon his kingdom, to order it, and to establish it with judgment and with justice from henceforth even forever. The zeal of the LORD of hosts will perform this" (Isaiah 9:6-7). His Majesty is the last of the Solomonic Kings there will be no other monarch to reign upon the throne of David. The reason being, this dynasty serves as the platform for which the Lord will establish his government on earth; the Ark of the Covenant also symbolizes God's presence. These two claims, which are both found in Ethiopia, have been justified by Haile Sellassie I. If we put our trust in the revelation then we would know that what we are looking for has been fulfilled by His Majesty. We would still be under the old covenant if we deny the divinity of the Emperor because we would remain under the veil of simplicity in following the philosophies of men who can only speculate concerning the Lord because they oppose the theocratic reign of Haile

---

[29] The Selected Speeches of His Imperial Majesty Haile Selassie I, page 75
[30] Tafia, Bairu, The Coptic encyclopedia, volume 4, CE:1197b-1199a
[31] Revelation 21:5

Sellassie I. But the prophecy has in fact been fulfilled, the times of ignorance are now behind us, the people must accept the divinity of His Majesty and implement his policies in order for humanity to progress; from him alone comes the true guidance that will save the world. Haile Sellassie I was a member of various organizations all across the globe and was held in high regards from people from all walks of life including the Jews, Christians, and Muslims. His association with these factions was to teach them what is right but we should not make the mistake of thinking that because His Majesty was a member of their group that means that they are who we should follow. Many times people make this mistake about the Emperor's alliance with the Ethiopian Orthodox Tewahedo Church, they believe that this religious assembly must be the true faith since he was a member of it. If that is your rationale then you also must apply this logic to all the other global organizations which Haile Sellassie I was part of. After careful study of His Majesty's policies we know that he never said to follow the Tewahedo Church but he did say to follow Christ. He beckoned us to read and study the Bible, and to accept the message of the scriptures with a clear conscience. It is important to also understand that the scriptures describe the church as your physical body not a concrete building.[32] As with all of his associations, His Majesty was directing its members in righteousness and teaching them to adopt better practices. The Orthodox Church as well as everyone else was advised by the Emperor on what they must do to adhere to the true faith. The world leaders as well as the clergy both fall short in their duties; no one should forget that the Ethiopian Church revolted against Haile Sellassie I and delivered the final consequential blow during the 1974 student rebellion which led to His Majesty's removal from office. If we follow the Tewahedo Church then we would be doing something which the Emperor never instructed us in, we would be supporting an institution which does not accept His Majesty's divinity, and we would be assimilating into an organization that fought against God.

"For the invisible things of him from the creation of the world are clearly seen, being understood by the things that are made, even his eternal power and Godhead; so that they are without excuse: because that, when they knew God, they glorified him not as God, neither were thankful; but became vain in their imaginations, and their foolish heart was darkened" (Romans 1:20-21). The only way to know the truth about the Lord is if we understand the doctrine of his prophet Jesus Christ. When the world knew God, they glorified him not as God because they did not know the

---

[32] John 2:19-21

Messiah's gospel. This is why Haile Sellassie I sent Abuna Yesehaq to the West so that those who admire Ethiopia can understand what the culture is all about. The Ethiopian patriarch was tutored personally by the Emperor and he advised the Rastafarians that we must accept Jesus Christ and the Bible. It is only through the Son of God that we can understand the mystery of the scriptures and properly explain how Haile Sellassie I is the Almighty. It is not acceptable to invent your own philosophy concerning the Emperor for the Lord will not hold him guiltless who takes his name in vain.[33] Anyone who believes in Haile Sellassie I must question themselves to ensure that they have the correct teachings regarding his divinity. The combination of the Rastafarian concept that His Majesty is God along with the Tewahedo Church's acceptance of the apostolical order together equates with the true gospel of Christ. This is also why the Emperor and the Abuna both rejected the Jamaican government's request for them to denounce the Rastafarian faith. Haile Sellassie I did not tell Yesehaq to inform the Rastafarians that we are wrong concerning our beliefs, His Majesty actually awarded the founders and leaders of the movement for their faith. This was a lesson for the Rastafarians as well as the Ethiopian Church, they both must learn from each other, that is why Haile Sellassie I put them together without denouncing either one. The Ethiopians must learn that His Majesty is God and the Rastafarians must learn to accept the gospel of Christ. It is only through Jesus that we will have the correct doctrine to answer all questions concerning the divinity of Emperor Haile Sellassie I.

"And immediately I was in the spirit: and, behold, a throne was set in heaven, and one sat on the throne" (Revelation 4:2). The Lord is both invisible and visible,[34] it all depends upon your faith and understanding. If you have the wrong interpretation of the scriptures then you will not know God but if you have the true message of Christ then you will. That is why you will be able to find scriptures which say that no one can see God, while also locating where it is written that we have seen the Lord. This is not a contradiction, it means that you can only understand God through Christ.[35] The Rastafarians acknowledge the divinity of the Emperor but fall short by creating their own philosophies and incorrectly attributing His Majesty with supernatural phenomenon; this demonstrates that they do not have the truth. When Haile Sellassie I visited Jamaica on April 21, 1966, he advised those who worship him that they must follow Jesus

---

[33] Deuteronomy 5:11
[34] Romans 1:20
[35] Colossians 1:15-19

Christ. This was done because only through the Messiah would you be able to see the Almighty; which means to correctly understand the mystery of God. It would raise doubts and confusion to associate His Majesty with things for which he did not do or advocate. The love which the Jamaican people have for the Emperor can be perfected if they accept the gospel of Jesus Christ. When His Majesty arrived at Norman Manley Airport, the Rastafarians stampeded onto the tarmac and surrounded the Emperor's plane. When Haile Sellassie I saw this reception he went back into his plane and began crying; some people incorrectly say that he was afraid but that is not an objective analysis. We do not know the congenital qualities of the Lord therefore no one should assume or imagine that they understand God's innate personality. We must become as children before His Majesty, which means to learn from him and adopt his philosophy instead of being high minded as if we already have all the answers. Many people do not understand that God can display emotion and live naturally according to the universal laws that he created; the Lord created the human condition therefore he is not separate from it. His Majesty cared about people which is why he cried when the Rastafarians displayed this tremendous adoration for him. The reception given to His Majesty would have moved anyone to tears if this were done for them. They held up signs acknowledging that he is the Almighty who sits upon the throne of David. The Rastafarians also put themselves into great danger by stampeding past the police onto the tarmac when His Majesty's plane landed. The huge crowd of people who surrounded his jet made it impossible for him to exit therefore he had to ask for security because he was not going to bogart through the people or mystically egress; the supernatural will prevent you from understanding God. It is written that the foolishness of the Lord is wiser than men[36] because the attributes of Haile Sellassie I which you do not understand or for which you believe are not qualities of the divine actually serve a significant purpose. God is the best teacher since he is perfect but it would not profit us if he displayed powers that we could not reciprocate; that is why His Majesty displayed natural affection and did not operate in an esoteric manner, he was teaching us how to live. The video footage from his visit to Jamaica clearly indicates that Haile Sellassie I was overcome with joy from this boisterous welcome and calmly exited the plane when it was safe to do so.

"As concerning therefore the eating of those things that are offered in sacrifice unto idols, we know that an idol is nothing in the world, and that there is none other

---

[36] 1 Corinthians 1:25

God but one. For though there be that are called gods, whether in heaven or in earth, (as there be gods many, and lords many), But to us there is but one God, the Father, of whom are all things, and we in him; and one Lord Jesus Christ, by whom are all things, and we by him" (1 Corinthians 8:4-6). When faced with a crisis most people will pray to God in hopes that he will solve their dilemmas through a paranormal medium. What Haile Sellassie I did was better than that, he took on the biggest challenges that mankind faces and demonstrated how you must conduct yourself in order to overcome your difficulties. We now have a real solution to our problems if we acknowledge that His Majesty is God and adopt his principles. Dwight Eisenhower spoke about the Emperor and said, "I read once that no individual can really be known to have greatness until he has been tested in adversity. By this test, our guest of honor has established new standards in the world."[37] This means that he was greater than all the rest; his bravery, wisdom, and ability was unmatched throughout all of human history. The twentieth century produced the biggest threat to humanity with the discovery of atomic energy and the advances of technology. Nationalistic leaders were on the verge of placing the entire globe under colonial rule and exterminating entire classes of people. The polarization of wealth produced the most inhumane conditions for those less fortunate and political parties have become more effective in deceiving the people into supporting their unjust policies. Haile Sellassie I was active in combating all of this corruption, in his speeches we will find a clear plan on what must be done to change the world. If the people would have listened to him back then, we would not be faced with our current crisis. But God was not going to force humanity to accept him, mankind was given free will therefore it is up to us to decide if we will accept his counsel. This has also been the case in 1974 when the Ethiopian students overthrew His Majesty during the revolution. God has articulated what we must do to create a better society but the people have rejected him. His Majesty taught us how to correctly handle adversity and that would be head on. He never ran from his problems, he faced all of his obstacles lion hearted. When his people revolted against him, he choose to face the charges rather than run away from them. His Majesty knew that he was innocent from any slander regarding corruption, embezzlement, negligence, or incompetence. During the eleven month investigation by the Derg from September 1974 to August 1975 they searched through all of his files and paperwork for any

---

[37] Eisenhower, Dwight D., Toasts of the President and Emperor Haile Selassie of Ethiopia, May 26, 1954

evidence of guilt to justify their allegations. Their initial intentions were to put Haile Sellassie I on trial, that is why he was placed under house arrest rather than executed on November 23, 1974, along with the sixty senior Imperial officials. To this date there have been no documents produced to justify the revolution but rather than free the Emperor when they did not find anything, they killed him because these rebels were dregs of the highest order. It turned out that his accusers were the real corrupt, incompetent, ineffective, cowardly, and stagnant rulers;[38] everything that they tried to pin on His Majesty, they were guilty of committing. It is also important to note that the same auspicious circumstances, pertaining to the Wollo famine, that led to the overthrow of the Imperial government was also witnessed in 1960. When Haile Sellassie I was made aware of the drought he mobilized a relief effort to help his people and to answer the claims of embezzlement he invited his accusers to audit his records. They found that not only was he using government funds appropriately, he was also using his own personal money to finance projects, which is how Addis Ababa University for one came into existence. He governed righteously during his entire reign which is why he said, "We are proud of what has been achieved during our reign and we thank God for it. We are content to let history judge the wisdom of our actions."[39] His Majesty has demonstrated the true qualities of bravery and leadership, we must confront our challenges confident in victory and free our hearts from all panic when it comes to doing what is right. During the Italian invasion he was on the front lines battling to save his nation, he said it is better to die free than to live as a slave;[40] when he spoke before the League of Nations it was to petition for more arms so that he could continue fighting. Coincidentally Haile Sellassie I and Dwight Eisenhower are the only two rulers of the twentieth century to lead troops in battle. As a result, their level of leadership has to be considered more formidable than those who lacked this same experience and we have read how Eisenhower lauded the Emperor. His Majesty is the true Savior, he has demonstrated what we must do in order to overcome. The old method of waiting for a miracle to solve our problems has been abolished for that is idolatry. There is only one God and from him alone comes salvation, we would only be destroying ourselves if we reject him.

---

[38] In reference of Mengistu Haile Mariam who fled into exile rather than answer for the atrocities committed during his administration.

[39] The Selected Speeches of His Imperial Majesty Haile Selassie I, page 416

[40] The Wisdom of Rastafari, page 52

"There is one body, and one Spirit, even as you are called in one hope of your calling; One Lord, one faith, one baptism; One God and Father of all, who is above all, and through all, and in you all" (Ephesians 4:4-6). The state religion of Ethiopia currently does not recognize the divinity of Haile Sellassie I, as a result this raises certain questions regarding the validity of admonishing His Majesty as the Almighty. It is important to understand that our faith is not justified through the Ethiopians neither is any truth contingent upon the approval of man. There is only one God therefore all of humanity will have to face this reality. If there be any who do not believe our message then they should do so based upon the fact that they can disprove our position not because their state religion did not tell them to follow it. What we have noticed concerning the Ethiopians is that many times they take a high minded position as if they know everything concerning the Emperor and could not be taught anything new. It is also common among the naysayers to support this point of view by stating that since Haile Sellassie I was from that country then his family and his people must have the best and most accurate analysis of him; but that is incorrect. The Ethiopians revolted against His Majesty and overthrew the Imperial government based upon an inaccurate scrutinization of his policies, trumped up by foreign influences who did not have the peoples best interest in mind. To this date there has been no evidence produced to justify the 1974 revolution but it is from this frame of mind that many of his people view him. The Derg spread baseless propaganda about Haile Sellassie I and suppressed any opposition to their regime. As a result the Ethiopians could not investigate what His Majesty accomplished; the books about him were burned, all information about the Emperor was censored, and a brain drain occurred. Many of the intellectuals, doctors, and ministers fled into exile or were killed. The generation who was cultivated by the Derg therefore have no knowledge of Haile Sellassie I although they are Ethiopian. This of course is not true for everyone, there are many who are from the country who know that His Majesty was a great and divine man, there also are many who repented of rebelling against him when they recognized their errors in judgment. But the analysis that the Ethiopians have been robbed of their history and do not know who Haile Sellassie I is has also been articulated by their own people. Tikher Teferra Kidane made a documentary about His Majesty and said, "Growing up, I never remember a day I heard anything good about him on government media and I never remember ever learning in school about any Ethiopian king [...] It is always politics and propaganda, well politics might be good; and propaganda might be something a government must do; but always?! [...] If you ask a guy in Addis about the

Emperor, he will know more about Bill Gates because he is part of a denied generation!"[41] The question of who is Haile Sellassie I is one that can only be answered through Christ. We all have been placed into the same category therefore we must become as children to the Lord and approach this subject with an open mind. If we have already decided that we know everything and cannot examine new ideas then this only demonstrates our incompetence. There is only one doctrine because there is only one God; everyone cannot be right if we hold different interpretations of righteousness. We must be able to examine religion objectively if we want to know the truth; simply following a tradition passed down to you by your parents or leaders will not be enough to merit your validity. The only way to justify your claim is through facts. We have explained that His Majesty is the one and only King of Kings and Lord of Lords; that is a historical truth which cannot be negated. Whether certain people choose to ignore this reality is a decision that they will have to give account for but we place the biblical emphasis upon the personage who has the titles of God by declaring that Emperor Haile Sellassie I is the Almighty.

"For after that in the wisdom of God the world by wisdom knew not God, it pleased God by the foolishness of preaching to save them that believe" (1 Corinthians 1:21). The common philosophies prevalent in the world all fall short of showing people the King of Kings and Lord of Lords in the flesh. This demonstrates that they do not know who God is, as a result they could never have the correct understanding of the scriptures. It is from this misguided perspective that they judge Emperor Haile Sellassie I which leads to them fighting against the Savior of humanity. It has been said that His Majesty was an autocrat despite the fact that he introduced Ethiopia's first written constitution which established a bicameral legislature and allowed for the ministers to manage various facets of the government. He said, "The Ethiopian people must share the burden of responsibility which in the past was borne by their monarch."[42] His Majesty relinquished his jurisdiction even further in 1955 when he revised the constitution to expand the powers of parliament. Even with these measures being provided it neither made the Emperor a figurehead or tolerated any disinclinations to his right to rule. Haile Sellassie I was still the most powerful man in the country but that does not make him a despot. The newly formed Ethiopian intelligentsia, created by His Majesty, travelled the world and witnessed how

---

[41] His Imperial Majesty Emperor Haile Selassie I: Man of the Millennium, 4th Avenue Films

[42] The Selected Speeches of His Imperial Majesty Haile Selassie I, page 411

various European governments subjugated their sovereigns into becoming constitutional monarchs; they then adopted this model as their standard of modernization. These students began demanding that Haile Sellassie I relinquish all authority but the Emperor would not concede because he knew that the measures he was taking were best for the nation. Besides the fact that the small functions which were already delved unto the people to administer, were not handled properly on their part, therefore it would be irresponsible for His Majesty to abdicate full control of the empire. Parliament opposed and prevented many of Haile Sellassie's key initiatives that would have benefited the country, such as the progressive tax schemes of 1941 and 1966. His Majesty petitioned that, "Land reform measures are calculated to affect and improve the living conditions of literally millions of Ethiopians;"[43] he also initiated a program of land and credit assistance on September 18, 1959 when he declared, "For those of you who possess the land and labour but lack capital, We have made credit available at low interest. For those of you who have the necessary capital but do not possess land to work on, We have, in accordance with Our Proclamation which entitled every Ethiopian to ownership of land, established offices in every province through which you may be able to acquire land. Those who have neither land nor money will be granted land and a financial loan at low interest. For those of you who possess land, who have financial resources and manpower, We have made experts available to furnish you with the necessary guidance and advice in your various undertakings."[44] If they invoked and appreciated the Emperor's policies, the criticism levied upon his government regarding land tenure and the condition of the poor farmers, would not have existed. But to change customs that have endured for thousands of years takes time to sanction and His Majesty was not going to heavy handily impose modifications upon his people because he governed respectfully and not as a colonist. Haile Sellassie I set out to address the issues which he was reproached on well before the revolution occurred but was rebuffed by his own parliament; how then can anyone say that he was an autocrat? The only definition of this term means absolute power, not subject to restrictions. Yet despite these glaring distortions with calling His Majesty a totalitarian, this is exactly what is happening; in defiance of the facts. There also are some concerns regarding his treatment of the Oromo population and the accusation that he deconstructed Ethiopian civilization, but the Emperor declared,

---

[43] Ibid, page 439
[44] Ibid, page 489

"Misguided people sometimes create misguided ideas. Some of my ancestors were Oromo. How can I colonize myself?"[45] The reforms made during his administration were necessary to ensure that his nation could compete in the modern world and to safeguard their independence. It was necessary for the various indigenous tribes in Ethiopia to unite as well as modernize, for the very survival of their country depended on it. Italy was able to exploit certain archaic customs in the Empire whereas Haile Sellassie I was working towards ensuring that this would never happen again. If we studied his administration from an objective point of view, we would understand that what he did was right for the people.

"I have manifested your name unto the men which you gave me out of the world: they were yours, and you gave them me; and they have kept your word. O righteous Father, the world has not known you: but I have known you, and these have known that you have sent me. I have declared unto them your name, and will declare it: that the love wherewith you have loved me may be in them, and I in them" (John 17:6, 25, 26). Because the world does not know God, when those who have accepted the true message of Christ declare the name of the Lord Emperor Haile Sellassie I, this is perceived as a foreign concept. Despite the numerous Bible verses that verify this doctrine, as well as the excellency of his personality which justify the claim. What has taken place is the incorruptible God is being looked upon as a corruptible man.[46] The slander associated with His Majesty has been devised to rob people of their salvation. It is therefore important that we become aware of what is best for us because what is popular oftentimes is not what is correct. In 1961 the Eritrean Assembly voted to abolish the federal stature which made Eritrea the fourteenth province of Ethiopia. This resulted in an armed conflict instigated by foreign interests seeking to control the flow of trade and injure the Ethiopians. The idea that Haile Sellassie I was unjustly forcing the people to assimilate was a propagandist piece devised to stir up strife between the different tribes and to rule over them by exploiting their division. It is very important to understand that on December 2, 1950, the United Nations adopted Resolution 390A (V) which incorporated this former Italian colony into Ethiopia because their ancestry is analogous, much in the same way that the Ogaden was granted; albeit through federation. His Majesty was adamant about his objection to this form of government which he viewed as a

---

[45] Haile Selassie I allegedly responding to accusations by dissidents. The authenticity of this quote is disputed yet His Majesty was Oromo and was illogically accused of colonizing his own people.

[46] Romans 1:22-25

colonial administration for which he was not a consul. The Emperor requested that the wishes of the people be respected for which the unionist movement was the largest but the UN was not able to reach a consensus on this therefore the federal stature was the next best resolution that could be adopted. The history of this region illustrates that these two countries was always one dating before the time of the ancient Kingdom of Aksum through 1889 when Italy conquered the northern territory and imposed an artificial boundary between the two regions. Ethiopians and Eritreans are the same geographically, economically, historically, and ethnically. Haile Sellassie I said that this is a well known fact among the indigenous population recognized by those who can read as well as the illiterate. But another important reason why it was necessary to consolidate these two territories has to due with the fact that Ethiopia's sovereignty was threatened twice using Eritrea as a launching pad for the offensive. Was it expected for the Emperor to take no precautions to ensure that this does not happen again and leave the door open for his country to finally be conquered? Menelik II did not pursue the Italians after his victory at the Battle of Adowa, he consolidated a lot of land that historically belonged to his Empire but because Eritrea was not incorporated the entire independent state of Ethiopia was almost lost. His Majesty said many times, "We should never have let them become established on our mountains. The hills are our natural frontier. They could never have hoped to attack us successfully from the plains [...] Menelek was so great an Emperor. Why did he make this one mistake?"[47] Haile Sellassie I was set to complete what was undone and he warned the people not to be swayed by alien influences whose desire was to maintain their colonial influence rather than to promote what was best for the people.[48] If the Italians were driven out of East Africa in 1892 after they lost at Adowa then the Eritreans would not have garnered foreign ideas that they are a separate entity from Ethiopia as the occupational period was only three years at that point, there would not have been enough time to erase thousands of years of history and alienate them from their indigenous heritage in such a short stint; the term "Eritrea" would have been eliminated. His Majesty was in exile for five years during the fascist offensive and was able to liberate his country without them losing their identity. But unfortunately European imperialism was allowed to cultivate in the northern province and many have been taken by their devious objectives of divide and rule; resulting in the separation,

---

[47] Princess Asfa Yilma, Haile Selassie: Emperor of Ethiopia, page 158
[48] Haile Selassie I, Visit to Eritrea, June 27, 1962

weakening, and exploitation of the region. Haile Sellassie I tried to prevent this by stating, "You know that there are a lot of reasons for Ethio-Eritrean oneness. The relation of the people of Eritrea with Ethiopia is not confined to the political aspect. Not only are the two people joined by culture, geography and language, but historically the Adoulis heritage shows that the other Ethiopian tribes originated from Eritrea. Throughout Ethiopia's long record as an independent entity, Eritrea was separated from us for only 60 years and even if we were separated by political and artificial barriers during this short span of time, we were unseparated in our way of life and mutual feeling."[49] The case which the Emperor made is one for African unity, the abolishment of colonial exploitation, and respect for the optimum lines of demarcation. Those who fought against these objectives do so without having the correct point of view; much in the same way that they fight against his divinity.

"And Jesus answered him, The first of all the commandments is, Hear, O Israel; The Lord our God is one Lord: And thou shall love the Lord thy God with all your soul, and with all your mind, and with all your strength: this is the first commandment" (Mark 12:29-30). It is not acceptable to give your opinion about the interpretation of scriptures unless you have first learned the gospel of Jesus Christ. It is written that only through the mediator comes the correct understanding of God. The religious world has only accepted Christ in the letter, which means only in theory, but they deny Christ the person and they reject his message. That is why they think the Lord is an invisible ectoplasm although he is described as a visible King. There is only one way to interpret the Bible so people must be careful that they are not at odds with the Lord in following a false man made philosophy. Often times we see this occurring when people take a literal analysis of the scriptures even though it is written that Jesus told Nicodemus that he greatly erred in this regard.[50] There are doomsday cults who preach that God will physically destroy the world and those who adhere to this point of view will never see this herald come to pass. They also have prevented themselves from knowing the truth in Emperor Haile Sellassie I because their perception of the Bible is false. This is why everyone must make sure that they know who Christ is so that they can know who God is. His Majesty is the ultimate summit of this most excellent path towards salvation. Those who question the rationale in God operating by ordinary means are very short sighted for this is the only way to offer tangible solutions. So let us not think

---

[49] The Selected Speeches of His Imperial Majesty Haile Selassie I, page 463
[50] John 3:1-21

of Haile Sellassie I as being just a regular man because he is the Almighty; his method of carrying out his objectives by natural means only justifies his ethos, humanity cannot benefit from the Lord's divine operation in any other way. The wisdom in God instructing mankind through common methods is extremely profound, it is correct in every way as a far sighted approach that could only have been fulfilled properly by the Almighty himself. Herbert Armstrong said, "All my life, from age 19, I have had more or less close contact with many of the great and the near great of the world - heads of large corporations, presidents and chairmen of major banks, publishers, educators - and in these recent years government heads and world leaders. But none had seemed a more outstanding personality than Emperor Haile Selassie."[51] He was better than the best, all of the exceptional men of the world admired him and understood that they could not be compared to him. African chieftains such as Kwame Nkrumah and Nelson Mandela were counseled by him. American Presidents like John F. Kennedy and Franklin D. Roosevelt admired him. European heads of state such as Winston Churchill and Marshall Tito looked up to him. Asian luminaries like Chairman Mao and Emperor Hirohito honored him. His Majesty was the leader of all leaders, his accolades and honors are immeasurable but unless you study his life objectively you will never be able to unlock the mysteries of God.

"Let God arise, let his enemies be scattered: let them also that hate him flee before him. As smoke is driven away, so drive them away: as wax melts before the fire, so let the wicked perish at the presence of God. But let the righteous be glad; let them rejoice before God: yea, let them exceedingly rejoice. Sing unto God, sing praises to his name: extol him that rides upon the heavens by his name JAH, and rejoice before him" (Psalm 68:1-4). If people knew God then they would have a better understanding of how he operates. Simply calling out a name such as Yahweh or Allah does not equate with knowing him in any logical way. If I never met my father but I knew his name, would you say that I know him just because I am able to say his name? Nobody could rationally conclude that I do; but people do not associate God with real life scenarios because they do not have the truth. It would destroy their faith if they incorporated reality into their religion because they adhere to the false concept of the supernatural which is pure fantasy. If your beliefs do not correlate with the real world then you have been deceived. This again shows the wisdom of the true God Emperor Haile Sellassie I revealing himself to the world through conventional means. There

---

[51] The Plain Truth, December 1973

are worldly phrases such as God makes no mistakes, everything happens for a reason, and what is meant to be will be. While all of this is true, the interpretation of it is not because people take this to mean that everything which occurs in the world is the will of the Lord but the reason why atrocities occur is not because God wanted these crimes to be committed. So if innocent people are murdered, if a certain group of people are enslaved, if a woman becomes pregnant after she was raped, if you do not get the job that you wanted, etc., are we supposed to believe that God has allowed this to happen? It therefore would be the Lord's fault for everything including all the evil which happens on earth but then how could he judge the world? Humanity has been given free will which contradicts the idea that God made our condition the way it is. If the Almighty has not programmed everyone to follow him, then the evil which men do is not because of the Lord's design. When bad things occur, the Lord's wish is that it did not happen, he has not established the universe for him to magically possess and control our bodies. Why would the saints be rewarded for their deeds if they had no choice in the matter and how could the sinner be condemned when he had no power over his own actions? The evil which occurs on earth is the result of man not God. The Lord has asked us to do good and follow his law; he would not have petitioned for the world to change their ways if this was not a quality confined solely within the individual. We therefore cannot blame God for the wickedness which plague the earth. His Majesty said, "Eritrea before the federal union with Ethiopia, stayed separated for 60 years by the design of imperialists and colonists and not by the will of God;"[52] therefore we ought not to think that everything which happens has been sanctioned by the Lord. Those who want to do evil misinterpret the Word to deceive people into accepting abominations because they want to spread darkness. We must be careful of not falling prey to this deceit and the only way to guard yourself against all the wiles of the devil is to put your faith in the Almighty God Emperor Haile Sellassie I.

"*Blessed are the pure in heart: for they shall see God*" (Matthew 5:8). To know God means that you know who he is. If your beliefs do not coincide with this reality then you are not adhering to the Bible which says that the righteous shall see the Almighty. Without fully knowing the Lord it becomes easy to fall victim to false doctrines and duplicity. It is possible to distort the scriptures to say take no thought for your life, do not eat or drink, neither care for your body, for ye are not of this world and God has chosen the poor. These verses are all

---

[52] The Selected Speeches of His Imperial Majesty Haile Selassie I, page 426

found in the Bible but the interpretation of them is not what you think. People such as King Leopold II and the pope have misused the scriptures to oppress and enslave the world. Being accepted by God does not mean that you must be a transient or destitute on earth. When it said that it is easier for a camel to go through the eye of a needle than for a rich man to enter the kingdom of the Lord, this was not referring to worldly possessions. It means that those who are high minded and act as if they already know everything about God, will never fully comprehend the heavenly mysteries. There is nothing wrong with living comfortably and maintaining your dignity in this life. Haile Sellassie I said, "Knowing that material and spiritual progress are essential to man, we must ceaselessly work for the equal attainment of both. Only then shall we be able to acquire that absolute inner calm, so necessary to our well-being."[53] The true interpretation is not for us to deny ourselves, it is okay to maintain your integrity. The devil wants to take that away from people but we must guard ourselves against this deception by adhering to the true message of God. It is only by incorporating what Haile Sellassie I has said and did, with the Bible that you can then understand the scriptures. This is the foundation of the doctrine of Christ and no other path will lead to salvation.

"And I saw heaven opened, and behold a white horse; and he that sat upon him was called Faithful and True, and in righteousness he does judge and make war. His eyes were as a flame of fire, and on his head were many crowns; and he had a name written, that no man knew, but he himself. And he was clothed with a vesture dipped in blood: and his name is called The Word of God. And the armies which were in heaven followed him upon white horses, clothed in fine linen, white and clean. And out of his mouth goes a sharp sword, that with it he should smite the nations: and he shall rule them with a rod of iron: and he treadeth the winepress of the fierceness and wrath of Almighty God. And he has on his vesture and on his thigh a name written KING OF KINGS, AND LORD OF LORDS" (Revelation 19:11-16). The truth about the Creator cannot be found within these overturned religions responsible for provoking nearly all the wars ever fought and spreading darkness instead of light. The essence of our dignity as human beings must lead us to reject any dogma which debases and persecutes people. Basic logic should bring us to conclude that they are wrong, for you cannot claim to be of God, yet act like the devil and expect to be counted among the righteous. We must also remember that these big religions gained their followers through force not reason. There must come a recognition of one's actions with their message but most of these institutions

---

[53] The Voice of Ethiopia, April 5, 1948

would be afraid to accept this reality because they are hypocrites. They preach that it is acceptable for them to wage war in the name of God, they use their religion to subjugate nations, and then they instruct their congregation to be pious; without ever obeying this principle themselves. That is why it is important to know that the true message of God will uplift humanity not oppress the world. The war in heaven is a battle to eradicate the false teachings that corrupt mankind. Napoleon Bonaparte said, "Religion is excellent stuff for keeping common people quiet."[54] This is due to the misinterpretation of the scriptures; they have used the Bible to pacify and manipulate humanity. The French leader also said that, "Religion is what keeps the poor from murdering the rich."[55] As much as your love for God may be genuine, no one can deny the fact that the end result of these religious institutions has dumbed-down the population and stripped its members of their common sense. God himself will never condone this malapropism or advocate their practices. It is written in Matthew 7:15-20 that we shall know them by their fruits, therefore if the culmination of their dogma hinders mankind's plight then it is clearly wrong. We cannot deny our human condition in hopes of a blessed afterlife. That is why Emperor Haile Sellassie I was a staunch human rights advocate who abolished slavery in Ethiopia and instructed his people to defend their sovereignty at all costs. His Majesty also gave assistance to those who were suffering under these inhumane regimes who disguise themselves as being godlike when they are actually the complete opposite. The false religions of the world are built upon empty promises and mythology; there is no way to prove their validity. In contrast, the truth about Rastafari is the only doctrine based upon historical facts and evidence; anyone with an objective point of view will recognize that Haile Sellassie I is the Almighty.

"And you are witnesses of these things. And, behold, I send the promise of my Father upon you: but tarry ye in the city of Jerusalem, until you be endued with power from on high" (Luke 24:48-49). The true definition of righteousness is found within God Emperor Haile Sellassie I. His Majesty said, "Human beings are precisely the same whatever color, race, creed, or national origin they may be."[56] In practice, this will lead to the abolishment of any racist philosophy which regards one group better than another based upon religious affiliation, nationality, wealth, etc. If we view each other as equals then the preservation of human rights and tolerance would only increase. The solution to our problems

---

[54] Adherents.com: Religious Affiliation of History's 100 Most Influential People
[55] Byrne, Robert, 1,911 Best Things Anybody Ever Said, 1988
[56] Haile Selassie I, Interview on Meet the Press, October 1963

has been articulated by Haile Sellassie I; there is no situation which you would not be counseled in the proper order by looking to His Majesty for guidance. The idea of any person being inherently better than another is false. This begs the question of how does the royal family fit into this equation and what were the Emperor's views of his own dynastic succession. It is written in his Constitution that power will be transferred to his Crown Prince upon his passing; but that is not what happened. When Haile Sellassie I died, the Solomonic incumbency was abolished. So how are we to interpret this if we know that he is God? Some call for the restoration of the royal family but this would only reinforce cultural prejudices that a certain set of people are born better than others. This position would only contradict His Majesty's speeches and mission. But if we dig a little deeper to understand these matters we will come to the conclusion that he was speaking of a spiritual succession which would then correlate with the Bible and his own philosophy. Only in a metaphysical aspect would it make sense for him to write that his heir must be a man not a woman; since the scriptures designates the male as Christ who leads the female (the church). The descendants of King Solomon are therefore those who acknowledge the truth in the Bible that Emperor Haile Sellassie I is the Almighty. It is this empire that will reign forever in righteousness which means that people throughout all generations will worship His Majesty for he is God. The rightful heir of the Lord is his prophet, that is why it is written that we are a royal priesthood, kings and priests before God who shall reign on earth.[57] Unless we study the Emperor's words and deeds from a theistic standpoint we would never understand what he meant because His Majesty frequently made references to males and females that was unrelated to a person's gender. He said, "It is Our steadfast aim that all citizens of the Empire shall live together as brothers, in one large family;"[58] here he calls all Ethiopians brothers which would also include women since they are citizens as well. In addition, the Emperor stated, "It is laboring to improve Ethiopia's judicial system so that speedy and impartial justice will be guaranteed to all. All men stand equal before the law. All men must be able to enforce their legal rights before the courts;"[59] the rights of everyone have been protected under this ordinance not just males. Gender equality during His Majesty's reign has been well documented therefore it would be grossly inaccurate to interpret his words as being sexist. "In

---

[57] Revelation 5:10
[58] The Selected Speeches of His Imperial Majesty Haile Selassie I, page 404
[59] Ibid, page 421

the eyes of the law, however, the woman of the country makes up for whatever of other sacrifices she is called on to make because of the social pattern. So far as property and other legal matters pertaining to her rights before the law, the Ethiopian woman suffers no form of injustice. If anything, she has the edge on her male counterpart before the law."[60] Before Haile Sellassie I instructed the world in righteousness, humanity formulated their own doctrines which was not in conjunction with the truth which then led to the implementation of unjust policies. This is one reason how the institution of a royal family came into existence, they misinterpret what "the seed" means,[61] but His Majesty refuted the idea of one set of people being better than another and basically told Herbert Armstrong that anyone could trace their lineage back to Solomon[62] because the seed is not a literal blood based descent. The administration of inherent rule by divine right has been abolished; we now must elect our leaders based upon their merit not their ancestry. The Lord alone is the only one who possess the innate rights of eminent domain; that is why Haile Sellassie I said that he was born a King. No one else is deserving of this same prestige for he alone is God; we all are equal under him and he is the only one supreme over us. It is also important to understand that David and Solomon did not reign in ancient times therefore it is impossible for anyone to actually trace their lineage back to them. Ethiopia, as well as the rest of the world, operated under a shadow of things to come, which means they did their best to follow what they believed was the way; but now that God was manifest in the flesh, we must learn from him if we want to know the truth. The real meaning of divine rule is open to anyone who is inspired by God to do what is right, it is not based upon your genealogy.

"For it is written, that Abraham had two sons, the one by a bondmaid, the other by a free woman. But he who was of the bondwoman was born after the flesh; but he of the free woman was by promise. Which things are an allegory: for these are the two covenants, the one from the mount Sinai, which genders to bondage, which is Agar. For this Agar is mount Sinai in Arabia, and answers to Jerusalem which now is, and is in bondage with her children. But Jerusalem which is above is free, which is the mother of us all" (Galatians 4:22-26). A careful investigation into the Bible reveals that many of the stories which are taken literally are actually parables. Legends have been constructed to add prominence to certain

---

[60] Talbot, David Abner, Contemporary Ethiopia, page 39
[61] Genesis 22:17-18
[62] The Plain Truth, December 1973

cultures who claim to be descendants of Abraham, Israel, or Solomon, etc. However there is no historical evidence that any of these people ever existed in antiquity. The true doctrine of God does not rest in fables and mythology. It is written that Abraham and his two sons are allegories. One covenant (Ishmael) transcribes to bondage while the other (Isaac) is the promised seed. This is referring to the religions of the world; for certain preachers will interpret the scriptures to mean that Jerusalem is in Arabia. As a result the conflict which has ensued between the Jews, Muslims, and Christians has been ongoing for over two millennia and threatens to destroy humanity. In contrast, the mother of us all, the cradle of civilization where mankind originated, along the Nile River - Ethiopia, has had a peaceful coexistence between Beta Israel, Muslims, and Christians from time immemorial. When you look to the Arab territory of Palestine there are only relics of a prior surmounted civilization which has been labeled with extravagant names such as Mount Zion and the Holy Land. But if you study Ethiopian history then you will notice that this country has never been conquered and that Emperor Haile Sellassie I is the King of Kings and Lord of Lords. The biblical analogies along with historical facts both demonstrate that His Majesty is who the prophecy is referring to. To be blessed with salvation is not found in your hemoglobin or nationality but in your faith. Therefore when Haile Sellassie I said that he was a descendant of Solomon this was also a parable which means that he supports the Bible and its true interpretation. Anyone who claims to be of David, Shem, or Judah, etc., must believe that His Majesty is God. Again Jesus said to drink his blood[63] for he was referring to his gospel; as no one can be saved by body fluids. The children and grandchildren of Haile Sellassie I are no different from anyone else born into this world. If they do not accept his divinity they would be falling under the category of Hagar but if they accept the gospel then they would be of Sarah. Under this order is the only means to properly explain the scriptures in its full context along with being able to judge the world fairly; this then would be the only acceptable interpretation of the Bible.

"Lift up your heads, O ye gates; and be lifted up, ye everlasting doors; and the King of glory shall come in. Who is this King of glory? The LORD strong and mighty, the LORD mighty in battle. Lift up your heads, O ye gates; even lift them up, ye everlasting doors; and the King of glory shall come in. Who is this King of glory? The LORD of hosts, he is the King of glory. Selah" (Psalm 24:7-10). It is known by those who study the scriptures that God will establish his kingdom

---

[63] John 6:55

on earth. What the dissimulators have undertaken is a coarse to prevent people from acknowledging the Lord at his coming. For they know that he will bring about an end to their deceptive dogmas which only oppresses humanity. One of the most powerful means of misleading the people is through science. The theory of evolution as well as the concept of the big bang have been presented as ideas to explain our existence without acknowledging God. What adds to their appeal is the logic found within the entire context of their subject; for it would be unavailing to dispute many of the concrete principles discovered by scientists such as gravity and photosynthesis. As a result it appears as if science stands to present the world according to the laws of nature and religion seeks to defy it through the notion of the supernatural. In such an argument it is clear to see why no one knows who God is; because the stance of the faithful is incorrect. The truth is discovered through facts, science and religion should not be polarized but galvanized by learning from each other. His Majesty said, "The progress of science can be said to be harmful to religion only in so far as it is used for evil aims and not because it claims a priority over religion in its revelation to man."[64] The scientists must accept that the universe could not have been formed without a catalyst; rocks, gasses, water, explosions, and organisms cannot just be present on their own. God is the only logical explanation for such an intricate creation and to believe that all beings evolved into their current state by chance is absurd. If there was no Creator then our reproductive system, for example, came into existence by itself; but how can something so sophisticated be devised without a guide? True science would have to accept God and true religion would have to abdicate from the supernatural. Only then could people speak on either of these topics properly because the truth is found within the middle ground, not through polarizing your opinion on these subjects. The idea of a paranormal Creator has been induced into the canon to prevent people from knowing God. Since the educated elite know that it is impossible to defy the laws of nature, they have used this concept, through religion, as a means to pacify the population and to oppose the Lord. Christ is the only one who could see through all the smoke screens and properly declare how Emperor Haile Sellassie I is the Almighty. Many others have failed in not understanding why His Majesty lived according to normal means, when this method validates his divinity and offers true knowledge.

"I beheld till the thrones were cast down, and the Ancient of days did sit, whose garment was white as snow, and the hair of his head like the pure wool: his throne

---

[64] The Selected Speeches of His Imperial Majesty Haile Selassie I, page 663

was like the fiery flame, and his wheels as burning fire. A fiery stream issued and came forth from before him: thousands ministered unto him, and ten thousand times ten thousand stood before him: the judgment was set, and the books were opened" (Daniel 7:9-10). Although Haile Sellassie I was one of the most popular celebrities of the twentieth century, there is an opinion that if he is in fact God then there should be more of an awareness and acceptance of him. We agree that the entire world should acknowledge his divinity but it is written that they fled away from his face.[65] This would indicate that they are not of God and do not want to acknowledge him. Christ was also tempted with the entire world by satan, this analogy demonstrates the power which the devil commands on earth. Because most common people believe in good and not evil, it would make them apprehensive to accept that they are following Lucifer; but this is what it means by the greatest trick satan ever pulled was convincing people that he does not exist, they are unaware that they are his subjects. It is the over-seers who are leading the people astray under the solace of a false religion and the guise of good government. What we are fighting against is the high science of psychology which imparts subliminal messages upon the general popu-lation which most are unaware of. They do not see the correlation between believing in supernatural concepts and pacification. Or the link between a lit-eral interpretation of the Bible and atheism. But what has been bestowed upon the people is a philosophy designed to prevent them from knowing God and to keep them oppressed under tyrannical rulership. The only liberation from this spiritual assault comes from the true Savior Emperor Haile Sellassie I. It there-fore would make sense for the leaders to prevent their subjects from accepting His Majesty. They know that if the people would acknowledge his divinity this will lead to a cultural revolution and a higher level of consciousness. Only God can free us from all of the deceit and dishonesty which is rampant throughout our society; he is the solution to all our problems. This is why it is written that the judgment was set, for we present before you this day life and death; there-fore choose life.[66] It is for you to decide whether your faith is real because if it is then you would accept Emperor Haile Sellassie I as God. His Majesty has es-tablished the universal principles which will save humanity, if we do not follow him then we would be subject to corruption and injustice. Because he was such a beacon of light, his outstanding personality made it possible for many to im-mediately recognize his divinity; the Rastafarian movement has grown faster

---

[65] Revelation 20:11
[66] Deuteronomy 30:19-20

than any other religion in its first seventy years. This is an everlasting devotion that will only increase, for now the power of Christ has been revealed to present unto us a perfect doctrine so that the world may know righteousness.

"*You are come unto Mount Zion, and unto the city of the living God, the heavenly Jerusalem, and to an innumerable company of angels, to the general assembly and church of the firstborn, which are written in heaven, and to God the Judge of all, and to the spirits of just men made perfect*" (Hebrews 12:22-23). The idea of going to heaven when you physically die is false. To put our hopes in the hereafter would prevent us from obtaining the inheritance promised to us in this life. The Bible describes Zion as the knowledge of God,[67] we are made perfect when we come unto him with reverence. Haile Sellassie I has addressed the nations in what must be done to build a better society. Instead of waiting to die to enter paradise, the challenge is for us to establish this now. That is why God established his kingdom on earth, this is a sign that we must not look elsewhere for a provision which has already been presented to us. No one can tell what will take place when we physically pass away and the scriptures also describe being dead as a certain mental state.[68] It is up to us to accept God Emperor Haile Sellassie I, because if we do not then nothing for which we hope for will ever be fulfilled. The interpretation and promises offered before His Majesty revealed himself to mankind have all been devised out of the people's own imagination; for they knew not God. We now have been given the opportunity to establish the true doctrine, for the Lord has magnified himself; with this calling also comes the responsibility of instituting Zion. Our dreams of paradise must become our existence. Haile Sellassie I has demonstrated what must to be done in order to change the world, he stated that, "Throughout history it has been the inaction of those who could have acted, the indifference of those who should have known better, the silence of the voice of justice when it mattered most, that has made it possible for evil to triumph. The glorious pages of human history have been written only in those moments when men have been able to act in concert to prevent impending tragedies. By the actions you take you can also illuminate the pages of history;"[69] it is expedient for us to follow his great example.

"*I know that, whatsoever God does, it shall be forever: nothing can be put to it, nor anything taken from it: and God does it, that men should fear before him. That which has been is now; and that which is to be has already been; and God requires*

---

[67] Revelation 21:1-7

[68] Colossians 3:1-3

[69] Haile Selassie I, United Nations security meeting, Addis Ababa, 1963

that which is past" (Ecclesiastics 3:14-15). The utopian example and teachings of Haile Sellassie I shall stand throughout all generations as the sole source of salvation for all of humanity to look to. His government is the first and the last administration to operate on earth under the titles King of Kings and Lord of Lords. No one will be successful in any attempt to distort this critical piece of history; for there will be no other sign given to find a correlation between the prophecies that we read in the holy books and our own human existence. His Majesty is the Almighty, through him peace will reign and all the problems which plague mankind will be solved. This is not a prospect solely for any specific group of people, whether they be Ethiopians, Africans, West Indians, etc.; the salvation of God is open for everyone to accept. Haile Sellassie I has spoken out against racism and xenophobia; he furthermore travelled around the world demonstrating love and compassion to all of mankind as a means to prove this point. Unless we learn to walk on earth as brothers and sisters, our existence will be marred by unnecessary conflicts that are all emulsifiable. It may be popular to think that heaven cannot be established on earth but that only means the people do not know who God is. Haile Sellassie I said, "This is only fitting and proper, for the church, as a symbol of peace, must follow the path of peace in all parts of the world. For world peace can only be made abiding by the grace of God, through the prayers of the Holy Fathers. The truth of this cardinal fact is evident to all mankind [...] Therefore, it has become the noble responsibility of Christians, and peoples of other faiths and their leaders throughout the world, to pray and to work hard for the preservation of world peace."[70] If these goals were unattainable then the Lord would be vain for asking us to seek it, the Bible would be false for teaching us to hope for salvation. We should not make the mistake of characterizing an objective that is difficult to achieve as being impossible. One of their best known philosophers, St. Francis of Assisi said, "Start by doing what's necessary; then do what is possible; and suddenly your doing the impossible." It will take the effort of all the world to work in a concerted effort to eradicate poverty, ignorance, disease, war, and corruption; but these are all feasible and noble aspirations. His Majesty also said, "We have no problem which is insurmountable. Let us work in unity and diligence [...] Unity gives strength and assures success."[71] God is the only one who can offer this real opportunity to be saved, in the truest sense of the term; which is according to our human condition and not merely rhetorically. These

---

[70] The Wisdom of Rastafari, page 3
[71] The Selected Speeches of His Imperial Majesty Haile Selassie I, page 95

are the factual promises of the Bible, let us all worship the only one who can make this manifest: Emperor Haile Sellassie I.

The Stumbling Block

Primus St. Croix is the mediator of a new covenant that speaks better things than that of Abel. Only through the Son can you know the Father, which means that he is the only one who can give you the proper understanding of the Word.

The message of the Bible is the same prophecy in the Quran, the Bhagavad-Gita, and all other religious scriptures. Haile Sellassie I said, "Your guide should therefore be the apostolic saying: study and examine all but choose and follow the good."[72] If we understood the parables then we would not remain divided in hostile camps; we would understand the remarkable unity of faith that is present within all the different religious denominations. Furthermore the Emperor has stated, "Above all, Ethiopia is dedicated to the principle of the equality of all men, irrespective of differences of race, color, or creed. As we do not practice or permit discrimination within our nation, so we oppose it wherever it is found. As we guarantee to each the right to worship as he chooses, so we denounce the policy which sets man against man on issues of religion. As we extend the hand of universal brotherhood to all, without regard to race or color, so we condemn any social or political order which distinguishes among God's children on this most specious of grounds." There is only one Creator, therefore only one can hear our prayers, which means that only one can be worshipped. To say that His Majesty is my God, but you worship someone else, is a delusional polytheistic viewpoint. The concept of monotheism means that there could only be one faith but it is our traditions and misinterpretations which have divided us; that is why it is written, *"Is he the God of the Jews only? Is he not also of the Gentiles? Yes, of the Gentiles also: Seeing it is one God, which shall justify the circumcision by faith, and uncircumcision through faith"* (Romans *3:29-30).* The right to worship as you choose is not a liberty to do as you please; if this was so, then there would be no rebuke for denominations who condone human sacrifice or slavery. Also keep in mind that many religions condemn those who are not part of their faith, therefore the freedom for everyone to practice their own beliefs rebukes their ideology. The principle of judgment

---

[72] Ibid, page 80

has not been lost, the struggle to advance continues to unfold, and the beacon of correction remains ever so poignant.

There is a popular citation from the Emperor that reads, "No one should question the faith of others, for no human being can judge the ways of God." Besides the fact that this saying is misquoted and taken out of context, the correct way to understand this comment is that we cannot question the level of consciousness which is cognizant with the Almighty; Haile Sellassie I was not speaking of a persons' religion. If the ways of mankind were the same as God then how could anyone lend correction, as God is perfect those who follow him would also be irreproachable. But we know that this ideal has not been reached by any denomination therefore the journey to achieve this level is an effort that can only be done through improving one's values and increasing in knowledge; which always requires a rebuttal of erroneous principals. The same circumstances surround the often quoted (but currently unverifiable saying) where it is referenced that His Majesty said, "We must stop confusing religion and spirituality. Religion is a set of rules, regulations, and rituals created by humans which were supposed to help people spirituality. Due to human imperfection religion has become corrupt, political, divisive, and a tool for power struggle. Spirituality is not theology or ideology. It is a simple way of life, pure and original as given by the Most High. Spirituality is a network linking us to the Most High, the universe, and each other." This falls in line with the same message which the Emperor spoke on in the address "Investiture of a New Patriarch" on May 11, 1971. We must push to correct those principles which do not commend the righteousness of God. If we make up our own beliefs without adhering to what the LORD has decreed then this will only lead to our downfall. In like manner, the proper understanding of the term "faith is personal" works in tandem with Matthew 6:1-13 which calls for us to develop a positive and genuine relationship with God; this does not mean that we are free to establish any form of theology. Our obedience to the Lord must be established upon his principles and not our own; only then could our faith be just and true before the Almighty; this is the only way for the world to find salvation. The goal of any religion or form of spirituality that is honest and sincere in its intentions, is to please God. In this pursuit, the devotee will be true to their heart and faithful to the commandments of the Lord; which would make their personal relationship with the Almighty definitive. In order to overcome the wiles of the devil, we must be willing to challenge ourselves to objectively determine if we have the truth. We cannot be afraid to study someone else's point of view, for if we come across some irrevocable facts that do not coincide with our present beliefs, our pride and sensibilities should not prevent us from accepting it.[73] Also if what we hold to be true was actually the truth then nothing could disprove it, we should therefore be able to analyze everything objectively and explain how our position is correct. Plato said, "Those who are able to see beyond the shadows and lies of their culture will never be understood, let alone believed, by the masses." This is evident when people form an allegiance to their traditions and refuse to consider different viewpoints regardless of the evidence and facts. But the love of God must be greater than our ego and if it is then we would be able to admit when we are wrong, we would be able to listen to each others beliefs to prove if our own convictions are valid. Only with an open mind can we be considered sincere seekers of the truth because God is not fallible and anyone looking for him without investigating all paths will almost certainly fail to find him. His Majesty advised us on this necessary exchange of ideas when he said, "Were the thoughts of Plato and Socrates, the beliefs of Christianity and Judaism not harmonized with Hindu philosophy; were Yoga and its various stages not exposed to Western thought; had Western religion and philosophy not been exposed to the philosophy and religion of the East through Your Excellency's persistent endeavor, how much the poorer would human thought have been!"[74]

Jesus Christ is the messenger of God, therefore all of the prophets, such as Enoch, Moses, Joshua, David, Mohammad, Arjuna, etc., are all referring to him.[75] Psalm 118:26 says, *"Blessed is he that comes in the name of the LORD: we have blessed you out of the house of the LORD."* All the various holy books throughout the world say that a righteous sage will lead the people to salvation by declaring who God is; this herald has been written from time immemorial. There is evidence of these sayings that go back before 2200 BC when the Egyptian deity Horus was proclaimed to have been born of a virgin on December 25th, taught in the temple as a child, had twelve disciples, performed miracles, healed the sick, walked on water, raised the dead, he was also crucified and resurrected after three days; Horus was referred to as God's anointed Son, the Messiah, the Son of Man, the Lamb of God, the good shepherd, the way, the truth, and the light. These same descriptions are also referenced in relation to the ancient Persian idol Mithra that the Romans later amalgamated into their culture. We have to understand the correct context of the harbinger

---

[73] Acts 10:28

[74] The Selected Speeches of His Imperial Majesty Haile Selassie I, page 133

[75] Acts 10:43

if we are to interpret the Bible correctly; these events did not transpire in antiquity, it is an omen, a promise made by the Lord that he will send a deliverer to teach the world in righteousness. This prophecy has been fulfilled in our times by Primus St. Croix: *"He was in the world, and the world was made by him, and the world knew him not. He came unto his own, and his own received him not. But as many as received him, to them gave he power to become the sons of God, even to them that believe on his name, which were born, not of blood, nor of the will of the flesh, nor of the will of man, but of God" (John 1:10-13).* We can become one of the chosen elect if we accept the testimony of the Messiah. The twelve disciples are referring to a certain level of understanding which, if we develop, would then lead to a perfection of character. It is not talking about a specific number of people as this analogy is used in many different ways and the opportunity to become one of his apostle's could only be an invitation open to everyone. There are twelve thrones, twelve angels, twelve tribes, twelve stars, twelve gates, twelve stones, twelve cubits long is the altar of the Lord.[76] A dozen represents our traditions; we all have a certain way of life, a present belief, a familiar culture, but our native ordinances will only be justified through the gospel of Jesus Christ. Because God would not have to send a mediator if our understanding of spiritual matters was already adequate. Without accepting the revelation of these heralds, our knowledge of sacred issues is limited and unreliable; the next step is to increase in knowledge to ensure that our faith is justified. It is this challenge that many avoid yet it is only natural that we ameliorate until we reach our apex. *"Do you hear what these say? Jesus said unto them, yes; have you not read, out of the mouth of babes and sucklings thou has perfected praise" (Matthew 21:16).* We are at twelve when we profess to love the Creator, when we claim to have the truth, when we follow ordinances that we think are acceptable to the Lord. But the prophet shall come to prove who is sincere in their faith, for he shall preach an indisputable message that cannot be denied by anyone who is honest with God. When you are able to combine your tradition with the fulfillment of prophecy then you would have implemented the true purpose of your religion; which represents perfection. Twelve squared is one hundred and forty four:[77] this number is also used to describe those who have overcome.[78] Which means that we have to hone our faith and the only way to accomplish this feat is if we do not place our customs above the truth. His

---

[76] Revelation 21:10-17
[77] Acts 12:24
[78] Revelation 7

Majesty said, "And the Apostles turned their efforts to the law of perfection and to that complete correction of the internal spiritual deeds which must be observed by a wise man, but over which judges have no power, such as the correction of conscience, character and internal impulses. Since it is the soul that moves the body, when the moving agent is corrected and perfect, the actions done by the moved object, that is, the body, are correct, because it is the instrument of the soul." Haile Sellassie I alone enacted the predestined functions of the LORD therefore the question of whose faith is real has been answered with those who either accept or deny the Emperor. Primus St. Croix was able to explain the Bible correctly, he put God and Christ into their proper context; from this foundation the entire book opens up. There is a parable written in Matthew 25:14-30 which says that unto the servant who had five talents, he was able to increase and gain five more, and he who had two, gained two more because he also neglected not his gifts; but unto him who used not his talent, he was cast out of the kingdom. This demonstrates that everyone's opinion is that their traditions are right but your faith is only justified when you accept the Father of all religions: Haile Sellassie I. If you are unable to connect your spirituality with the real God then you are not using your talents and your veneration would be in vain. It is this increase, to combine the prophecy with its fulfillment, that is the ultimate summit of every spiritual denomination.[79] His Majesty is the Almighty, when the world is able to challenge their traditions and prove the validity of their beliefs then they will be moving closer to understanding God. The Emperor said, "A man who says, 'I have learned enough and will learn no further,' should be considered as knowing nothing at all."

The names of the disciples change due to this quest to be accepted by God. Simon Peter was given the name Cephas after he followed Jesus Christ.[80] This reflects his adoption from being a fisherman to now becoming a fisher of men. If we should increase in knowledge, by accepting the revelation of God, then this would lead to the perfection of faith. *"Jesus said unto him, if you will be perfect, go and sell what you have, and give to the poor, and you shall have treasure in heaven: and come and follow me" (Matthew 19:21).* We would be advancing our faith by doing away with the false philosophies that prevent us from accepting Haile Sellassie I as God; this is what it means by selling your riches. His Majesty said, "We must look into ourselves, into the depth of our souls. We must become something we have never been and for which our education

---

[79] Acts 9:31
[80] John 1:42

and experience and environment have ill-prepared us. We must become bigger than we have been, more courageous, greater in spirit, larger in outlook."[81] The twelve apostles have nothing to do with a certain amount of people, it is referring to a certain level of understanding.[82] By rejecting the misinformation that prevents you from knowing God, you can then become one of the disciples and obtain the true knowledge. When Judas Iscariot betrayed the Lord this signifies those who claim to be of God but reject the Word because their faith is not sincere. The other side to this would be Saul who was at first against the faith but later repented and became the apostle Paul.[83] These are all representations of what is occurring in the world today. When the people claim to be of God yet reject Haile Sellassie I they fulfill Judas Iscariot. If they were not of Rastafari but later accepted His Majesty then they are like Paul. This is also demonstrated with Joses as he was then called Barnabas[84] after he believed the gospel and Lebbaueus, whose surname was Thaddaeus[85] when he followed Christ. We also read how Simon (this is not Simon Peter) was called Zelotes[86] and Lebbaueus was called Judas[87] (this is not Judas Iscariot). The change of name represents a change in understanding, we must always strive to ameliorate, this is the lesson and the mission. The parable is written for all people to find themselves inside of the holy book, it is not referring to an ancient myth that occurred thousands of years ago. Revelation 2:17 says, *"He that has an ear, let him hear what the spirit says unto the churches; to him that overcomes will I give to eat of the hidden manna, and will give him a white stone, and in the stone a new name written, which no man knows saving he that receives it."* This representation of receiving a new moniker when you have obtained a higher learning, is repeated over and over again throughout the scriptures, Abram became Abraham[88] when God established his covenant with him and Jacob was named Israel[89] when he submitted to the Lord.

The final prod to this analogy concerning the names is understanding the correct context of the prophet. All of the depictions of the messenger describes

---

[81] The Selected Speeches of His Imperial Majesty Haile Selassie I, page 378

[82] Acts 6:1-3

[83] Acts 13:9

[84] Acts 4:36-37

[85] Matthew 10:3

[86] Luke 6:15

[87] Luke 6:16

[88] Genesis 17:5

[89] Genesis 35:10

a person who was chosen by God to preach the true Word unto the people. Although each story is the same in its purpose and portrayal of the seer, the world has been disillusioned to believe that it is talking about different people who lived in antiquity. The lie that the Bible unfolded during prehistoric times was devised to confuse the world and rob them of their salvation. All of the names of the prophets are talking about one person, that is the mystery of the transfiguration; people misinterpret it to be three separate individuals - Moses, Elijah, and Jesus, but it actually is the same person: the Son of God.[90] Acts 4:12 says, *"Neither is there salvation in any other: for there is no other name under heaven given among men, whereby we must be saved."* This explanation of how all the prophets are synonymous is elaborated on in Hebrews 11, when it says that they all upheld the true faith, a description for which has been designated for only one person. We can read about how Jacob[91] and Moses[92] have seen God but it says that only Christ can see the Lord;[93] this means that the Messiah is every last prophet. So when Jesus said that he will fulfill all the laws and the prophets,[94] this means that he will do everything that is written about God's messenger because all of the stories are depictions of him; he is the only one who can carry out what is written concerning the anointed seer. The narratives of Abraham, David, Job, Isaiah, Muhammad, Arjuna, etc., are all prophesies that tell of a person chosen by God to deliver the true message of salvation unto the world. *"And when Abram was ninety years old and nine, the LORD appeared to Abram, and said unto him, I am the Almighty God, walk before me, and be thou perfect"* (Genesis 17:1). The fulfillment of this prophecy has been accomplished by Primus St. Croix who both seen God and declared him unto us. The antiquated harbinger about the messenger has a manifestation that has come to pass, if we reject the person for whom the portend is referring to, then we have only been pretending to believe in these sacred chronicles. It is written in Revelation 3:12 that Christ will come in a new name and will proclaim who God is. We are now able to understand that Emperor Haile Sellassie I is the Almighty because his Son has risen and revealed the mystery. The new name of the prophet represents the manifestation, we can no longer associate the sages with prehistoric fables which lack evidence and coherency. Primus St. Croix has taught us the scriptures so that we may know that His Majesty is the

---

[90] Matthew 17:1-8
[91] Genesis 32:30
[92] Deuteronomy 5:4
[93] John 1:18
[94] Matthew 5:17

true and living God. It is also important to note that when Tafari Makonnen became the Emperor of Ethiopia, he changed his name to Haile Sellassie I. This also depicts the Biblical exemplification of obtaining a new moniker when you have reached a higher level which is a demonstration of becoming a new man; obtaining a new life. His Majesty proclaimed his regnal name on April 3, 1930, after Empress Zewditu died, but his reign did not officially begin until the Coronation. The Bhagavad-Gita says, "The Lord has different names according to His different activities" (Gita 1:15). His Majesty cautioned everyone to continue learning as education and the quest for knowledge stops only at the grave: "A mountain top is reached, beyond, on the far slope, there are new lands to explore, and new peaks to scale. As each goal along life's path is reached, new vistas open before us, and new challenges are made. It is indeed, an immutable law of life that man's strivings can never end, that to pause in life's struggle is to slip back along the road to progress."[95]

If we were not afraid to question our beliefs and to increase in knowledge then we would find solace in the doctrine of Christ because it unifies all religions. Not only regarding spiritual matters but the same is true concerning secular issues, for we all have much more in common than we do differently. To focus upon what sets us apart leads to conflict but to build upon our similarities fosters unity. It is evident that everyone cannot be right with all the divergent doctrines in the world; but there are valid points found within each denomination. These topics must be used to bring people together so we can increase in knowledge; as we all can learn from one another. Haile Sellassie I said, "We don't consider our religion alone valid and have granted the people the freedom to observe any religion they please."[96] The only way to reach this level of consciousness would be to fully grasp the concept of monotheism and to understand that everyone has a role in the gospel. If there is only one God, how can anyone show differentiation towards an alternative belief? The different variations of religions does not change the fact that there is one all powerful Creator who rules over everyone. In this light, let us understand the difference between correcting and renouncing as concerning the faith. If we tell someone who believes in animism that they are wrong concerning how they view the spirit world, this must be done with the intention of teaching them what is right. In this sense it is not a condemnation, which implies a renunciation of their faith; but rather an improvement to their existing beliefs.

---

[95] The Selected Speeches of His Imperial Majesty Haile Selassie I, page 57
[96] The Wisdom of Rastafari, page 3

If anyone is against advancing their religion then this indicates that they are contrary to their own faith. There is no reason to ask a Christian to convert to being a Muslim, or for a Buddhist to become a Rastafarian, etc. This is why Paul said, *"And unto the Jews I became as a Jew, that I might gain the Jews; to them that are under the law, as under the law, that I might gain them that are under the law; To them that are without law, as without law, (being not without law to God, but under the law to Christ,) that I might gain them that are without law. To the weak became I as weak, that I might gain the weak: I am made all things to all men, that I might by all means save some"* (1 Corinthians 9:20-22). The truth is that if we all truly understood our religion then everyone would agree on the same thing; for there is only one God. Therefore we cannot be afraid of correction, we cannot be prideful and think that our customs are already perfect. Because if it was, then this supreme gospel would overshadow all the vain dogmas and unite all people; this is the ultimate culmination of the question of theology. Our present existence must demonstrate that this realization has not yet been met; either due to a lack of acceptance or knowledge of the truth, therefore we all should be seeking to achieve that perfection. The prophesies have foretold that this faultless gospel will be preached by Jesus Christ. The term "Son of God" means that he is the mediator between God and man; not that he is the biological child of the Almighty. All of the stories about the messenger are referring to him; that is why it is written in Matthew 5:17 that he will fulfill the entire law and prophets. *"And he said unto them, these are the words which I spoke unto you, while I was yet with you, that all things must be fulfilled, which were written in the law of Moses, and in the prophets, and in the psalms, concerning me"* (Luke 24:44).

"I have raised up one from the north, and he shall come: from the rising of the sun shall he call upon my name: and he shall come upon princes as upon mortar, and as the potter treads clay. Who hath declared from the beginning, that we may know? And beforetime, that we may say, He is righteous? Yea, there is none that shows, yea, there is none that declares, yea, there is none that hears your words. The first shall say to Zion, Behold, behold them: and I will give to Jerusalem one that brings good tidings. For I beheld, and there was no man; even among them, and there was no counselor, that, when I asked of them, could answer a word. Behold, they are all vanity; their works are nothing: their molten images are wind and confusion" (Isaiah 41:25-29). After His Majesty's Coronation on November 2, 1930, the Rastafarian tradition was established but the fullness was not revealed until Christ preached his gospel concerning the Father. Anyone who declares that Emperor Haile Sellassie I is the Almighty, is sitting in Moses seat, for you are

assuming to carry forth the works of the prophet. This task must be carried out correctly, with the proper care and thought; otherwise you would be playing with fire. It is written that, *"No man has seen the Father, save he which is of God, he has seen the Father" (John 6:46)*; this indicates that there was no counselor, there was no one who understood the mysteries, therefore God had to send his Son. For Jesus said, *"Though you do not know him, I know him; and if I should say I know him not, I shall be a liar like you are, but I know him and keep his word" (John 8:55)*. The people are able to see God but because they do not follow his Word, this leads to them being spiritually blind and void of the truth. It is for this reason that all religions must challenge themselves to ensure that they have it correct; otherwise it serves no beneficial purpose to consider spirituality. Matthew 5:48 says, *"Be ye therefore perfect, even as your Father which is in heaven is perfect."* If the people were committed to accepting the truth then the entire world would unite and understand that Haile Sellassie I is the Almighty. The prophecy concerning the revelation is the same story in different languages and allegories but the only way to understand their connection is if you know certain fundamental principles which the Messiah first preached. Studying any of the various sacred books from the correct perspective will lead the sincere devotee before the Throne of the Almighty. Primus St. Croix articulated this universal doctrine which binds all religions; upon this basis alone, he is justified as being the true Christ.[97] What we have seen and heard from him, is the same testimony which we preach to you concerning the Most High. The Father and the Son are two different people, they are not consubstantial. It is an incorrect viewpoint to think that multiple beings are somehow the same entity. This position could only be explained by believing in the supernatural. It would be impossible to explain the concept of being consubstantial using real terms such as facts, history, human nature, or the scriptures. That is why it is written that the truth about the LORD can only be found in Jesus.

"Behold, I will send my messenger, and he shall prepare the way before me: and the Lord, whom ye seek, shall suddenly come to his temple, even the messenger of the covenant, whom ye delight in; behold, he shall come, saith the LORD of hosts. But who may abide the day of his coming? And who shall stand when he appears? For he is like a refiners fire, and like fullers soap. And he shall sit as a refiner and purifier of silver: and he shall purify the sons of Levi, and purge them as gold and silver, that they may offer unto the LORD an offering in righteousness" (Malachi 3:1-3). The purpose of Christ is to proclaim the name of the Lord; it is written that he is the messenger

---

[97] Luke 24:45

of God. Jesus did not speak of himself, the doctrine regarding "God the Father, God the Son" is not found in the scriptures. There is only one God not two and two cannot be one; furthermore three cannot be one. How is that not evident, when it bears no logic or evidence? That which is popular is not necessarily right; and that which is right is not necessarily popular. The only reference in the Bible regarding the trinity is found in 1 John 5:7 where it says, *"There are three that bear record in heaven, the Father, the Word, and the Holy Ghost: and these three are one."* This describes three attributes of one person, not three people with the same attributes. It is inaccurate to say that three objects can all encapsulate the same matter, but you can describe one object in three different ways. We also must understand the very important reason why it says Word and not Son. Jesus said that the Word which he preaches is not his but the Father's (John 14:24). Christ speaks the truth about God therefore he carries the Word; but his message is not about himself.[98] It is an open invitation for everyone to become one of the Son's of God.[99] Therefore the designation of being the Son of God could never mean that you are God. For the same power which Jesus possessed, it is written that this is given to anyone who accepts the gospel.[100] Therefore he is not God because the ability which the Almighty is endowed with cannot be shared with other people. Matthew 28:19 asks us to teach the world about the Father, the Son, and the Holy Ghost; these three are not the same entity. The Father is God Almighty, the Son is the prophet who taught us about God, and the Holy Spirit is the gospel which will enable you to understand the parables of the Bible. Without accepting this foundation, which Primus St. Croix taught, it would be impossible to formulate any coherency in the scriptures.

"Speak unto all the people of the land, and to the priests, saying, when you fasted and mourned in the fifth and seventh month, even those seventy years, did you fast unto me, even to me; saith the Lord. And when you did eat, and when you did drink, did not you eat for yourselves and drink for yourselves" (Zechariah 7:5-6). From 1930 the world has witnessed the power of Haile Sellassie I but has not followed his example. His principals have not been emulated which demon-strates that the people do not accept God. Seventy years after the Coronation the entire world remains without the truth, including the Rastafarian com-munity because they never implemented the Emperor's principles. Primus St. Croix was the first one to accept the true message of the Bible and to live his

---

[98] John 5:31-32
[99] Romans 8:14
[100] John 1:12

life according to the Word of God. His Majesty said, "I have the highest respect for the Bible as a whole. We also recognize the rightful name the Bible bears [...] My advice to all is to fulfill the Ten Commandments. You are aware of the contents of the Ten Commandments and can elaborate on it. If the nation for which I am their Emperor follows and accepts this, since this is also what I accept and follow, I would believe our country to not only be historically Christian but actively Christian [...] He taught us that all men are equal regardless of sex, their national origin, and tribe. And He also taught us all who seek him shall find him. To live in this healthy life, a Christian life, is what makes me follow Jesus Christ."[101] Many of the Rastafarian leaders have introduced different forms of spirituality which flies in the face of the teachings of Haile Sellassie I. They are against the Bible, they advocate black supremacy, they oppose following the laws of Moses, and they deny Jesus Christ. The struggle to gain independence from their colonizers has somehow led to them compromising the principles of His Majesty although the Emperor was the most effective opponent of colonization. As we stated before it is important to give careful thought to your role if you claim to represent Haile Sellassie I. Primus St. Croix faced strong resistance from many Rastafarian leaders but his message was for us to implement the ecclesiastical order. He preached how the Sabbath must be observed, His Majesty also said to uphold the ten commandments but they refused to take heed to this admonition. Primus broke the idols of satan, just as Moses was commanded by God to destroy graven images, but they say that this was a foolish act despite the fact that Haile Sellassie I supports the Bible as a whole. When the day of reckoning arrived the Rastafarians found themselves contrary to God and Christ. The scriptures are pertaining to our present conditions, it is not a far removed fable that played out in antiquity. That is why it is written during those seventy years, from 1930 to 2000, did you fast unto me, or did you not eat and drink for yourselves? Which means that they did not observe the instructions and laws of Haile Sellassie I, they made up their own customs. Why is Bob Marley the common image of Rastafari and not the Emperor himself? Bob Marley said, "What direction we need? We need direction towards our own self. I mean find our self that god live in a man. Rastafari is God." His advice to look into ourselves for God essentially contradicts saying that His Majesty is the Almighty. Because if Haile Sellassie I lived inside of everyone, then everyone would already do as he did and adhere to his precepts. The realities of life indicate that this is not the case and that no

---

[101] Haile Selassie I, Interview with Dr. Oswald Hoffman, December 25, 1968

one is like His Majesty therefore we cannot look inside of ourselves for him; we must look to the actual person Ras Tafari for guidance. Bob Marley was double talking, which is common among those who claim to be of Rastafari, they look to their own self for direction despite saying that they follow His Majesty. You can either follow yourself or you can follow Haile Sellassie I but to claim to do both is a contradiction, yielding confusion; because looking to your conscience for instruction only defies the counsel of the LORD. The Rastafarians do not look to the Emperor because they do not accept his Word, they would rather look towards their own selves and follow whatever their heart desires. Did the smoking of cannabis come from Haile Sellassie I, or the dreadlock hairstyle, or being promiscuous? Why are these traditions so prevalent within a movement which claims to follow a man (Ras Tafari) who did not advocate or observe any of these customs? Are they aware that it is illegal to smoke weed in Ethiopia, therefore if Babylon is unjustly fighting against the sensimilla then His Majesty is also. Marijuana can be used for various medical purposes and this should only inform us not to use it; the opposite of consuming it liberally. All medicine whether it be agrarian or industrial is prescribed to a patient who is suffering from some sort of aliment, if you do not have any complications then abusing these medications will only harm you. The kava plant is used to cure urinary tract infections but can induce sever liver damage if consumed orally, senna is good for constipation but it can cause your bowels to stop functioning if you take it for longer than two weeks, ephedra has been used in China and India for over 5,000 years to cure the common cold but if you take this plant when you have no medical necessity then it can kill you; these are all natural herbs which will have a negative effect upon anyone who is not taking these prescriptions properly. And this is true for every kind of drug on earth, cannabis is not excluded, to think otherwise is a slap in the face of science and facts. Even over the counter medications, which are deemed safe enough for everyone to buy, will have negative consequences upon anyone who takes these remedies openhandedly; so how is it that we do not apply this logic to cannabis if we understand that it is medicine? Haile Sellassie I reigned as Emperor from 1930 to1974 and it is written, *"Harden not your hearts, as in the provocation, in the day of temptation in the wilderness: when your fathers tempted me, proved me, and saw my works forty years. Wherefore I was grieved with that generation, and said, they do always error in their heart; and they have not known my ways"* (Hebrews 3:8-10). The Rastafarians choose not to implement the teaching of His Majesty although they was present during his lifetime and were eyewitnesses to his reign which lasted forty four years. Haile Sellassie

I said that he has always been religious but they state that they are not into religion; the Emperor was a politician, being that he was the head of state, but they say that they are not into politics. These glaring contradictions have left them without the truth, they do always error and have not known his ways; as a result Primus St. Croix had to do what no other man did, which is to follow God in spirit and in truth.

It is written that the Lord has put his words into the mouth of the prophet[102] therefore we will know who is the true Messiah by his message; which will be of God and not his own. The Rastafarian elders had every opportunity to be justified in their works if they simply followed what Haile Sellassie I advocated; but they fell short of the promises because the only direction they feel they need, is direction towards their own selves. Instead of becoming educated in Western institutions like His Majesty recommended, they label these schools as Babylon which means evil establishments. The Emperor set up scholarships and sent Ethiopians to the West to receive training but the Rastafarians who already live in America and England, by in large, shun these opportunities. Being a vegetarian is a healthy lifestyle but it is important to understand that Haile Sellassie I ate meat occasionally and served it to his guests and his people. Yet the Rastafarians disdain carnivores as if that is the message of the Lord. Matthew 15:8-9 says, *"These people draw near unto me with their mouth, and honor me with their lips; but their heart is far from me. In vain they do worship me, teaching for doctrines the commandments of men."* Primus St. Croix understood these contradictions and saw the necessity of teaching the people what His Majesty really stood for. His own infirmities he did not try to coax or justify, he is a vegetarian who smokes cannabis, listens to Bob Marley and has dreadlocks; but he never stated that this is what identifies a person as being a Rastafarian. Primus placed these subjects into their proper context by stating that people can keep their traditions as long as they do not place their customs above the teachings of God Emperor Haile Sellassie I. This means that a Muslim can continue to wear his shemagh, a Hindu can continue to abstain from eating beef, a Jew can keep his yamaka, etc., because none of these outward customs can justify anyone within their faith. *"Render your heart and not your garments, and turn unto the LORD your God: for he is gracious and merciful, slow to anger, and of great kindness, and ready to repent of the evil"* (*Joel 2:13*). What makes one approved is the spirit, when you accept the divinity of the Emperor and adhere to his precepts, then you would know what traditions

---

[102] Jeremiah 1:9

and beliefs are unprofitable and profitable; the true devotee will abandon his unproductive ways so that he may serve the Lord wholeheartedly. It is this journey to be accepted by God which has led Primus to see past his own traditions and to analyze the Word objectively.

Haile Sellassie I was asked if he was Jesus Christ on several occasions, most notably by Bill McNeil in 1967, and he always said no. Instead of giving a false interpretation of what His Majesty said, Primus St. Croix accepted this reality and read the scriptures which explain that the Father and Son are two different people.[103] Primus knew that the pope is a deceiver therefore he did not accept the vatican theory of God and Christ being consubstantial, rather he was able to come into the full realization of the truth by correlating what Haile Sellassie I said with the Bible. God the Father alone is the Almighty, Jesus Christ is a different person, a prophet who preaches the true message of the LORD.[104] This universal message cannot be denied through the scriptures and it will unite all people. The Muslims have long held a similar view that Christ could not be God according to the Bible but rather a prophet. The Bhagavad-Gita tells of the same relationship between Krsna and Arjuna, as one being the Supreme Godhead and the other his messenger. Primus St. Croix fulfilled this ancient prophecy by declaring that Emperor Haile Sellassie I is who the scriptures appertain to and Christ is the mediator who preaches the message correctly. The different religions can now see the manifestation of their beliefs, anyone whose faith is sincere will accept the revelation. This beckons one to look beyond allegiances to family, friends, culture, customs, etc., and to place

---

[103] John 8:17-18
[104] Romans 15:6-8

God above everything. Matthew 10:32-39 says, *"Whosoever therefore shall confess me before men, him will I confess also before my Father which is in heaven. But whosoever shall deny me before men, him will I also deny before my Father which is in heaven. Think not that I am come to send peace on earth: I came not to send peace but a sword. For I am come to set a man at variance against his father, and the daughter against her mother, and the daughter in law against her mother in law. And a man's foes shall be they of his own household. He that loves father or mother more than me is not worthy of me: he that loves son or daughter more than me is not worthy of me. And he that takes not his cross, and follows after me, is not worthy of me. He that finds his life shall lose it: and he that loses his life for my sake shall find it."* This means that the validity of our customs will be tested when Christ declares unto us who God is. If you are a true Muslim, Hindu, Jew, etc., then you will accept the divinity of Emperor Haile Sellassie I. The truth will set you at odds with those who place their customs above the Word, that is why it is written that your foes shall be they of your own household. For the people and the religion that you was born into will disavow you despite the fact that the texts which they adhere to are referring to His Majesty. This is the sword sent into the world and not peace, because Jesus did not come to appease those who refuse to progress and follow the LORD. Only those whose spiritual sense has been heightened, through faith, will be able to understand this phenomenon. When you know God, you can comprehend the universal message found in all the religions; because he is the tie that binds us. Since the knowledge of man cannot be compared to that of the Almighty, we should be humble enough to continue learning and make adjustments when it relates to refining our spirituality. It is this journey to be accepted by God which led Primus St. Croix to break the Catholic idols. Because this signifies a renunciation of false principles, the courage to do what is right regardless of the consequences or public opinion. He said, "My act was not an act of hatred but an act of love because God always sends people to save humanity before he destroys them."[105] Primus gave this interview to the national newspaper of St. Lucia, and his words reflect Luke 10:8-12, *"And into whatsoever city you enter, and they receive you, eat such things as are set before you: heal the sick that are there, and say unto them, the kingdom of God is come near unto you. But into whatsoever city you enter, and they receive you not, go your way out into the streets of the same, and say, even the very dust of your city, which cleaves on us, we do wipe off against you: notwithstanding be ye sure of this, that the kingdom of God is come near unto*

---

[105] The Voice, Vol. 114 No. 8,729, St. Lucia

you. But I say unto you, that it shall be more tolerable in that day for Sodom, than for that city." Certain people would interpret his judgments incorrectly that he was creating unnecessary problems or that it was not of God for him to break the statues. But the true meaning of this skirmish is for us to let go of our false ideologies which do not coincide with the real message of the LORD. The act of smashing idols was merely a sign, we are not to mimic his deeds by breaking sculptures, if anyone truly wants to follow his example then they must repent from all their falsehoods and worship Emperor Haile Sellassie I according to his commandments.

Primus St. Croix went on to say, "I am from Marigot. I am married with two sons. I did destroy statues of the Roman Catholic Church in New York for which I was charged with. Idol worship is of the devil as explained in the Bible. I was commanded by God to destroy the statues of the Catholic churches in New York. My duty is to preach the gospel of Selassie to all the people. If I see a wrong it is my duty to point out the wrong. I cannot be seen to preach the gospel yet at the same time wreak destruction on people and structures. It does not work that way."[106] He conducted this interview to give clarification regarding his actions because some people believed that he was advocating a physical war against the Catholics. But Ephesians 6:12 says, *"For we wrestle not against flesh and blood, but against principles and powers, against the rulers of the darkness of this world, against spiritual wickedness in high places."* His objective was for the people to take heed to the gospel so that their faith may be made whole. He plainly said that this engagement was not to wreak destruction on people and structures, which means that there is a deeper motivation and gist to his mission. If you only examine the surface of these events then you would never understand its true meaning. Primus also left notes for investigators during the time these incidents were occurring, explaining his reasons for engaging in these activities. It was from this correspondence that the vatican was alerted and the bounty for his capture was raised. Because the year 2000 was the Catholic jubilee celebration and the pope was parading around the world appearing to make amends and offer guidance to the people. But Primus knew that this was a farce and the breaking of idols corresponded to the events of the pontiff. For example, on March 12, 2000, the pope made a historic appeal seeking forgiveness for the sins of the church and they received their answer that same night as idols were found smashed at several of their cathedrals. They cannot be forgiven when they blatantly going against what the Bible stands for.

---

[106] Ibid

Isaiah 44:10-11 says, *"Who has formed a god, or molten a graven image that is profitable for nothing? behold, all his fellows shall be ashamed: and the workmen, they are of men: let them all be gathered together, let them stand up; yet they shall fear and they shall be ashamed together."* Many Catholics were outraged when their relics were attacked and they tried to justify their existence by stating that they do not worship these statues. But this overlooks a very important point: the scriptures commanded that these images were not to be made, the vatican is guilty because they have constructed these idols; you are condemned regardless of what you do with them because they were never supposed to be produced. When you construct an image of God and the prophets those who follow you will believe that this likeness is actually how these people appear. This myth will prevent those who accept it from knowing the truth because they have put their trust in a false image therefore when the prophecy comes to pass, no matter how factual it is, they will deny it because it does not match with the likeness of their phantasm. In Acts 17:29 it says, *"Therefore since we are God's offspring, we ought not to think that the Godhead is like unto gold, or silver, graven by art and the imagination of man."* If the pope was truly sincere in seeking forgiveness then he would renounce his deceitful dogma which is adjudged throughout the entire Bible; but he will not do this. Primus was fighting against spiritual wickedness in high places for he knew that the intentions of the vatican are to deceive humanity; this was not a petty crime.

It is not enough just to read the Bible, we must live according to the example written in the scriptures and each of us must fulfill our own unique purpose given to us by God. The only way to know your mission is to first acknowledge the Lord; for the knowledge of self is always synonymous with the knowledge of God. If the world understood that Emperor Haile Sellassie I is the Creator then they would live according to his standard; which will lead to true righteousness. Primus St. Croix understood that his purpose was to combat the pope during that critical moment in time, when the Catholics were celebrating their jubilee in the year 2000, and to appeal for them to stop the charade and come clean regarding the faith. The vatican has rewritten history to claim that Jesus Christ was born in ancient Arabia, which then resulted in the necessity for a land holding in that area to support their falsifications. This led to the Inquisitions and the establishment of Israel in 1948; which resulted in the unjust murder and oppression of millions of innocent people indigenous to that region. This conflict has the potential to destroy humanity for it demonstrates the relentless pursuit of evil doers to subject the world under heinous tribulations. The only way that the Catholic Church can be forgiven is if they renounce their pagan gospel and stop misleading the public; the world severely suffers as a result of their deceitful policies. The millions of people under their sectarian dominion appear clueless as to their treachery although history is clearly candid on troves of major transgressions committed by the vatican; including war, torture, homosexuality, pedophilia, censorship, idolatry, and heresy. At what point do we raise concerns if we notice their actions completely contradict their purpose? Or do we mindlessly follow customs despite their hallow exactitude and pernicious design? When Primus St. Croix was arrested on May 18, 2000, he quoted Deuteronomy 12:3, *"And ye shall overthrow their altars, and break their pillars, and burn their groves with fire; and ye shall hew down the graven images of their gods."* This was a plea for them to abandon their false principles which are contrary to the Word of God. Anyone who is sincere in seeking forgiveness cannot do so by continuing in the same practices which condemned them to begin with. After the events with Primus, the media reported on numerous cases of rape and molestation across America and around the world in Catholic Churches. This led to a series of arrests (John Geoghan) and convictions as cops discovered that the vatican had been paying off victims for years not to prosecute their priests. Rather than defend the innocent by prosecuting their victimizers, they merely shuffled their predator priests from one guild to another which only allowed them to continue preying upon defenseless children (Mario Pezzotti). How can anyone forgive the pope, remember that if this story were not made public those pedophiles would still be in office as Catholic missionaries committing their crimes. That is why Primus sough to crush their order because the pope is a liar and a deceiver.

"Now we beseech you, brethren, by the coming of our Lord Jesus Christ, and by our gathering together unto him. That you be not soon shaken in mind, or be troubled, neither by spirit, nor by word, nor by letter as from us, as that the day of Christ is at hand. Let no man deceive you by any means: for that day shall not come, except there come a falling away first, and that man of sin be revealed, the son of perdition. Who opposes and exalts himself above all that is called God, or that is worshipped, so that he as God sitteth in the temple of God, showing himself that he is God" (2 Thessalonians 2:1-4). If you seek forgiveness from the LORD this must be done earnestly and not from a Machiavellian standpoint. The judgment is upon those who handle the Word of God deceitfully and walk in craftiness. You cannot abide in darkness and pretend to be holy; this deception will only lead to your demise. Primus St. Croix had to condemn the pope because they are insincere and sinister. *"Because he has appointed a day, in the which he will judge the world in righteousness by that man whom he has ordained; whereof he has given assurance*

unto all men, in that he has raised him from the dead" (Acts 17:31). The vatican has been successful in deceiving millions of people by pretending to follow Christ but God knows that satan is a liar. When John Paul II became the pope on October 16, 1978, he set out to mimic the deeds of Emperor Haile Sellassie I and erase his legacy. His Majesty was the most travelled and the most photographed person on earth before the Ethiopians deposed him in 1974. After his passing, the pontiff then travelled, in like manner, all around the world trying to gain the admiration of the people but to what avail? Before Haile Sellassie I, nobody ever journeyed on a regular basis from country to country because prior to the twentieth century the technology was not yet up to standard to support this type of endeavor. The question then is, why did the Emperor take his trips and what was the pope trying to accomplish by mimicking his deeds; also why are these two leaders the only people who have journeyed on this massive level? For the uncircumcised, the relationship between Haile Sellassie I and John Paul II is unrecognizable because they do not view the world based upon the divinity of His Majesty, but we who do, have been able to understand the great prophecy regarding the dragon who exalted himself against God. Rome has always been at odds with Ethiopia, they tried to destroy the Ark of the Covenant many times through war and corruption. The vatican understands the significance of the Solomonic Dynasty and in order for them to succeed in covering the world in darkness with their Machiavellian version of Christianity, they would have to erase the truth. Fortunately it is not possible to prevail against the LORD therefore the pope has undertaken a vain cause in fighting against His Majesty. It is a spiritual war being carried out where the vatican is seeking to get as many people as possible under their armada which means that Haile Sellassie I would not be recognized since the pontiff is called "the holy father" and "lord god the pope" according to the official decretum of Catholicism; in fact the word "pope" means father.[107] Many people do not understand that the See of Rome considers the pontifex to be supreme and they consider themselves to be the mother of all churches. This constitutes a grave danger in the world since their institution is grounded in paganism and ungodliness. The pope is pretending to be God and in committing this most diabolical of all crimes, he denies the authority of the true and living Creator. John Paul II was seeking to persuade the people to forget about Haile Sellassie I and to remain steadfast in their ancient customs; never increasing in knowledge, never validating their faith through the revelation, and never receiving

---

[107] Matthew 23:9

the promises of Christ. His Majesty was enormously popular when he was alive and there was a huge growing consensus inside of Ethiopia and worldwide that he was in fact God incarnate. The pontiff who came into power in 1978 took drastic measures to crush that movement through the spread of propaganda; he travelled around the world trying to persuade people to believe in him, and invoked popular ancient pagan deities such as the Queen of heaven (Virgin Mary), so that he could win over and deceive as many people as possible.

"He that commits sin is of the devil; for the devil sins from the beginning. For this purpose the Son of God was manifested, that he might destroy the works of the devil" (1 John 3:8). The role of Christians and those who claim to love God is to accept the revelation for this is the only way to be justified, through evidence. When the Almighty was manifest in the flesh on earth, those who are sincere in their beliefs accepted the divinity of His Majesty but those who are not had to be judged for their pomposity. The religious members who reject God are held more accountable than the agnostics who reject Haile Sellassie I. Because the pious proclaim to support the LORD whereas those who are secular openly confess not to be part of the faithful. While the goal is for all people to know who God is and those who are irreligious could never escape their condemnation, it is particularly painstaking and disappointing to be faced with hypocrisy because their objectives are convoluted between being either ignorant or outright deceitful. It is for this reason we know that the pope is the devil and that Mengistu Haile Mariam was a tyrant. Both of them sought to erase His Majesty's legacy but one is an atheist and one pretends to be the vicar of Christ. When God comes on earth, we would expect the fight against his reverence to come from the unbelievers not those who proclaim to love the LORD. The pope is not ignorant but deceitful, for his study in the Bible has led him to take an active interest in Ethiopia not to be a guardian of the Ark of the Covenant but to destroy it. Colonel Mengistu was a power hungry atheist who is not found in the Bible; he fought Haile Sellassie I out of envy and his own incompetence. The vatican fights against the divinity of His Majesty due to a selfish and ungodly desire to destroy the truth in the Bible. Satan is described as being the one who exalts himself against God so that he can show himself to be God.[108] Mengistu Haile Mariam did not seek to persuade people that he is the Almighty but the pope did. The world was supposed to take notice of His Majesty and direct all of their activities to him for he is the King of Kings and Lord of Lords. If the vatican was sincere in the faith then they would have

---

[108] 2 Thessalonians 2

renounced their hidden doctrine of dishonesty, which is their pagan agenda of pretending that the papacy is divine. But they have not, instead they bear the awesome responsibility of being the largest Christian Church in the world and they mislead their flock because they do not want the people to know the truth. This threat must not go unchecked, while the pope is deceiving the world we cannot sit by silent and allow this to happen. That is why Primus St. Croix had to take action and wage a spiritual war against the serpent.

"If the world hate you, ye know that it hated me before it hated you. If ye were of the world, the world would love his own: but because ye are not of the world, but I have chosen you out of the world, therefore the world hates you. Remember the word that I said unto you, The servant is not greater than his lord. If they have persecuted me, they will also persecute you; if they have kept my saying, they will keep yours also. But all these things will they do unto you for my name's sake, because they know not him that sent me. If I had not come and spoken unto them, they had not had sin: but now they have no cloak for their sin. He that hates me hates my Father also. If I had not done among them the works which none other man did, they had not had sin: but now have they both seen and hated both me and my Father. But this cometh to pass, that the word might be fulfilled that is written in their law, They hated me without a cause" (John 15:18-25). The vatican orchestrated a major world event in the year 2000 that blatantly sought to defy the sovereignty of the LORD Emperor Haile Sellassie I. Beginning on December 24, 1999, and lasting until January 6, 2001, the size and magnitude of this celebration led to this ceremony being known as the Great Jubilee for it was bigger than all the previous Christian and Judaic festivals. John Paul II indicated that he had desired to orchestrate this grand spectacle since the beginning of his pontificate. For the world was expecting for Jesus Christ to return in the year 2000 therefore the antichrist needed to counteract that revelation to prevent people from knowing the truth. Preparations for the Catholic jubilee began in 1997 with a three year exploration of the trinity, each year was marked by a special prayer to the Virgin Mary, over forty events were eventually arranged with millions in attendance for each occasion, various nations were involved including Israel which plays a vital role in the deception. The pope was trying to ensnare the world to remain stagnant in their old customs whereas the message of the Bible and the revelation of Haile Sellassie I represent an increase in knowledge, a new earth (which is a new understanding), positive reformation towards proficiency. Primus St. Croix was aware of the devil's plot to deceive humanity and he immediately recognized the deceit of this jubilee scheme. When John Paul II was carrying out these misleading ceremonies, Primus

was combating these lies with the truth. The first letter was mailed to the authorities in December 1999, warning the vatican to abdicate from their plans and to turn to the living God Emperor Haile Sellassie I. Unfortunately the pope did not take heed and proceeded to open the doors of the basilica which officially kicked off their jubilee celebration. Primus responded by breaking idols at several Catholic Churches in January 2000 and he sent another note explaining that Rome must repent and accept the divinity of His Majesty. The vatican did not comply but only increased the bounty to capture Primus to one of the highest stipends on law enforcements most wanted list during that time in North America. To the common man the smashing of statues may have seemed insignificant but the gravity of these events was found within his letters which explained the doctrine. Rome was afraid of his message because they knew it had the potential to change the world for the better and destroy their erroneous faith; in rejecting the true gospel of Christ which declares that Emperor Haile Sellassie I is the Almighty, they fulfilled their part as being the dragon. Satan went about his business, seeking to align as many people as possible underneath his circle of treachery, covertly declaring himself to be God, instituting Machiavellian Christianity, and presenting himself as an angel of light yet behind closed doors administering pure evil. The vatican carried out their jubilee of artists, deacons, and Roman Curia in February 2000; with Primus St. Croix responding by destroying their relics. This back and forth continued until Primus was eventually arrested in May 2000.

"For God so loved the world, that he gave his only begotten Son, that whosoever believes in him should not perish, but have everlasting life. For God sent not his Son into the world to condemn the world; but that the world through him might be saved" (John 3:16-17). The reason that Primus put his life on the line was not to terrorize the public but to get the leaders to adopt better policies so that we can make this world a better place. From the correct spiritual standpoint we would be able to maximize our potential and develop a truly robust society for everything would be in its proper order. The pope wishes to oppress and exploit the people which is why Primus St. Croix challenged him; we must get rid of those obstacles which prevent us from moving forward. The media is owned by vatican consorts so their depiction of these events were to favor the pontiff. But something very interesting is to be learned from their depiction of Primus St. Croix because they inadvertently declared him to be Jesus Christ when they sought to belittle him. That is what Mark 15:17-20 means, "And they clothed him with purple, and platted a crown of thorns, and put it on his head, and began to salute him, Hail, King of the Jews! And they smote him on the head with *a reed, and did spit upon him, and bowing their knees worshipped him. And when they had mocked him, they took off the purple from him, and put his own clothes on him, and led him out to crucify him."* The crucifixion of Christ was not a physical assault, for it is not possible for anyone to literally rise from the dead and fly into the sky; these scriptures are parables which describe how they rejected the gospel. The media ridiculed the actions of Primus St. Croix and portrayed him to be a delusive minister. The only problem with their portrayal is that all the slander which they labeled him to be coincides with the descriptions of the Messiah and the accusations against the Son of God. "The Brooklyn district attorney's office announced Friday that a Manhattan man (Primus St. Croix) had pleaded guilty to vandalizing five statues at Roman Catholic churches in Brooklyn."[109] This trial is the herald for it is written in Matthew 12:39-40, *"An evil and adulterous generation seeks after a sign; and no sign shall be given it except the sign of the prophet Jonah; for as Jonah was three days and three nights in the whale's belly; so shall the Son of man be three days and three nights in the heart of the earth."* This means that the prophet was condemned by man yet God raised him above their reproach for everything he did was correct according to the scriptures; there shall be no other sign given.

"The Brooklyn district attorney announced the indictment yesterday of a man accused of vandalizing five statues at Roman Catholic churches in Brooklyn. The man, Primus St. Croix, 33, was charged with criminal mischief and other crimes."[110] The first thing that stood out to us was his name because we all knew him as Kenyatta Felix before his arrest. Maybe he used an alias because he was an illegal immigrant in America but whatever his reasons were, the meaning of his real name is quite striking. Primus St. Croix means the First Saint of the Cross and his proper appellation fits perfectly with his purpose. Jesus is called the first begotten whom all mankind must follow, for his cross is the true gospel.[111] We mentioned before how the Bible uses monikers to designate a certain position which a person holds and when you rise to a higher level then your epithet changes. This is what His Majesty did on November 2, 1930, and this is also what happened with Kenyatta, in the year 2000, when it was revealed that he is Primus St. Croix. In Revelation 3:12 it says that Jesus shall come in a new name. The second coming of Christ does not mean that he walked the earth thousands of years ago and has returned. The first man is

---

[109] New York Times, October 2, 2000

[110] New York Times, May 27, 2000

[111] Hebrews 1:5-13

earthly but the second man came from heaven.[112] This indicates that the first understanding of Jesus and the Bible was wrong, the supernatural interpretations and the ancient historical analysis of the scriptures is not what the oracle exemplifies. The second man, which is the second coming, is the actual person who the prophecy is referring to. He will give the proper perspective of spiritual matters and will fulfill all the prophecies foretold of him.

"A man who the police said cited the biblical commandment against graven images has been arrested on charges of vandalizing statues at several Catholic churches in Brooklyn, the authorities said. The suspect, Primus St. Croix, 33, told investigators that he had smashed the statues with a sledgehammer as a protest against idolatry, Police Commissioner Howard Safir said."[113] We also must recognize his age, because being that he was 33 years old when these events transpired, this is the exact moment in time when it was prophesied that Jesus would be crucified. The Bible describes death as being rejected not as a physical elimination. God rose Christ from the dead because his message is true and although in the eyes of man he was called a fool, in the sight of the LORD he was correct and granted all authority in heaven and earth. Paul most famously affirmed this in 1 Corinthians 15:31 when he said that he dies daily. It cannot then be perceived that he was literally being killed every day; the scriptures are written in parables. The crucifixion of Christ was the sign of his advent for Jesus lived a long life on earth well after this event. John 21:25 asserts this fact, *"And there are also many other things which Jesus did, the which if they should be written every one, I suppose that even the world itself could not contain the books that should be written. Amen."* This verse is referring to his deeds after the resurrection because the message cannot be destroyed for it is the Word of God.

"Primus St. Croix, 33, allegedly worked with a dozen people to deface statues across Brooklyn."[114] We also recognized the association when he was referred to as being the head of twelve followers. The correlation between Christ and the twelve disciples matches perfectly based upon this description. *"And when he had called unto him his twelve disciples, he gave them power against unclean spirits, to cast them out, and to heal all manner of sickness and all manner of disease (Matthew 10:1)."* The body of Christ are those who emulate his deeds and adhere to his message; which is exactly the same way that they portrayed

---

[112] 1 Corinthians 15:47

[113] New York Times, May 18, 2000

[114] Catholic World News, May 18, 2000

these events with Primus and his cohorts. "Although statues have been van-dalized outside a dozen Catholic churches and organizations in the last year, the police said Mr. St. Croix had confessed to participating in only five attacks. Mr. Safir however said that Mr. St. Croix might have been part of a larger group of perhaps a dozen people who shared his beliefs and carried out similar at-tacks at other churches in Brooklyn."[115] His disciples were questioned about the idols being broken for they was given the same commandment as him; the power to become the sons of God and the power over serpents.[116]

"An anonymous tip led the police to Mr. St. Croix, who was arrested Tuesday."[117] It is also very consistent with the prophecy that he was betrayed to the authorities for a bounty. "Shortly after Hamilton came forward, Primus St. Croix of Brooklyn was apprehended in May of 2000 and confessed to assisting or personally chopping off the hands or decapitating over a dozen Catholic church statues. The $25,000 in reward money was combined with other smaller reward offers from the Police Department, the Brooklyn Diocese, the Anti-Defamation League and the Brooklyn District Attorney's Office."[118] We earlier explained how the disciples have a broad definition, Judas Iscariot is fulfilled by anyone who denies Christ. Not only has the snitch who turned in Primus St. Croix carried out that role but everyone who does not accept the gospel as well. *"Then one of the twelve, called Judas Iscariot, went unto the chief priests, and said unto them, What will you give me, and I will deliver him unto you? And they covenanted with him for thirty pieces of silver. And from that time he sought opportunity to betray him"* (Matthew 26:14-16). We are fighting against our intrinsic salvation if we deny Jesus, that is why it is written that he was betrayed by one of his own. The world takes on the role of discipleship when they profess to love God but they fail in this endeavor when they oppose the revelation.

"A charismatic, Bible-quoting construction worker known to followers as 'Master' confessed yesterday to desecrating statues at Catholic churches around Brooklyn, police said."[119] It has been foretold that Jesus was a carpenter and for Primus to do construction work correlates with the descriptions of the Messiah. At some point the similarities have to be understood as being more than just coincidences but of exactitude if the entire prophecy runs parallel

---

[115] New York Times, May 18, 2000
[116] John 1:12
[117] New York Times, May 18, 2000
[118] Canarsie Courier, December 13, 2001
[119] Daily News, May 18, 2000

with the manifestation. Also notice how he was referred to as 'Master.' No one who was around him every called him that but the media portrayed him this way to ridicule him. Matthew 10:24-25 says, *"The disciple is not above his master, nor the servant above his lord. It is enough for the disciple that he be as his master, and the servant as his lord. If they have called the master of the house Beelzebub, how much more shall they call them of his household?"* In labeling him this way, they was mocking him and calling his fight a crock. This is the crown of thorns, an unjust condemnation against the messenger of God. It was reported that, "The suspect sometimes walked the streets of Flatbush wearing a white robe and was called 'master' by his followers. There was a whole bunch of them, and they had their own religion. They'd say 'Fxck the white man,' stomp their feet and shout."[120] None of this ever happened, Primus did not walk the streets in a robe and we do not condone racism but even the libel which they used to try to discredit our movement has worked to our benefit. For it is written that he would be called Beelzebub but God will not suffer his holy child to see corruption. The propaganda which they tried to use against us has been written into the prophecy concerning Jesus therefore Primus St. Croix has been given the victory over their slander for these are all the descriptions of Christ; his justification is the resurrection.

"St. Croix was born in St. Lucia, roughly 400 miles from Puerto Rico in the eastern Caribbean."[121] The misconception of Jesus leads people to the wrong conclusion concerning the nationality of Christ. Some think that he is Caucasian, Oriental, Mesopotamian, African, or Arabian. Even the popular stereotypes of who are the real Rastafarians, would be the Jamaicans. No one would have guessed that the Messiah would come from St. Lucia. Keep in mind that the nationality of Primus St. Croix holds no significance only in so far as mankind would take issue with these subjects. Because no matter what country he was born in, the true measure of his validity is found in his doctrine not his visa but the Bible says that Christ rose up out of a stock which no one knew of. *"If therefore perfection were by the Levitical priesthood, (for under it the people received the law,) what further need was there that another priest should rise after the order of Melchisedec, and not be called after the order of Aaron? For the priesthood being changed, there is made of necessity a change also of the law. For he of whom these things are spoken pertains to another tribe, of which no man gave attendance at the altar. For it is evident that our Lord sprang out of Juda; of which*

---

[120] Ibid
[121] Ibid

Moses spoke nothing concerning priesthood. And it is yet far more evident: for that after the similitude of Melchesidec there arises another priest, Who is made, not after the law of a carnal commandment, but after the power of an endless life" (Hebrews 7:11-16). Jesus Christ came from a different association than what people were expecting. He was not of the Levitical priesthood which is the way mankind commonly views spirituality for their interpretation is false. Therefore Jesus came with an unrepresentative doctrine that was after the power of an endless life, which signifies that he spoke the truth about God; he was from a different tribe (the scriptures designate land to mean a certain understanding: for example, Egypt is the house of bondage as opposed to Jerusalem which is Holy Mt Zion). Therefore if it seems strange to you that we declare that Jesus was born in St. Lucia, you can find comfort in the scriptures for it is written that he came from a different lot, of which no man gave attendance at the altar. This does not mean that we are saying that everyone from St. Lucia is of Judah for we have already explained that the children of Israel are those who are of the faith. But concepts such as nationality, race, traditions, class, etc., can also be applied to this topic since the descriptions of Christ illustrate that he comes in a manner which no one will expect (a thief in the night). Also keep in mind that the fact that he is black and smokes cannabis would in itself be a tremendous disassociation, for some, because of how they perceived Jesus to be as opposed to who he really is.

"Well-spoken and calm, St. Croix quoted from the Bible with an ease and expertise that impressed detectives. He quoted Chapter 5 of the book of Deuteronomy, which decrees against idolatry by saying, 'Smash their sacred stones [...] cut down the idols of their gods.'"[122] It had to be mentioned, despite their vain attempt to portray Primus as being crazy, that he actually is an expert in the Bible. He quotes the book with a masterful brilliance, anyone who has had the opportunity to hear him speak can attest to his ecclesiastical acumen regardless of if they are his friends or enemies. The cops who arrested him certainly were not on his side but they had to confess that he is greatly proficient in the scriptures. *"The officers answered, No one ever spoke like this man" (John 7:46).* Christ is described as a preacher with a greater message than what is found in the world, only through him can you know God. *"For he taught them as one having authority, and not as the scribes" (Matthew 7:29).* Primus is the only one who understood the parables, above all it is his doctrine that makes him the Christ, all of the prophesies are signs which point you to accepting his

---

[122] Ibid

gospel. "St. Croix, according to police, was a charismatic Rastafarian preacher who offered interpretations of the Bible to his followers, many of them young men who considered him an elder. In particular, he warned against worshipping graven images."[123] If we are sincere in our love for God then we would be able to recognize and accept the Messiah. We will know that these are the proper ordinances by the keenness and dexterity of the prophet's message; for no other postulate is greater than his testimony.

"During the interrogation, St. Croix quoted passages from the Bible to explain why he believed the statues are sacrilegious, investigators said."[124] If anyone thinks that Primus was wrong for breaking the idols then it must be understood that the Bible advocated for these works to be done. According to the scriptures there would be no way to prove him incorrect. "St. Croix's feelings echo the words in the Biblical passage quoted in the letters - Deuteronomy, chapter 16, verses 21 and 22 - which falls under the heading 'Pagan Worship.'"[125] Therefore if the customs of humanity have softened them up to accept idolatry then this is tolerable only to man but not to God. 1 Corinthians 12:2 says, *"You know that when you were pagans, you were led astray to dumb idols which have no voice."* If Primus is ostracized for what he did then we are against the Bible which instructed him to carry out these acts. God commanded us not to make icons, nor any likeness of anything that is in heaven, do not put your trust in graven images. *"Dear children, keep yourselves from idols. Amen" (1 John 5:21).* Moses was instructed to crush their statues because the LORD abhors sacrilege,[126] Jesus has further stated that he would fulfill everything written about the prophets.[127] That is why Primus St. Croix carried out all that has been foreseen regarding the messenger whether that be the story of Moses, Jesus, Jacob, David, etc.; he has carried out everything envisioned regarding God's anointed.

"A scripture-spouting Rastafarian yesterday admitted smashing up religious statues at five Catholic sites - telling detectives he was carrying out orders from a higher authority."[128] His allegiance was not to man but to God just as Frederick Douglass said, "I prefer to be true to myself, even at the hazard of incurring the ridicule of others, rather then to be false, and incur my own

---

[123] Ibid

[124] Ibid

[125] New York Post, September 6, 2000

[126] Leviticus 26:30

[127] Luke 24:44

[128] Daily News, May 18, 2000

abhorrence."[129] Primus considered it to be more important to follow what is written in the scriptures than to adhere to the popular worldly customs which are contrary to the commandments of the LORD. He speaks and exemplifies the Word of God because he does what the Bible has instructed us to uphold. The newspapers tried to make it appear as if he suffered from a schizophrenic disorder by writing that he was hearing voices. "Police Commissioner Howard Safir said the man told the police God had told him to do it; that the Bible suggested to him that he should not worship graven images, Safir said."[130] Primus was not going crazy, the media was trying to make him appear this way so that the public would write him off without investigating these matters. God put his Word into the prophets' mouth by the devotee being true to that which is written throughout the holy books. *"And the LORD said unto Moses, Thus shall you say to the children of Israel, You have seen that I have talked with you from heaven. You shall not make gods of silver neither shall you make gods of gold" (Exodus 20:22-23).* Through reading and studying the scriptures, he understood what the LORD wanted him to do, which would be to obey his commandments. Breaking statues was only one act of a much larger operation because the gravity to his purpose lies in the enlightenment which he has shed in the scriptures not the vandalism of sculptures. If you want to follow Christ and combat idolatry then you must renounce your false customs and follow Emperor Haile Sellassie I.

"It is not in dispute that St. Croix is mentally competent to stand trial. Indeed he even promised yesterday that when released, he will continue his crusade to get Catholics to get rid of religious statues. This is not the voice of someone who admits wrongdoing."[131] The media sensationalized this event to manipulate the public so that people would view Primus as being demented. But if we examine this case in conjunction with the Bible then we will notice certain similarities which could not be denied. *"And Pilate wrote a title, and put it on the cross. And the writing was, JESUS OF NAZARETH THE KING OF THE JEWS. This title then read many of the Jews: for the place where Jesus was crucified was near to the city: and it was written in Hebrew, and Greek, and Latin. Then said the chief priests of the Jews to Pilate, Write not, The King of the Jews; but that he said, I am King of the Jews. Pilate answered, What I have written will stay as it is" (John 19:19-22).* The Bible describes how they attempted to

---

[129] Douglass, Frederick, Narrative of the Life of Frederick Douglass, page 27

[130] Catholic World News, May 18, 2000

[131] Catholic League President William Donohue, October 11, 2000

portray Christ as being false, but despite this distortion, what was recorded of him identified him as the Son of God. We now can understand how all the slander that has been inscribed regarding Primus St. Croix only confirms his legitimacy because there is no way to ignore the fact that they depicted him as being Jesus. *"And when they had platted a crown of thorns, they put it upon his head, and a reed in his right hand: and they bowed the knee before him, and mocked him, saying, Hail, King of the Jews! And they spit upon him, and took the reed, and smote him on the head"* (Matthew 27:28-30). They ridiculed Primus by representing him as being mentally unstable when in fact he was completely competent and skillful in his craft. *"Then did they spit in his face, and buffeted him; and others smote him with the palms of their hands, saying, prophesy unto us, thou Christ, Who is he that smote thee"* (Matthew 26:67-68). The crucifixion is not literal, it is describing the scorn which they displayed towards the Son of God but the propaganda which has been broadcast surrounding Primus St. Croix is not going to be able to discredit who he is. This is how God raised him from the dead because the media's schemes has only worked against them because their own stories only prove that he is the Messiah. For it is written that they would lampoon Christ which is exactly what they did and in doing so they only confirmed his veneration.

"Primus St. Croix, an immigrant from the Caribbean, recently received a whopping 5 years probation after destroying statuary in five Brooklyn churches. Mr. St. Croix, who is presumably an idiot, pleaded guilty, said he was sorry, and that his motives for the vandalism were religious in nature. Since he won't be doing any time in the stir, why not offer this goof a one-way ticket to Afghanistan? Sounds like the Taliban could use a guy with his talents these days."[132] It must be understood that Primus never said that he was sorry for what he did. He never blinked in the face of adversity and remained steadfast in the fight against ungodliness. I was in the courtroom during his sentencing and what he said to the judge was, "I am sorry for how they took it." Which attests that he never admitted any wrongdoing and that his undertakings were to benefit society but they never understood it that way; he continued by saying, "If I see a bomb and do not warn the people about it, then when they die their blood will be on me." This is also what is written in Ezekiel 33; the judge understood that Primus St. Croix carried out his actions in an effort to save the world which is why he received probation instead of jail time. *"Pilate said unto him, What is truth? And when he had said this, he went out again unto the Jews, and said*

---

[132] The Bryan H. Roberts Gallery, March 2001

unto them, I find no fault in him" (John 18:38). It is very rare not to be imprisoned on a high profile multifarious felonious conviction but Justice Ann Feldman, who levied the sentence, sided with reason and could not find any occasion to condemn him; despite the fact that he pleaded guilty to six counts of Criminal Mischief in the Second Degree, five counts of Aggravated Harassment in the First Degree, three counts of Criminal Interference with Health Care Services or Religious Worship in the Second Degree, two counts of Criminal Trespass in the Third Degree, and Tampering with Physical Evidence.[133] This decision went against the recommendations of the District Attorney's Office and popular opinion at the time. The only rationalization why the judge could not send Primus to jail is because her conscience would not allow her to conclude that this man should be repudiated after she heard his defense. In this manner, Pontius Pilate's role has been carried out, for despite the Jews murmurings to crucify Christ, the judge found no fault in him and washed her hands from his reproach. *"Pilate therefore went forth again, and said unto them, Behold, I bring him forth to you, that you may know that I find no fault in him" (John 19:4).* This personification is also applied to anyone who accepts the gospel of Christ; as with any principle it is valid in various scenarios.

"Now as far as I am concerned, Mr. St. Croix is welcome to his beliefs that Catholics are guilty of the sin of idolatry because they venerate statues of holy people. And if that is the case, cast me with that lot as well. I am a Greek Catholic, and I hold icons as something sacred."[134] The uproar which ensued over the desecration of religious relics revolved primarily around the Catholics defense that they do not worship statues. They said that Primus St. Croix did not know what he was talking about and that his actions were in vain but we found the opposite to be true. The pope has instituted Machiavellian Christianity which means that they say whatever it takes to please the people without being true to their word and concealing their real intentions; which essentially means they lie. When Primus St. Croix went on his mission in the year 2000, it would not have suited the vatican's objective of deceiving the world if they admitted that they have the people worshipping graven images. But they cannot hide their transgressions because the culture of the church openly displays these atrocities. After a Catholic confesses their sin, they are told to go before these icons and Hail Mary a certain number of times; these are regular practices within their cathedrals. Those who are subject to these ordinances understand that

---

[133] The Brooklyn DA, News Releases 2001
[134] Nicholas Sanches CNS Commentary, October 13, 2000

they are being told to venerate the sculptures, if not there would not have been any discord when their idols were smashed. Primus merely stated the obvious that the pope has the people putting their trust in statues. *"But you shall destroy their altars, break their images, and cut down their groves: For you shall worship no other god but the LORD, whose name is Jealous, he is a jealous God: Lest thou make a covenant with the inhabitants of the land, and they go whoring after their gods, and do sacrifice unto their gods, and one call thee, and you eat of his sacrifice; And you take their daughters unto your sons, and their daughters go whoring after their gods, and make your sons to go whoring after their gods. Do not make molten images of gods for yourself"* (Exodus 34:13-17). Christ has executed the judgment prescribed from the LORD for their pagan customs hinder the world from knowing that Emperor Haile Sellassie I is the Almighty.

"At yesterdays hearing, Lance Ogiste, the district attorneys executive assistant, said, 'The people are asking for a sentence of two and one-third to seven years. The defendant terrorized not only Brooklyn but all New York City and not only Catholics but people of all religious faiths.' The district attorney's office is currently investigating six other crimes of a similar nature; the 12 suspects may be connected to a religious group led by St. Croix, who is a Rastafarian."[135] It is important that we do not analyze these events from a myopic standpoint because if we do then we would never understand the full gravity of this juncture. Idolatry refers to anyone who does not accept the true gospel of Christ that Emperor Haile Sellassie I is the Almighty. Primus attacked the pope because he is a liar and the father of lies but we should not be limited in scope to think that he was only addressing Catholicism. The vatican allows the world to observe backwards customs because their dominion is not threatened by this, for as long as the people follow darkness they are happy. It is only the light, the truth, that threatens their authority and prompts a response which is always carried out through clandestine means because the true nature of the papacy is kept hidden from the public. But the devil must realize that the LORD would not allow evil to triumph and destroy humanity, that is why he sent forth his son Jesus Christ to execute the real judgment whose ripple effects will tear down the walls of Jericho. Nelson Mandela said, "Education is the most powerful weapon which you can use to change the world;"[136] once the people know who God is, this will solve all problems. *"And after these things I*

---

[135] Catholic League, October 11, 2000
[136] Speech delivered by Nelson Mandela at the launch of Mindset Network, July 16, 2003

saw another angel come down from heaven, having great power; and the earth was lightened with his glory. And he cried mightily with a strong voice, saying, Babylon the great is fallen, is fallen, and is become the habitation of devils, and the hold of every foul spirit, and a cage of every unclean and hateful bird. For all nations have drunk of the wine of the wrath of her fornication, and the kings of the earth have committed fornication with her, and the merchants of the earth are waxed rich through the abundance of her delicacies. And I heard another voice from heaven, saying, Come out of her, my people, that you be not partakers of her sins; and that you receive not of her plagues. For her sins have reached unto heaven, and God has remembered her iniquities" (Revelation 18:1-5). Satan has to be crushed in order for the kingdom of God to take root in the hearts of men because you cannot follow the truth if you hold onto false beliefs. The first step is to repent, destroy your idols, do away with improper philosophies, lose your life to gain it. Only from this standpoint would you be able to accept Emperor Haile Sellassie I as the Almighty; for his genius is the embodiment of salvation. It was to this end that Primus St. Croix labored and sacrificed everything for the gospel's sake.

"Now of the things which we have spoken this is the sum: We have such a high priest, who is set on the right hand of the throne of the Majesty in the heavens. A minister of the sanctuary, and of the true tabernacle, which the Lord pitched, and not man" (Hebrews 8:1-2). Primus St. Croix preached the correct interpretation of the Bible; anyone who denies the gospel will never know God and cannot be saved. His message is not what is commonplace in the world because the popular perception of theism is unreal. The Word of Life does not need approval from mankind in order for it to be valid, it is right based upon its own accreditation. We have not set out to explain every verse in the Bible, only to provide the proper foundation for people to build upon and increase in understanding. For example, in Revelation 1:7 it says that he comes with the clouds and every eye shall see him. We have previously explained how the supernatural is a false concept therefore no one should view this from a literal standpoint. The peculiar advent of both the Father and the Son coming in modern times has afforded all of humanity the opportunity to research these events. The information age has opened the gates of enlightenment, now anyone can learn about whatever topic they are interested in, students can take virtual classes on the internet and be connected with a professor who is giving his lecture on the other side of the planet. As such, this juncture has afforded all of humanity the opportunity to learn about Haile Sellassie I and Primus St. Croix. If you are not familiar with these people all you have to do is look them up and you will be connected to archived newspapers that recorded their affairs, photographs of them, as well as you would be able to hear their voices as they speak on different topics. It is the uniqueness of the revelation taking place in this era that justifies the Word because the evidence of our faith is not found in art or man's devices. The Bible classifies the paintings and images of Jesus Christ as idolatry, the dogma which states that the scriptures are referring to ancient events does not correlate with the message and purpose of the book. *"Knowing this first, that no prophecy of the scripture is of any private interpretation. For the prophecy came not in old time by the will of man: but holy men of God spoke as they were moved by the Holy Ghost" (2 Peter 1:20-21).* It is written that we must know who Christ is, because only through his gospel can we see God, therefore we must be familiar with the person and that cannot be accomplished through icons, sculptures, or fables.

"Beloved, believe not every spirit, but try the spirits whether they are of God: because many false prophets are gone out into the world. Hereby know ye the Spirit of God: Every spirit that confesses that Jesus Christ is come in the flesh is of God. And every spirit that confesses not that Jesus Christ is come in the flesh is not of God: and this is the spirit of antichrist, whereof you have heard that it should come; and even now already is it in the world" (1 John 4:1-3). The accusation that we are cherry picking verses to fit our interpretation is a quaint misrepresentation. First of all, no one can successfully quote any verse in the Bible to prove a point that is invalid. Those who attempt to do this can easily be proven wrong because their interpretation does not coincide with the prophecy. Jesus has demonstrated this during his confrontation with the devil in Luke 4:1-13. Furthermore, it is written that Christ selected key scriptures to teach his lessons and prove his point.[137] Therefore if this is the example of the Messiah then I am keen to follow it. It also is quite absurd to ask someone to quote the whole Bible, you can just purchase a copy of that book if you are looking to read all the letters. But if you do pick up that publication, you will read in 1 Corinthians 14 how it beckons us to explain what the verses mean and that is what we did. It is only natural to be skeptical when you study a different religion but there comes a point where doubt must translate into acceptance after the facts have been established. We must not be intellectually lazy and caulk up every notion that we do not like as being incorrect without doing an objective analysis of the circumstances first. Because the highest form of ignorance is to reject something that you know nothing about.[138] When it says that there are many false prophets in the world

---

[137] Luke 4:16-21
[138] Quote from Dr. Wayne W. Dyer

this should only lead us to examine our own beliefs more closely to ensure that we are not one of them; as well as everyone else's. In this pursuit it would be inappropriate to dismiss all theories regarding the return of Jesus as being impostors; especially when it is written that those who are antichrist are they who deny that he has come in the flesh. Somewhere in the world the truth has to be found because the Bible is valid and the prophecies written beforehand will be fulfilled; you are now fortunate to come across the manifestation in Emperor Haile Sellassie I and his prophet Primus St. Croix.

"And I saw a new heaven and a new earth: for the first heaven and the first earth were passed away; and there was no more sea" (Revelation 21:1). The end of the world signifies the abolition of idolatry, the old false interpretation of the scriptures has been shattered by the truth delivered by the Son of God. Primus St. Croix preached the message of salvation, that Emperor Haile Sellassie I is the Father of Jesus Christ. If anyone should deny this doctrine then in them is fulfilled the prophecy of Ezekiel 12:2, *"Son of man, you dwell in the midst of a rebellious house, which have eyes to see and see not; they have ears to hear and hear not: for they are a rebellious house."* They resist because they love lies more than the truth. His Majesty's reign as well as the arrival of Primus St. Croix seventy years after the Coronation follows all the signs and descriptions found in the Bible. *"And it shall come to pass, when seventy years are accomplished, that I will punish the king of Babylon, and that nation, says the LORD, for their iniquity, and the land of the Chaldeans, and will make it perpetual desolations" (Jeremiah 25:12).* Those who adhere to false principles are spiritually blind (desolate), that is why it is written, *"They that make idols are like unto them, so is everyone who puts their trust in them" (Psalm 115:8).* The old testament represents the period before the fulfillment of prophecy,[139] mankind was free to hypothesize on what they believed the parables meant; this is the first earth. But now that Christ has come, we are able to see God in the flesh and understand that His Majesty is the Almighty; this is the new world, the new testament. We must accept the revelation, for the LORD has proclaimed his holy power to all nations, the grace of God that brings salvation has appeared to all men. *"The preaching of the cross is to them that perish foolishness; but unto us which are saved it is the power of God. For it is written, I will destroy the wisdom of the wise, and will bring to nothing the understanding of the prudent. Where is the wise? where is the scribe? where is the disputer of this world? has not God made foolish the wisdom of this world? For after that in the wisdom*

---

[139] Acts 14:15-17

of God the world by wisdom knew not God, it pleased God by the foolishness of preaching to save them that believe. For the Jews require a sign, and the Greeks seek after wisdom: but we preach Christ crucified, unto the Jews a stumbling block, and unto the Greeks foolishness; but unto them which are called, both Jews and Greeks, Christ the power of God, and the wisdom of God. Because the foolishness of God is wiser than men; and the weakness of God is stronger than men. For you see your calling brethren, how that not many wise men after the flesh, not many mighty, not many noble, are called: but God has chosen the foolish things of the world to confound the wise; and God has chosen the weak things of the world to confound the things which are mighty; And base things of the world, and things which are despised, has God chosen, yes, and things which are not, to bring to nothing things that are: that no flesh should glory in his presence. But of him are you in Christ Jesus, who of God is made unto us wisdom, and righteousness, and sanctification, and redemption: that, according as it is written, He that glories, let him glory in the Lord" (1 Corinthians 1:18-31). It has been ordained that the doctrine of this lowly minister would be established as the authority on theology; the sole means by which humanity can be saved. Primus St. Croix, a virtual unknown in the world yet mighty in the Bible, has been chosen, based upon the accuracy of his message, to destroy all false religious concepts so that humanity may know that Haile Sellassie I is the Creator. This decree has been written beforehand to be bestowed upon the mustard seed, the smallest of all sects, the least esteemed in the sight of man; this body has been chosen by God to bear the supreme gospel, for it is written that broad is the way that leads to destruction but straight is the way unto life and there be few that find it.[140] Our Heavenly Father, in his infinite wisdom, has deemed it expedient to call base things of the world to rebuke that which is popular, things which are despised to bring to nothing that which is acceptable, foolish things to confound the wise, the weaker elements to crush the mighty; just as David and Goliath. This is the LORD's doings and it is marvelous in our eyes. Blessed be Jah Ras Tafari, the Most High God, Emperor Haile Sellassie I; through his Son, the prophet, Jesus Christ Primus St. Croix. *"And he said also to the people, When you see a cloud rise out of the west, straightway you say, There comes a shower, and so it is. And when you see the south wind blow, you say, There will be heat; and it comes to pass. You hypocrites, you can discern the face of the sky and of the earth; but how is it that you can not discern these times? Then he left them and departed"* (Luke 12:54-56).

---

[140] Matthew 7:13-14

For it is Written

"He that speaks in an unknown tongue, speaks not unto men, but unto God: for no man understands him; howbeit in the spirit he speaks mysteries. But he that prophesies, speaks unto men to edification, and exhortation, and comfort" (1 Corinthians 14:2-3).

"Now, brethren, if one come unto you speaking with tongues, what shall he profit you, except he speak to you either by revelation, or by knowledge, or by prophesying, or by doctrine" (1 Corinthians 14:6).

Introduction

We have seen many things happen in the 20th century. There have been two world wars and countless other conflicts that have killed millions of people, evil rulers have reigned, and deadly diseases have spread plagues over the earth. But there also have been a lot of progressive developments such as various nations gaining their independence from the yoke of colonization, mental chains were broken, and walls crumbled. We have even seen the fulfillment of biblical prophecy; God established his kingdom on earth. He rested on the seventh day and magnified his holy name to all of mankind. He was crowned King of Kings, Lord of Lords, Conquering Lion of the Tribe of Judah, Elect of God, Light of the Universe. Emperor Haile Selassie First said, "The world is today passing through a period of such rapid and profound change that it is difficult to point to another era in recorded history when so many movements and events have so rapidly and profoundly shaped the lives of a single generation. Such an observation applies no less to Ethiopia than to other countries. The progress achieved since Our Coronation has been the cause of humble and profound gratification."[1] The Lord visited the nations, seeking a peaceful solution to the problems in the world; he defeated many of the enemies of humanity, and showed that he is the Most High by mighty signs and wonders. The devil has also showed his ugly face by exalting himself against God, fighting against the Almighty, and deceiving all who follow him. Therefore God sent forth his Prophet, to save the world from sin and ignorance. Jesus Christ came preaching in the name of his Father, showing us who is worthy to be praised. He warned us that unless we accept God as our Savior, we would be destroying our lives.

The Doctrine

You may ask is there any truth to these statements? When did God show his face? Who is Jesus Christ? How is the devil deceiving everyone? In 2 Peter 1:20 it says, "Knowing this first, that no prophesy of the scripture is of any private interpretation," therefore we must show the evidence of our claims. In 1 Timothy 3:16 it says, "And without controversy great is the mystery of godliness: God was manifested in the flesh, justified in the spirit, seen of angels, preached unto the Gentiles, believed on in the world, received up into glory." Biblical prophecy was intended to be tangible and irrevocable so that there will be no excuse for not believing. Acts 17:26-29 says, "God hath made of one blood all nations of men for to dwell on all the face of the earth, and hath determined the times before appointed, and the bounds of their habitations; that they should seek the Lord, if haply they might feel after him, and find him, though he be not far from every one of us. For in him we live, and move, and have our being; as certain also of your own poets have said, for we are also his offspring, forasmuch then as we are the offspring of God, we ought not to think that the Godhead is like unto gold, or silver, or stone, graven by art and man's device." We are made in the image of God physically, but the true blessing of the Lord is to be made in his image spiritually by following his word and instructions.

---

[1] The Selected Speeches of His Imperial Majesty Haile Selassie I, page 393

Romans 1:20 says, "For the invisible things of him (God) from the creation of the world are clearly seen, being understood by the things that are made even his eternal Power and Godhead so that they are without excuse." On November 2, 1930, in Ethiopia (the oldest nation in the world) King Ras Teferi was crowned Emperor Haile Selassie First, King of Kings, Lord of Lords, Conquering Lion of the Tribe of Judah, Elect of God, Light of the Universe. Many nations were present such as Britain, France, Germany, Italy, Belgium, Sweden, Netherlands, USA, Japan, Egypt, and Greece. The Ethiopian people along with the entire world witnessed the accession of His Imperial Majesty to the supreme rite of lordship in a truly magnificent ceremony befit for the Negus Negast. It says in Isaiah 52:10, "The Lord hath made bare his holy arm in the eyes of all the nations; and all the ends of the earth shall see the salvation of our God." Psalm 68:24 says, "They have seen thy goings, O God; even the goings of our God and King in the sanctuary," this happened at the Coronation in Addis Ababa. Psalm 87:1-6 says, "His foundation is in the holy mountains. The Lord loveth the gates of Zion more than all the dwellings of Jacob. Glorious things are spoken of thee O city of God. I will make mention of Rahab and Babylon to them that know me: behold Philisita and Tyre with Ethiopia; this man was born there. And of Zion it shall be said, this and that man was born in her: and the Highest himself shall establish her. The Lord shall count when he writes up the people, that this man was born there." Haile Selassie First is that man the Bible is referring to, he was born in Ethiopia, the Highest himself who established Zion. Hebrews 4:4 says, "For he (God) spake in a certain place of the seventh day on this wise, and God did rest the seventh day from all his works." The Sabbath is a memorial to commemorate the day that the Lord established his kingdom on earth that is why it said to remember God. November 2, 1930, is the seventh day, that is the day the Lord did bless and make holy. We should fear God and keep his commandments.

In this present historical time when there are numerous mediums to record events, such as camera's and camcorders, we have actual evidence of the Lord's work. Therefore those who believe are justified and all nonbelievers are left without any excuse which makes it a righteous judgment. Paintings and graven images are not a sufficient record of God, the Bible said not to believe in them because this is art and man's device. In this modern age when news travels from one end of the earth to the other in seconds, everyone can research these events that we are referring to and understand what is truth and myth. On November 2, 1930, God rested and made the law most honorable by showing the world his face. Zechariah 14:9 says, "The Lord shall be King over all the earth; in that day shall there be one Lord and his name <u>One</u>:" Haile Selassie <u>First</u>, his name means Power of the Trinity. In 1 John 5:7 it says, "For there are three that bear record in heaven, the Father, the Word, and the Holy Ghost: and these three are <u>One</u>." This scripture is not referring to three people but one person: Emperor Haile Selassie First. Our God is One, the Word is God, it is he whom the scriptures appertain to. John 1:1 says, "In the beginning was the Word, and the Word was with God, and the Word was God:" His Majesty, who on November 2, 1930, proved to be the Alpha and Omega, before him there was no god formed and after him there shall be none. Remember that Romans 1:20 says, "For the invisible things of him from the creation (the beginning) of the world are clearly seen, being understood by the things that are made (those who believe), even his Eternal Power and Godhead, so that they are without excuse." Haile Selassie First is the One who beareth record in heaven (Ethiopia) before all the nations of the earth. He is the One who Jesus Christ testifies of, the King of Glory (like it says in Revelation 19:10, the spirit of prophesy). Jesus said, don't worship me but worship him that sent me (John 7:16), Emperor Haile Selassie First, the King of Heaven whose name is One. Isaiah 61:1-2 says, "The spirit (the word) of the Lord is upon me; because the Lord hath anointed me to preach good tidings unto the meek; he hath sent me to bind up the brokenhearted, to proclaim liberty to the captives and the opening of the prison to them that are bound; <u>to proclaim the acceptable year of the Lord and the day of vengeance of our God</u>." This is again referring to November 2, 1930, the grand occasion at St. George Cathedral in Addis Ababa, this is the acceptable year and dwelling place of God. In Revelation 19:11-13 it says, "I saw heaven opened, and behold a white horse; and he that sat upon him was called Faithful and True, and in righteousness he doth judge and make war. His eyes were as a flame of fire, and on his head were many crowns; and he had a name written, that no man knew, but he himself. And he was clothed with a vesture dipped in blood (the spirit of prophesy): and his name is called The Word of God:" Emperor Haile Selassie First, Power of the Trinity First. In Matthew 23:9 Jesus said, "Call no man your Father upon the earth: for <u>One</u> is your Father, which is in heaven." Psalm 50:1-2 says, "The Mighty God, even the Lord, hath spoken (Hebrews 4:4 says, he spoke in a certain place on the seventh day on this wise), and he called the earth from the rising of the sun unto the going down thereof. <u>Out of Zion (Ethiopia) the perfection of beauty, God has shined</u>." The Bible is telling us that God is going to appear on earth so that we may follow him and be saved. Psalm 48:1-3 says, "Great is the Lord, and greatly to be praised in the city of our God, in the mountain of his holiness. Beautiful for situation, the joy of the whole earth, is mount Zion, on the sides of the north, the city of the great King (Haile Selassie First), for he is known in her palaces for a refuge;" and in verses 12-14 it says, "Walk about Zion, and go round about her: tell the towers thereof. Mark ye well her bulwarks, consider her palaces; that ye may tell it to the generation following. For this God is our God forever and ever: he will be our guide even unto death."

Haile Selassie First is the Almighty, he was born in Ethiopia (Psalm 87), the Highest himself who did establish Zion on November 2, 1930, the heavenly Jerusalem, free from bondage. In Hebrews chapter 12 verses 18, 22, & 23, it says, "For ye are not come unto the mount that might be touched, and that burned with fire, nor unto blackness, and darkness, and tempest (falsehoods). But ye are come unto mount Sion, and unto the city of the living God, the heavenly Jerusalem, and to an innumerable company of angels, to the general assembly and church of the firstborn, which are written in heaven, and to God the Judge of all, and to the spirits of just men made perfect." Psalm 11:4 says, "The Lord is in his holy temple, the Lord's Throne is in Heaven" (Ethiopia), also in Matthew 23:22 Jesus says, "He that shall swear by heaven, sweareth by the throne of God, and him that sitteth thereon." Revelation 4:2 says, "Immediately I was in the spirit (according to the word): and, behold, a throne was set in heaven, and One sat on the throne." Haile Selassie First, he is the One who sits on the throne; the Father, the Word, and the Holy Ghost (these three are One), who beareth record in Heaven, on the Sabbath day. In Isaiah 52:6 the Lord says, "Therefore my people shall know my name: therefore they shall know in that day that I am he that doth speak: behold it is I," Emperor Haile Selassie I (First). In Psalm 118:23-24 it says, "This is the Lord's doing, it is marvelous in our eyes. This is the day that the Lord hath made (November 2, 1930); we will rejoice and be glad in it." Again in Psalm 47:1-2 it says, "Clap your hands, all ye people, shout unto God with the voice of triumph. For the Lord Most High is terrible, he is a great King over all the earth" also verses 7 & 8 says, "God is the King of all the earth: sing praises with understanding. God reigneth over the heathen: God sitteth upon the throne of his holiness." Therefore it is not enough just to say God rhetorically because with this we still don't know who is the Supreme Being. You have to bring it into manifestation with sound doctrine and show who the Lord is. The entire chapter of 1 Corinthians 14 says that it is better to prophesy than to speak in tongues, verse 2 says, "For he that speaketh in an unknown tongue speaketh not unto men, but unto God: for no man understandeth him; howbeit in the spirit he speaketh mysteries." Remember that in 1 Timothy 3:16, it says, "Great is the mystery – God was manifested in the flesh and justified in the Spirit (the Bible)." He is not invisible, as many believe (this is how Christ cured the blind). Romans 1:20 says, "The invisible things of him from the creation of the world are clearly seen, being understood by the things that are made, even his Eternal Power and Godhead so that they are without excuse." Acts 17:27-31 says, "That they should seek the Lord, if haply they might feel after him, <u>and find him though he be not far from every one of us</u>: for in him we live, and move, and have our being; as certain also of your own poets have said, for we are also his offspring. Forasmuch then as we are the offspring of God, we ought not to think that the Godhead is like unto gold, or silver, or stone graven by art and man's device. And the times of this ignorance God winked at; but now commandeth all men everywhere to repent: <u>because he hath appointed a day, in the which he will judge the world in righteousness</u>." Isaiah 43:10-11 says, "Ye are my witnesses, said the Lord, and my servants whom I have chosen: that ye may know and believe me, and understand that I am he: before me there was no God formed, neither shall there be after me, I even I, am the Lord; besides me there is no savior," also in verses 18 & 19 the Lord says, "Remember ye not the former things, neither consider the things of old. Behold, I will do a new thing; now it shall spring forth; shall ye not know it? I will even make a way in the wilderness, and rivers in the deserts." In Revelation 21:1-6 it says, "And I saw a new heaven and a new earth (a new doctrine which is the manifestation of the scriptures): for the first heaven and the first earth were passed away; and there was no more sea. And I saw the holy city, new Jerusalem, coming down from God out of heaven, prepared as a bride adorned for her husband. And I heard a great voice out of heaven saying, behold, the tabernacle of God is with men, and he will dwell with them, and they shall be his people, <u>and God himself shall be with them, and will be their God</u>. And God shall wipe away all tears from their eyes; and there shall be no more death, neither sorrow, nor crying, neither shall there be any more pain: for the former things are passed away. And he that sat upon the throne said, behold, I make all things new. And he said unto me, write: for these words are true and faithful. And he said unto me, it is done, I am Alpha and Omega, the beginning and the end. I will give unto him that is athirst of the fountain of the water of life freely." In Isaiah 44:6 the Lord declares, "I am the First and I am the Last, and besides me there is no other God." Isaiah 45:19 also says, "I have not spoken in secret, in a dark place of the earth: I said not unto the seed of Jacob, seek ye me in vain: I the Lord speak righteousness, I declare things that are right;" and verses 22 & 23 proclaim, "Look unto me, and be ye saved, all the ends of the earth: for I am

God, and there is none else. <u>I have sworn by myself</u> (the Elect of God), the word is gone out of my mouth in righteousness, and shall not return, that unto me every knee shall bow, every tongue shall swear."

The Lord commandeth all people everywhere to repent, for the old philosophies concerning religion have been proven fraudulent. Emperor Haile Selassie First is the Eternal God, the healing of the nations; this is the new earth. Acts 14:15-17 says, "The living God, which made heaven and earth (November 2, 1930), and the sea, and all things that are therein: who in times past suffered all nations to walk in their own ways. Nevertheless he left not himself without witness, in that he did good, and gave us rain from heaven, and fruitful seasons, filling our hearts with food and gladness." Therefore we should no longer pray in tongues to God, but prophesy, for the Lord showed his face and is clearly seen in Ethiopia. Seek his face, like it says in Psalm 24:6, we will praise the living God: Emperor Haile Selassie First and no one else. In Deuteronomy 10:20-21 it says, "Thou shalt fear the Lord thy God; him shalt thou serve and to him shalt thou cleave, and swear by his name. He is thy praise, and he is thy God, that hath done for thee these great and terrible things, which thine eyes have seen." We are witnesses to these events in Addis Ababa, anyone can look up the Coronation and learn about what happened. On November 2, 1930, God magnified himself therefore we ought not to think that he is a graven image or invisible. We know that it is hard to break with tradition, it says in Jeremiah 10:3-8, "For one cutteth a tree out of the forest, the work of the hands of the workman, with the axe. They deck it with silver and with gold; they fasten it with nails and with hammer, that it move not. They are upright as the palm tree, but speak not: they must needs be borne because they cannot go. Be not afraid of them; for they cannot do evil, neither also is it in them to do good. Forasmuch as there is none like unto thee, O Lord; thou art great, and thy name is great in might. Who would not fear thee, O King of nations? (Haile Selassie First) For to thee doth it appertain (not to wood or stone): forasmuch as among all the wise men of the nations, and in all their kingdoms, there is none like unto thee. But they are altogether brutish and foolish: their stock is a doctrine of vanities," because in Romans 1:21 it says, "That when they knew God, they glorified him not as God, neither were thankful; but became vain in their imagination, and their foolish heart was darkened." Romans 10:3 says, "For they being ignorant of God's righteousness, and going about to establish their own righteousness, have not submitted themselves unto the righteousness of God," also read Mark 7:6-8 and Isaiah 29:13. In Jeremiah 4:22-25 the Lord says, "For my people are foolish, they have not known me; they are sottish children, and they have no understanding: they are wise to do evil, but to do good they have no knowledge. I beheld the earth, and, lo, it was without form, and void (no comprehension of the Lord): and the heaven, and they had no light. I beheld the mountains, and, lo, they trembled, and all the hills moved lightly. I beheld, and, lo, there was no man, and all the birds of the heavens were fled." Revelation 20:11 says, "I saw a great white throne, and him that sat on it, from whose face the earth and the heavens fled away; and there was found no place for them," because the people of the world do not believe in Haile Selassie First. Psalm 82:5 says, "They know not, neither will they understand; they walk on in darkness: all the foundations of the earth are out of course," because they do not believe in the true and living King of Glory. The people of the world are confused because they do not worship His Majesty yet they claim to believe in God. Exodus 20:4-6 says, "Thou shalt not make unto thee any graven image, or any likeness of any thing that is in heaven above, or that is in the earth beneath, or that is in the water under earth; thou shalt not bow down thyself to them, nor serve them; for I the Lord thy God am a jealous God, visiting the iniquity of the fathers upon the children unto the third and fourth generation of them that hate me; and showing mercy unto thousands of them that love me, and keep my commandments." By not worshipping Emperor Haile Selassie First, the people abide in sin and are dead to the law. Remember that the first commandment is to love the Lord with all your heart and to follow his instructions. The Sabbath is the day that God established his kingdom on earth: November 2, 1930. The religious world is trying to establish their own law by neglecting His Majesty, but God blessed his own special day (Genesis 2:2-3, Exodus 31:14-17, Hebrews 4:4). Jesus Christ observed the seventh day of the Lord, which means that he praised Emperor Haile Selassie First in spirit and in truth (read John 15:10 and John 5:19-20). Mark 2:27-28 says, "The Sabbath was made for man, and not man for the Sabbath: therefore the Son of Man is also lord of the Sabbath." Christ wants us to observe the day that the Lord magnified himself before the eyes of the nations and not to make up our own conception of God. Matthew 5:17-19 says, "Think not that I am come to destroy the law, or the Prophets: I am not come to destroy, but to fulfill. For verily I say unto you, till heaven and earth pass, one jot or one tittle shall in no wise pass from the law, till all be fulfilled. Whosoever therefore shall break one of these least commandments and shall teach men so, he shall be called the least in the kingdom of heaven: but whosoever shall do and teach them, the same shall be called great in the kingdom of heaven."

Sunday Worship

Those leaders who break the law of the Lord and teach men to do the same, speak blasphemy and have no light in them. 2 Corinthians 11:13-15 says, "False apostles, deceitful workers, transforming themselves into the apostles of Christ. And no marvel; for Satan himself is transformed into an angel of light. Therefore it is no great thing if his ministers also be transformed as ministers of righteousness; whose end shall be according to their works." In Isaiah 24:1-6, it says, "Behold, the Lord maketh the earth empty, and maketh it waste, and turneth it upside down, and scattereth abroad the inhabitants thereof. And it shall be, as with the people, so with the priest; as with the servant, so with his master; as with the maid, so with her mistress; as with the buyer, so with the seller; as with the lender, so with the borrower; as with the taker of usury, so with the giver of usury to him. The land shall be utterly emptied, and utterly spoiled: for the Lord hath spoken this word. The earth mourneth and fadeth away, the world languisheth and fadeth away, the haughty people of the earth do languish. The earth also is defiled under the inhabitants thereof; because they have transgressed the laws, changed the ordinance, broken the everlasting covenant. Therefore hath the curse devoured the earth, and they that dwell therein are desolate: therefore the inhabitants of the earth are burned, and few men left." The pope of Rome has deceived his people into praising an invisible god during Sunday service. The Catholic hierarchy is aware that this is wrong but they encourage their followers to believe in idolatry. They are following a long tradition of paganism for that is the foundation of their church. In John 8:44 Jesus says, "Ye are of your father the devil, and the lusts of your father ye will do. He was a murderer from the beginning, and abode not in the truth, because there is no truth in him. When he speaketh a lie, he speaketh of his own: for he is a liar, and the father of it." The pope will never praise Haile Selassie First but he claims to follow the Bible. 2 Thessalonians 2:3-10 says, "Let no man deceive you by any means: for that day shall not come except there come a falling away first, and that man of sin be revealed, the son of perdition; who opposeth and exalteth himself above all that is called God, or that is worshipped; so that he as God sitteth in the temple of God, shewing himself that he is God. For the mystery of iniquity doth already work: only he who now letteth will let, until he be taken out of the way. And then shall that wicked be revealed, whom the Lord shall consume with the spirit of his mouth, and shall destroy with the brightness of his coming: even him, whose coming is after the workings of Satan with all power and signs and lying wonders, and with all deceivableness of unrighteousness in them that perish; because they received not the love of the truth, that they might be saved."

The Roman Church has been stamping their false religion over the earth for thousands of years, grounded in paganism, discouraging heterosexual relationships, claiming that Jesus came in old times, worshipping the pope, crafting idols, inventing purgatory, and drawing paintings for people to venerate (this is the mother of harlots). In the year 2000, during the Catholics so called jubilee year, Pope John Paul 2 traveled throughout the world claiming to mend rifts and make friends, only to release a statement claiming that those same people have deficiencies and defects because they do not praise him. Daniel 11:36 says, "He shall exalt himself, and magnify himself above every god, and shall speak marvelous things against the God of gods, and shall prosper till the indignation be accomplished," also in Daniel 7:25, it says, "He shall speak great words against the Most High, and shall wear out the saints of the Most High, and think to change time and laws." Sunday law has been established thousands of years ago in Rome but now when God has shown his face the churches need to update their philosophy. The Lord is no longer invisible therefore we should not believe that he is in the sky. Sunday worship is set up for people who are deceived and do not believe in Haile Selassie First. Isaiah 1:10 says, "Hear the word of the Lord, ye rulers of Sodom; give ear unto the law of our God, ye people of Gomorrah," verses 14-15 says, "Your new moons (sabbaths) and your appointed feasts (traditions) my soul hateth: they are a trouble unto me; I am weary to bear them. And when ye spread forth your hands, I will hide mine eyes from you; yea, when ye make many prayers, I will not hear: your hands are full of blood." How can you receive the blessings of the Lord if you do not adhere to his precepts? 1 John 5:19 says that, "The whole world lieth in wickedness, (for they have transgressed the law of God and broken the everlasting covenant therefore the curse devoured the earth and they that dwell therein are desolate)." If you are not following Emperor Haile Selassie First then you have not the true guidance towards righteousness.

Instead of repenting when the Lord revealed himself on earth, they continued in their false religion and deceived the world. Revelation 17:1-5 says, "Come hither; I will shew unto thee the judgment of the great whore that sitteth upon many waters: with whom the kings of the earth have committed fornication, and the inhabitants of the earth have been made drunk with the wine of her fornication. So he carried me away in the spirit into the wilderness: and I saw a woman sit upon a scarlet colored beast, full of names of blasphemy, having seven heads and ten horns. And the woman was arrayed in purple and scarlet color, and decked with gold and precious stones and pearls, having a golden cup in her hand full of abominations and filthiness of her fornication: and upon her forehead was a name written, Mystery, Babylon the Great, The Mother of Harlots and Abominations of the Earth." This is the Catholic Church whose influence spreads over the whole globe for the purpose of evil. Isaiah 47:5-11 says, "Sit thou silent, and get thee into darkness, O daughter of the Chaldeans: for thou shalt no more be called, the lady of kingdoms. I was wroth with my people, I have polluted mine inheritance, and given them into thine hand: thou didst shew them no mercy; upon the ancient hast thou heavily laid thy yoke. And you said, I shall be a lady forever: so that thou didst not lay these things to thy heart, neither didst remember the latter end of it. Therefore hear now this, thou that art given to pleasures; that dwellest carelessly, that sayest in thine heart, I am, and none else besides me; I shall not sit as a widow, neither shall I know the loss of children: but these two things shall come to thee in a moment in one day, the loss of children, and widowhood, they shall come upon thee in their perfection for the multitude of thy sorceries, and for the great abundance of thine enchantments. For thou hast trusted in thy wickedness: thou hast said, none seeth me. Thy wisdom and thy knowledge, it hath perverted thee; and thou hast said in thine heart, I am, and none else besides me. Therefore shall evil come upon thee; thou shalt not know from whence it riseth: and mischief shall fall upon thee; thou shalt not be able to put it off: and desolation shall come upon thee suddenly, which thou shalt not know." Jeremiah 50:35-38 says, "A sword is upon the Chaldeans, saith the Lord, and upon the inhabitants of Babylon, and upon her princes, and upon her wise men. A sword is upon the liars; and they shall dote: a sword is upon her mighty men; and they shall be dismayed. A sword is upon their horses, and upon their chariots, and upon all the mingled people that are in the midst of her; and they shall become as women: a sword is upon her treasures; and they shall be robbed. A drought is upon her waters; and they shall be dried up: for it is the land of graven images, and they are mad upon their idols." Psalm 115:4-8 says, "Their idols are silver and gold, the works of men's hands. They have mouths, but they speak not: eyes have they, but they see not: they have ears, but they hear not: noses they have, but they smell not: they have hands, but they handle not: feet have they, but they walk not: neither speak they through their throat. They that make them are like unto them, so is every one that trusteth in them (just as Arthur Matuszewski, a Polish immigrant, who blinded himself in an unsuccessful attempt to repair the relics that Primus St. Croix broke)."[2] Jesus on the cross is a popular image that many Catholics worship but the Bible calls this witchcraft.

In Isaiah 41:21-29, it says, "Produce your cause, saith the Lord; bring forth your strong reasons, saith the King of Jacob. Let them bring them forth, and shew us what shall happen: <u>let them shew the former things, what they be, that we may consider them, and know the latter end of them</u>; or declare us things for to come. Shew the things that are to come hereafter, that we may know that ye are gods: yea, do good, or do evil, that we may be dismayed, and behold it together. Behold, ye are of nothing, and your work of nought: an abomination is he that chooses you. I have raised up one from the north, and he shall come: from the rising of the sun shall he call upon my name; and he shall come upon princes as upon morter, and as the potter treadeth clay. Who hath declared from the beginning, that we may know? And beforetime, that we may say, He is righteous? Yea, there is none that sheweth, yea, there is none that declareth, yea, there is none that heareth your words. The first shall say to Zion, behold them: and I will give to Jerusalem one that bringeth good tidings. For I beheld, and there was no man; even among them, and there was no counselor, that, when I asked of them, could answer a word. Behold, they are all vanity; their works are nothing: their molten images are wind and confusion." There was no one who declared the righteousness of the Lord by praising Haile Selassie First on the seventh day. Acts 17:29-30 says that since we are, "The offspring of God, we ought not to think that the Godhead is like unto gold, or silver, or stone, graven by art and man's device. And the times of this ignorance God winked at; but now commandeth all

---

[2] Daily News, March 27, 2000

men everywhere to repent: because he hath appointed a day, in the which he will judge the world in righteousness by that man whom he hath ordained." Again in Isaiah 46:5-13 it says, "To whom will ye liken me, and make me equal, and compare me, that we may be like? They lavish gold out of the bag, and weigh silver in the balance, and hire a goldsmith; and he maketh it a god: they fall down, yea, they worship. They bear him upon the shoulder, they carry him, and set him in his place, and he standeth; from his palace shall he not remove: yea, one shall cry unto him, yet can he not answer, nor save him out of his trouble. Remember this, and shew yourselves men: bring it again to mind, O ye transgressors. Remember the former things of old: for I am God, and there is none else; I am God, and there is none like me. Declaring the end from the beginning, and from ancient times the things that are not yet done, saying, My counsel shall stand, and I will do all my pleasure: calling a ravenous bird from the east, the man that executeth my counsel from a far country: yea, I have spoken it, I will also bring it to pass; I have purposed it, I will also do it." Malachi 4:1-4 says, "Behold, the day cometh, that shall burn as an oven; and all the proud, yea, and all that do wickedly, shall be stubble: and the day that cometh shall burn them up, saith the Lord of hosts, that it shall leave them neither root nor branch. But unto you that fear my name shall the Sun of righteousness arise with healing in his wings; and ye shall go forth, and grow up as calves of the stall. And ye shall tread down the wicked; for they shall be ashes under the soles of your feet in the day that I shall do this, saith the Lord of hosts." Remember the law of Moses, which the Lord commanded unto him in Horeb for all Israel, concerning the statutes and judgments. Deuteronomy 12:1-3 says, "These are the statutes and judgments, which ye shall observe to do in the land, which the Lord God of thy father giveth thee to possess it, all the days that ye live upon the earth. Ye shall utterly destroy all the places, wherein the nations which ye shall possess serve their gods, upon the high mountains, and upon the hills, and under every green tree: and ye shall overthrow their altars, and break their pillars, and burn their groves with fire; and ye shall hew down the graven images of their gods, and destroy the names of them out of that place." For the Lord God is a jealous God, visiting the iniquity of the fathers upon the children unto the third and fourth generation of them that hate him (Exodus 20:5). Therefore we should observe the law handed down to us by Moses in the Bible and stay away from anything contrary. 1 John 3:4 says, "Whosoever committeth sin transgresseth also the law: for sin is transgression of the law," also verse 8 says, "He that committeth sin is of the devil; for the devil sinneth from the beginning. For this purpose the Son of God was manifested, that he might destroy the works of the devil." But how shall we know what is the work of satan? Isaiah 44:10-11 says, "Who hath formed a god, or molten a graven image that is profitable for nothing? Behold, all his fellows shall be ashamed: and the workmen, they are of men: let them all be gathered together, let them stand up; yet they shall fear, and they shall be ashamed together."

Primus St. Croix

In May 2000, a Rastafarian named Primus St. Croix was arrested for breaking statues outside of numerous Catholic churches in Brooklyn, NY. The authorities questioned him as to why would he do this and he responded that he was commanded by God to execute the judgment. He said that we should not praise idols but the living God Emperor Haile Selassie First. Religious leaders from all denominations have called this man a heretic but he was trying to send a message of peace through re-pentance. He studied from popular sacred texts such as, The Holy Bible and The Noble Quran. He preached that Haile Selassie First was the God of all religions but the people did not receive him; they condemned him. Ecclesiastical and political leaders in the year 2000 combined their efforts to offer a reward of one hundred thousand dollars to imprison Primus St. Croix for breaking statues. Exodus 11:6 says, "There shall be a great cry throughout all the land of Egypt, such as there was none like it, nor shall be like it any more." This cry did not happen in the Middle East but in New York City when Primus St. Croix was protesting against idolatry.[3] When a person is murdered the reward to catch the suspect is usually between five to twenty thousand dollars, so why was the bounty for this crime so high? The Vatican City knew that this occurrence was a direct threat to their very survival and therefore sought to ensure that this troublemaker was silenced. They sought to kill the message of the Prophet but the Word is above any condemnation. Revelation 11:8 says, "The great city, which spiritually is called Sodom and Egypt, where also our lord (Jesus Christ) was crucified," also in Revelation 17:15 it says, "The waters which thou sawest, where the whore sitteth, are peoples, and multitudes, and nations, and tongues." In Isaiah 19:1 it says, "The burden of Egypt. Behold, the Lord rideth upon a swift cloud, and shall come into Egypt: and the idols

---

[3] Daily News, March 17, 2000

of Egypt shall be moved at his presence, and the heart of Egypt shall melt in the midst of it," also verses 19 & 20 says, "In that day shall there be an altar to the Lord in the midst of the land of Egypt, and a pillar at the border thereof to the Lord. And it shall be for a sign and for a witness unto the Lord of host in the land of Egypt: for they shall cry unto the Lord because of the oppressor, and he shall send them a savior and a great one, and he shall deliver them." In New York City, where you can find almost every culture and kindred of people, there is a temple that praises His Majesty in plain view for the world to bear witness. This sanctuary is the "Church of Haile Selassie The First through the Body of Jesus Christ," which was founded by Primus St. Croix in the year 2000 (not to be confused with the congregation of Ascento Foxe). The earth lies in sin and for this reason Primus did his work to save us from condemnation. For the Lord said in Deuteronomy 18:18-19, "I will raise them up a Prophet from among their brethren, like unto thee, and I will put my words in his mouth; and he shall speak unto them all that I shall command him. And it shall come to pass, that whosoever will not hearken unto my words which he shall speak in my name, I will require it of him." John 3:16-21 says, "For God so loved the world, that he gave his only begotten Son, that whosoever believeth in him should not perish, but have everlasting life. For God sent not his Son into the world to condemn the world; but that the world through him might be saved. He that believeth on him is not condemned: but he that believeth not is condemned already, because he hath not believed in the name of the only begotten Son of God (Primus St. Croix). And this is the condemnation, that light is come into the world, and men loved darkness rather than light, because their deeds were evil. For everyone that doeth evil hateth the light, neither cometh to the light, lest his deeds should be reproved. But he that doeth truth cometh to the light, that his deeds may be made manifest, that they are wrought in God." Primus was trying to warn people that they were following Satan if they did not believe in Haile Selassie First. Isaiah 14:24 says, "The Lord of hosts hath sworn, saying, surely as I have thought, so shall it come to pass; and as I have purposed, so shall it stand," verses 26 & 27 says, "This is the purpose that is purposed upon the whole earth: and this is the hand that is stretched out upon all the nations. For the Lord of hosts hath purposed, and who shall disannul it? And his hand is stretched out, and who shall turn it back?" Isaiah 42:1-8 says, "Behold my servant, whom I uphold; mine elect, in whom my soul delight; I have put my spirit upon him: he shall bring forth judgment to the Gentiles. He shall not cry, nor lift up, nor cause his voice to be heard in the street. A bruised reed shall he not break, and the smoking flax shall he not quench: he shall bring forth judgment unto truth. He shall not fail nor be discouraged, till he has set judgment in the earth: and the isles shall wait for his law. Thus saith God the Lord, he that created the heavens, and stretched them out; he that spread forth the earth, and that which cometh out of it, he that giveth breath unto the people upon it, and spirit to them that walk therein: I the Lord have called thee in righteousness, and will hold thine hand, and will keep thee, and give thee for a covenant of the people, for the light of the Gentiles; to open the blind eyes, to bring out the prisoners from the prison, and them that sit in darkness out of the prison house. I am the Lord: that is my name, and my glory will I not give to another, neither my praise to graven images."

In John 5:20-27 it says, "For the Father loveth the Son, and showed him all things that himself doeth: and he will show him greater works than these, that you may marvel. For as the Father raised up the dead, and quicken them; even so the Son quickenth whom he will. <u>For the Father judgeth no man, but have committed all judgment to the Son</u>: That all men should honor the Son, even as they honor the Father. He that honors not the Son, honors not the Father which have sent him. Verily, verily, I say unto you, he that heareth my word, and believeth on him that sent me, hath everlasting life, and shall not come into condemnation; but is passed from death unto life. <u>Verily, verily, I say unto you, the hour is coming, and now is, when the dead shall hear the voice of the Son of God: and they that hear shall live. For as the Father has life in himself; so hath he given to the Son to have life in himself; and hath given him authority to execute judgment also, because he is the Son of man</u>." In Psalm 2:1-2 it says, "Why do the heathen rage, and the people imagine a vain thing? The kings of the earth set themselves, and the rulers take counsel together, against the Lord, and against his anointed (Jesus Christ)." Again John 1:4-5 says, "In him was life; and the life was the light of men. <u>And the light shineth in darkness; and the darkness comprehends it not</u>" also verses 10-14 says, "He was in the world, and the world was made by him (according to the scriptures), <u>and the world knew him not. He came unto his own, and his own received him not. But as many as received him, to them gave he power to become the sons of God, even to them that believe on his name</u>: Which were born, not of blood, nor of the will of the flesh, nor of the will of man (false doctrines), but of God." 1 John 5:4-7 says, "For whatsoever is born of God overcometh the world, and this is the victory that overcometh the world: even our faith. Who is he that overcometh the world, but he that believeth that Jesus (Primus St. Croix) is the Son of God, this is he that came by water and blood, even Jesus Christ; not by water only, but by water and blood. And it is the spirit that beareth witness, because the spirit is truth. For there are three that beareth record in heaven, the Father, the Word, and the Holy Ghost: and these three are One (Haile Selassie First). And there are three that bear witness in earth, the spirit, the water, and the blood: and these three agree in one (Primus St. Croix)." For the Son testifies of his Father in Ethiopia, preaching to all people that our God is One – Emperor Haile Selassie First. John 1:18 says that, "No man has seen God at any time; the only begotten Son, which is in the bosom of the Father, he hath declared him." It is written in Romans 1:20, Psalm 68:24, and Isaiah 52:10, that all have seen the goings of our Lord, you have beheld God in all his glory but have not recognized that he is the Creator. On November 2, 1930, H.I.M. Haile Selassie First showed the world that he is worthy to be praised but because the people have no understanding of the scriptures they did not recognize that he is God. They look to the sky for their sign and await supernatural occurrences therefore they will never see the manifestation of truth and inherit the promises.

Revelation 5:1-6 says, "I saw in the right hand of him that sat on the throne (God the Father) a book written within and on the backside, sealed with seven seals (The Holy Bible). And I saw a strong angel proclaiming with a loud voice, Who is worthy to open the book, and to loose the seals thereof? And no man in heaven, nor in earth, neither under the earth, was able to open the book (understand the book), neither to look thereon. And I wept much, because no man was found worthy to open and to read the book, neither to look thereon. And one of the elders saith unto me, Weep not: behold, the Lion of the tribe of Judah, the root of David (the Son of God), hath prevailed to open the book, and to loose the seven seals thereof. And I behold, and, lo, in the midst of the throne and of the four beasts, and in the midst of the elders, stood a Lamb as it had been slain, having seven horns and seven eyes, which are the seven spirits of God sent forth into all the earth." This is the Lamb of God who takes away sins, he came to save us from condemnation, he was found worthy to open the Bible, to give us the true meaning of the scriptures so that we may be found acceptable before the eyes of him who sits upon the Throne of Heaven. Primus St. Croix declared the name of the Lord (Mark 12:29), showing us that the Sabbath day is November 2, 1930, the day that God established his kingdom on earth (Isaiah 61:1-2). He did heal and cure those who were seeking God so that we may be free from sin in knowing him who is true. John 6:63 says, "It is the spirit that quickeneth; the flesh profiteth nothing: the words that I speak unto you, they are spirit, and they are life." Also in John 12:44-46 it says, "He that believeth on me, believeth not on me, but on him that sent me. And he that seeth me, seeth him that sent me. I am come a light into the world, that whosoever believeth on me should not abide in darkness." Therefore we should not think that God is invisible when Jesus said that we shall see the Lord. Hebrews 1:1-3 says, "God, who at sundry times and in divers manners spake in time past unto the fathers by the prophets, hath in these last days spoken unto us by his Son, whom he hath appointed heir of all things, by whom also he made the worlds; who being the brightness of his glory, and the express things of his person, and upholding all things by the word of his power, when he had by himself purged our sins, sat down on the right hand of the Majesty on high." In 1 John 4:9-10 it says, "In this was manifested the love of God towards us, because that God sent his only begotten Son into the world, that we might live through him. Herein is love, not that we loved God, but that he loved us, and sent his Son to be the propitiation for our sins." Philippians 2:5-11 says, "Let this mind be in you, which was also in Christ Jesus: who, being in the form of God, thought it not robbery to be equal with God: but made himself of no reputation, and took upon him the form of a servant, and was made in the likeness of men: and being found in fashion as a man, he humbled himself, and became obedient unto death, even the death of the cross. Wherefore God also hath highly exalted him, and given him a name which is above every name: that at the name of Jesus (Primus St. Croix) every knee should bow, of things in heaven, and things in earth, and things under the earth; and that every tongue should confess that Jesus Christ is Lord (concerning the gospel), to the glory of God the Father (Emperor Haile Selassie First)." This man, Primus St. Croix is the Son of the living God, he came to destroy the works of the devil so that we may live and inherit the promise of salvation.

In John 12:31-32 Jesus says, "Now is the judgment of this world: now shall the prince of this world be cast out. And I, if I be lifted up from the earth, will draw all men unto me," also verses 49 & 50 says, "I have not spoken of myself; but the Father which sent me, he gave me a commandment, what I should say, and what I should speak. And I know that his commandment is life everlasting: whatsoever I speak therefore, even as the Father said unto me, so I speak." When Primus St. Croix was arrested, he told the authorities that the people were worshipping idols and that he had to warn them of their ungodly deeds (Ezekiel 33:1-7). Revelation 12:7-12 says, "There was war in heaven: Michael and his angels fought against the dragon; and the dragon fought and his angels, and prevailed not; neither was their place found any more in heaven, And the great dragon was cast out, that old serpent, called the Devil (the pope) Satan, which deveiveth the whole world: he was cast out into the earth, and his angels were cast out with him. And I heard a loud voice saying in heaven, now is come salvation, and strength, and the kingdom of our God, and the power of his Christ: for the accuser of our brethren is cast down, which accused them before our God day and night. And they overcame him by the blood (the gospel) of the Lamb, and by the word of their testimony; and they loved not their lives unto the death. Therefore rejoice, ye heavens, and ye that dwell in them. Woe to the inhabiters of the earth and of the sea! For the devil is come down unto you, having great wrath, because he knoweth that he hath but a short time." 1 John 3:10-16 says, "In this the children of God are manifest, and the children of the devil: whosoever doeth not righteousness is not of God, neither he that loveth not his brother (Primus St. Croix). For this is the message that ye heard from the beginning, that we should love one another. Not as Cain, who was of that wicked one, and slew his brother. And wherefore slew he him? Because his own works were evil, and his brothers righteous. Marvel not, my brethren, if the world hate you. We know that we have passed from death unto life, because we love the brethren. He that loveth not his brother abideth in death. Whosoever hateth his brother is a murderer: and ye know that no murderer hath eternal life abiding in him. Hereby perceive we the love of God, because he laid down his life for us: and we ought to lay down our lives for the brethren." 1 John 4:1-4 says, "Beloved, believe not every spirit, but try the spirits whether they are of God: because many false prophets are gone out into the world. Hereby know ye the spirit of God: every spirit that confesseth that Jesus Christ is come in the flesh is of God: and every spirit that confesseth not that Jesus Christ is come in the flesh is not of God; and this is that spirit of antichrist, whereof ye have heard that it should come; and even now already is it in the world. Ye are of God, little children, and have overcome them: because greater is he that is in you, than he that is in the world. They are of the world: therefore speak they of the world, and the world heareth them. We are of God: he that knoweth God heareth us; he that is not of God heareth not us. Hereby know we the spirit of truth, and the spirit of error." 1 John 2:18 says, "Little children, it is the last time: and as ye have heard that the antichrist shall come, even now are there many antichrist; whereby we know that it is the last time." Also 1 John 5:19-20 says, "And now we know that we are of God, and the whole world lieth in wickedness. And we know that the Son of God is come, and hath given us an understanding, that we may know him that is true (Haile Selassie First), and we are in him that is true, even in his Son Jesus Christ (Primus St. Croix)." Ecclesiastes 12:13-14 says, "Let us hear the conclusion of the whole matter: fear God, and keep his commandments: for this is the whole duty of man. For God shall bring every work into judgment, with every secret thing, whether it be good, or whether it be evil."

I had to give my testimony on what has taken place the seventy years from 1930 - 2000. God has shown his face and everyone shall be given according to their work. Emperor Haile Selassie First is the Almighty, there is no one else that we can look to for our survival, this is the true message of Christ. Let us follow after that which makes for peace.

The Letters of
Primus Saint Croix

"Examine yourselves, whether you be in the faith; prove your own selves. Know you not your own selves, how that Jesus Christ is in you, except you be reprobates? But I trust that you shall know that we are not reprobates. Now I pray to God that you do no evil; not that we should appear approved, but that you should do that which is honest, although we be as reprobates. For we can do nothing against the truth, but for the truth. For we are glad, when we are weak, and you are strong: and this also we wish, even your perfection" (2 Corinthians 13:5-9).

The First Letter

Greetings to all in the name of the Most High Emperor Haile Sellassie The First. To all my beloved brothers and sisters that fear Haile Sellassie The First of Israel. Praise his name. Israel you are the salt of the earth. It is you my brethrens and sisthrens, the heirs of salvation, the children of God through Christ. It is you that will declare the glory of His Majesty, the God of Israel, Elohim Sabbath, the Holy One of Zion. Brethrens and sisthrens, the people of Israel who fear the Most High, that went through great tribulation for his name sake. You are the ones that want to see his holy name, Haile Sellassie The First, praised on the Sabbath Day, the Seventh Day, on that glorious day. The day Haile Sellassie The First became King of Kings and Lord of Lords over all the earth; and there was One Lord and his name One. The day he clothed himself in majesty and wore an everlasting crown of gold, he sat on his heavenly throne in Zion. He blessed and sanctified the Seventh Day and hallowed it. He made it holy from that time forth even forever more, world without end. It is you Israel that come on the Sabbath Day before his holy presence with thanksgiving to hallow his holy name. It is you Israel that unified his name by saying, "Our Father who are in Heaven Ethiopia, Hallowed be Thy Name Emperor Haile Sellassie The First." For you Israel have walked through the valley of trials and tribulation and have not lost the faith of our brethren Joshua The Christ, the Son of the Living God, the Holy One of Israel. God has led us in the path of righteousness for his name sake: Lij Tafari, Ras Tafari, Emperor Haile Sellassie The First. Israel you are the children that keep the commandments of Haile Sellassie The First and the faith of the brethren Joshua The Christ, the Son of the Most High. Israel you are the ones that preach and teach the people to fear the true and living God, with the word that Christ left with us, the truth of Haile Sellassie The First. Your spirit testifies the same testimony that Joshua The Christ testified concerning the everlasting Father Haile Sellassie The First of Ethiopia Zion. Let us make our boast in the Lord. Let us be joyful in HIM His Imperial Majesty. Let us come before his presence with praise and magnify his name, for we are his children. Only know that Haile Sellassie The First is the Almighty and we are the heirs of salvation who have the same faith of Joshua The Christ. Let us exalt and extol the Lord's name together: Emperor Haile Sellassie The First is the God of the whole world. Amen. Praise the Lord Emperor Haile Sellassie The First. This is a note written by me, Malchinjah (Primus St. Croix), a servant of Haile Sellassie The First, brethren of the brethren Joshua The Christ to the saints; the children of Israel, my beloved ones. My brothers and sisters of the faith of Joshua The Christ, those that keep the Commandments of God, Elohim Sabbath, Haile Sellassie The First. I want to tell you all that it is a great joy to hear of the wonderful works that you are all doing so that His Majesty's name may be praised. And for the gospel that you are all preaching to the whole world that they may understand and know that the teachings of Christ testify that Haile Sellassie The First is the true God. It is a blessing to know brethrens and sisthrens who dwell together in unity and praise the name of the Most High. Just continue in what you are doing, this is salvation and the joy of our children here after. Whatever you all may do, whether bound or free, do for the holy name of His Imperial Majesty and for the glorious gospel of Christ. You all will be rewarded with life everlasting. For the gift of Haile Sellassie The First is eternal life. Peace be with you and I know that you are the blessed ones of His Majesty. Just be strong and take courage in him for he is our joy, our salvation, our praise, our help, and most of all he is our God Emperor Haile Sellassie The First. Read his Word:

Part One:

"But my God shall supply all your needs according to his riches in glory by Jesus Christ" (Philippians 4:19).

"If ye abide in me, and my words abide in you, ye shall ask what you will, and it shall be done unto you. Herein is my Father glorified, that you bear much fruit; so shall you be my disciples. As the Father has loved me, so have I loved you: continue in my love. If you keep my commandments, you shall abide in my love; even as I have kept my Father's commandments, and abide in his love" (John 15:7-10).

"Now unto God and our Father be glory forever and ever. Amen" (Philippians 4:20).

Emperor Haile Sellassie The First is the Father of Jesus Christ, to love this testimony, which is the true message of the Bible, saves those who accept the Word therefore we must increase in the knowledge of God. The hopes and prayers of mankind is that they might be saved, they all ask for his salvation, and the opportunity to be accepted by the Lord has been made available to all when His Majesty fulfilled the prophecy on November 2, 1930. We must bear much fruit in the gospel, which is the demonstration of our faith through the scriptures, for herein is our Father glorified: Haile Sellassie The First.

"And as many as walk according to this rule, peace be on them, and mercy, and upon the Israel of God. From henceforth let no man trouble me: for I bear in my body the marks of the Lord Jesus. Brethren, the grace of our Lord Jesus Christ be with your spirit. Amen" (Galatians 6:16-18).

"Now unto him that is able to keep you from falling, and to present you faultless before the presence of his glory with exceeding joy" (Jude 1:24).

"The LORD shall establish you as a holy people unto himself, as he has sworn unto you, if you shall keep the commandments of the LORD thy God, and walk in his ways. And all people of the earth shall see that you are called by the name of the LORD; and they shall be afraid of you" (Deuteronomy 28:9-10).

"And there shall be no more curse: but the throne of God and of the Lamb shall be in it; and his servants shall serve him. And they shall see his face; and his name shall be in their foreheads" (Revelation 22:3-4).

"Wherefore, let them that suffer according to the will of God commit the keeping of their souls to him in well doing, as unto a faithful Creator" (1 Peter 4:19).

"Only let your conversation be as it becometh the gospel of Christ: that whether I come and see you, or else be absent, I may hear of your affairs, that you stand fast in one spirit, with one mind striving together for the faith of the gospel; And in nothing terrified by your adversaries: which is to them an evident token of perdition, but to you of salvation, and that of God. For unto you it is given in the behalf of Christ, not only to believe in him, but also to suffer for his sake" (Philippians 1:27-29).

The Rastafarians are the children of Israel according to the Bible because the chosen people are those who can see the face of the Almighty and have his name written in their conscious. We are not afraid of those who oppose the gospel because they all are false, this election is according to faith not works, it is an open invitation to all. There shall be no curse on us, which is the wrong understanding, from henceforth we must study to present ourselves acceptable before the Lord. We must know that this is the real doctrine, these are the marks of Christ for which we suffer by preaching to the world, if we may save some by the blood of sprinkling: for Emperor Haile Sellassie The First is the Almighty Creator of heaven and earth.

"And Jesus answered him, The first of all the commandments is, Hear, O Israel; the Lord our God is one Lord" (Mark 12:29).

"And the LORD shall be King over all the earth: in that day shall there be one LORD, and his name One" (Zechariah 14:9).

"This is the LORD's doing; it is marvelous in our eyes. This is the day which the LORD has made; we will rejoice and be glad in it" (Psalm 118:23-24).

November 2, 1930, is the day which the LORD has made, when God revealed himself to the world. This is the Sabbath for which the children of Israel must enter into his rest, this means to remember what we saw in Ethiopia when Emperor Haile Sellassie The First was crowned King of Kings and Lord of Lords. The Coronation is marvelous to us because his appearance perfectly aligns with the prophecy written beforehand concerning the LORD. We must rejoice in his commandments, which is to accept the oracle that His Majesty alone is God.

"Thou are my servant, O Israel, in whom I will be glorified. Then I said, I have labored in vain, I have spent my strength for naught, and in vain: yet surely my judgment is with the LORD, and my work with my God. And now, says the LORD that formed me from the womb to be his servant, to bring Jacob again to him, Though Israel be not gathered, yet shall I be glorious in the eyes of the LORD, and my God shall be my strength. And he said, It is a light thing that thou should be my servant to raise up the tribes of Jacob, and to restore the preserved of Israel: I will also give thee for a light to the Gentiles, that you may be my salvation to the ends of the earth. Thus says the LORD, the redeemer of Israel, and his Holy One, to him whom man despiseth, to him whom the nation abhoreth, to a servant of rulers, Kings shall see and arise, princes also shall worship, because of the LORD that is faithful, and the Holy One of Israel, and he shall choose thee" (Isaiah 49:3-7).

"For your Maker is your husband; the LORD of hosts is his name; and your Redeemer the Holy One of Israel; The God of the whole earth shall he be called" (Isaiah 54:5).

The Bible teaches us that we must be faithful to God, for he is our husband, do not fornicate which is to lust after other gods. Emperor Haile Sellassie The First is the Holy One of Israel, our King, we have been chosen by him to declare his praise so that the whole world may know him who is true.

"Praise ye the LORD. Sing unto the LORD a new song, and his praise in the congregation of saints. Let Israel rejoice in him that made him: let the children of Zion be joyful in their King" (Psalm 149:1-2).

"Let them praise the name of the LORD: for his name alone is excellent; his glory is above the earth and heaven. He also exalteth the horn of his people, the praise of all his saints; even of the children of Israel, a people near unto him. Praise ye the LORD" (Psalm 148:13-14).

"He showeth his word unto Jacob, his statutes and his judgments unto Israel. He has not dealt so with any nation: and as for his judgments, they have not known them. Praise ye the LORD" (Psalm 147:19-20).

"For our heart shall rejoice in him, because we have trusted in his holy name. Let your mercy, O LORD, be upon us, according as we hope in thee" (Psalm 33:21-22).

"Surely the righteous shall give thanks unto thy name: the upright shall dwell in thy presence" (Psalm 140:13).

If we take a survey of all the religions on earth, there is only one sect that declares that the King of Kings and Lord of Lords was manifest in the flesh, he sits upon the Throne of David, and his name is One. It is this religion that the Bible describes as Israel, a people who rejoice in Yahweh, a people near unto him because they accept the manifestation of the Word. Let the righteous praise thy name, for you alone art the true and living God: Emperor Haile Sellassie The First.

"But you that did cleave unto the LORD your God are alive every one of you this day. Behold, I have taught you statutes and judgments, even as the LORD my God commanded me, that you should do so in the land whither ye go to possess it. Keep therefore and do them; for this is your wisdom and your understanding in the sight of the nations, which shall hear all these statues, and say, Surely this great nation is a wise and understanding people. For what nation is there so great, who has God so near unto them, as the LORD our God is in all things that we call upon him for? And what nation is there so great, that has statutes and judgments so righteous as all this law, which I set before you this day" (Deuteronomy 4:4-8).

"Unto thee it was shown, that you might know that the LORD he is God; there is none else beside him" (Deuteronomy 4:35).

"Beware that thou forget not the LORD thy God, in not keeping his commandments, and his judgments, and his statutes, which I command thee this day" (Deuteronomy 8:11).

Besides Rastafari there is no other religion which has a living example of righteousness and guidance. They all adhere to ancient myths, idolatry, or divination, none of which can offer any tangible solutions to save mankind. But

His Majesty has personally shown us the path to salvation by his own deeds. This makes the children of Israel a great nation and a peculiar people unto him, for we have been called to deliver the true message of the Bible, that Emperor Haile Sellassie The First is God.

"But I said unto their children in the wilderness, Walk ye not in the statutes of your father, neither observe their judgments, nor defile yourselves with their idols: I am the LORD your God; walk in my statues, and keep my judgments, and do them; And hallow my Sabbath; and they shall be a sign between me and you, that you may know that I am the LORD your God" (Ezekiel 20:18-20).

"The counsel of the LORD stands forever, the thoughts of his heart to all generations. Blessed is the nation whose God is the LORD; and the people whom he has chosen for his own inheritance" (Psalm 33:11-12).

"For as many as are led by the Spirit of God, they are the sons of God. For you have not received the spirit of bondage again to fear; but you have received the Spirit of adoption, whereby we cry, Abba, Father. The Spirit itself bears witness with our spirit, that we are the children of God: And if children, then heirs; heirs of God, and joint-heirs with Christ; if so be that we suffer with him, that we may be also glorified together" (Romans 8:14-17).

"Who are Israelites; to whom pertaineth the adoption, and the glory, and the covenants, and the giving of the law, and the service of God, and the promises; Whose are the fathers, and of whom concerning the flesh Christ came, who is over all, God blessed forever. Amen. Not as though the word of God has taken none effect. For they are not all Israel, which are of Israel: Neither, because they are the seed of Abraham, are they all children: but the children of the promise are counted for the seed" (Romans 9:4-6).

"Wherefore come out from among them, and be ye separate, says the Lord, and touch not the unclean thing; and I will receive you, And will be a Father unto you, and you shall be my sons and daughters, says the Lord Almighty" (2 Corinthians 6:17-18).

Now that we have been so fortunate as to taste of the living waters, we shall not sin again and walk in the ways of the heathen. Our forefathers, the common spiritual guides, have not the truth therefore if any man love the world, the love of God is not in them. But we have been called to be separate from their false doctrine and to cleave unto the LORD. The Israel of God are those who inherit the promises and give service to Emperor Haile Sellassie The First. The common perception of Israel is unjustly defined based upon biased terms such as nationality, race, ethnicity, or ancestry. But we know that the judgments of the LORD are true and righteous altogether, therefore his chosen people have been elected based upon the only justifiable term which is their faith; just as it is written in the scriptures.

"For this is the covenant that I will make with the house of Israel after those days, says the Lord; I will put my laws into their mind, and write them in their hearts: and I will be to them a God, and they shall be to me a people: And they shall not teach every man his neighbor, and every man his brother, saying, Know the Lord: for all shall know me, from the least to the greatest" (Hebrew 8:10-11).

"Save us, O LORD our God, and gather us from among the heathen, to give thanks unto thy holy name, and to triumph in thy praise. Blessed be the LORD God of Israel from everlasting to everlasting: and let all the people say, Amen. Praise ye the LORD" (Psalm 106:47-48).

"In thy name shall they rejoice all the day: and in thy righteousness shall they be exalted. For thou art the glory of their strength: and in thy favor our horn shall be exalted. For the LORD is our defense; and the Holy One of Israel is our King" (Psalm 89:16-18).

"Who is this King of Glory? The LORD strong and mighty, the LORD mighty in battle. Lift up your heads, O ye gates; even lift them up, ye everlasting doors; and the King of glory shall come in. Who is this King of glory? The LORD of hosts, he is the King of glory. Selah" (Psalm 24:8-10).

"For the LORD is our judge, the LORD is our lawgiver, the LORD is our king; he will save us" (Isaiah 33:22).

"Blessed be the LORD God of Israel from everlasting, and to everlasting. Amen, and Amen" (Psalm 41:13).

"O LORD of hosts, God of Israel, that dwells between the cherubims, thou art the God, even thou alone, of all the kingdoms of the earth: thou has made heaven and earth" (Isaiah 37:16).

"Give ear, O Shepherd of Israel, thou that leads Joseph like a flock; thou that dwells between the cherubims, shine forth. Before Ephraim and Benjamin and Manasseh stir up thy strength, and come and save us. Turn us again, O God, and cause your face to shine; and we shall be saved" (Psalm 80:1-3).

Emperor Haile Sellassie The First carries all the designations and assurances of the Almighty. Those who submit unto him receive the blessings of Israel. It is normal to wrestle with the idea that His Majesty is God, you will have to study the Bible and the history of Ethiopia in order to be convinced of the doctrine; but after this is done you must put all the pieces together and submit unto him whom the profile portrays. There is only one person who fits all the descriptions of the Most High; who is this King of Glory? He that dwells between the cherubims, cause your face to shine upon us and we shall be saved, for you alone are God: Emperor Haile Sellassie The First.

"Keep not thou silence, O God: hold not thy peace, and be not still, O God. For, lo, thine enemies make a tumult: and they that hate thee have lifted up the head. They have taken crafty counsel against thy people, and consulted against thy hidden ones. They have said, Come, and let us cut them off from being a nation; that the name of Israel may be no more in remembrance. For they have consulted together with one consent: they are confederate against thee: The tabernacles of Edom, and the Ishmaelites; of Moab, and the Hagarenes; Gebal, and Ammon, and Amalek; the Philistines with the inhabitants of Tyre; Assur also is joined with them: they have helped the children of Lot. Selah. Do unto them as unto the Midianites; as to Sisera, as to Jabin, at the brook of Kison: Which perished at Endor: they became as dung for the earth. Make their nobles like Oreb, and like Zeeb: yea, all their princes as Zebah, and as Zalmunna: Who said, Let us take to ourselves the houses of God in possession. O my God, make them like a wheel; as the stubble before the wind. As the fire burneth a wood, and as the flame setteth the moutains on fire; So persecute them with thy tempest, and make them afraid with thy storm. Fill their faces with shame; that they may seek thy name, O LORD. Let them be confounded and troubled forever; yea, let them be put to shame, and perish: That men may know that thou, whose name alone is JEHOVAH, art the most high over all the earth" (Psalm 83:1-18).

"There is none like unto the God of Jeshurun, who rideth upon the heaven in thy help, and in his excellency on the sky. The eternal God is thy refuge, and underneath are the everlasting arms: and he shall thrust out the enemy from before thee; and shall say, Destroy them. Israel then shall dwell in safety alone: the fountain of Jacob shall be upon a land of corn and wine; also his heaven shall drop down dew. Happy art thou, O Israel: who is like unto thee, O people saved by the LORD, the shield of thy help, and who is the sword of thy excellency! And thine enemies shall be found liars unto thee; and thou shall tread upon their high places" (Deuteronomy 33:26-29).

The devil pope and his minions rob the people of their salvation because they do not teach the people that His Majesty is God even though this is the message of Jesus Christ. Academic scholars seek to portray the Emperor as a tyrant which totally distorts the facts, they deny His Majesty's significance and impact upon the 20th Century in defiance of the reality that he was the most powerful, effective, and popular leader on earth during his time. George Orwell said, "He who controls the past controls the future. He who controls the present controls the past." Their endeavor to rewrite history and whitewash the tremendous works of the Emperor has been concocted out of ignorance, error, or envy. Haile Sellassie The First deserves his recognition for he has merited the acclaim and the right to this supreme honor and privilege; he is the Most High and his adoration is validated by his fidelity. Our own progress is halted if we oppose him, His Majesty has decreed an indefectible order that stands as the sole means of attaining salvation. In this we know that the gates of hell shall not prevail against the gospel, as the truth cannot be buried, changed, hidden, or fractioned; Emperor Haile Sellassie The First is the Almighty Father, justified in the spirit and not by men, for an everlasting covenant that God indeed was manifest in the flesh and we bear witness of his marvelous works: Worship Ababa Janhoy.

Part Two:

"I know your works, and your labor, and your patience, and how you cannot bear them which are evil: and thou has tried them which say they are apostles, and are not, and have found them liars" (Revelation 2:2).

"Fear not; for I am with you: I will bring your seed from the east, and gather you from the west: I will say to the north, Give up; and to the south, Keep not back: bring my sons from afar, and my daughters from the ends of the earth; Even everyone that

is called by my name: for I have created them for my glory, I have formed them; yea, I have made them. Bring forth the blind people that have eyes, and the deaf that have ears. Let all the nations be gathered together, and let the people be assembled: who among them can declare this, and show us former things? Let them bring forth their witnesses, that they may be justified: or let them hear, and say, It is truth. You are my witnesses, says the LORD, and my servant whom I have chosen; that you may know and believe me, and understand that I am he: before me there was no God formed, neither shall there be after me. I, even I, am the LORD; and beside me there is no savior. I have declared, and have saved, and I have shown, when there was no strange god among you: therefore you are my witnesses, says the LORD, that I am God. Yea, before the day was I am he; and there is none that can deliver out of my hand: I will work, and who shall let it? Thus says the LORD, your redeemer, the Holy One of Israel; For your sake I have sent to Babylon, and have brought down all their nobles, and the Chaldeans, whose cry is in the ships. I am the LORD, your Holy One, the Creator of Israel, your King" (Isaiah 43:5-15).

"Thus says the LORD the King of Israel, and his redeemer the LORD of hosts; I am the first, and I am the last; and beside me there is no God. And who, as I, shall call, and shall declare it, and set it in order for me, since I appointed the ancient people? And the things that are coming, and shall come, let them show unto them. Fear ye not, neither be afraid: have not I told you from that time, and have declared it? You are even my witnesses. Is there a God beside me? Yea, there is no God; I know not any. They that make a graven image are all of them vanity; and their delectable things shall not profit; and they are their own witnesses; they see not, nor know; that they may be ashamed. Who has formed a god, or molten a graven image that is profitable for nothing? Behold, all his fellows shall be ashamed; and the workmen, they are of men: let them all be gathered together, let them stand up; yet they shall fear, and they shall be ashamed together" (Isaiah 44:6-11).

The scriptures are warning everyone not to be taken by false doctrines because there is only one God: Emperor Haile Sellassie The First, the Creator of Israel (the true religion). We all must study to be approved which is to ensure that our beliefs coincides with the Bible; for there are many who say that they follow God and Christ but are liars. Just because society or your family has passed down a certain religious custom unto you is not enough evidence to conclude that you have the correct interpretation. The descriptions of the Holy One indicate that he is a great King who shall proclaim his divinity before the world, the children of Israel bear witness to his advent and declare his glory.

We must not turn away from His Majesty because everything else is idolatry which cannot save anyone.

"The secret things belong unto the LORD our God: but those things which are revealed belong unto us and to our children forever, that we may do all the words of this law" (Deuteronomy 29:29).

"If you will not observe to do all the words of this law that are written in this book, that thou may fear this glorious and fearful name, THE LORD THY GOD" (Deuteronomy 28:58).

"Thou shalt not take the name of the LORD thy God in vain: for the LORD will not hold him guiltless that takes his name in vain. Keep the Sabbath day to sanctify it, as the LORD thy God has commanded you" (Deuteronomy 5:11-12).

"Surely the Lord God will do nothing, but he revealeth his secret unto his servants the prophets. The lion has roared, who will not fear? The Lord GOD has spoken, who can but prophesy" (Amos 3:7-8).

We must worship who the Bible describes as God for only then could we be found holy on the Sabbath; for the seventh day indicates praise. All the prophecies of the LORD cumulates to the revelation of Emperor Haile Sellassie The First on November 2, 1930, when he proved to be the one and only King of Kings and Lord of Lords. All religions and omens are referring to him because he alone is the Creator. This mystery has been revealed to those who are true to the Word of God (Israel) but for those who are not sincere in their faith the manifestation of the LORD shall remain an anomaly.

"And swear by him that lives forever and ever, who created heaven, and the things that therein are, and the earth, and the things that therein are, and the sea, and the things which are therein, that there should be time no longer: But in the days of the voice of the seventh angel, when he shall begin to sound, the mystery of God should be finished, as he has declared to his servants the prophets. And the voice which I heard from heaven spoke to me again, and said, Go and take the little book which is open in the hand of the angel which stands upon the sea and upon the earth. And I went unto the angel, and said unto him, Give me the little book. And he said unto me, Take it, and eat it up; and it shall make your belly bitter, but it shall be in your mouth sweet as honey. And I took the little book out of the angel's hand, and ate it

up; and it was in my mouth sweet as honey; and as soon as I had eaten it, my belly was better. And he said unto me, Thou must prophesy again before many people, and nations, and tongues, and kings" (Revelation 10:6-11).

"Grace be unto you, and peace, from God our Father, and from the Lord Jesus Christ. I thank my God always on your behalf, for the grace of God which is given you by Jesus Christ; That in everything you are enriched by him, in all utterance, and in all knowledge; Even as the testimony of Christ was confirmed in you: So that you come behind in no gift; waiting for the coming of our Lord Jesus Christ: who shall also confirm you unto the end, that you may be blameless in the day of our Lord Jesus Christ. God is faithful, by whom you were called unto the fellowship of his Son Jesus Christ our Lord. Now I beseech you, brethren, by the name of our Lord Jesus Christ, that you all speak the same thing, and that there be no divisions among you; but that you be perfectly joined together in the same mind and in the same judgment" (1 Corinthians 1:3-10).

"For the perfecting of the saints, for the work of the ministry, for the edifying of the body of Christ: Till we all come in the unity of the faith, and of the knowledge of the Son of God, unto a perfect man, unto the measure of the stature of the fullness of Christ: That we henceforth be no more children, tossed to and fro, and carried about with every wind of doctrine, by the sleight of men, and cunning craftiness whereby they lie in wait to deceive; but speaking the truth in love, may grow up into him in all things, which is the head, even Christ. From whom the whole body fitly joined together and compacted by that which every joint supplies, according to the effectual working in the measure of every part, maketh increase of the body unto the edifying of itself in love. This I say therefore, and testify in the Lord, that you henceforth walk not as other Gentiles walk, in the vanity of their mind, having the understanding darkened, being alienated from the life of God through the ignorance that is in them, because of the blindness of their heart: Who being past feeling have given themselves over unto lasciviousness, to work all uncleanness with greediness. But you have not so learned Christ. If so be that you have heard him, and have been taught by him, as the truth is in Jesus" (Ephesians 4:12-21).

The Bible is a guide that leads you to the Almighty, we know that the Word is true because the promises of salvation have come to pass. The theories which question the existence of the Creator of the Universe have been put to rest by Emperor Haile Sellassie The First because he is God. It was never intended for humanity to struggle with proving the validity of the Most High because the scriptures have mentioned in numerous different verses and books that God will appear on earth. Now the only question is do we accept the revelation, do we believe in God? Mankind has been given full assurance that all the mysteries of theology will be answered; that is why Jesus Christ was sent into the world. Haile Sellassie The First was not going to teach the people how he is God and explain how the Bible is talking about him; he sent forth his Prophet to do that. At this point it is up to us to accept the gospel, only then would we have the vital evidence necessary to justify our faith.

"Seeing then that we have a great high priest, that is passed into the heavens, Jesus the Son of God, let us hold fast our profession. For we have not a high priest which can not be touched with the feeling of our infirmities; but was in all points tempted like as we are, yet without sin. Let us therefore come boldly unto the throne of grace, that we may obtain mercy, and find grace to help in time of need" (Hebrew 4:14-16).

"And whoso shall swear by the temple, swears by it, and by him that dwells therein. And he that shall swear by heaven, swears by the throne of God, and by him that sits thereon" (Matthew 23:21-22).

"Remember, I beseech you, the word that you commanded thy servant Moses, saying, If you transgress, I will scatter you abroad among the nations. But if you turn unto me, and keep my commandments, and do them; though there were of you cast out unto the uttermost part of the heaven, yet will I gather them from thence, and will bring them unto the place that I have chosen to set my name there. Now these are thy servants and thy people, whom thou has redeemed by your great power, and by your strong hand" (Nehemiah 1:8-10).

"And you has he quickened, who were dead in trespasses and sins; Wherein in time past you walked according to the course of this world, according to the prince of the power of the air, the spirit that now worketh in the children of disobedience: Among whom also we all had our conversation in times past in the lusts of our flesh, fulfilling the desires of the flesh and of the mind; and were by nature the children of wrath, even as others. But God, who is rich in mercy, for his great love wherewith he loved us, Even when we were dead in sins, hath quickened us together with Christ, (by grace you are saved;) And has raised us up together, and made us sit together in heavenly places in Christ Jesus: That in the ages to come he might show the exceeding riches of his grace, in his kindness toward us, through Christ Jesus" (Ephesians 2:1-7).

The job of Jesus Christ is to teach people to put their trust in God who sits upon the throne of heaven. This revelation is not a supernatural phenomenon that will take place in the sky after we physically die. There was a time when we used to believe in these false concepts, when we walked according to the curse of this world, for the pope who oversees the regulation of all religions has made it a point to authorize an incorrect doctrine into canon. But through the grace of the Almighty we are saved, we have been made to recognize that the manifestation of the Bible is none other than Emperor Haile Sellassie The First of Ethiopia. This is the real message of Jesus Christ which has quickened us from dead conversations (false religions) and enabled us to swear by the throne of God and by him who sits thereon: Blessed be Jah Rastafari.

"These all died in faith, not having received the promises, but having seen them afar off, and were persuaded of them, and embraced them, and confessed that they were strangers and pilgrims on the earth. For they that say such things declare plainly that they seek a country. And truly, if they had been mindful of that country from whence they came out, they might have had opportunity to have returned. But now they desire a better country, that is, a heavenly: wherefore God is not ashamed to be called their God: for he has prepared for them a city" (Hebrew 11:13-16).

"For I reckon that the sufferings of this present time are not worthy to be compared with the glory which shall be revealed in us. For the earnest expectation of the creature waits for the manifestation of the sons of God. For the creature was made subject to vanity, not willingly, but by reason of him who has subjected the same in hope. Because the creature itself also shall be delivered from the bondage of corruption into the glorious liberty of the children of God" (Romans 8:18-21).

"Of his own will begat he us with the word of truth, that we should be a kind of firstfruits of his creatures" (James 1:18).

"Listen, my beloved brethren, Has not God chosen the poor of this world rich in faith, and heirs of the kingdom which he has promised to them that love him" (James 2:5).

"Thou shall arise, and have mercy upon Zion: for the time to favor her, yea, the set time, is come. For thy servants take pleasure in her stones, and favor the dust thereof. So the heathen shall fear the name of the LORD, and all the kings of the earth your glory. When the LORD shall build up Zion, he shall appear in his glory. He will regard the prayer of the destitute, and not despise their prayer. This shall be

written for the generation to come: and the people which shall be created shall praise the LORD" (Psalm 102:13-18).

The world prays for God to help them and they hope for the promises of the Bible to come to pass. If they had been mindful of the teachings of Rastafari then they would be delivered from the bondage of a corrupt religion and would be transformed into the glorious liberty of the children of God. Because the sons of God are those who know and accept the divinity of Emperor Haile Sellassie The First for he is the Father of Jesus Christ. The sufferings of this world, which is the criticism of skeptics, is not going to deter our mission in the gospel because their argument is false whereas our position is valid. The truth cannot be vanquished, this promise comes from God, who has appeared on earth in his full glory to justify the Bible. Emperor Haile Sellassie The First is worthy to be praised for he has fulfilled the entire prophecy.

"For whatsoever things were written aforetime were written for our learning, that we through patience and comfort of the scriptures might have hope. Now the God of patience and consolation grant you to be likeminded one toward another according to Christ Jesus: That you may with one mind and one mouth glorify God, even the Father of our Lord Jesus Christ. Wherefore receive ye one another, as Christ also received us, to the glory of God" (Romans 15:4-7).

"Now of the things which we have spoken this is the sum: We have such an high priest, who is set on the right hand of the throne of the Majesty in the heavens" (Hebrew 8:1).

"If you then be risen with Christ, seek those things which are above, where Christ sits on the right hand of God. Set your affection on things above, not on things on the earth. For you are dead, and your life is hid with Christ in God. When Christ, who is our life, shall appear, then shall you also appear with him in glory. Mortify there-fore your members which are upon the earth; fornication, uncleanness, inordinate affection, evil concupiscence, and covetousness, which is idolatry: For which things sake the wrath of God cometh on the children of disobedience: In the which ye also walked sometime, when ye lived in them. But now you also put off all these; anger, wrath, malice, blasphemy, filthy communication out of your mouth. Lie not one to another, seeing that you have put off the old man with his deeds; And have put on the new man, which is renewed in knowledge after the image of him that created him" (Colossians 3:1-10).

In order to understand the Bible, it is paramount that you can correctly identify the relationship between God and his Prophet. All of the scriptures are centered on this analogy. It is written that Jesus Christ sits at the right hand of His Majesty. This means that the Son of God has preached that Emperor Haile Sellassie The First is the Almighty. The deceiver has misused the Bible to entice the world into accepting a false interpretation that Jesus is God despite the fact that he is labeled as a Prophet. The people will never know God if they accept idolatrous, unclean, and inordinate dogmas. But we do not adhere to a blasphemous gospel because we accept God the Father and his Son as they are. Emperor Haile Sellassie The First alone is the Almighty and Jesus Christ is the man who declared his glory.

"And let the peace of God rule in your hearts, to the which also you are called in one body; and be ye thankful. Let the word of Christ dwell in you richly in all wisdom; teaching and admonishing one another in psalms and hymns and spiritual songs, singing with grace in your hearts to the Lord. And whatsoever you do in word or deed, do all in the name of the Lord Jesus, giving thanks to God and the Father by him" (Colossians 3:15-17).

"And the glory which you gave me I have given them; that they may be one, even as we are one: I in them, and you in me, that they may be made perfect in one; and that the world may know that you have sent me, and has loved them, as you have loved me. Father, I will that they also, whom thou has given me, be with me where I am; that they may behold my glory, which you have given me: for you loved me before the foundation of the world. O righteous Father, the world has not known you: but I have known you, and these have known that you have sent me. And I have declared unto them your name, and will declare it: that the love wherewith you have loved me may be in them, and I in them" (John 17:22-26).

"For it became him, for whom are all things, and by whom are all things, in bringing many sons unto glory, to make the captain of their salvation perfect through sufferings. For both he that sanctifies and they who are sanctified are all of one: for which cause he is not ashamed to call them brethren, Saying, I will declare your name unto my brethren, in the midst of the church will I sing praise unto thee. And again, I will put my trust in him. And again, Behold I and the children which God has given me" (Hebrew 2:10-13).

It is written for us all to become one with God just as Jesus Christ is one with the Father. It is preordained for many to inherit salvation and become one of the sons of God because the power which Jesus possesses is available for anyone to receive. Christ accepts God and declared the name of the Father unto his disciples. If we should accept his gospel then our faith would be perfect for we would know God Emperor Haile Sellassie The First. The world does not know who God is because the pope has deceived them with a backwards dogma but anyone who rises to the level of becoming one of the sons, is able to see the Almighty.

"The Grace of our Lord Jesus Christ be with you all. Amen. Now to him that is of power to establish you according to my gospel, and the preaching of Jesus Christ, according to the revelation of the mystery, which was kept secret since the world began, But now is made manifest, and by the scriptures of the prophets, according to the commandment of the everlasting God, made known to all nations for the obedience of faith: To God only wise, be glory through Jesus Christ forever. Amen" (Romans 16:24-27).

"Whereby, when you read, ye may understand my knowledge in the mystery of Christ; Which in other ages was not made known unto the sons of men, as it is now revealed unto his holy apostles and prophets by the Spirit; That the Gentiles should be fellowheirs, and of the same body, and partakers of his promise in Christ by the gospel: Whereof I was made a minister, according to the gift of the grace of God given unto me by the effectual working of his power. Unto me, who am less than the least of all saints, is this grace given, that I should preach among the Gentiles the unsearchable riches of Christ; And to make all men see what is the fellowship of the mystery, which from the beginning of the world has been hid in God, who created all things by Jesus Christ: To the intent that now unto the principalities and powers in heavenly places might be known by the church the manifold wisdom of God, According to the eternal purpose which he purposed in Christ Jesus our Lord: In whom we have boldness and access with confidence by the faith of him. Wherefore I desire that ye faint not at my tribulations for you, which is your glory. For this cause I bow my knees unto the Father of our Lord Jesus Christ, Of whom the whole family in heaven and earth is named, That he would grant you, according to the riches of his glory, to be strengthened with might by his Spirit in the inner man; That Christ may dwell in your hearts by faith; that ye, being rooted and grounded in love, May be able to comprehend with all saints what is the breadth, and length, and depth, and height; And to know the love of Christ, which passeth knowledge,

that you might be filled with all the fullness of God. Now unto him that is able to do exceeding abundantly above all that we ask or think, according to the power that worketh in us, Unto him be glory in the church by Christ Jesus throughout all ages, world without end. Amen" (Ephesians 3:4-21).

The parables can only be comprehended properly if we are able to explain each verse in conjunction with the entire scenario. We accept the Bible as a whole therefore our interpretation of individual scriptures must correlate with the full testimony without contradiction. The only one who is able to provide this accurate analysis is Christ, that is why it is written that God created all things by Jesus. If you are not picking and choosing what verses you pay attention to but study everything then you would understand that Christ is the Lord's messenger. Therefore what Jesus created was the true gospel, which then aligns with the other scriptures that calls for you to comprehend the heights of all wisdom; this makes a man whole, the knowledge of God gives you life and without it you are spiritually dead.

"Praise waits for thee, O God, in Sion: and unto thee shall the vow be performed. O thou that hears prayer, unto thee shall all flesh come" (Psalm 65:1-2).

"Praise ye the LORD: for it is good to sing praises unto our God; for it is pleasant; and praise is comely" (Psalm 147:1).

"Whither the tribes go up, the tribes of the LORD, unto the testimony of Israel, to give thanks unto the name of the LORD. For there are set thrones of judgment, the thrones of the house of David" (Psalm 122:4-5).

"We will go into his tabernacles: we will worship at his footstool. Arise, O LORD, into thy rest; thou, and the ark of thy strength. Let thy priests be clothed with righteousness; and let thy saints shout for joy. For your servant David's sake turn not away the face of your anointed" (Psalm 132:7-9).

"One thing have I desired of the LORD, that will I seek after; that I may dwell in the house of the LORD all the days of my life, to behold the beauty of the LORD, and to enquire in his temple" (Psalm 27:4).

"The LORD sitteth upon the flood; yea, the LORD sitteth King forever. The LORD will give strength unto his people; the LORD will bless his people with peace" (Psalm 29:10-11).

The Bible describes who God is and everything points to Emperor Haile Sellassie The First. Christ came to bear witness of His Majesty for he kept us in the name of his Father. This is eternal life because the gospel shall stand the test of time, it will remain accurate under any scrutiny. Let us Praise the Lord whose glory shall endure forever: Emperor Haile Sellassie The First.

"Now set your heart and your soul to seek the LORD your God; arise therefore, and build ye the sanctuary of the LORD God, to bring the ark of the covenant of the LORD, and the holy vessels of God, into the house that is to be built to the name of the LORD" (1 Chronicles 22:19).

"Again he said, Therefore hear the word of the LORD; I saw the LORD sitting upon his throne, and all the host of heaven standing on his right hand and on his left" (2 Chronicles 18:18).

"Glory and honor are in his presence; strength and gladness are in his place. Give unto the LORD, ye kindreds of the people, give unto the LORD glory and strength. Give unto the LORD the glory due unto his name: bring an offering, and come before him: worship the LORD in the beauty of holiness" (1 Chronicles 16:27-29).

Those who are created in the image of God are the ones who acknowledge the fact that Emperor Haile Sellassie The First is the Almighty. Their inner morale has been awakened because they are able to accept their Creator and give him the glory due unto his name. Anyone who seeks him shall find him for he is not far from us. All of the guidance which humanity needs to better themselves, His Majesty has demonstrated. Let us follow and worship the King of Zion who sat upon his holy throne on the seventh day, November 2, 1930: Rastafari praise his name.

"I bring near my righteousness; it shall not be far off, and my salvation shall not tarry: and I will place salvation in Zion for Israel my glory" (Isaiah 46:13).

"Thus says the LORD, Keep ye judgment, and do justice: for my salvation is near to come and my righteousness to be revealed. Blessed is the man that doeth this, and

the son of man that lays hold on it; that keepeth the Sabbath from polluting it, and keepeth his hand from doing evil. Neither let the son of the stranger, that has joined himself to the LORD, speak, saying, The LORD has utterly separated me from his people: neither let the eunuch say, Behold, I am a dry tree. For thus says the LORD unto the eunuchs that keep my Sabbath, and choose the things that please me, and take hold of my covenant; Even unto them will I give in mine house and within my walls a place and a name better than of sons and of daughters: I will give them an everlasting name, that shall not be cut off. Also the sons of the stranger, that join themselves to the LORD, to serve him, and to love the name of the LORD, to be his servants, everyone that keepeth the Sabbath from polluting it, and taketh hold of my covenant; Even them will I bring to my holy mountain, and make them joyful in my house of prayer: their burnt offerings and their sacrifices shall be accepted upon mine altar; for mine house shall be called a house of prayer for all people. The Lord GOD, which gathers the outcasts of Israel saith, Yet will I gather others to him, beside those that are gathered unto him" (Isaiah 56:1-8).

The children of Israel, which are those who praise Emperor Haile Sellassie The First, shall be rewarded with heavenly gifts which are the oracles of God. They will comprehend the mysteries of the Bible for they are ordained by the Lord to show forth his praise which delivers salvation. We should not be ashamed of this high office or allow the devil to rob us of our saving grace. Those who can endure through the tribulations and remain faithful shall be made pillars in the house of the Lord; they will win favor from the Most High.

"And speak unto him, saying, Thus speaketh the LORD of hosts, saying, Behold the man whose name is The BRANCH; and he shall grow up out of his place, and he shall build the temple of the LORD: Even he shall build the temple of the LORD; and he shall bear the glory, and shall sit and rule upon his throne; and he shall be a priest upon his throne: and the counsel of peace shall be between them both. And the crowns shall be to Helem, and to Tobijah, and to Jedaiah, and to Hen the son of Zephaniah, for a memorial in the temple of the LORD. And they that are far off shall come and build in the temple of the LORD, and ye shall know that the LORD of hosts has sent me unto you. And this shall come to pass, if you will diligently obey the voice of the LORD your God" (Zechariah 6:12-15).

"For thou art an holy people unto the LORD thy God: the LORD thy God has chosen you to be a special people unto himself, above all people that are upon the face of the earth. The LORD did not set his love upon you, nor choose you, because

you were more in number than any people; for you were the fewest of all people"
(Deuteronomy 7:6-7).

"Wherefore he says, Awake thou that sleeps, and arise from the dead, and Christ
shall give you light. See then that you walk circumspectly, not as fools, but as wise,
Remembering the time, because the days are evil. Wherefore be ye not unwise, but
understand what the will of the Lord is. And be not drunk with wine, wherein is
excess; but be filled with the Spirit; Speaking to yourselves in psalms and hymns
and spiritual songs, singing and making melody in your heart to the Lord; Giving
thanks always for all things unto God and the Father in the name of our Lord Jesus
Christ" (Ephesians 5:14-20).

Temptation is all around us but we must learn to resist it at all costs; the
times are evil so we have to arm ourselves with the knowledge of God. The
world is under the veil of ignorance because they deny their Creator Emperor
Haile Sellassie The First. But we have been called to be holy as the Lord is holy
therefore anyone who loves the world has not the love of God in them. Crowns
of wisdom shall be given unto those who can overcome the wiles of the devil;
just as Jesus did. Walk uprightly, according to the divination of the Bible.

"And came and preached peace to you which were afar off, and to them that were
near. For through him we both have access by one Spirit unto the Father. Now there-
fore you are no more strangers and foreigners, but fellow citizens with the saints,
and of the household of God; And are built upon the foundation of the apostles and
prophets, Jesus Christ himself being the chief corner stone; In whom all the building
fitly framed together grows unto a holy temple in the Lord: In whom ye also are built
together for a habitation of God through the Spirit" (Ephesians 2:17-22).

"To whom coming, as unto a living stone, disallowed indeed of men, but chosen
of God, and precious, You also, as lively stones, are built up a spiritual house, a
holy priesthood, to offer up spiritual sacrifices, acceptable to God by Jesus Christ.
Wherefore also it is contained in the scripture, Behold, I lay in Sion a chief corner
stone, elect, precious, and he that believes on him shall not be confused. Unto you
therefore which believe he is precious: but unto them which be disobedient, the stone
which the builders disallowed, the same is made the head of the corner, And a stone
of stumbling, and a rock of offense, even to them which stumble at the word, being
disobedient: whereunto also they were appointed. But you are a chosen generation,
a royal priesthood, a holy nation, a peculiar people; that you should show forth the

praises of him who has called you out of darkness into his marvelous light: Which in time past were not a people, but are now the people of God: which had not obtained mercy, but now have obtained mercy. Dearly beloved, I beseech you as strangers and pilgrims, abstain from fleshly lusts, which war against the soul; Having your conversation honest among the Gentiles: that, whereas they speak against you as evildoers, they may by your good works, which they shall behold, glorify God in the day of visitation. Submit yourselves to every ordinance of man for the Lord's sake: whether it be to the king, as supreme; Or unto governors, as unto them that are sent by him for the punishment of evildoers, and for the praise of them that do well. For so is the will of God, that with well doing you may put to silence the ignorance of foolish men: As free, and not using your liberty for a cloke of maliciousness, but as the servants of God. Honor all men. Love the brotherhood. Fear God. Honor the king" (1 Peter 2:4-17).

Do you not know that your body is the temple of God? Therefore when the Bible speaks about those who built the house of the Lord, it is referring to those who were sincere in their faith. Everyone must look into their heart to ensure that they are doing all that they can to please God because if we did then we would be familiar with the scriptures which would lead us to accept the King of Glory. The revelation of the Creator is not an event encapsulated fully through traditions passed down from generation to generation, it is a job that one must perform faithfully by learning the Bible and applying its wisdom. Those who excel in this undertaking shall become a royal priesthood, a holy nation, having the proper counsel; and no weapon formed against them shall prosper: Blessed be Jah Rastafari.

The Second Letter

The words of our Lord and savior, Iyesus Kristos, native Son of the Most High Haile Sellassie The First and a few words from our brethren Paul. The gospel is pertaining to His Majesty:

"Believe thou not that I am in the Father, and the Father in me? The words that I speak unto you I speak not of myself: but the Father that dwelleth in me, he doeth the works" (John 14:10).

"It is written in the prophets, and they shall be all taught of God. Every man therefore that has heard, and has learned of the Father, cometh unto me" (John 6:45).

"They are not of the world, even as I am not of the world. Sanctify them through your truth: Your word is truth" (John 17:16-17).

"Jesus answered and said unto him, If a man love me, he will keep my words: and my Father will love him, and we will come unto him, and make our abode with him. He that loves me not keeps not my sayings: and the word which you hear is not mine, but the Father's which sent me" (John 14:23-24).

Iyesus Kristos preached the true Word of God, if we accept his testimony then we shall know that Haile Sellassie The First is the Supreme Sovereign of Heaven and earth. This edification is the eternal guide to understanding all the prophecies. Humanity cannot be saved metaphysically, salvation must be tangible in order for it to be substantial. In like manner, people cannot learn mystically, education must be holistic in order for it to be effective. The Son of God is different from the common preachers because he is the only one who can manifest the actualization of the Bible. Everyone else merely speculates and hypothesizes on what they think the scriptures mean, whereas Iyesus reveals who the prophecy is referring to because he has full command of the Word.

"I have many things to say and to judge of you: but he that sent me is true; and I speak to the world those things which I have heard of him" (John 8:26).

"And what he has seen and heard, that he testifies; and no man receives his testimony. He that has received his testimony has set to his seal that God is true. For he whom God has sent speaks the words of God: for God gives not the Spirit by measure unto him" (John 3:32-34).

"They understood not that he spoke to them of the Father" (John 8:27).

The world has rejected the message of the Messiah that Emperor Haile Sellassie The First is the Almighty God of the Sabbath because they have been blinded by popery. Those who have overcome the deception of the devil are able to see God; they know that His Majesty is the Almighty. Iyesus Kristos preached about his Father, the disciples acknowledge the mystery that Haile Sellassie The First is the Almighty. This is the seal, the evidence and manifestation of the prophecies. The only person who can reveal the mystery is Christ but there are those who want to kill this message because they love the old testament, which represents an incorrect approach that they refuse to reform.

"If you abide in me, and my words abide in you, you shall ask what you will, and it shall be done unto you. Herein is my Father glorified, that you bear much fruit; so shall you be my disciples" (John 15:7-8).

"Then said Jesus to those Jews which believed on him, If you continue in my word, then are you my disciples indeed" (John 8:31).

"In the beginning was the Word, and the Word was with God, and the Word was God. The same was in the beginning with God" (John 1:1-2).

"Then said they unto him, Who are you? And Jesus said unto them, Even the same that I said unto you from the beginning" (John 8:25).

Iyesus Kristos is God's Preacher, he has declared that Emperor Haile Sellassie The First is the Almighty. Those who abide in his doctrine shall know who the Father is, they will be able to see the LORD. The Word is God Emperor Haile Sellassie The First, Iyesus Kristos is the messenger of the Word (the Prophet of God). When it says that he was in the beginning with God, this means that he is one with the LORD, he acknowledges His Majesty's divinity, he loves the Almighty. The Son sits on the right hand side of the Father, this demonstrates his obedience to the LORD as well as the power and command which he possesses in the Word (the gospel of God).

"Say ye of him, who the Father has sanctified, and sent into the world, Thou blasphemest; because I said, I am the Son of God? If I do not the works of my Father, believe me not. But if I do, though you believe not me, believe the works: that you may know, and believe, that the Father is in me, and I in him" (John 10:36-38).

"He that is of God hears God's words: you therefore hear them not, because you are not of God" (John 8:47).

"And it came to pass, as he spoke these things, a certain woman of the company lifted up her voice, and said unto him, Blessed is the womb that bare you, and the paps which you have sucked. But he said, Yea, rather, blessed are they that hear the word of God, and keep it" (Luke 11:27-28).

"And heal the sick that are there, and say unto them, the kingdom of God is come near unto you. But into whatsoever city you enter, and they receive you not, go your

ways out into the streets of the same, and say, Even the very dust of your city, which cleaves on us, we do wipe off against you; notwithstanding be ye sure of this, that the kingdom of God is come near unto you" (Luke 10:9-11).

Iyesus Kristos was rejected because they do not believe in the Father Emperor Haile Sellassie The First. The true gospel of the Messiah leads you before the Throne of the Almighty and HIM that sits thereon, these are the descriptions of the Son of God; he declares the King of Zion. We who accept his testimony inherit the promises and live according to the Word; this is how we know that His Majesty is God. There are a lot of different theories about who Christ is and what do the parables mean; that is why it is essential to study the Bible to understand the characterization of Iyesus Kristos. By their works we will know who is true because only the Son can reveal the Father.

"Now you are clean through the word which I have spoken unto you" (John 15:3).

"I am come a light into the world, that whosoever believes on me should not abide in darkness. And if any man hear my words, and believe not, I judge him not: for I came not to judge the world, but to save the world" (John 12:46-47).

"But I receive not testimony from man: but these things I say, that you might be saved" (John 5:34).

"He that rejects me, and receives not my words, has one that judges him: the word that I have spoken, the same shall judge him in the last day" (John 12:48).

If we accept the testimony of Iyesus Kristos then we will know that Haile Sellassie The First is the Almighty. It is his gospel which justifies you before the LORD because only by acknowledging the divinity of the Emperor would our faith be concurrent with the message of the Bible. Haile Sellassie The First is the King of Kings and Lord of Lords, that is a historical reality which we all must recognize and understand. It is not feasible to compromise the Word of God to win favor with men and to fit in with what the rest of the world follows. Anyone who says that they love Iyesus Kristos must believe in His Majesty for he is the Almighty Father who searches the veins of our hearts and knows our sincerity in the faith.

"Jesus answered, If I honor myself, my honor is nothing: It is my Father that honors me; of whom you say, that he is your God: Yet you have not known him; but I know him: and if I should say, I know him not, I shall be a liar like unto you: but I know him, and keep his sayings" (John 8:54-55).

"For I have not spoken of myself; but the Father which sent me, he gave me a commandment what I should say, and what I should speak. And I know that his commandment is life everlasting: whatsoever I speak therefore, even as the Father said unto me, so I speak" (John 12:49-50).

"Pilate therefore said unto him, Are you a king then? Jesus answered; You say that I am a king. To this end was I born, and for this cause came I into the world, that I should bear witness unto the truth. Every one that is of the truth hears my voice" (John 18:37).

"This is he that came by water and blood, even Jesus Christ; not by water only, but by water and blood. And it is the Spirit that bears witness, because the Spirit is truth" (1 John 5:6).

"And to Jesus the mediator of the new covenant, and to the blood of sprinkling, that speaks better things than that of Abel" (Hebrew 12:24).

If the testimony of Iyesus Kristos equated with him being God then that would make him a liar and the entire Bible would be a contradiction. The scriptures have stated that he did not speak of himself because anyone who does preach their own exaltation is a false prophet. Emperor Haile Sellassie The First did not teach us how he is the Almighty, his works prove his divinity and the Bible says that the correct pattern is for the LORD to send forth his mediator to declare the mystery of God.

"Remember them which have the rule over you, who have spoken unto you the word of God: whose faith follow, considering the end of their conversation. Jesus Christ the same yesterday, today, and forever. Be not carried about with divers and strange doctrines: for it is a good thing that the heart be established with grace; not with meats, which have not profited them that have been occupied therein" (Hebrews 13:7-9).

"Whosoever transgresses, and abides not in the doctrine of Christ, has not God. He that abides in the doctrine of Christ, he has both the Father and the Son. If there come any unto you, and bring not this doctrine, receive him not into your house, neither bid him God speed: For he that bids him God speed is partaker of his evil deeds" (2 John 1:9-11).

"Who being past feeling have given themselves over unto lasciviousness, to work all uncleanness with greediness. But you have not so learned Christ; If so be that you have heard him, and have been taught by him, as the truth is in Jesus: That you put off concerning the former conversation the old man, which is corrupt according to the deceitful lusts; And be renewed in the spirit of your mind; And that you put on the new man, which after God is created in righteousness and true holiness" (Ephesians 4:19-24).

"That their hearts might be comforted, being knit together in love, and unto all riches of the full assurance of understanding, to the acknowledgement of the mystery of God, and of the Father, and of Christ; In whom are hid all the treasures of wisdom and knowledge. And this I say, lest any man should beguile you with enticing words. For though I be absent in the flesh, yet am I with you in the spirit joying and beholding your order and the steadfastness of your faith in Christ. As you have therefore received Christ Jesus the Lord, so walk ye in him: Rooted and built up in him, and established in the faith, as you have been taught, abounding therein with thanksgiving. Beware lest any man spoil you through philosophy and vain deceit, after the tradition of men, after the rudiments of the world, and not after Christ. For in him dwells all the fullness of the Godhead bodily" (Colossians 2:2-9).

"Therefore, seeing we have this ministry, as we have received mercy, we faint not; But have renounced the hidden things of dishonesty, not walking in craftiness, nor handling the word of God deceitfully; but, by manifestation of the truth, commending ourselves to every man's conscience in the sight of God. But if our gospel be hid, it is hid to them that are lost; In whom the god of this world has blinded the minds of them which believe not, lest the light of the glorious gospel of Christ, who is the image of God, should shine unto them" (2 Corinthians 4:1-4).

"Till we all come in the unity of the faith, and of the knowledge of the Son of God, unto a perfect man, unto the measure of the stature of the fullness of Christ: That we henceforth be no more children, tossed to and fro, and carried about with every wind of doctrine, by the sleight of men, and cunning craftiness whereby they lie in *wait to deceive; but speaking the truth in love, may grow up into him in all things, which is the head, even Christ: From who the whole body fitly joined together and compacted by that which every joint supplies, according to the effectual working in the measure of every part, maketh increase of the body unto the edifying of itself in love. This I say therefore, and testify in the Lord, that you henceforth walk not as other Gentiles walk, in the vanity of their mind" (Ephesians 4:13-17).*

"Let as many servants as are under the yoke count their own masters worthy of all honor, that the name of God and his doctrine be not blasphemed. And they that have believing masters, let them not despise them, because they are brethren; but rather do them service, because they are faithful and beloved, partakers of the benefit. These things teach and exhort. If any man teach otherwise, and consent not to wholesome words, even the words of our Lord Jesus Christ, and to the doctrine which is according to godliness; he is proud, knowing nothing, but doting about questions and strife, railings, evil surmising, perverse disputings of men of corrupt minds, and destitute of the truth, supposing that gain is godliness: from such withdraw thyself. But godliness with contentment is great gain. For we brought nothing into this world, and it is certain we can carry nothing out" (1 Timothy 6:1-7).

We must ensure that our obedience is to the correct pattern of the Bible and not a man made philosophy. Iyesus Kristos is the Son of God, his descriptions of being the Prophet of the LORD cannot be changed, if anyone preaches that he is God then they are wrong and we must guard ourselves against these corrupt doctrines by studying the Word so that we may know the truth; those who read the Bible know that the Messiah is the one who will teach the world the truth about the Father, he did not preach himself. It may be popular to believe that Iyesus Kristos is God but that is not the message found in the scriptures. It is time for us to renounce these deceitful philosophies because they cannot offer salvation.

"Grace be unto you, and peace, from God our Father, and from the Lord Jesus Christ. I thank my God always on your behalf, for the grace of God which is given you by Jesus Christ; that in everything you are enriched by him, in all utterance, and in all knowledge; Even as the testimony of Christ was confirmed in you: So that you come behind in no gift; waiting for the coming of our Lord Jesus Christ: who shall also confirm you unto the end, that you may be blameless in the day of our Lord Jesus Christ. God is faithful, by whom you were called unto the fellowship of his Son Jesus Christ our Lord. Now I beseech you, brethren, by the name of our

Lord Jesus Christ, that you all speak the same thing, and that there be no divisions among you; but that you be perfectly joined together in the same mind and in the same judgment" (1 Corinthians 1:3-10).

"When Christ, who is our life, shall appear, then shall you also appear with him in glory" (Colossians 3:4).

"Even so we, when we were children, were in bondage under the elements of the world: But when the fullness of the time was come, God sent forth his Son, made of a woman, made under the law, to redeem them that were under the law, that we might receive the adoption of sons. And because you are sons, God has sent forth the Spirit of his Son into your hearts, crying, Abba, Father. Wherefore you are no more a servant, but a son; and if a son, then an heir of God through Christ" (Galatians 4:3-7).

"For our exhortation was not of deceit, nor of uncleanness, nor in guile: But as we were allowed of God to be put in truth with the gospel, even so we speak; not as pleasing men, but God, which tries our hearts. For neither at any time used we flattering words, as you know, nor a cloke of covetousness; God is witness: Nor of men sought we glory, neither of you, nor yet of others, when we might have been burdensome, as the apostles of Christ. But we were gentle among you, even as a nurse cherishes her children: so being affectionately desirous of you, we were willing to have imparted unto you, not the gospel of God only, but also our own souls, because you were dear unto us" (1 Thessalonians 2:3-8).

We have been allowed to know the true gospel through God who has appeared on earth and taught us the law of righteousness; he also sent forth his Son for further edification. No longer are we subject to bondage under any false counsel for we have been made blameless by acknowledging the divinity of Emperor Haile Sellassie The First. The aspirations of our faith are not to please men but God, this should also be the aim of all those who claim to follow Iyesus Kristos. Anyone who is real with the LORD will be able to renounce their traditions if they are proven contrary to the truth as well as adopt new customs that are found to be pleasing to the Almighty.

"Therefore, brethren, we were comforted over you in all our affliction and distress by your faith: for now we live, if you stand fast in the Lord. For what thanks can we render to God again for you, for all the joy wherewith we joy for your sakes before our God; night and day praying exceedingly that we might see your face, and might

perfect that which is lacking in your faith? Now God himself and our Father, and our Lord Jesus Christ, direct our way unto you. And the Lord make you to increase and abound in love one toward another, and toward all men, even as we do toward you: to the end he may establish your hearts unblameable in holiness before God, even our Father, at the coming of our Lord Jesus Christ" (1 Thessalonians 3:7-13).

"Now the Spirit speaks expressly, that in the latter times some shall depart from the faith, giving heed to seducing spirits, and doctrines of devils; speaking lies in hypocrisy, having their conscience seared with a hot iron. If you put the brethren in remembrance of these things, you shall be a good minister of Jesus Christ, nourished up in the words of faith and of good doctrine, whereunto you have attained" (1 Timothy 4:1, 2, 6).

"Grace be to you, and peace, from God the Father, and from our Lord Jesus Christ, who gave himself for our sins, that he might deliver us from this present evil world, according to the will of God and our Father: To whom be glory forever and ever. Amen. I marvel that you are so soon removed from him that called you into the grace of Christ unto another gospel: which is not another; but there be some that trouble you, and would pervert the gospel of Christ. But though we, or an angel from heaven, preach any other gospel unto you than that which we have preached unto you, let him be accursed. As we said before, so say I now again, If any man preach any other gospel unto you than that you have received, let him be accursed. For do I now persuade men, or God? Or do I seek to please men? For if I yet pleased men, I should not be the servant of Christ. But I certify you, brethren, that the gospel which was preached of me is not after man. For I neither received it of man, neither was I taught it, but by the revelation of Jesus Christ" (Galatians 1:3-12).

Our gospel is based upon the evidence of the Bible, the fulfillment of prophecy; there is no testimony more definitive. But even as we see God in the flesh as Iyesus Kristos declared him, some will turn away from the truth because they are men pleasers and weak hearted. Emperor Haile Sellassie The First is the Almighty Father, if anyone opposes the Godhead they shall be broken and torn asunder, according to the scriptures, because it is impossible to prove the LORD false.

"And he that searches the hearts knows what is the mind of the Spirit, because he makes intercession for the saints according to the will of God. And we know that all things work together for good to them that love God, to them who are the called

according to his purpose. For whom he did foreknow, he also did predestinate to be conformed to the image of his Son, that he might be the firstborn among many brethren" (Romans 8:27-29).

"Even him, whose coming is after the working of Satan with all power and signs and lying wonders, and with all deceivableness of unrighteousness in them that perish; because they received not the love of the truth, but had pleasure in unrighteousness. But we are bound to give thanks always to God for you, brethren beloved of the Lord, because God has from the beginning chosen you to salvation through sanctification of the Spirit and belief of the truth: whereunto he called you by our gospel, to the obtaining of the glory of our Lord Jesus Christ. Therefore, brethren, stand fast, and hold the traditions which you have been taught, whether by word, or our epistle. Now our Lord Jesus Christ himself, and God, even our Father, which has loved us, and has given us everlasting consolation and good hope through grace, comfort your hearts, and establish you in every good word and work" (2 Thessalonians 2:9-17).

"But as many as received him, to them gave he power to become the sons of God, even to them that believe on his name" (John 1:12).

Those who are honest to God will accept the gospel of Iyesus Kristos that Emperor Haile Sellassie The First is the Almighty. We have been renewed into the image of the Son of God, which means that we see and know the Father. The children of Israel are those who inherit the promises of the Bible, those who carry the fulfillment of the ordinances, and preach salvation unto the world for a witness. Our brethren Iyesus Kristos gave us the same power which he possessed; which is the gospel.

"The next day John seeth Jesus coming unto him, and said, Behold the Lamb of God, which takes away the sin of the world" (John 1:29).

"But all these things will they do unto you for my name's sake, because they know not him that sent me. If I had not come and spoken unto them, they had not had sin; but now they have no cloke for their sin. He that hates me hates my Father also. If I had not done among them the works which none other man did, they had not had sin: but now have they both seen and hated both me and my Father" (John 15:21-24).

"*The LORD is good, a strong hold in the day of trouble; and he knows them that trust in him*" (Nahum 1:7).

"*Nevertheless the foundation of God stands sure, having this seal, The Lord knows them that are his. And, Let everyone that names the name of Christ depart from iniquity*" (2 Timothy 2:19).

"*I have manifested your name unto the men which you gave me out of the world: yours they were, and you gave them me; and they have kept your word*" (John 17:6).

"*But he that enters in by the door is the shepherd of the sheep. To him the porter opens; and the sheep hear his voice; and he calls his own sheep by name, and leads them out. And when he puts forth his own sheep, he goes before them, and the sheep follow him: for they know his voice. And a stranger will they not follow, but will flee from him: for they know not the voice of strangers. This parable spoke Jesus unto them; but they understood not what things they were which he spoke unto them. Then said Jesus unto them again, Verily, verily, I say unto you, I am the door of the sheep. All that ever came before me are thieves and robbers: but the sheep did not hear them. I am the door: by me if any man enter in, he shall be saved, and shall go in and out, and find pasture. The thief cometh not, but for to steal, and to kill, and to destroy: I am come that they might have life, and that they might have it more abundantly. I am the good shepherd: the good shepherd gives his life for the sheep. But he that is a hireling, and not the shepherd, whose own the sheep are not, sees the wolf coming, and leaves the sheep, and flees: and the wolf catches them, and scatters the sheep. The hireling flees, because he is a hireling, and cares not for the sheep. I am the good shepherd, and know my sheep, and am known of mine. As the Father knows me, even so know I the Father: and I lay down my life for the sheep*" (John 10:2-15).

Iyesus Kristos healed the blind and cured the lame by teaching us who the Father is; this is how our reproach has been removed. The false preachers of the world claim to follow the Bible but they are unable to show us God incarnate because this is the distinction between those who are approved and those who are false. It is written that you must acknowledge that both the Father and the Son have come in the flesh or else you are antichrist. Paintings and idolatry is not sufficient evidence that the prophecies have come to pass. We must ensure that our faith is in accordance with the Bible's depiction; the only way to be approved through the scriptures is to praise Emperor Haile Sellassie The First through his Prophet Iyesus Kristos.

"*Therefore we ought to give the more earnest heed to the things which we have heard, lest at any time we should let them slip. For if the word spoken by angels was stedfast, and every transgression and disobedience received a just recompense of reward; how shall we escape, if we neglect so great salvation; which at the first began to be spoken by the Lord, and was confirmed unto us by them that heard him. But we see Jesus, who was made a little lower than the angels for the suffering of death, crowned with glory and honor; that he by the grace of God should taste death for every man. For it became him, for whom are all things, and by whom are all things, in bringing many sons unto glory, to make the captain of their salvation perfect through sufferings. For both he that sanctifies and they who are sanctified are all one: for which cause he is not ashamed to call them brethren, saying, I will declare your name unto my brethren, in the midst of the church will I sing praise unto thee. And again, I will put my trust in him. And again, Behold I and the children which God has given me. Forasmuch then as the children are partakers of flesh and blood, he also himself likewise took part of the same; that through death he might destroy him that had the power of death, that is, the devil; And deliver them, who through fear of death were all their lifetime subject to bondage. For verily he took not on him the nature of angels; but he took on him the seed of Abraham. Wherefore in all things it behoved him to be made like unto his brethren, that he might be a merciful and faithful high priest in things pertaining to God, to make reconciliation for the sins of the people*" (Hebrew 2:1-3, 9-17).

"*As every man has received the gift, even so minister the same one to another, as good stewards of the manifold grace of God. If any man speak, let him speak as the oracles of God; if any man minister, let him do it as of the ability which God giveth: that God in all things may be glorified through Jesus Christ, to whom be praise and dominion forever and ever. Amen. Beloved, think it not strange concerning the fiery trial which is to try you, as though some strange thing happened unto you: But rejoice, inasmuch as you are partakers of Christ's sufferings; that, when his glory shall be revealed, you may be glad also with exceeding joy. If you be reproached for the name of Christ, happy are you; for the Spirit of glory and of God rests upon you: on their part he is evil spoken of, but on your part he is glorified. But let none of you suffer as a murderer, or as a thief, or as an evil doer, or as a busybody in other men's matters. Yet if any man suffer as a Christian, let him not be ashamed; but let him glorify God on this behalf. For the time is come that judgment must begin at the house of God: and if it first begin at us, what shall the end be of them that obey not the gospel of God? And if the righteous scarcely be saved, where shall the ungodly and the sinner appear? Wherefore, let them that suffer according to the will of God*

commit the keeping of their souls to him in well doing, as unto a faithful Creator"
(1 Peter 4:10-19).

We ought to lay our treasures in heaven and not on earth, this means to
please God and not man. Iyesus Kristos has preached the message of salvation
that Emperor Haile Sellassie The First is the Almighty Father; the devil has
sought out ways to kill this gospel but we know that he will have no success.
It has been predestinated that those who work for His Majesty shall not fall
victim to Satan's entrapping. We must remain steadfast in the true doctrine of
Iyesus Kristos which is to know that Haile Sellassie The First is God. Although
many people will fight against us because they have been led astray, we shall
remain vigilant because our testimony is true.

"That which was from the beginning, which we have heard, which we have seen with
our eyes, which we have looked upon, and our hands have handled, of the Word of
life; For the life was manifested, and we have seen it, and bear witness, and show
unto you that eternal life, which was with the Father, and was manifested unto us"
(1 John 1:1-2).

"For all the promises of God in him are yea, and in him Amen, unto the glory of
God by us. Now he which established us with you in Christ, and has anointed us,
is God; who has also sealed us, and given the earnest of the Spirit in our hearts"
(2 Corinthians 1:20-22).

"For we are not as many, which corrupt the word of God: but as of sincerity, but as
of God" (2 Corinthians 2:17).

"And such trust have we through Christ to God-ward: Not that we are sufficient
of ourselves to think anything as of ourselves; but our sufficiency is of God; Who
also has made us able ministers of the new testament; not of the letter, but of the
spirit: for the letter killeth, but the spirit gives life. But if the ministration of death,
written and engraven in stones, was glorious, so that the children of Israel could not
stedfastly behold the face of Moses for the glory of his countenance; which glory was
to be done away: How shall not the ministration of the spirit be rather glorious" (2
Corinthians 3:4-8).

"It is the spirit that quickens; the flesh profits nothing: the words that I speak unto
you, they are spirit, and they are life" (John 6:63).

We are living in biblical times for the prophecies have come to pass: God has established his kingdom on earth. Through the blood (the testimony) of Iyesus Kristos we have come to know that Emperor Haile Sellassie The First is the Almighty Creator. Our gospel is valid because we bear witness of that which we preach; we are able to see the Father and the Son. Although it is common to deny the revelation, the Bible has indicated that those who do this shall receive eternal damnation. The LORD is not far from us and his Prophet was sent to gather all those whose faith is sincere to inherit the promises of salvation prepared from the foundation of the world: Blessed be Jah Rastafari.

The Third Letter

Those that put their trust in idols, the work of men hands, those followers of Satan; our brethren Iyesus Kristos was sent to destroy the works of the devil and his followers.

Part One:

"Cursed be the man that maketh any graven or molten image, an abomination unto the LORD, the work of the hands of the craftsman, and putteth it in a secret place: And all the people shall answer and say, Amen" (Deuteronomy 27:15).

"And you have seen their abominations, and their idols, wood and stone, silver and gold, which were among them" (Deuteronomy 29:17).

"Take heed unto yourselves, lest you forget the covenant of the LORD your God, which he made with you, and make you a graven image, or the likeness of any thing, which the LORD your God has forbidden. For the LORD your God is a consuming fire, even a jealous God" (Deuteronomy 4:23-24).

"And go not after other gods to serve them, and to worship them and provoke me not to anger with the works of your hands; and I will do you no hurt. Yet you have not listened to me, says the LORD; that you might provoke me to anger with the works of your hands to your own hurt" (Jeremiah 25:6-7).

The pope has committed the greatest atrocity against God because he presents himself as being the "holy father," this false representation is classified as idolatry according to the Bible. The authority which he yields around the world puts him in a position of enormous influence but rather than portraying the correct image of Christ, he deceives the people. When anyone professes incorrect theological principles these beliefs must be admonished because the wrong understanding will not lead you to the truth about God. The vatican is more than an institution subject to vanity, they know that they are wrong and actively advocate ungodliness, and they do this under the guise of being the vicar of Christ. The LORD shall not hold him guiltless for he is the source of all the heretical interpretations of the Bible.

"But this thing commanded I them, saying, Obey my voice, and I will be your God, and you shall be my people: and walk ye in all the ways that I have commanded you, that it may be well unto you. But they listened not, nor inclined their ear, but walked in the counsels and in the imagination of their evil heart, and went backward, and not forward. Since the day that your father came forth out of the land of Egypt unto this day, I have even sent unto you all my servants the prophets, daily rising up early and sending them: Yet they listened not to me, nor inclined their ear, but hardened their neck; they did worse than their fathers. Therefore you shall speak all these words unto them; but they will not listen to you: you shall also call them; but they will not answer you" (Jeremiah 7:23-28).

"They shall be turned back, they shall be greatly ashamed, that trust in graven images, that say to the molten images, Ye are our gods" (Isaiah 42:17).

"They shall be ashamed, and also confounded, all of them: they shall go to confusion together that are makers of idols" (Isaiah 45:16).

"Shall a man make gods unto himself, and they are no gods? Therefore, behold, I will this once cause them to know, I will cause them to know mine hand and my might; and they shall know that my name is The LORD" (Jeremiah 16:20-21).

John Paul II became very popular by invoking ancient pagan customs such as the worship of Virgin Mary; he also beatified more people than any other pope in history (up to that point). When God revealed himself on November 2, 1930, in Ethiopia, this marked the beginning of a new spiritual awakening for all of mankind. We was supposed to turn away from our old false way of thinking and learn the true meaning of righteousness from Emperor Haile Sellassie The First. But John Paul II has fought against the revelation by pulling the world back into darkness and ignoring the savior of the world. He deceived the people into keeping those customs which they are familiar with, despite the fact that they are wrong, and incorporated idolatrous beliefs into Christianity. The queen of heaven is an ancient pagan deity that the Bible condemns but the pope has invoked this spirit by worshiping the Virgin Mary and calling her the Mother of God; which is not advocated in any scripture. John Paul II also travelled all around the world and appealed to the different nations by making many of their heroes into idols so that they can pray to them. This appealed to their traditions and nationality which made it very easy for people to like him and obey. But their is a problem with that because God has challenged us to think on a higher level and do away with those teachings which are not in line with the Bible. The vatican is the antithesis of the Word of God because their mission is to preserve those ancient traditions that are grounded in idolatry and falsehoods; which makes them antichrist.

"And what agreement has the temple of God with idols? For you are the temple of the living God, as God has said, I will dwell in them, and walk in them; and I will be their God, and they shall be my people. Wherefore come out from among them, and be ye separate, says the Lord, and touch not the unclean thing; and I will receive you, And will be a Father unto you, and you shall be my sons and daughters, says the Lord Almighty" (2 Corinthians 6:16-18).

"But if any man love God, the same is known of him. As concerning therefore the eating of those things that are offered in sacrifice unto idols, we know that an idol is nothing in the world, and that there is none other God but one" (1 Corinthians 8:3-4).

"What say I then? That the idol is anything, or that which is offered in sacrifice to idols is anything? But I say, that the things which the Gentiles sacrifice, they sacrifice to devils, and not to God: and I would not that you should have fellowship with devils" (1 Corinthians 10:19-20).

We must not adhere to ungodly customs if we desire to please the Almighty. It is important that we judge spiritual matters according to the laws of God and reject everything that is contrary. The pope presents himself to be the vicar of Christ yet all of his actions are contradictory to the message of the Bible. We must read and study the scriptures so that we know what is right and wrong. The LORD has pleaded with us not to follow idolatrous principles so that we are free from evil. As sons and daughters of God we must know our Father who is in heaven, hallowed be thy name: Emperor Haile Sellassie The First.

"He smote also all the firstborn in their land, and devoured the fruit of their ground. He smote also all the firstborn in their land, the chief of all their strength" (Psalm 105:36-37).

"This I say therefore, and testify in the Lord, that you henceforth walk not as other Gentiles walk, in the vanity of their mind, Having the understanding darkened, being alienated from the life of God through the ignorance that is in them, because of the blindness of their heart: Who being past feeling have given themselves over unto lasciviousness, to work all uncleanness with greediness. But you have not so learned Christ; If so be that you have heard him, and have been taught by him, as the truth is in Jesus" (Ephesians 4:17-21).

"And we know that we are of God, and the whole world lies in wickedness. And we know that the Son of God is come, and has given us an understanding, that we may know him that is true, and we are in him that is true, even in his Son Jesus Christ. This is the true God, and eternal life. Little children, keep yourselves from idols. Amen" (1 John 5:19-21).

"Lest ye corrupt yourselves, and make you a graven image, the similitude of any figure, the likeness of male or female" (Deuteronomy 4:16).

The world has been condemned because they are contrary to the Word of God. If you are awaiting for the promises of the Bible to come to pass this only demonstrates that you have not the truth because the parables can only be understood after Christ has appeared on earth; that is why he is called the Messiah (the teacher). Furthermore there would be no need for a mediator between God and man if the world already knew the truth concerning the LORD. But the world is covered in darkness, there are evil forces at work who seek to deceive the people by teaching a false interpretation of the scriptures. The vatican is the head of this spiritual wickedness for the pope has instituted graven images as Biblical depictions which seeks to bastardize the sacred Word of God.

"Verily, verily, I say unto you, He that hears my word, and believes on him that sent me, has everlasting life, and shall not come into condemnation; but is passed from death unto life" (John 5:24).

"And it came to pass, as he spoke these things, a certain woman of the company lifted up her voice, and said unto him, Blessed is the womb that bare thee, and the paps which you have sucked. But he said, Yea, rather, blessed are they that hear the word of God, and keep it" (Luke 11:27-28).

"But he answered and said unto them, An evil and adulterous generation seeks after a sign; and there shall no sign be given to it, but the sign of the prophet Jonas: for as Jonas was three days and three nights in the whale's belly; so shall the Son of man be three days and three nights in the heart of the earth. The men of Nineveh shall rise in judgment with this generation, and shall condemn it: because they repented at the preaching of Jonas; and behold, a greater than Jonas is here. The queen of the south shall rise up in the judgment with this generation, and shall condemn it: for she came from the uttermost parts of the earth to hear the wisdom of Solomon; and, behold, a greater than Solomon is here. When the unclean spirit is gone out of a man, he walks through dry places, seeking rest, and finds none. Then he says, I will return into my house from which I came out; and when he is come, he finds it empty, swept, and garnished. Then goes he, and takes with himself seven other spirits more wicked than himself, and they enter in and dwell there: and the last state of that man is worse than the first. Even so shall it be also unto this wicked generation. While he yet talked to the people, behold, his mother and his brethren stood without, desiring to speak with him. Then one said unto him, Behold, your mother and your brethren stand without, desiring to speak with you. But he answered and said unto him that told him, Who is my mother? And who are my brethren? And he stretched forth his hand toward his disciples, and said, Behold my mother and my brethren! For whosoever shall do the will of my Father which is in heaven, the same is my brother, and sister, and mother" (Matthew 12:39-50).

"And when you pray, you shall not be as the hypocrites are: for they love to pray standing in the synagogues and in the corners of the streets, that they may be seen of men. Verily I say unto you, They have their reward. But you, when you pray, enter into your closet, and when you have shut your door, pray to your Father which is in secret; and your Father which sees in secret shall reward you openly. But when you pray, use not vain repetitions, as the heathen do: for they think that they shall be heard for their much speaking. Be not ye therefore like unto them: for your Father knows what things you have need of, before you ask him. After this manner therefore pray: Our Father which art in heaven, Hallowed be thy name" (Matthew 6:5-9).

The message of Iyesus Kristos is for us to know who the LORD is. If we say that we follow the Son but are unable to see the Father then we do not conform with the Word of God. If we say that Iyesus Kristos is the Almighty then we are not following the Bible. It is necessary to study the scriptures so that we know what is the message of salvation, so that we can guard ourselves against false teachings. The true gospel of Iyesus Kristos is greater than the common misinterpretation prevalent in the world concerning the Son of God. But we know that we hold the truth according to the scriptures because we follow the Almighty Emperor Haile Sellassie The First.

"For in six days the LORD made heaven and earth, the sea, and all that in them is, and rested the seventh day: wherefore the LORD blessed the Sabbath day, and hallowed it" (Exodus 20:11).

"Because they despised my judgments, and walked not in my statutes, but polluted my Sabbaths: for their heart went after their idols. Nevertheless mine eye spared them from destroying them, neither did I make an end of them in the wilderness. But I said unto their children in the wilderness, Walk ye not in the statutes of your fathers, neither observe their judgments, nor defile yourselves with their idols. I am the LORD thy God; walk in my statutes, and keep my judgments, and do them; and hallow my Sabbaths, and they shall be a sign between me and you, that you may know that I am the LORD your God" (Ezekiel 20:16-20).

"For he spoke in a certain place of the seventh day on this wise, And God did rest the seventh day from all his works. And in this place again, If they shall enter into my rest. Seeing therefore it remains that some must enter therein, and they to whom it was first preached entered not in because of unbelief: Again, he limited a certain day, saying in David, Today, after so long a time; as it is said, Today if you will hear his voice, harden not your hearts. For if Jesus had given them rest, then would he not afterward have spoken of another day. There remains therefore a rest to the people of God. For he that is entered into his rest, he also has ceased from his own works, as God did from his. Let us labor therefore to enter into that rest, lest any man fall after the same example of unbelief. For the word of God is quick, and powerful, and sharper than any two edged sword, piercing even to the dividing asunder of soul and spirit, and of the joints and marrow, and is a discerner of the thoughts and intents of the heart. Neither is there any creature that is not manifest in his sight: but all things are naked and opened unto the eyes of him with whom we have to do. Seeing then that we have a great high priest, that is passed into the heavens, Jesus the Son

of God, let us hold fast our profession. For we have not a high priest which cannot be touched with the feeling of our infirmities; but was in all points tempted like as we are, yet without sin. Let us therefore come boldly unto the throne of grace, that we may obtain mercy, and find grace to help in time of need" (Hebrew 4:4-16).

"And he that shall swear by heaven, swears by the throne of God, and by him that sits thereon" (Matthew 23:22).

The promise of Iyesus Kristos and the Bible is for us to see and know who God is. Only the Father can direct the world in righteousness; that is why he is the Savior and although Haile Sellassie The First is the one and only King of Kings and Lord of Lords, many people ignore this sign despite the message of the Bible which says that God is the first and the last person to come in this name. If the preachers or your friends and family do not accept the divinity of the Emperor then most people would not recognize His Majesty as being the Almighty; despite what the Bible says. If they was not born into this culture then a lot of people would feel as if it does not relate to them. This demonstrates that they put their trust in man and not God. But we also must admonish leaders such as the pope who has been heralded with papal supremacy, the ruler of the largest religious sect on earth with over a billion members worldwide, to direct those who look up to him accurately. This necessary edict has not been honored and as a result the people are led astray. If the world kept the commandments of God they would know that Haile Sellassie The First is the Almighty Father because the Sabbath Day signifies the fulfillment of prophecy.

"God, who at sundry times and in divers manners spoke in time past unto the fathers by the prophets, has in these last days spoken unto us by his Son, whom he has appointed heir of all things, by whom also he made the worlds; Who being the brightness of his glory, and the express image of his person, and upholding all things by the word of his power, when he had by himself purged our sins, sat down on the right hand of the Majesty on high" (Hebrew 1:1-3).

"Now of the things which we have spoken this is the sum: We have such a high priest, who is set on the right hand of the throne of the Majesty in the heavens" (Hebrew 8:1).

"That the God of our Lord Jesus Christ, the Father of glory, may give unto you the spirit of wisdom and revelation in the knowledge of him: The eyes of your

understanding being enlightened; that you may know what is the hope of his call-
ing, and what the riches of the glory of his inheritance in the saints, and what is the
exceeding greatness of his power to us-ward who believe, according to the working
of his mighty power, which he wrought in Christ, when he raised him from the dead,
and set him at his own right hand in the heavenly places" (Ephesians 1:17-20).

"And to make all men see what is the fellowship of the mystery, which from the be-
ginning of the world has been hid in God, who created all things by Jesus Christ:
To the intent that now unto the principles and powers in heavenly places might be
known by the church the manifold wisdom of God, according to the eternal purpose
which he purposed in Christ Jesus our Lord: in whom we have boldness and access
with confidence by the faith of him. Wherefore I desire that you faint not at my trib-
ulations for you, which is your glory. For this cause I bow my knees unto the Father
of our Lord Jesus Christ, of whom the whole family in heaven and earth is named,
that he would grant you, according to the riches of his glory, to be strengthened with
might by his Spirit in the inner man; that Christ may dwell in your hearts by faith;
that you, being rooted and grounded in love, may be able to comprehend with all
saints what is the breadth, and length, and depth, and height" (Ephesians 3:9-18).

To be a Christian is more than just wearing your faith on your sleeve. It
is important to first fully understand the gospel of Iyesus Kristos so that the
principles which we relay to others are correct and in line with the message
of the Bible. If anyone professes to be a Christian then they must declare that
the Almighty Father has come in the flesh because that is what the scriptures
foretold. It does not say that Iyesus Kristos is God therefore a lot of people
fall short of following the Word. The vatican is the chief institution of erroneous theology (idolatry) and they disseminate false information intentionally.
If you cannot show the people who God is then you are not a real Christian;
unfortunately paintings and graven images are not sufficient evidence according to the scriptures. The only way to be one of the sons or daughters of God is
to declare that Emperor Haile Sellassie The First is the Almighty. We will be
on the right hand side of the LORD, just as Iyesus Kristos is, if we accept the
revelation.

"By this we know that we love the children of God, when we love God, and keep his
commandments. For this is the love of God, that we keep his commandments: and
his commandments are not grievous" (1 John 5:2-3).

"And hereby we do know that we know him, if we keep his commandments. He that says, I know him, and keeps not his commandments, is a liar, and the truth is not in him. But whoso keeps his word, in him verily is the love of God perfected: hereby know we that we are in him" (1 John 2:3-7).

"The Grace of our Lord Jesus Christ be with you all. Amen. Now to him that is of power to establish you according to my gospel, and the preaching of Jesus Christ, according to the revelation of the mystery, which was kept secret since the world began, But now is made manifest, and by the scriptures of the prophets, according to the commandment of the everlasting God, made known to all nations for the obedience of faith: To God only wise, be glory through Jesus Christ forever. Amen" (Romans 16:24-27).

"Look to yourselves, that we lose not those things which we have wrought, but that we receive a full reward. Whosoever transgresses, and abides not in the doctrine of Christ, has not God. He that abides in the doctrine of Christ, he has both the Father and the Son. If there come any unto you, and bring not this doctrine, receive him not into your house, neither bid him God speed: For he that bids him God speed is partaker of his evil deeds" (2 John 1:8-11).

The commandments indicate that we must believe in God therefore you must know who God is before you can praise him; for the LORD is greater than any rhetorical statement. All the names and titles attributed to the Almighty are descriptions of him but it is only when you can identify the Supreme Being that you would be following the message of Iyesus Kristos. The Son has declared the Father unto us, so that we may know him who is true: Emperor Haile Sellassie The First.

"For these are wells without water, clouds that are carried with a tempest; to whom the mist of darkness is reserved forever. For when they speak great swelling words of vanity, they allure through the lusts of the flesh, through much wantonness, those that were clean escaped from them who live in error. While they promise them liberty, they themselves are the servants of corruption: for of whom a man is overcome, of the same is he brought in bondage. For if after they have escaped the pollutions of the world through the knowledge of the Lord and Savior Jesus Christ, they are again entangled therein, and overcome, the latter end is worse with them than the beginning. For it had been better for them not to have known the way of righteousness,

than, after they have known it, to turn from the holy commandment delivered unto them" (2 Peter 2:17-21).

"The LORD is well pleased for his righteousness' sake; he will magnify the law, and make it honorable" (Isaiah 42:21).

"For the truth's sake, which dwells in us, and shall be with us forever" (2 John 1:2).

"Let them give glory unto the LORD, and declare his praise in the islands" (Isaiah 42:12).

We know that November 2, 1930, in Ethiopia is the Sabbath of God. For that is the day that Emperor Haile Sellassie The First was crowned King of Kings and Lord of Lords. The devil and his angels seek to exalt themselves above His Majesty and change time and law by denying the revelation. It is common to refer to Haile Sellassie The First as being King of Kings, Elect of God, Conquering Lion of the Tribe of Judah, but these are not all of his commendations. There is a secret agenda ordered by the vatican to discredit the Emperor's name and accomplishments; that is why they seem to cleverly omit the fact that His Majesty held the title of Lord of Lords. They do admit that Haile Sellassie The First is King of Kings because there is a long list of rulers who held this rank and they want to associate him with being an ordinary leader like the rest of them. But His Majesty was greater than them all and he held the highest titles as the King of Kings and Lord of Lords. If we shall turn from this herald and seek another sign, then the only thing that shall be given is bondage and retribution. Haile Sellassie The First is the Almighty and besides him there is no Savior.

"Grace be with you, mercy, and peace, from God the Father, and from the Lord Jesus Christ, the Son of the Father, in truth and love. I rejoiced greatly that I found of your children walking in truth, as we have received a commandment from the Father" (2 John 1:3-4).

"He sends forth his commandment upon earth: his word runs very swiftly" (Psalm 147:15).

"I cried with my whole heart; hear me, O LORD: I will keep your statutes" (Psalm 119:145).

"Your word is true from the beginning: and every one of your righteous judgments endures forever" (Psalm 119:160).

"Concerning your testimonies, I have known of old that you have founded them forever" (Psalm 119:152).

"Forever, O LORD, your word is settled in heaven" (Psalm 119:89).

"Your righteousness is an everlasting righteousness, and your law is the truth" (Psalm 119:142).

The message of the Bible and the commandments of God are for us to worship the LORD in spirit and in truth. This means that we must put our trust in the true and living God Emperor Haile Sellassie The First. The sign of the first and the last King of Kings and Lord of Lords is an everlasting covenant that cannot be erased or proven wrong because we are referring to historical facts not theory. This is a judgment that shall stand forever because it is the truth; that is why he is called the eternal God. Generation after generation shall learn about His Majesty and realize that his philosophy is the saving grace for all humanity. Haile Sellassie The First does not live forever in the flesh because he is not a charlatan and His Majesty cautioned us not to associate him with idolatrous beliefs. God has left us an enduring legacy, that is why Haile Sellassie The First was referred to as being an immortal; we must learn from his high example so that we can also make a lasting positive contribution towards the advancement of civilization.

"Blessed are they that do his commandments, that they may have right to the tree of life, and may enter in through the gates into the city" (Revelation 22:14).

"Open to me the gates of righteousness: I will go into them, and I will praise the LORD: This gate of the LORD, into which the righteous shall enter" (Psalm 118:19-20).

"Let us hear the conclusion of the whole matter: Fear God, and keep his commandments: for this is the whole duty of man. For God shall bring every work into judgment, with every secret thing, whether it be good, or whether it be evil" (Ecclesiastes 12:13-14).

"I counsel thee to keep the king's commandment, and that in regard of the oath of God. Be not hasty to go out of his sight: stand not in an evil thing; for he does whatsoever pleases him. Where the word of a king is, there is power: and who may say unto him, What doest thou? Whoso keeps the commandments shall feel no evil thing: and a wise man's heart discerns both time and judgment" (Ecclesiastes 8:2-5).

"What! Know ye not that your body is the temple of the Holy Ghost which is in you, which you have of God, and you are not your own" (1 Corinthians 6:19).

"Wherefore the law is holy, and the commandment holy, and just, and good" (Romans 7:12).

"Seeing it is one God, which shall justify the circumcision by faith, and uncircumcision through faith. Do we then make void the law through faith? God forbid: yea, we establish the law" (Romans 3:30-31).

We will worship Emperor Haile Sellassie The First because the Bible says that the King of Kings and Lord of Lords is the Almighty Father. There is only one God and we will honor his Word and keep his commandments. If the whole world goes astray and neglects his saving grace, we shall be separate from the evil. His Majesty is worthy to be praised, the Bible is a narrative of his glory from beginning to end. Iyesus Kristos has kept us in the name of his Father: Emperor Haile Sellassie The First. We shall do well in keeping the testimony of the only begotten Son of God; Blessed be Jah Rastafari, the Most High King of Glory, Creator of Heaven and earth.

Part Two:

"They that forsake the law praise the wicked: but such as keep the law contend with them. Evil men understand not judgment: but they that seek the LORD understand all things" (Proverbs 28:4-5).

"For I delight in the law of God after the inward man" (Romans 7:22).

"And the smoke of their torment ascendeth up forever and ever: and they have no rest day nor night, who worship the beast and his image, and whosoever receives the mark of his name. Here is the patience of the saints: here are they that keep the commandments of God, and the faith of Jesus" (Revelation 14:11-12).

The mark of the beast signifies those who are in bondage spiritually. The vatican has made it a point to oversee all the religions in the world by proclaiming that everyone must go through the pope in order to get to God; Rome investigates all theological sects to ensure that their authority is not threatened. If your faith is not true to the LORD then this is categorized as idolatry for which the pope is the head. False doctrines will not free the world from the corrupt ideologies which cause people to suffer. The vatican is the mastermind behind all the chaos on earth; their history illustrates their intentions and because Rome knows that they are engaged in a devilish plot to oppress humanity, they must keep an eye out for the LORD's trumpet which has been prophesied to stop them. Common people are unaware of this spiritual war and this illustrates that you cannot initiate a change in policy without first invoking peoples consciousness. The pope wishes for the world to remain asleep, subject to bondage and corruption, because under this veil evil shall continue to thrive and further debase humanity. But God has offered us salvation in sending forth Jesus Christ to give us the gospel of salvation which shall destroy all the snares of the devil and introduce heaven on earth.

"So then they that are in the flesh cannot please God. But you are not in the flesh, but in the Spirit, if so be that the Spirit of God dwell in you. Now if any man have not the Spirit of Christ, he is none of his. And if Christ be in you, the body is dead because of sin; but the Spirit is life because of righteousness. But if the Spirit of him that raised up Jesus from the dead dwell in you, he that raised up Christ from the dead shall also quicken your mortal bodies by his Spirit that dwells in you. For as many as are led by the Spirit of God, they are the sons of God. For you have not received the spirit of bondage again to fear; but you have received the Spirit of adoption, whereby we cry, Abba, Father. The Spirit itself bears witness with our spirit, that we are the children of God: And if children, then heirs; heirs of God, and joint-heirs with Christ; if so be that we suffer with him, that we may be also glorified together. For I reckon that the sufferings of this present time are not worthy to be compared with the glory which shall be revealed in us" (Romans 8:8-11, 14-18).

"Now the God of patience and consolation grant you to be likeminded one toward another according to Christ Jesus: That you may with one mind and one mouth glorify God, even the Father of our Lord Jesus Christ" (Romans 15:6-8).

"The Spirit of the Lord is upon me, because he has anointed me to preach the gospel to the poor; he has sent me to heal the brokenhearted, to preach deliverance to the

captives, and recovering of sight to the blind, to set at liberty them that are bruised, To preach the acceptable year of the Lord" (Luke 4:18-19).

"Howbeit then, when you knew not God, you did service unto them which by nature are no gods. But now, after you have known God, or rather are known of God, how turn you again to the weak and beggarly elements, whereunto you desire again to be in bondage? Ye observe days, and months, and times, and years. I am afraid of you, lest I have bestowed upon you labor in vain. Brethren, I beseech you, be as I am; for I am as you are: ye have not injured me at all" (Galatians 4:8-12).

The spirit of bondage, for which the pope is at the helm, represents the incorrect dogmas which prevent mankind from following their Creator Emperor Haile Sellassie The First to the hilt. This mettle is found in every religious sect including Christianity, Islam, Jewish, and even our Rastafarian kinsmen who all adhere to false principles such as the supernatural which leads to a false interpretation of scripture and an amoral perspective on life. Leonard Howell, who is historically referred to as being the first Rastaman, did an amazing job of organizing and centralizing the people but he fell short of teaching them the fullness about His Majesty. He, along with Joseph Nathaniel Hibbert, are recognized as being the pioneers of the movement and they viewed themselves as being modern day Melchizedeks,[1] which in principle would be suitable, only if they knew how to interpret the King of Salem correctly. But they viewed the scriptures as being literal which led them to believe that man can live forever in the flesh. This belief defies the teachings and the reality of Emperor Haile Sellassie The First. Our Rastafarian elders deserve great credit for their brave efforts in raising awareness to His Majesty's divinity but the only one who can teach us the true knowledge of God is Jesus Christ. That is why the scriptures have forewarned us to be of one mind in the faith because even those who claim to be of Rastafari do not follow His Majesty. Haile Sellassie The First has instructed the world in righteousness, there is no better counsel for us to adhere to, all we have to do is follow his commandments instead of making up our own philosophy.

"The Spirit of the LORD GOD is upon me; because the LORD has anointed me to preach good tidings unto the meek; he has sent me to bind up the brokenhearted,

---

[1] Murrell, Nathaniel Samuel, Afro-Caribbean Religions: An Introduction to their Historical, Cultural, and Sacred Traditions, page 306

to proclaim liberty to the captives, and the opening of the prison to them that are bound; To proclaim the acceptable year of the LORD, and the day of vengeance of our God; to comfort all that mourn; To appoint unto them that mourn in Zion, to give unto them beauty for ashes, the oil of joy for mourning, the garment of praise for the spirit of heaviness; that they might be called trees of righteousness, the planting of the LORD, that he might be glorified" (Isaiah 61:1-3).

"And you shall know that I have sent this commandment unto you, that my covenant might be with Levi, says the LORD of hosts. My covenant was with him of life and peace; and I gave them to him for the fear wherewith he feared me, and was afraid before my name. The law of truth was in his mouth, and iniquity was not found in his lips: he walked with me in peace and equity, and did turn many away from iniquity. For the priest's lips should keep knowledge, and they should seek the law at his mouth: for he is the messenger of the LORD of hosts" (Malachi 2:4-7).

"But ye shall be named the Priests of the LORD: men shall call you the Ministers of our God: you shall eat the riches of the Gentiles, and in their glory shall you boast yourselves" (Isaiah 61:6).

"Wherefore, holy brethren, partakers of the heavenly calling, consider the Apostle and High Priest of our profession, Christ Jesus" (Hebrew 3:1).

For the most part, the first time you attempt to do something you are not really proficient, as compared to a person who has experience doing it. Whatever the task may be, people become efficient through trial and error; by learning from their mistakes. This same depiction is prophesied in the Bible, that the first man is dust but the latter is the Lord from heaven. Which means that the first understanding of God was carnal but Jesus Christ was sent to correct their errors. Therefore no one should be offended if we state that the entire religious world, along with the Rastafarian elders, have an inaccurate understanding of spiritual matters; Haile Sellassie The First himself instructed everyone to follow the Son of Man for this same reason. Christ is the high priest of God who preached the law of truth and saved us from unsound doctrines.

"For God is not unrighteous to forget your work and labor of love, which you have showed toward his name, in that you have ministered to the saints, and do minister" (Hebrew 6:10).

"And no man takes this honor unto himself, but he that is called of God, as was Aaron. So also Christ glorified not himself to be made a high priest; but he that said unto him, Thou art my Son, today have I begotten thee. As he said also in another place, Thou art a priest forever after the order of Melchisedec" (Hebrew 5:4-6).

"The LORD has sworn, and will not repent, Thou art a priest forever after the order of Melchizedek" (Psalm 110:4).

"Forasmuch as ye know that you were not redeemed with corruptible things, as silver and gold, from your vain conversation received by tradition from your fathers; But with the precious blood of Christ, as of a lamb without blemish and without spot: Who verily was foreordained before the foundation of the world, but was manifest in these last times for you. Who by him do believe in God, that raised him up from the dead, and gave him glory; that your faith and hope might be in God" (1 Peter 1:18-21).

Every intention of the sincere devotee of the LORD is not to please men but the Almighty. Therefore if we find that we have been led astray by spurious philosophies, how can we continue to observe these false ordinances; or do we consider ourselves to be legitimate without investigating the validity of our faith? Jesus Christ is a priest after the highest order which means that he is the only one qualified to teach us about the LORD Emperor Haile Sellassie The First. Those who came before him are thieves and robbers, which means their doctrine had blemishes (inaccuracies), therefore His Majesty had to send forth his Son because the world knew not righteousness. After we have learned about Haile Sellassie The First, how can we turn away from his most excellent counsel, back to the irrational dogmas found throughout the world? The Rastafarian elders were supposed to repent from their erroneous beliefs which do not coincide with the teachings of His Majesty, instead they tried to incorporate agnostic ideas into the faith, in the same manner that the pope included paganism with Christianity, but this endeavor has been destined for failure because our brethren Jesus Christ executes an impartial judgment upon all the inhabitants on earth.

"But there were false prophets also among the people, even as there shall be false teachers among you, who privily shall bring in damnable heresies, even denying the Lord that bought them, and bring upon themselves swift destruction. And many

shall follow their pernicious ways; by reason of whom the way of truth shall be evil spoken of" (2 Peter 2:1-2).

"Now the Spirit speaks expressly, that in the latter times some shall depart from the faith, giving heed to seducing spirits, and doctrines of devils; Speaking lies in hypocrisy; having their conscience seared with a hot iron" (1 Timothy 4:1-2).

"For then shall be great tribulation, such as was not since the beginning of the world to this time, no, nor ever shall be. And except those days should be shortened, there should no flesh be saved: but for the elect's sake those days shall be shortened. Then if any man shall say unto you, Lo, here is Christ, or there; believe it not. For there shall arise false Christs, and false prophets, and shall show great signs and wonders; insomuch that, if it were possible, they shall deceive the very elect. Behold, I have told you before. Wherefore if they shall say unto you, Behold, he is in the desert; go not forth: behold, he is in the secret chambers; believe it not" (Matthew 24:21-26).

Leonard Howell wrote a book called "The Promised Key" which is predominately a carbon copy of "The Royal Parchment Scroll for Black Supremacy" but it also includes his views regarding the fact that Rastafari is the living God. He taught that black people are the chosen based upon their skin color which is a concept that Haile Sellassie The First never condoned. In fact His Majesty actively challenged the world to look past race because it is a superficial and artificial method of judgment. Howell also viewed himself as being Melchizedek which makes him a false Christ because that is one of the titles of the Messiah; who did not glorify himself. The high priest of the LORD who has no father or mother is referring to Jesus, the preacher of a better covenant, not made by man; which means not conceived under incorrect precepts. Howell also authored his work under the pen name "Gangunguru Maragh" which means King of Kings in the Hindi language.[2] This demonstrates his sentiments that he considered himself to be equal with Haile Sellassie The First, he has expressed this position on many occasions which contradicts the idea of declaring Rastafari to be the Supreme God. The Bible has declared that there will be false teachers, false Christ's who shall do great works but shall not follow the instructions of His Majesty.

---

[2] Howell, Leonard P., The Promised Key, page xv

"Unto the pure all things are pure: but unto them that are defiled and unbelieving is nothing pure; but even their mind and conscience is defiled. They profess that they know God; but in works they deny him, being abominable, and disobedient, and unto every good work reprobate" (Titus 1:15-16).

"For this ye know, that no whoremonger, nor unclean person, nor covetous man, who is an idolater, has any inheritance in the kingdom of Christ and of God. Let no man deceive you with vain words: for because of these things comes the wrath of God upon the children of disobedience. Be not ye therefore partakers with them. For you were sometimes darkness, but now are you light in the Lord: walk as children of light: For the fruit of the Spirit is in all goodness and righteousness and truth" (Ephesians 5:5-9).

"That their hearts might be comforted, being knit together in love, and unto all riches of the full assurance of understanding, to the acknowledgement of the mystery of God, and of the Father, and of Christ; In whom are hid all the treasures of wisdom and knowledge. And this I say, lest any man should beguile you with enticing words. For though I be absent in the flesh, yet am I with you in the spirit, joying and beholding your order, and the stedfastness of your faith in Christ. As you have therefore received Christ Jesus the Lord, so walk ye in him: Rooted and built up in him, and established in the faith, as you have been taught, abounding therein with thanksgiving. Beware lest any man spoil you through philosophy and vain deceit, after the tradition of men, after the rudiments of the world, and not after Christ. For in him dwells all the fullness of the Godhead bodily" (Colossians 2:2-9).

Leonard Howell is also credited with establishing the principles and structure of the "Nyabinghi Order" which is currently the largest faction of the different Rastafari sects. Howell called for the hatred of white people and to exact revenge upon them due to their imperialistic ways and false religion. Nyabinghi emerged to define itself under a similar terminology: "death to all white and black down-pressers." With this we must take into account the fact that Emperor Haile Sellassie The First operated on a higher level for which those who claim to follow him never exacted. When the Italians sought to annihilate all of Ethiopia, His Majesty did not seek revenge or call upon his people to hate them. After he regained control of his country, he told the Ethiopians not to render evil for evil, not to harm them, and he allowed the Italians to stay in his country if they would assist him in rebuilding; that is a perfect example to emulate but the strength to follow his precepts seem to be lost. We must be careful to study these issues objectively because rhetorically a person can claim to follow Rastafari but that does not mean that they actually do. Someone can wear a certain hairstyle and appear to be part of the movement yet their heart is far from the Lord. It would be in our best interest to avoid unclean doctrines which will only continue the cycle of hatred and corruption; Jesus Christ is the only one who can preach the true gospel of Rastafari.

"Therefore, seeing we have this ministry, as we have received mercy, we faint not; But have renounced the hidden things of dishonesty, not walking in craftiness, nor handling the word of God deceitfully; but, by manifestation of the truth, commending ourselves to every man's conscience in the sight of God. But if our gospel be hid, it is hid to them that are lost: In whom the god of this world has blinded the minds of them which believe not, lest the light of the glorious gospel of Christ, who is the image of God, should shine unto them" (2 Corinthians 4:1-4).

"For I am not ashamed of the gospel of Christ: for it is the power of God unto salvation to everyone that believes; to the Jew first, and also to the Greek. For therein is the righteousness of God revealed from faith to faith: as it is written, The just shall live by faith. For the wrath of God is revealed from heaven against all ungodliness and unrighteousness of men, who hold the truth in unrighteousness; Because that which may be known of God is manifest in them; for God has showed it unto them. For the invisible things of him from the creation of the world are clearly seen, being understood by the things that are made, even his eternal power and Godhead; so that they are without excuse" (Romans 1:16-20).

"Be it known therefore unto you, that the salvation of God is sent unto the Gentiles, and that they will hear it" (Acts 28:28).

"God that made the world and all things therein, seeing that he is Lord of heaven and earth, dwells not in temples made with hands; Neither is worshipped with men's hands, as though he needed any thing, seeing he gives to all life, and breath, and all things. And has made of one blood all nations of men for to dwell on all the face of the earth, and has determined the times before appointed, and the bounds of their habitation; That they should seek the Lord, if haply they might feel after him, and find him, though he be not far from every one of us: For in him we live, and move, and have our being; as certain also of your own poets have said, For we are also his offspring. Forasmuch then as we are the offspring of God, we ought not to

think that the Godhead is like unto gold, or silver, or stone, graven by art and man's device" (Acts 17:24-29).

The real representation of Rastafari must be according to the principles and high example of the Emperor and not corresponding to a man made tradition that has nothing to do with the mission of Haile Sellassie The First. We are not afraid to tell it like it is because His Majesty said, "During Our lifetime, We have unfailingly done what We have felt, before Almighty God, to be Our duty to Our people and Our nation, no matter what the cost to Ourself. You must do likewise."[3] We will die for the gospel's sake because we put God first, above the vanity of man, and above the allure of this world. Jesus Christ did what no other man would do and that is to follow God Emperor Haile Sellassie The First in spirit and in truth; his message is the healing of the nations, the saving grace for all mankind, redemption from the corrupt doctrines that lead the world astray and trigger the vile policies that destroy humanity.

Part Three:

"Thus says the LORD the King of Israel, and his redeemer the LORD of hosts; I am the first, and the last; and beside me there is no God. And who, as I, shall call, and shall declare it, and set it in order for me, since I appointed the ancient people? And the things that are coming, and shall come, let them show unto them. Fear ye not, neither be afraid: have not I told you from that time, and have declared it? You are even my witnesses. Is there a God beside me? Yea, there is no God; I know not any. They that make a graven image are all of them vanity; and their delectable things shall not profit; and they are their own witnesses; they see not, nor know; that they may be ashamed. Who has formed a god, or molten a graven image that is profitable for nothing? Behold, all his fellows shall be ashamed; and the workmen, they are of men: let them all be gathered together, let them stand up; yet they shall fear, and they shall be ashamed together" (Isaiah 44:6-11).

"Whosoever commits sin transgresses also the law: for sin is the transgression of the law" (1 John 3:4).

"For in that day every man shall cast away his idols of silver, and his idols of gold, which your own hands have made unto you for a sin" (Isaiah 31:7).

---

[3] The Selected Speeches of Haile Selassie I, page 415

"Thou shall not make unto thee any graven image, or any likeness of any thing that is in heaven above, or that is in the earth beneath, or that is in the water under the earth" (Exodus 20:4).

The world has turned their backs on God Emperor Haile Sellassie The First because they would rather formulate their own doctrines rather than follow what His Majesty instructed us to do. Those who have made a graven image (devised untrue articles of faith) shall be put to shame by Christ who shall expose all those who take the LORD's name in vain. Iyesus has been sent to defend the truth about Rastafari by waging a spiritual battle against every misrepresentation of God. The ancient people appointed to declare his glory and crush the wicked is referring to the people who was with him in the beginning; meaning those who worship Haile Sellassie The First in spirit and in truth. Your faith is not real if you do not follow His Majesty's precepts. Although Ethiopia is the oldest nation on earth, the Emperor was a reformer, he sought to liberate the farmers from their cumbersome daily operation so that his county can compete in the global economy. Therefore we ought not to hold onto obsolete customs which hinder our progress in these modern times and disavow the teachings of Haile Sellassie The First.

"Then shall it be for a man to burn: for he will take thereof, and warm himself; yea, he kindles it, and bakes bread; yea, he makes a god, and worships it; he makes it a graven image, and falls down to it. And the residue thereof he maketh a god, even his graven image: he falls down unto it, and worships it, and prays to it, and says, Deliver me; for thou art my god. They have not known nor understood: for he has shut their eyes, that they cannot see; and their hearts, that they cannot understand" (Isaiah 44:15, 17-18).

"Beloved, believe not every spirit, but try the spirits whether they are of God: because many false prophets are gone out into the world. We are of God: he that knows God hears us; he that is not of God hears not us. Hereby know we the spirit of truth, and the spirit of error." (1 John 4:1, 6).

"Every man is brutish by his knowledge; every founder is confounded by the graven image: for his molten image is falsehood, and there is no breath in them. They are vanity, the work of errors: in the time of their visitation they shall perish" (Jeremiah 51:17-18).

The Nyabinghi council claims to uphold the ancient traditions but this is a form of idolatry because it defies everything that Haile Sellassie The First was working towards. Our goal should not be to plant a garden in the mountains but rather to modernize all aspects of industry so that our country does not lag behind and suffer. His Majesty also was highly educated and spoke properly, we therefore should be the same way instead of using slang words like *InI, Ises, Idren,* etc. The sad reality is that this culture was developed by many illiterate and reprobate elders. That is where the heavy usage of the letter "I" comes from, it is a contortion of His Majesty's name "Selassie I." They mistook this to be a regular "I" but it really means "The First;" they also mispronounce His Majesty's name using the letter "I" because they did not understand the correct context or definition of this term.

"Set up the standard upon the walls of Babylon, make the watch strong, set up the watchmen, prepare the ambushes: for the LORD has both devised and done that which he spoke against the inhabitants of Babylon. O thou that dwells upon many waters, abundant in treasures, your end is come, and the measure of your covetousness" (Jeremiah 51:12-13).

"And there came one of the seven angels which had the seven vials, and talked with me, saying unto me, Come hither; I will show unto you the judgment of the great whore that sits upon many waters: with whom the kings of the earth have committed fornication, and the inhabitants of the earth have been made drunk with the wine of her fornication" (Revelation 17:1-2, 5).

"A drought is upon her waters; and they shall be dried up: for it is the land of graven images, and they are mad upon their idols" (Jeremiah 50:38).

"Therefore, behold, the days come, that I will do judgment upon the graven images of Babylon: and her whole land shall be confounded, and all her slain shall fall in the midst of her" (Jeremiah 51:47).

The whole earth is immersed in popery for the spiritual sense in humanity is lost; they do not know what is right. Satan has polluted the earth through false religious precepts and as a result the people are blind to the truth in the Bible that Emperor Haile Sellassie The First is God. Christ has been sent to put the world in remembrance of His Majesty The Father because the LORD is the judgment. The current calamities that we are faced with is directly related to the absence of the Almighty. But it is not God who is oblivious to his creation, it is mankind that has turned away from him and neglected his saving grace. We have found that there is none righteous because those who acknowledge His Majesty as well as the disbelievers, have both disregarded his instructions and failed where it matters the most. If we do not observe the principles of Emperor Haile Sellassie The First then we will be vain in all of our pursuits which always constitutes a miserable existence.

"Thy name, O LORD, endures forever; and your memorial, O LORD, throughout all generations. For the LORD, will judge his people, and he will repent himself concerning his servants. The idols of the heathen are silver and gold, the work of men's hands. They have mouths, but they speak not; eyes have they, but they see not; They have ears, but they hear not; neither is their any breath in their mouths" (Psalm 135:13-18).

"Confounded be all they that serve graven images, that boast themselves of idols: worship him, all ye gods. Zion heard, and was glad; and the daughters of Judah rejoiced because of your judgments, O LORD. For you, LORD, art high above all the earth: you art exalted far above all gods. Ye that love the LORD, hate evil: he preserves the souls of his saints; he delivers them out of the hand of the wicked" (Psalm 97:7-10).

"The LORD has brought forth our righteousness: come, and let us declare in Zion the work of the LORD our God. Make bright the arrows; gather the shields: the LORD has raised up the spirit of the kings of the Medes: for his device is against Babylon, to destroy it; because it is the vengeance of the LORD, the vengeance of his temple" (Jeremiah 51:10-11).

Haile Sellassie The First deserves to be glorified with the most holy of all sacraments for he alone is God. We have to make sure that we do not take his name in vain by associating him with falsehoods or idolatry. The LORD will judge the world through his Prophet Jesus Christ and eliminate all of those cunningly devised fables which do not agree with the truth. For example: the term "Nyabinghi" originates from Uganda, where it was a women's liberation front created to oppose British colonization. These female warriors would intreat the supernatural force of a mythical amazon queen called Nya Binghi to help them defeat the invading Europeans. But this could not reasonably be justified as being an honest representation of Haile Sellassie The First. Because

His Majesty was an ardent opponent of imperialism yet he did not instruct his people to pray for magical powers when the Italians attacked their country or to call upon false deities for assistance. The Emperor was a staunch advocate of education so people can analyze the world logically which would enable us to solve our problems effectively. The supernatural is a false concept, this is not of God but the devil, His Majesty has spoken out against these type of delusive interpretations. We cannot associate Nyabinghi with Rastafari and win favor from the LORD; Haile Sellassie The First is not pleased with sacrilege. Our Rasta kinsfolk have also falsely asserted that His Majesty is the head of the Nyabinghi and that he sanctioned their order. Now if the energy we put into formulating lies was redirected towards obeying the LORD's commands then righteousness would prevail and the name of Emperor Haile Sellassie The First would be sanctified with the rightful dignity due unto his person.

"And I heard a great voice out of the temple saying to the seven angels, Go your ways, and pour out the vials of the wrath of God upon the earth. And the first went, and poured out his vial upon the earth; and there fell a noisome and grievous sore upon the men which had the mark of the beast, and upon them which worshipped his image" (Revelation 16:1-2).

"The burden of Babylon, which Isaiah the son of Amoz did see. Lift ye up a banner upon the high mountain, exalt the voice unto them, shake the hand, that they may go into the gates of the nobles. I have commanded my sanctified ones, I have also called my mighty ones for mine anger, even them that rejoice in my highness" (Isaiah 13:1-3).

"And when the LORD thy God shall deliver them before you; you shall smite them, and utterly destroy them; you shall make no covenant with them, nor show mercy unto them: Neither shall you make marriages with them; your daughter you shall not give unto his son, nor his daughter shall you take unto your son. For they will turn away your son from following me, that they may serve other gods: so will the anger of the LORD be kindled against you, and destroy you suddenly. But thus shall ye deal with them; ye shall destroy their altars, and break down their images, and cut down their groves, and burn their graven images with fire. For you art a holy people unto the LORD thy God: the LORD thy God has chosen thee to be a special people unto himself, above all people that are upon the face of the earth. The LORD did not set his love upon you, nor choose you, because you were more in number than any people; for you were the fewest of all people" (Deuteronomy 7:2-7).

The judgment of God Emperor Haile Sellassie The First is upon everyone who has fallen short of his glory and that would entail the entire world. Those whose love for the LORD is sincere will accept correction so that they may be accepted by His Majesty but those who are reprobate will harden their hearts and seek to fight against the truth. It has been commanded by God to destroy all the false philosophies which prevent the people from entering into the true light of Haile Sellassie The First. We therefore would have to rebuke Nyabinghi and all other fraudulent representations of Rastafari. Frederico Philos, an Italian journalist, sought to justify the Italian invasion of Ethiopia by writing a newspaper article in 1934 which said that His Majesty was elected as the head of the Nyabinghi Order. Philos claimed that Haile Sellassie The First was seeking to go to war against the Europeans due to their pillage of the black continent and that the Emperor was elected by all the African leaders to be their God, Messiah, and Savior of the Negro race.[4] This propaganda piece was written to discredit His Majesty but instead of being rejected by the Rastafarians due to its grossly inadequate portrayal of the Emperor, it somehow has been incorporated as one of the main pillars of the movement. It must be understood that Haile Sellassie The First was not organizing a race war against the Europeans and he never invoked false deities. The article by Frederico Philos was written to portray His Majesty as an infidel, incompetent, and dangerous leader who needed to be removed from office; the Fascists were trying to justify their invasion. It is therefore an unsound meditation on the part of the Rastafarians to accept the notion that Haile Sellassie The First is the head of the Nyabinghi Order when this idea was devised by those who sought to destroy Ethiopia.

"And I saw another sign in heaven, great and marvelous, seven angels having the seven last plagues; for in them is filled up the wrath of God. And I saw as it were a sea of glass mingled with fire: and them that had gotten the victory over the beast, and over his image, and over his mark, and over the number of his name, stand on the sea of glass, having the harps of God. And they sing the song of Moses the servant of God, and the song of the Lamb, saying, Great and marvelous are thy works, Lord God Almighty; just and true are your ways, thou King of saints. Who shall not fear you, O Lord, and glorify your name? For thou only art holy: for all nations shall come and worship before thee; for your judgments are made manifest" (Revelation 15:1-4).

---

[4] Murrell, Nathaniel Samuel, Afro-Caribbean Religions, page 305

"These are the statues and judgments, which you shall observe to do in the land, which the LORD God of your father gives you to possess it, all the days that you live upon the earth. You shall utterly destroy all the places, wherein the nations which ye shall possess served their gods, upon the high mountains, and upon the hills, and under every green tree: And ye shall overthrow their altars, and break their pillars, and burn their groves with fire; and ye shall hew down the graven images of their gods, and destroy the names of them out of that place" (Deuteronomy 12:1-3).

"So that not only this our craft is in danger to be set at nought; but also that the temple of the great goddess Diana should be despised, and her magnificence should be destroyed, whom all Asia and the world worships" (Acts 19:27).

Emperor Haile Sellassie The First was an excellent statesman, as such he was graceful and debonair in conducting his business and resolving disputes. The purpose and character which His Majesty God the Father displayed is different from his Prophet whom it is written will carry out the judgement.[5] The scriptures calls for the destruction of idols because the false philosophies that corrupt the conscience of men manifests itself through the immorality, injustice, and ignorance which debase humanity. Being that Haile Sellassie The First accepts the Bible he therefore would not condemn the breaking of statues for which it is written that his messenger was commanded to execute. Everyone has a unique purpose, this is what it means by different members in the body of Christ.[6] Haile Sellassie The First fought against wickedness in his own way, Moses will fight in his respective manner, Christ according to his custom, and each disciple will have to use their own disposition to combat Satan. We all are distinct, working towards the same objective of good over evil. Therefore it should not come as a shock if Iyesus has a distinct approach in administering the gospel; his peculiar role is suited for his personality and only the true Christ could carry out that mission properly. The Prophet must preach that Haile Sellassie The First is God and invalidate all other religious doctrines because they are all vanity. His Majesty was not going to teach the world how he is the Almighty, he sent forth his Son to do that. They have two different approaches yet their objective is one and the same - to establish the Kingdom of God on earth.

---

[5] John 5:22
[6] 1 Corinthians 12:12-27

"Now I beseech you, brethren, mark them which cause divisions and offenses contrary to the doctrine which you have learned; and avoid them. For they that are such serve not our Lord Jesus Christ, but their own belly; and by good words and fair speeches deceive the hearts of the simple. For your obedience is come abroad unto all men. I am glad therefore on your behalf: but yet I would have you wise unto that which is good, and simple concerning evil. And the God of peace shall bruise Satan under your feet shortly. The grace of our Lord Jesus Christ be with you. Amen" (Romans 16:17-20).

"But rise, and stand on your feet: for I have appeared to you for this purpose, to make you a minister and a witness both of these things which you have seen, and of those things in the which I will appear unto thee; Delivering you from the people, and from the Gentiles, unto whom now I send you, To open their eyes, and to turn them from darkness to light, and from the power of Satan unto God, that they may receive forgiveness of sins, and inheritance among them which are sanctified by faith that is in me" (Acts 26:16-18).

The Bible will teach you who is the true and living God; the intentions of all religions are the same in this purpose. Therefore when you come into the full assurance of the LORD, the next level of comprehension will be to abolish those false edicts which challenge his authority; because if we do not accept the Savior then humanity is destined for failure. Emperor Haile Sellassie The First must be accorded his rightful honor and dignity in order for the world to be saved and peace to reign. Those who question his divinity and slander his relevance cannot be allowed to succeed because His Majesty is the only one who can establish the true definition of righteousness. Haile Sellassie The First is the Father of Jesus Christ, he must be accorded the Highest and Supreme rites for he alone is the Almighty. The Bobo Shanti division of Rastafari believes that the trinity means "prophet, priest, and king;" thus decreeing Marcus Garvey, Charles Edwards, and His Majesty to be three in one and one in three. In this they have made two other men to be comparable with Haile Sellassie The First which is not true in theory or in deeds; His Majesty has no equal for he is the Most High. Marcus Garvey famously repudiated his support for Haile Sellassie The First therefore no one could honestly say that they worked in tandem with each other. Furthermore the idea that the trinity is "prophet, priest, and king," is not supported by any farfetched interpretation of the Bible; it is an apocryphal credence devised by a narcissistic usurper. Charles Edwards included himself into his trinity concept which entails gallant haughtiness on his part as to worship himself and to direct his followers to do the same. If these selfish and arrogant acts go unchecked His Majesty will not be recognized for who he is and the world shall remain in darkness. That is why the true Christ has been commanded to destroy idolatry and to condemn those who do not correspond with the Word of God.

"But we see Jesus, who was made a little lower than the angels for the suffering of death, crowned with glory and honor; that he by the grace of God should taste death for every man. For it became him, for whom are all things, and by whom are all things, in bringing many sons unto glory, to make the captain of their salvation perfect through sufferings. For both he that sanctifies and they who are sanctified are all of one: for which cause he is not ashamed to call them brethren, Saying, I will declare your name unto my brethren, in the midst of the church will I sing praise unto you. And again, I will put my trust in him. And again, Behold, I and the children which God has given me. Forasmuch then as the children are partakers of flesh and blood, he also himself likewise took part of the same; that through death he might destroy him that had power of death, that is, the devil" (Hebrews 2:9-14).

"And if I by Beelzebub cast out devils, by whom do your sons cast them out? Therefore shall they be your judges." (Luke 11:19).

"Servants, be obedient to them that are your masters according to the flesh, with fear and trembling, in singleness of your heart, as unto Christ; Not with eye service, as men pleasers; but as the servants of Christ, doing the will of God from the heart; with good will doing service, as to the Lord, and not to men: Knowing that whatsoever good thing any man does, the shame shall he receive of the Lord, whether he be bond or free. And, ye masters, do the same things unto them, forbearing threatening: knowing that your Master also is in heaven; neither is there respect of persons with him. Finally, my brethren, be strong in the Lord, and in the power of his might. Put on the whole armor of God, that you may be able to stand against the wiles of the devil" (Ephesians 6:5-11).

All of the corruption and immorality on earth originates from ignorance and neglecting God the Savior. In order to correct this, the Lord sent his minister to destroy the devil's philosophy which depreciates the human condition. Any belief that is not absolute in truth is idolatry because it contains some level of deceit which gives room for wrongdoing; it therefore would have to be abolished. The LORD commanded Christ to reprove every false viewpoint for this same reason. The leader of Bobo Shanti, Charles Edwards, calls himself Prince Emmanuel and is worshipped as being the black Christ. Their interpretation of Iyesus Kristos is identical to the vatican council who state that the Father and Son are the same entity. Therefore in actuality, their position is that Charles Edwards is God which then gives him a higher classification over Haile Sellassie The First whom they designate to be Abraham or Solomon. They must understand that in order to observe the Sabbath you would have to praise the LORD in spirit and in truth; meaning that you worship the true and living God according to his commandments. If this is not being done then you are not observing the seventh day and your faith is vain. We have been called to render our hearts and not our garments, it is necessary to praise His Majesty according to the lawful edicts that we have been instructed to acknowledge in the Bible. We can only venerate the King of Glory because he alone is God.

Part Four:

"Little children, let no man deceive you: he that does righteousness is righteous, even as he is righteous" (1 John 3:7-8).

"For though we walk in the flesh, we do not war after the flesh: (For the weapons of our warfare are not carnal, but mighty through God to the pulling down of strong holds;) Casting down imaginations, and every high thing that exalts itself against the knowledge of God, and bringing into captivity every thought to the obedience of Christ" (2 Corinthians 10:3-5).

"For we wrestle not against flesh and blood, but against principalities, against powers, against the rulers of the darkness of this world, against spiritual wickedness in high places. Wherefore take unto you the whole armor of God, that you may be able to withstand in the evil day, and having done all, to stand. Stand therefore, having your loins girt about with truth, and having on the breastplate of righteousness; And your feet shod with the preparation of the gospel of peace; Above all, taking the shield of faith, wherewith ye shall be able to quench all the fiery darts of the wicked. And take the helmet of salvation, and the sword of the Spirit, which is the word of God: Praying always with all prayer and supplication in the Spirit, and watching thereunto with all perseverance and supplication for all saints; And for me, that utterance may be given unto me, that I may open my mouth boldly, to make known the mystery of the gospel. For which I am an ambassador in bonds; that therein I may speak boldly, as I ought to speak" (Ephesians 6:12-20).

Religious tolerance does not mean that people can believe whatever they want to without being corrected on their wrong ideologies. It means that we do not physically assault anyone or deprive them of their basic human rights based upon spiritual matters. In order for the world to progress and evolve we must be courageous in challenging our own viewpoints to ensure that what we hold is true. If people never evolve from the predilections of paganism, false deities, superstition, etc., then the salvation of God cannot be realized and we would remain subject to malignancy. Anyone whose faith is rebuked should not respond carnally as to cause physical harm to their accuser because this type of reaction does not correspond with your vindication. God corrects those who he loves as a father chastises his son;[7] any worthwhile guardian will instruct his subjects in the right way and censure their improper ways. How can you love someone and allow them to destroy themselves? If we have admonished anyones beliefs this is done to save them not out of malice. That is why it is written that Jesus came to save the world and not to condemn because his reproach is a honest correction that will redeem anyone who takes heed unto his message. Emperor Haile Sellassie The First wishes for all of his creation to acknowledge the truth so that heaven may be realized not just in theory but through the manifestation of our deeds.

"So that we ourselves glory in you in the churches of God, for your patience and faith in all your persecutions and tribulations that you endure: Which is a manifest token of the righteous judgment of God, that you may be counted worthy of the kingdom of God, for which you also suffer: Seeing it is a righteous thing with God to recompense tribulation to them that trouble you; And to you who are troubled rest with us, when the Lord Jesus shall be revealed from heaven with his mighty angels, In flaming fire taking vengeance on them that know not God, and that obey not the gospel of our Lord Jesus Christ: Who shall be punished with everlasting destruction from the presence of the Lord, and from the glory of his power; When he shall come to be glorified in his saints, and to be admired in all them that believe (because our testimony among you was believed) in that day" (2 Thessalonians 1:4-10).

"I write unto you, little children, because your sins are forgiven you for his name's sake. I write unto you, fathers, because ye have known him that is from the beginning. I write unto you, young men, because you have overcome the wicked one. I write unto you, little children, because you have known the Father" (1 John 2:13-14).

---

[7] Proverbs 3:12

"And we know that we are of God, and the whole world lies in wickedness. And we know that the Son of God is come, and has given us an understanding, that we may know him that is true, and we are in him that is true, even in his Son Jesus Christ. This is the true God, and eternal life. Little children, keep yourselves from idols. Amen" (1 John 5:19-21).

The world only impairs itself by neglecting Haile Sellassie The First, this has proven to be true at the League of Nations, after the Ethiopian Revolution in 1974, and most significantly theistically. There is no other God besides His Majesty the King of Kings and Lord of Lords. We know that the prophecy concerning the coming of the LORD can only be fulfilled by the person to whom it is referring to; therefore Haile Sellassie The First must be revered for who he truly is which is the Almighty Father. There is no one else who can offer salvation, not even his wife Empress Menen. It is common among certain Rastafarian sects to regard her as Queen Omega or a celestial being. While her morality and religious adherence were of a strict noble class, the reality is that it would be idolatrous to worship the Empress. Just because she was married to His Majesty does not make her a deity. The Bible has warned us against these type of doctrines[8] and cautioned us to adhere to the Word of God so that we may know the truth about the LORD Emperor Haile Sellassie The First.

"And the rest of the men which were not killed by these plagues yet repented not of the works of their hands, that they should not worship devils, and idols of gold, and silver, and brass, and stone, and of wood: which neither can see, nor hear, nor walk: Neither repented they of their murders, nor of their sorceries, nor of their fornication, nor of their thefts" (Revelation 9:20-21).

"Jesus said unto them, If God were your Father, you would love me: for I proceeded forth and came from God; neither came I of myself, but he sent me. Why do you not understand my speech? Even because you cannot hear my word. You are of your father the devil, and the lusts of your father you will do. He was a murderer from the beginning, and abode not in the truth, because there is no truth in him. When he speaketh a lie, he speaks of his own: for he is a liar, and the father of it. And because I tell you the truth, you believe me not. Which of you convinceth me of sin? And if I say the truth, why do you not believe me? He that is of God hears God's words: you therefore hear them not, because you are not of God" (John 8:42-47).

---

[8] Jeremiah 44

The revelation of God on earth signifies that the factual precepts of the LORD have finally been established. Now that Haile Sellassie The First has revealed that he is the Almighty Father, we no longer need to imagine how we think God looks or make up our own version of righteousness to justify our unpleasant ambitions. From His Majesty we have the definition of all that is good. If anyone cannot accept the wise counsel of Emperor Haile Sellassie The First then this means that their deeds are evil and they do not want to repent. When people are allowed to continue in folly this creates a cruel world but the LORD wishes for us to live a healthy enjoyable life that is why he sent his Son to execute a righteous judgment on earth. The renunciation of idolatry entails all false tenants which affects everyone's ideology whether they are spiritual or irreligious. The time has arrived for the perfect doctrine of God to be accepted because His Majesty's counsel is irrefutable and absolute. We as Rastafarians should be vigilant in adhering to the precepts that we have learned from the Emperor. We have to accept the Bible, we must venerate Jesus Christ, and we need to become educated in the manner in which Haile Sellassie The First instructed us in. There are some who claim to be of Rastafari yet do not adhere to the teachings of His Majesty but this type of contradiction is destined to be invalidated. No one can reject Jesus Christ and accept Haile Sellassie The First, you cannot deny the Bible and claim to be of Rastafari. His Majesty was clear on numerous occasions that we must accept Iyesus Kristos along with the holy book for two cannot walk together except they be agreed.[9]

"You who I have taken from the ends of the earth, and called you from the chief men thereof, and said to you, You are my servant; I have chosen you, and will not cast you away. Fear thou not; for I am with you: be not dismayed; for I am your God: I will strengthen you; yea, I will help you; yea, I will uphold you with the right hand of my righteousness. Behold, all they that were incensed against you shall be ashamed and confounded: they shall be as nothing; and they that strive with you shall perish. You shall seek them, and shall not find them, even them that contended with you: they that war against you shall be as nothing, and as a thing of naught. For I the LORD thy God will hold your right hand, saying unto you, Fear not; I will help you. Fear not, thou worm of Jacob, and your men of Israel; I will help you, says the LORD, and your redeemer, the Holy One of Israel. Behold, I will make you a new sharp threshing instrument having teeth: you shall thresh the mountains, and beat them small, and shall make the hills as chaff. You shall fan them, and the wind

---

[9] Amos 3:3

shall carry them away, and the whirlwind shall scatter them: and you shall rejoice in the LORD, and shall glory in the Holy One of Israel. When the poor and needy seek water, and there is none, and their tongue fails for thirst, I the LORD will hear them, I the God of Israel will not forsake them. I will open rivers in high places, and fountains in the midst of the valleys: I will make the wilderness a pool of water, and the dry land springs of water. I will plant in the wilderness the cedar, the shittah tree, and the myrtle, and the oil tree; I will set in the desert the fir tree, and the pine, and the box tree together: That they may see, and know, and consider, and understand together, that the hand of the LORD has done this, and the Holy One of Israel has created it. Produce your cause, says the LORD; bring forth your strong reasons, says the King of Jacob. Let them bring them forth, and show us what shall happen: let them show the former things, what they be, that we may consider them, and know the latter end of them; or declare us things for to come. Show the things that are to come hereafter, that we may know that ye are gods: yea, do good, or do evil, that we may be dismayed, and behold it together. Behold, you are nothing, and your work of naught: an abomination is he that chooses you. I have raised up one from the north, and he shall come: from the rising of the sun shall he call upon my name: and he shall come upon princes as upon mortar, and as the potter treads clay. Who has declared from the beginning, that we may know? And beforetime, that we may say, He is righteous? Yea, there is none that shows, yea, there is none that declares, yea, there is none that hears your words. The first shall say to Zion, Behold, behold them: and I will give to Jerusalem one that brings good tidings. For I beheld, and there was no man; even among them, and there was no counselor, that when I asked of them, could answer a word. Behold, they are all vanity; their works are nothing: their molten images are wind and confusion" (Isaiah 41:9-29).

"Behold my servant, whom I uphold; mine elect, in whom my soul delights; I have put my spirit upon him: he shall bring forth judgment to the Gentiles. He shall not cry, nor lift up, nor cause his voice to be heard in the street. A bruised reed shall he not break, and the smoking flax shall he not quench: he shall bring forth judgment unto truth. He shall not fail nor be discouraged, till he has set judgment in the earth: and the isles shall wait for his law. Thus says God the LORD, he that created the heavens, and stretched them out; he that spread forth the earth, and that which cometh out of it; he that gives breath unto the people upon it, and spirit to them that walk therein: I the LORD have called you in righteousness, and will hold your hand, and will keep you, and give you for a covenant of the people, for a light of the Gentiles; To open the blind eyes, to bring out the prisoners from the prison, and them that sit in darkness out of the prison house. I am the LORD;

that is my name: and my glory will I not give to another, neither my praise to graven images" (Isaiah 42:1-8).

The true calling of God Emperor Haile Sellassie The First is for us to separate ourselves from the false philosophies which hinder our progress and corrupt humanity. Everything that His Majesty has instructed the world to emulate has proven to be honest and faithful. The tenants which Haile Sellassie The First introduced were established to save the world. Jesus Christ, the Prophet of Rastafari, defended the principles of his Father and warned the people that it is essential for us to follow everything that His Majesty stood for. If we turn away from this counsel then we would be eliminating our own salvation. But the LORD does not seek our destruction, he wants us to progress and manifest heaven on earth (which is within our power to do so). We therefore should not be idle hoping for the nations to fail and for humanity to become depraved. If countries like America, Israel, or Rome are engaged in sinister activity then we must remedy the situation and challenge them to adopt the commandments of God. Haile Sellassie The First revealed himself on earth to teach us the real definition of righteousness because he does not want to see us ruin ourselves. We must follow his example and work to save mankind instead of wishing for the world to end. His Majesty takes no pleasure in seeing people killed or suffering.

"And now come I to thee; and these things I speak in the world, that they might have my joy fulfilled in themselves. I have given them your word; and the world has hated them, because they are not of the world, even as I am not of the world. I pray not that you should take them out of the world, but that you should keep them from the evil" (John 17:13-15).

"Love not the world, neither the things that are in the world. If any man love the world, the love of the Father is not in him. For all that is in the world, the lust of the flesh, and the lust of the eyes, and the pride of life, is not of the Father, but is of the world. And the world passes away, and the lust thereof: but he that does the will of God abides forever. Little children, it is the last time: and as you have heard that antichrist shall come, even now are there many antichrists; whereby we know that it is the last time. They went out from us, but they were not of us; for if they had been of us, they would no doubt have continued with us: but they went out, that they might be made manifest that they were not all of us" (1 John 2:15-19).

"The world cannot hate you; but me it hates, because I testify of it, that the works thereof are evil" (John 7:7).

It was Mortimer Planno's idea that reggae music should be used as the chief medium to exemplify the message of Rastafari. As a result the popular image of the Rastafarians is not Emperor Haile Sellassie The First but rather Bob Marley. The culture that has been created is not emulated from the high example of the King of Kings but rather that of a musician. People now believe that to be of Rastafari means to grow dreadlocks, smoke ganja, and sing songs but these characteristics have nothing to do with the mission of Emperor Haile Sellassie The First. If our focus was upon cadences then how short sighted our purpose would be; it also should be noted that His Majesty's favorite musical genre was jazz not reggae. We ought not to adopt the ways of the world because people have a tendency to take the easy way out; it is essential to raise the standard by which we judge ourselves. We need to put ourselves in a position where we can effect policy and create institutions that advances progress. His Majesty is the real exemplar for the world to follow for he is the only one good. Let us not become comfortable in our own immorality and make excuses for our folly.

"When the Son of man shall come in his glory, and all the holy angels with him, then shall he sit upon the throne of his glory: And before him shall be gathered all nations: and he shall separate them one from another, as a shepherd divides his sheep from the goats: And he shall set the sheep on his right hand, but the goats on the left. Then shall the King say unto them on his right hand, Come, you blessed of my Father, inherit the kingdom prepared for you from the foundation of the world: For I was an hungered, and you gave me meat: I was thirsty, and you gave me drink: I was a stranger, and you took me in: Naked, and you clothed me: I was sick, and you visited me: I was in prison, and you came unto me. Then shall the righteous answer him, saying, Lord, when saw we thee an hungered, and fed thee? Or thirsty, and gave thee drink? When saw we thee a stranger, and took thee in? or naked, and clothed thee? Or when saw we thee sick, or in prison, and came unto thee? And the King shall answer and say unto them, Verily I say unto you, Inasmuch as you have done it unto one of the least of these my brethren, you have done it unto me. Then shall he say also unto them on the left hand, Depart from me, ye cursed, into everlasting fire, prepared for the devil and his angels: For I was an hungered, and ye gave me no meat: I was thirsty, and ye gave me no drink: I was a stranger, and ye took me not in: naked, and ye clothed me not: sick, and in

prison, and ye visited me not. Then shall they also answer him, saying, Lord, when saw we thee a hungered, or athirst, or a stranger, or naked, or sick, or in prison, and did not minister unto thee? Then shall he answer them, saying, Verily, I say unto you, Inasmuch as you did it not to one of the least of these, you did it not to me. And these shall go away into everlasting punishment: but the righteous into life eternal" (Matthew 25:31-46).

"He that hears you hears me; and he that despises you despises me; and he that despises me despises him that sent me. And the seventy returned again with joy, saying, Lord, even the devils are subject unto us through thy name. And he said unto them, I beheld Satan as lightning fall from heaven. Behold, I give unto you power to tread on serpents and scorpions, and over all the power of the enemy: and nothing shall by any means hurt you" (Luke 10:16-19).

"You have not chosen me, but I have chosen you, and ordained you, that you should go and bring forth fruit, and that your fruit should remain: that whatsoever you shall ask of the Father in my name, he may give it you" (John 15:16).

We must be obedient to the Word of God, as all of the descriptions of the prophecies indicate that Emperor Haile Sellassie The First is the Almighty Father. If we choose not to obey his commandments then it would be impossible to develop the correct perspective on life and spirituality. The manifestation of the Word determines whose faith is sincere; if you believe the Bible then you would accept the fact that Emperor Haile Sellassie The First is God. From him we will learn the true principles of righteousness which we will then have to dedicate the rest of our lives to enforce. The clear logic that His Majesty demonstrated throughout his entire life should be our model of discourse. No longer are we subject to impractical superstitious interpretations of the Bible. If we follow what Haile Sellassie The First has directed us in and apply those tenants with the message of the Bible then we would be able to explain the parables with wisdom and evidence. From this position it will be clear who has the truth and who has a false man made philosophy. God and the Bible are supposed to be explained logically, with a command of the scriptures that makes sense. The order of the universe follows a methodical intelligent design therefore the Creator must be organized and rational; we would have to explain his dominion in such manner. If this level of acumen is not present in their explanation of the Lord then neither is the truth.

"For through him we both have access by one Spirit unto the Father"
(Ephesians 2:18).

"These things I command you, that you love one another. If the world hate you,
you know that it hated me before it hated you. If you were of the world, the world
would love his own: but because you are not of the world, but I have chosen you
out of the world, therefore the world hates you. Remember the word that I said
unto you, The servant is not greater than his lord. If they have persecuted me,
they will also persecute you; if they have kept my saying, they will keep yours
also. But all these things will they do unto you for my name's sake, because they
know not him that sent me. If I had not come and spoken unto them, they had
not had sin; but now they have no cloke for their sin. He that hates me hates my
Father also. If I had not done among them the works which none other man did,
they had not had sin: but now have they both seen and hated both me and my
Father" (John 15:17-24).

"Let a man so account of us, as of the ministers of Christ, and stewards of the mys-
teries of God. For I know nothing by myself; yet am I not hereby justified: but he
that judges me is the Lord" (1 Corinthians 4:1&4).

The doctrine of Christ shall be recognized as being the truth because only
the Prophet can understand the parables of the Bible. That is why it said that
wisdom is justified by all her children[10] because although we are persecuted
for preaching the gospel of Rastafari, the evidence and clarity of the message
of Iyesus Kristos cannot be denied. Haile Sellassie The First is the Almighty
but since the world does not know the Father, or rather have denied him,
they will likewise reject the words of the Prophet who speaks in the name of
the Emperor of Ethiopia. We are justified in our sayings because we accept
the message of the Bible; although it does not yet appear that way. Our focus
remains upon pleasing the LORD which leads us to follow his Word and
Prophet. The theories of men concerning spirituality lack rational because
they was devised without acknowledging that Emperor Haile Sellassie The
First is God, making it impossible for them to form any type of coherency in
the scriptures. It is now time to repent from all forms of false beliefs which
would be classified as idolatry. His Majesty has made a way for us, all we

---

[10] Luke 7:35

must do is follow his guidance and we shall understand the real doctrine of life. Blessed be Ababa Janhoy.

Part Five:

"Yea, and all that will live godly in Christ Jesus shall suffer persecution. But evil men and seducers shall wax worse and worse, deceiving, and being deceived. But continue thou in the things which thou has learned and has been assured of, knowing of whom thou has learned them" (2 Timothy 3:12-15).

"To whom coming, as unto a living stone, disallowed indeed of men, but chosen of God, and precious, ye also, as lively stones, are built up a spiritual house, a holy priesthood, to offer up spiritual sacrifices, acceptable to God by Jesus Christ. Wherefore also it is contained in the scripture, Behold, I lay in Sion a chief corner stone, elect, precious: and he that believes on him shall not be confounded. Unto you therefore which believe he is precious: but unto them which be disobedient, the stone which the builders disallowed, the same is made the head of the corner" (1 Peter 2:4-7).

"And came and preached peace to you which were afar off, and to them that were near. For through him we both have access by one Spirit unto the Father. Now therefore ye are no more strangers and foreigners, but fellow citizens with the saints, and of the household of God; And are built upon the foundation of the apostles and prophets, Jesus Christ himself being the chief corner stone; In whom all the building fitly framed together grows unto a holy temple in the Lord: In whom ye also are built together for a habitation of God through the Spirit" (Ephesians 2:17-22).

We know that Christ has risen and given us an understanding so that we may know that His Majesty is the Almighty God over all gods. The persecution which we suffer cannot be compared to the glory which shall be revealed in us for we carry the true cross of salvation. Our intentions are not to please men but the LORD Emperor Haile Sellassie The First. We must make sure that the tenants that we adhere to are the same principles which His Majesty stood for because only through him comes deliverance from the falsehoods that abound on earth. Haile Sellassie The First was by far the most powerful and wisest leader of all time; although there are some who refute this reality, it is not possible to prevail against God's truth. His impact can be identified in many aspects, for it was his case which dismantled the League of Nations, I have yet to hear about another person who was able to nullify a global organization consisting of nearly every country; this demonstrates that he was stronger than the nations united. We also can recognize his enormous influence by identifying all the various countries around the world who acknowledge him by adopting certain elements of the Ethiopian flag. The national banners of Senegal, Cameroon, Mali, Benin, Guinea, Ghana, Guinea-Bissau, Republic of Congo, Persia-Iran, Bolivia, Guyana, Italy, Mexico, Burkina Faso, Madagascar, Jamaica, Bulgaria, Chad as well as others, all used certain elements of the Sendek Alama.[11] In fact it can be argued that every flag originated from Ethiopia because their Bandira[12] is the oldest in the world.

"Unto you therefore which believe he is precious: but unto them which be disobedient, the stone which the builders disallowed, the same is made the head of the corner, And a stone of stumbling, and a rock of offence, even to them which stumble at the word, being disobedient: whereunto also they were appointed. But ye are a chosen generation, a royal priesthood, a holy nation, a peculiar people; that you should show forth the praises of him who has called you out of darkness into his marvelous light: Which in time past were not a people, but are now the people of God: which had not obtained mercy, but now have obtained mercy. Dearly beloved, I beseech you as strangers and pilgrims, abstain from fleshly lusts, which war against the soul; Having your conversation honest among the Gentiles: that, whereas they speak against you as evildoers, they may by your good works, which they shall behold, glorify God in the day of visitation. Submit yourselves to every ordinance of man for the Lord's sake: whether it be to the king, as supreme; Or unto governors, as unto them that are sent by him for the punishment of evildoers, and for the praise of them that do well. For so is the will of God, that with well doing you may put to silence the ignorance of foolish men: As free, and not using your liberty for a cloke of maliciousness, but as the servants of God. Honor all men. Love the brotherhood. Fear God. Honor the king. Servants, be subject to your masters with all fear; not only to the good and gentle, but also to the forward. For this is thankworthy, if a man for conscience toward God endure grief, suffering wrongfully. For what glory is it, if, when you be buffeted for your faults, you shall take it patiently? But if, when you do well, and suffer for it, you take it patiently, this is acceptable with God. For even hereunto were ye called: because Christ also suffered for us, leaving us an example, that you

---

[11] Ethiopian Flag
[12] National Banner

should follow his steps: Who did no sin, neither was guile found in his mouth: who, when he was reviled, reviled not again; when he suffered, he threatened not; but committed himself to him that judges righteously: Who his own self bare our sins in his own body on the tree, that we, being dead to sins, should live unto righteousness: by whose stripes ye were healed. For ye were as sheep going astray; but are now returned unto the Shepherd and Bishop of souls" (1 Peter 2:7-25).

"And who is he that will harm you, if you be followers of that which is good? But and if you suffer for righteousness' sake, happy are you: and be not afraid of their terror, neither be troubled; But sanctify the Lord God in your hearts: and be ready always to give an answer to every man that asks you a reason of the hope that is in you, with meekness and fear: having a good conscience; that, whereas they speak evil of you, as of evildoers, they may be ashamed that falsely accuse your good conversation in Christ. For it is better, if the will of God be so, that you suffer for well doing, than for evil doing. For Christ also has once suffered for sins, the just for the unjust, that he might bring us to God, being put to death in the flesh, but quickened by the Spirit: By which also he went and preached unto the spirits in prison" (1 Peter 3:13-19).

"Beloved, think it not strange concerning the fiery trial which is to try you, as though some strange thing happened unto you: But rejoice, Inasmuch as you are partakers of Christ's sufferings; that when his glory shall be revealed, you may be glad also with exceeding joy. If you be reproached for the name of Christ, happy are ye; for the Spirit of glory and of God rests upon you: on their part he is evil spoken of, but on your part he is glorified. But let none of you suffer as a murderer, or as a thief, or as an evil doer, or as a busybody in other men's matters. Yet if any man suffer as a Christian, let him not be ashamed; but let them glorify God on this behalf. For the time is come that judgment must begin at the house of God: and if it first begin at us, what shall the end be of them that obey not the gospel of God? And if the righteous scarcely be saved, where shall the ungodly and the sinner appear? Wherefore, let them that suffer according to the will of God commit the keeping of their souls to him in well doing, as unto a faithful Creator" (1 Peter 4:12-19).

If you do something wrong then you are supposed to suffer for your crime but if you do that which is right then you should be praised for your righteous deeds. Yet we see that those who believe the gospel of Jesus Christ are crucified because people do not accept the fact that Haile Sellassie The First is God. For this cause we will overcome our afflictions, because His Majesty also was rejected by the world for his righteous deeds, so we are not ignorant of the ungrateful nature of men. The Emperor did more to save the world than anyone else, he came during the most pivotal era in all of human history and if it were not for him nationalism would have triumphed over the Allies thus destroying civilization. He deserves for someone to stand up for him, just as he did for us, so if we are persecuted for doing that which is right, it must be known that nothing shall ever stop our mission. What we are defending is not an abstract concept about a Savior who has no face or actuality, we worship the genuine article of faith, the manifestation of glory Emperor Haile Sellassie The First whose deeds justify his acclaim. His Majesty travelled all over the world so that everyone may be saved: the God of the whole earth shall he be called. Yet he was reviled for these good works, as many Ethiopians accustomed to their native tradition of isolationism could not understand why their King felt the need to travel at such great lengths. But shall salvation only be offered to a limited group or should everyone be given the opportunity to know God? The absurdity found in their reasons for fighting Haile Sellassie The First demonstrates that it is futile to try to please men and that we cannot allow ignorance to halt our mission.

"Feed the flock of God which is among you, taking the oversight thereof, not by constraint, but willingly; not for filthy lucre, but of a ready mind; Neither as being lords over God's heritage, but being examples to the flock. And when the chief Shepherd shall appear, you shall receive a crown of glory that fadeth not away. Likewise, you younger, submit yourselves unto the elder. Yea, all of you be subject one to another, and be clothed with humility: for God resisteth the proud, and gives grace to the humble. Humble yourselves therefore under the mighty hand of God, that he may exalt you in due time: Casting all your care upon him; for he cares for you. Be sober, be vigilant; because your adversary the devil, as a roaring lion, walks about, seeking whom he may devour: Whom resist stedfast in the faith, knowing that the same afflictions are accomplished in your brethren that are in the world. But the God of all grace, who has called us unto his eternal glory by Christ Jesus, after that you have suffered a while, make you perfect, establish, strengthen, settle you. To him be glory and dominion forever and ever. Amen" (1 Peter 5:2-11).

"Now the Spirit speaks expressly, that in the latter times some shall depart from the faith, giving heed to seducing spirits, and doctrines of devils; Speaking lies in hypocrisy; having their conscience seared with a hot iron; Forbidden to marry, and commanding to abstain from meats, which God has created to be received with thanksgiving of them which believe and know the truth. For every creature of

God is good, and nothing to be refused, if it be received with thanksgiving: For it is sanctified by the word of God and prayer. If you put the brethren in remembrance of these things, you shall be a good minister of Jesus Christ, nourished up in the words of faith and of good doctrine, whereunto thou has attained. But refuse profane and old wives' fables, and exercise thyself rather unto godliness. For bodily exercise profits little: but godliness is profitable unto all things, having promise of the life that now is, and of that which is to come. This is a faithful saying, and worthy of all acceptation. For therefore we both labor and suffer reproach, because we trust in the living God, who is the Savior of all men, especially of those that believe. These things command and teach. Let no man despise thy youth; but be thou an example of the believers, in word, in conversation, in charity, in spirit, in faith, in purity. Till I come, give attendance to reading, to exhortation, to doctrine. Neglect not the gift that is in you, which was give thee by prophecy, with the laying on of the hands of the presbytery. Meditate upon these things; give thyself wholly to them; that thy profiting my appear to all. Take heed to yourself, and unto the doctrine; continue in them: for in doing this you shall save both yourself, and them that hear you" (1 Timothy 4:1-16).

To be of Rastafari means that we must subject ourselves to the highest order and most meticulous principles, for His Majesty was a man of a solemn morality and astute intelligence. It is imperative that our actions and values coincide with the mission and tenants of Haile Sellassie The First. There are many false doctrines in the world and we must study to be approved so that we do not incorporate any fallacies into our faith. All forms of superstition, magic, witchcraft, sorcery, or the supernatural are all sacrilegious and idolatrous. The earth is the Lord's and the fullness thereof, as such we need to understand that the workings of the universe (otherwise called science) will always correspond with the operation of the real God who created everything; this is also known as true knowledge. Haile Sellassie The First always gave practical advice, void of any hocus pocus because he is the true Savior whose message has merit and tact. If we study him, we will find that he has provided us with all the answers to our questions as well as the means of transforming the world into a better place. His Majesty has guided us in what we must do to manifest heaven on earth and he did not point us to the afterlife or to an alternate reality. The power to either destroy or advance humanity is in our hands, human beings are responsible for their fate. There will not be an alien invasion or a heavenly divination that annihilates all of mankind, we will determine our outcome and survival. If we believe in nonexistent factors such as magic or space creatures then we would only be deceiving ourselves and hindering our own progress. Haile Sellassie The First is the only one who can teach the true principles of life for he alone is God.

"Now this I say, that everyone of you who says, I am of Paul; and I of Apollos; and I of Cephas; and I of Christ. Is Christ divided? Was Paul crucified for you? Or were you baptized in the name of Paul? I thank God that I baptized none of you, but Crispus and Gaius" (1 Corinthians 1:12-14).

"For what is our hope, or joy, or crown of rejoicing? Are not even ye in the presence of our Lord Jesus Christ at his coming" (1 Thessalonians 2:19).

"When he shall come to be glorified in his saints, and to be admired in all them that believe (because our testimony among you was believed) in that day. Wherefore also we pray always for you, that our God would count you worthy of this calling, and fulfill all the good pleasure of his goodness, and the work of faith with power: That the name of our Lord Jesus Christ may be glorified in you, and you in him, according to the grace of our God and the Lord Jesus Christ" (2 Thessalonians 1:10-12).

"Grace be unto you, and peace, from God our Father and from the Lord Jesus Christ. I thank my God upon every remembrance of you. Always in every prayer of mine for you all making request with joy, For your fellowship in the gospel from the first day until now; Being confident of this very thing, that he which has begun a good work in you will perform it until the day of Jesus Christ: Even as it is meet for me to think this of you all, because I have you in my heart; inasmuch as both in my bonds, and in the defense and confirmation of the gospel, you all are partakers of my grace. For God is my record, how greatly I long after you all in the bowels of Jesus Christ. And this I pray, that your love may abound yet more and more in knowledge and in all judgment; That you may approve things that are excellent; that you may be sincere and without offence till the day of Christ; Being filled with the fruits of righteousness, which are by Jesus Christ, unto the glory and praise of God. But I would you should understand, brethren, that the things which happened unto me have fallen out rather unto the furtherance of the gospel; So that my bonds in Christ are manifest in all the palace, and in all other places; And many of the brethren in the Lord, waxing confident by my bonds, are much more bold to speak the word without fear. Some indeed preach Christ even of envy and strife; and some also of good will: The one preach Christ of contention, not sincerely, supposing to add afflic-tion to my bonds: But the other of love, knowing that I am set for the defense of the

gospel. What then? Notwithstanding, every way, whether in pretence, or in truth, Christ is preached; and I therein do rejoice, yea, and will rejoice. For I know that this shall turn to my salvation through your prayer, and the supply of the Spirit of Jesus Christ, According to my earnest expectation and my hope, that in nothing I shall be ashamed, but that with all boldness, as always, so now also Christ shall be magnified in my body, whether it be by life, or by death. For to me to live is Christ, and to die is gain. But if I live in the flesh, this is the fruit of my labor: yet what I shall choose I wot not. For I am in a strait betwixt two, having a desire to depart, and to be with Christ; which is far better: nevertheless to abide in the flesh is more needful for you. And having this confidence, I know that I shall abide and continue with you all for your furtherance and joy of faith; That your rejoicing may be more abundant in Jesus Christ for me by my coming to you again. Only let your conversation be as it becomes the gospel of Christ: that whether I come and see you, or else be absent, I may hear of your affairs, that you stand fast in one spirit, with one mind striving together for the faith of the gospel; And in nothing terrified by your adversaries: which is to them an evident token of perdition, but to you of salvation, and that of God. For unto you it is given in the behalf of Christ, not only to believe on him, but also to suffer for his sake" (Philippians 1:2-29).

It only makes sense for you to do that which you profess or else your faith is in vain. If we are of Rastafari then we must mirror the Emperor in all our activities and principles. Satan lies in wait to deceive humanity with a false interpretation of the scriptures, we have read how he quotes the Bible carnally.[13] Humanity must guard themselves against this predicament by ensuring that your outlook complies with the revelation of the LORD and wisdom. People have been taught to follow their cultural traditions and not to question the religion of their forefathers; and if this be the case then how can anyone determine what is right or wrong? We would all be mindless sheep, blind towards the truth and pacified. As scary as it might be to find out that your religion is false, it is more scary to be subject unto the devil. Therefore it is necessary to question your faith and ask the hard questions so that we may verify our own beliefs. The truth about God shall stand eternally through any inquisition because it is absolute, it is only the traditions of men that are flawed. The vatican, who stands as the head of all religious charlatanism, captivates the masses with their familiarity and pageantry, not because of their validity or acumen. Anyone who has taken the time to study the history of the pope of Rome will know unequiv-

---

[13] Matthew 4

ocally that it is an elongated tyrannical narrative embedded with all the major catastrophes and devious schemes of the world; yet this is who people go to for the Word of God. But we shall not conform to such diabolism, we will follow the trustworthy teachings of Emperor Haile Sellassie The First.

"For you suffer, if a man bring you into bondage, if a man devour you, if a man take of you, if a man exalt himself, if a man smite you on the face. I speak as concerning reproach, as though we had been weak. Howbeit, whereinsoever any is bold, (I speak foolishly,) I am bold also. Are they Hebrews? So am I. Are they Israelites? So am I. Are they the seed of Abraham? So am I. Are they ministers of Christ? (I speak as a fool) I am more; in labors more abundant, in stripes above measure, in prisons more frequent, in deaths often. Of the Jews fives times received I forty stripes save one. Thrice was I beaten with rods, once was I stoned, thrice I suffered shipwreck, a night and a day I have been in the deep; In journeys often, in perils of waters, in perils of robbers, in perils of mine own countrymen, in perils by the heathen, in perils in the city, in perils in the wilderness, in perils in the sea, in perils among false brethren; In weariness and painfulness, in watching often, in hunger and thirst, in fasting often, in cold and nakedness. Beside those things that are without, that which cometh upon me daily, the care of all the churches. Who is weak, and I am not weak? Who is offended, and I burn not" (2 Corinthians 11:20-31).

"And above all these things put on charity, which is the bond of perfectness. And let the peace of God rule in your hearts, to the which also you are called in one body; and be ye thankful. Let the word of Christ dwell in you richly in all wisdom; teaching and admonishing one another in psalms and hymns and spiritual songs. And whatsoever you do in word or deed, do all in the name of the Lord Jesus, giving thanks to God and the Father by him" (Colossians 3:14-17).

"Be ye therefore followers of God, as dear children; and walk in love, as Christ also has loved us, and has given himself for us an offering and a sacrifice to God for a sweet smelling savour. But fornication, and all uncleanness, or covetousness, let it not be once named among you, as becometh saints; Neither filthiness, nor foolish talking, nor jesting, which are not convenient: but rather giving of thanks. For this you know, that no whoremonger, nor unclean person, nor covetous man, who is an idolater, has any inheritance in the kingdom of Christ and of God. Let no man deceive you with vain words: for because of these things comes the wrath of God upon the children of disobedience. Be not ye therefore partakers with them. For you were sometimes darkness, but now are you light in the Lord: walk as children of light:

(For the fruit of the Spirit is in all goodness and righteousness and truth;) Proving what is acceptable unto the Lord. And have no fellowship with the unfruitful works of darkness, but rather reprove them. For it is a shame even to speak of those things which are done of them in secret. But all things that are reproved are made manifest by the light: for whatsoever does make manifest is light. Wherefore he said, Awake thou that sleeps, and arise from the dead, and Christ shall give you light. See then that you walk circumspectly, not as fools, but as wise. Redeeming the time, because the days are evil" (Ephesians 5:1-16).

We are at peace, being granted the high honor of knowing God Emperor Haile Sellassie The First. In this we have manifested the true purpose of all religions for there is only one Creator; he is the same for Christians, Muslims, Jews, and atheists alike. We have inherited the earth by attaining the promises of all religions in finding favor with the LORD. Those who question the divinity of Haile Sellassie The First for the most part cannot understand what makes him celestial if he functioned by natural means. Their understanding, given to them by unworthy teachers who interpret the scriptures literally, leads them to believe that God is supernatural, so therefore he operates like a magician; but this is all contrary to fact. His Majesty would have to operate through conventional methods so that we can emulate his deeds; if he taught us salvation what would be the purpose of it if we could not reciprocate his actions? Therefore he was born on earth through a father and mother who had intercourse for him to be produced. His father, Ras Makonnen, was the hero of the Battle of Adowa and heir-apparent to the throne of Ethiopia; unfortunately his untimely death prevented him from obtaining the crown. Instead of believing in an unreal ideology ironclad in illusion and witchcraft which states that someone could be born without the amalgamation of a male and female, we should read the Bible with a sound mind and seek to understand the parables logically. For it profits nothing for the Lord to demonstrate a skill which no one else can learn or obtain; that would be completely useless, especially if we are to emulate his actions. From His Majesty's natural birth we learn an important lesson in parenthood and life. The influence of Ras Makonnen over his young son was very significant in his upbringing and perspective. He took steps to ensure that his child was educated properly in addition to being a positive role model and a strong father figure. We must now incorporate these lessons into our child bearing and do everything to ensure that our youths have a bright future. These are valuable lessons that we can learn from and imitate in our daily lives which would improve our lot and benefit future generations; the sound guidance that comes from studying Haile Sellassie The First objectively always leads to the pronouncement of his perfect operation. Let him be praised.

"Lord, they have killed your prophets, and digged down thine altars; and I am left alone, and they seek my life. But what says the answer of God unto him? I have reserved to myself seven thousand men, who have not bowed the knee to the image of Baal. Even so then at this present time also there is a remnant according to the election of grace" (Romans 11:3-5).

"And I was with you in weakness, and in fear, and in much trembling. And my speech and my preaching was not with enticing words of man's wisdom, but in demonstration of the Spirit and of power: That your faith should not stand in the wisdom of men, but in the power of God. Howbeit we speak wisdom among them that are perfect: yet not the wisdom of this world, nor of the princes of this world, that come to naught: But we speak the wisdom of God in a mystery, even the hidden wisdom, which God ordained before the world unto our glory: Which none of the princes of this world knew: for had they known it, they would not have crucified the Lord of glory" (1 Corinthians 2:3-8).

"And they smote him on the head with a reed, and did spit upon him, and bowing their knees worshipped him. And when they had mocked him, they took off the purple from him, and put his own clothes on him, and let him out to crucify him" (Mark 15:19-20).

"Ye men of Israel, hear these words; Jesus of Nazareth, a man approved of God among you by miracles and wonders and signs, which God did by him in the midst of you, as ye yourselves also know: Him, being delivered by the determinate counsel and foreknowledge of God, you have taken, and by wicked hands have crucified and slain: Whom God has raised up, having loosed the pains of death: because it was not possible that he should be holden of it" (Acts 2:22-24).

Despite the clear and thoughtful position of Iyesus Kristos, the people rejected his message because they are not of God. They themselves know the defects of their traditions yet they are afraid to change because they are complacent. If we never venture out to learn more then there would never be any progress and if we cannot accept that which is both sensible and spiritual then we have not the truth. The path towards enlightenment is a triumph of knowledge over absurdity, we must push ourselves towards rationality and civility even along religious lines. As spirituality is at the foundation of the conscious of men it is important that we are wise and prudent in regards to this realm. Christ is the Son of God because only he can give us the proper teachings of the Father; this knowledge is a mystery to the rest of the world. That is why the churches are filled with unreasonable canons brimming with superstition and delusion; their interpretation lacks any form of logic or coherency yet people accept their doctrine because they cannot see past their traditions. Christ will stand out from the rest because only he will be able to make sense out of the Bible. Those who are allured by Satan will reject his message because they prefer lies over the truth; they will do this despite the clearcut mastery over the parables which Iyesus Kristos will demonstrate.

The Fourth Letter

The words of Yesus dari Nazaret and Paulos concerning us who believe the gospel:

"Preserve me, O God: for in thee do I put my trust. O my soul, thou has said to the LORD, You are my LORD: my goodness extendeth not to thee; But to the saints that are in the earth, and to the excellent, in whom is all my delight" (Psalm 16:1-3).

"I have glorified you on the earth: I have finished the work which you gave me to do. And now, O Father, glorify me with thine own self with the glory which I had with you before the world was. I have manifested your name unto the men which you gave me out of the world: thine they were, and you gave them me; and they have kept your word. Now they have known that all things whatsoever you have given me are of thee. For I have given unto them the words which you gave me; and they have received them, and have known surely that I came out from you, and they have believed that you did send me. I pray for them: I pray not for the world, but for them which you have given me; for they are yours. And all mine are yours, and yours are mine; and I am glorified in them. And now I am no more in the world, but these are in the world, and I come to you. Holy Father, keep through your own name those whom thou has given me, that they may be one, as we are. While I was with them in the world, I kept them in your name: those that you gave me I have kept, and none of them is lost, but the son of perdition; that the scripture might be fulfilled. And now come I to you; and these things I speak in the world, that they might have my joy fulfilled in themselves. I have given them your word; and the world has hated them, because they are not of the world, even as I am not of the world. I pray not that

you should take them out of the world, but that you should keep them from the evil. They are not of the world, even as I am not of the world. Sanctify them through your truth: your word is truth. As you have sent me in the world, even so have I also sent them into the world. And for their sakes I sanctify myself, that they also might be sanctified through the truth. Neither pray I for these alone, but for them also which shall believe on me through their word; That they all may be one; as you, Father, are in me, and I in thee, that they also may be one in us: that the world may believe that you have sent me. And the glory which you gave me, I have given them; that they may be one, even as we are one: I in them, and you in me, that they may be made perfect in one; and that the world may know that you have sent me, and has loved them, as you have loved me. Father, I will that they also, whom thou has given me, be with me where I am; that they may behold my glory, which you have given me: for you loved me before the foundation of the world. O righteous Father, the world has not known you: but I have known you, and these have known that you have sent me. And I have declared unto them your name, and will declare it: that the love where-with you have loved me may be in them, and I in them" (John 17:4-26).

The gospel of Jesus Christ is to know that Emperor Haile Sellassie The First is God. It is written that the Prophet has kept us in the name of his Father; not in his own name. As Christ and his Father are one, we all must become one with God by accepting His Majesty for who he really is and that is the Almighty. We are not of the world, for the doctrines which abound on earth do not enable you to see the LORD, which is the defining characteristic of having the truth. Despite the fact that all religious books direct you to Emperor Haile Sellassie The First, the people are unable to understand the parables because their spiritual sense has been corrupted through incorrect interpretations of the Word. The Jehovah's Witness organization states that Jesus Christ was crowned as the king of heaven in 1914. Although the genealogical evidence deduced to calculate this date stem from apocryphal sources, the year is not far from the true vestige. This prophecy aligns with the delegation of Rastafari becoming the head of Ethiopia in 1917. We should not be looking in the sky for the manifestation of the promises; for it is written thy kingdom come, thy will be done on earth as it is in heaven.[14] All the heralds guide us to Emperor Haile Sellassie The First but only with the correct outlook and understanding would you be able to recognize this.

---

[14] Matthew 6:9-13

"And have put on the new man, which is renewed in knowledge after the image of him that created him" (Colossians 3:10).

"Now I say, That the heir, as long as he is a child, differs nothing from a servant, though he be lord of all; But is under tutors and governors until the time appointed of the father. Even so we, when we were children, were in bondage under the elements of the world: But when the fullness of the time was come, God sent forth his Son, made of a woman, made under the law, To redeem them that were under the law, that we might receive the adoption of sons. And because you are sons, God has sent forth the Spirit of his Son into your hearts, crying, Abba, Father. Wherefore you are no more a servant, but a son; and if a son, then an heir of God through Christ" (Galatians 4:1-7).

"Who delivered us from so great a death, and does deliver: in whom we trust that he will yet deliver us; You also helping together by prayer for us, that for the gift bestowed upon us by the means of many persons thanks may be given by many on our behalf. For our rejoicing is this, the testimony of our conscience, that in simplicity and godly sincerity, not with fleshly wisdom, but by the grace of God, we have had our conversation in the world, and more abundantly to you-ward, For we write none other things unto you, than what you read or acknowledge; and I trust you shall acknowledge even to the end; As also you have acknowledged us in part, that we are your rejoicing, even as you also, are ours in the day of the Lord Jesus" (2 Corinthians 1:10-14).

The Bible is admonishing everyone to acquire a new understanding so that we may know that Emperor Haile Sellassie The First is the Almighty. The old man represents those vain supernatural doctrines which leave us void of the LORD; their outlook is tainted because they do not teach the correct judgment. For this reason we must put on the new man, that is adopt a new understanding of the Bible with facts and evidence. His Majesty holds the titles for which the prophecy clearly states only God can assert; he is the first and the last King of Kings and Lord of Lords. The propaganda used to try to discredit Haile Sellassie The First are baseless lies which only deny the people of their salvation. It is a common myth to hear that His Majesty was a thief who embezzled enormous sums of money. Although the Ethiopians audited his records and found no evidence of this being true, as well as they travelled to European banks in search of this treasure and was told that no such bank accounts exist.[15] We also must ask if he was such a greedy tyrant, who cared not for his people, why did he refuse enormous sums of money from Italy during his most desolate and desperate interval so he could liberate his country? The reality is that Emperor Haile Sellassie The First spent his money wisely and did not mismanage any state funds; the accusation of him being a despot was circulated by a committee of jar-heads who proved to be enemies of humanity. Currently the royal family all lead regular lives and have to work traditional jobs to make a living; so where is this fabulous wealth that His Majesty supposably hoarded, what proof do we have to validate this insinuation? Some people would accept certain statements that have no merit when it complements their traditions or because they are too intellectually lazy to do the necessary research to substantiate the claim but those who want to know the LORD will investigate these allegations so that they may know what is right and wrong. This is the sole path to understanding the full gravity of the kingdom of God which would lead you to accepting the total eminence of Emperor Haile Sellassie The First.

"For what is our hope, or joy, or crown of rejoicing? Are not even you in the presence of our Lord Jesus Christ at his coming" (1 Thessalonians 2:19).

"But we are bound to give thanks always to God for you, brethren beloved of the Lord, because God has from the beginning chosen you to salvation through sanctification of the Spirit and belief of the truth: Whereunto he called you by our gospel, to the obtaining of the glory of our Lord Jesus Christ. Therefore, brethren, stand fast, and hold the traditions which you have been taught, whether by word, or our epistle. Now our Lord Jesus Christ himself, and God, even our Father, which has loved us, and has given us everlasting consolation and good hope through grace, Comfort your hearts, and establish you in every good word and work" (2 Thessalonians 2:13-17).

"Knowing, brethren beloved, your election of God. For our gospel came not unto you in word only, but also in power, and in the Holy Ghost, and in much assurance; as you know what manner of men we were among you for your sake. And you became followers of us, and of the Lord, having received the word in much affliction, with joy of the Holy Ghost: So that you were examples to all that believe in Macedonia and Achaia" (1 Thessalonians 1:4-8).

---

[15] Del Boca, Angelo, The Negus, page 35

We have been called unto the full assurance of understanding and wisdom in accepting the true God Emperor Haile Sellassie The First. The LORD established his kingdom on earth so that humanity may be saved from the corrupt doctrines and principles that afflict humanity. The only deliverance from these beguiling tenants is the gospel of Christ which acknowledges the divinity of Haile Sellassie The First. Much has been done to deceive the public so that the people do not recognize and accept His Majesty; because the devil is seeking to keep the world in darkness. The propaganda that has been circulated that Haile Sellassie The First starved his people yet fed his dogs are empty rumors. To say that the Emperor was a thief who did not have the peoples best interest in mind is an illusory accusation without verity. When these allegations first began to circulate during the failed coup d'etat against the Imperial government on December 13, 1960, His Majesty urged everyone to have faith in their Sovereign as well as he commissioned an independent investigation into the validity of these claims. Beriun Kebede, an Imperial Parliamentarian said, "Since the Emperor's victorious return in 1941 how much money has the Ethiopian government borrowed from outside? Let them submit documentation and we're going to inquire how each of the loans was utilized. But first, let's see the ledgers. This motion that I set forth found many supporters and was adopted by a majority vote. They brought the report in 7 days! Do you know the annual budget of Ethiopia at that time? It was $300 million. If I'm not mistaken the aggregate amount of all the loans was about $750 million. They were outraged when they saw this amount. Where did all the money go to? The Emperor summoned us and we went. 'You have a right to ask at the governments expense. I urge you to divide into groups, and go by plane, by boat, and by car; and using a list provided by the government go see the schools and hospitals funded with this money. Go and assess what's been done.' He commanded. We agreed to record how many rooms each hospital had, how many employees they hired, how many students each school enrolled, how many classrooms each school had, how many workers each factory employed, how much each factory cost. After we collected and examined our records we discovered that the loans had been insufficient and that the government had covered the deficit. We found that instead of having embezzled the loans, the government had been subsidizing the shortfalls from their budget. We [then] apologized to the Emperor."[16]

---

[16] Twilight Revelations: Episodes in the Life & Times of Emperor Haile Selassie, 2009

"Grace be unto you, and peace, from God our Father, and from the Lord Jesus Christ. I thank my God always on your behalf, for the grace of God which is given you by Jesus Christ; That in every thing you are enriched by him, in all utterance, and in all knowledge; Even as the testimony of Christ was confirmed in you: So that you come behind in no gift; waiting for the coming of our Lord Jesus Christ: Who shall also confirm you unto the end, that you may be blameless in the day of our Lord Jesus Christ. God is faithful, by whom you were called unto the fellowship of his Son Jesus Christ our Lord. Now I beseech you, brethren, by the name of our Lord Jesus Christ, that you all speak the same thing, and that there be no divisions among you; but that you be perfectly joined together in the same mind and in the same judgment" (1 Corinthians 1:3-10).

"If you put the brethren in remembrance of these things, you shall be a good minister of Jesus Christ, nourished up in the words of faith and of good doctrine, whereunto you have attained" (1 Timothy 4:6).

"Behold, I and the children whom the LORD has given me are for signs and for wonders in Israel from the LORD of hosts, which dwells in mount Zion" (Isaiah 8:18).

Our brethren Iyesus Kristos has offered us salvation by teaching us the correct interpretation of the Bible so that we may know that Emperor Haile Sellassie The First is the Almighty. The gospel which Christ has preached is the perfect testimony of the LORD, the only valid source to understand the parables of the scriptures; for he is the door into heaven. Those who follow his testimony can teach other people the doctrine and this saves all those who believe. With all the historical and Biblical evidence that directs the world to worship Haile Sellassie The First, people will still resist this edict because it is a new concept for many. Human nature in general opposes all changes, even those reforms which are clearly beneficial. His Majesty is the true definition of righteousness, every instance where the people have turned their backs on him has proven to be a detrimental mistake. This has been the case at the League of Nations, after the Ethiopian Revolution, and most notably in the Bible. When people reject the fact that Emperor Haile Sellassie The First is God, they are choosing to remain dormant in a counterfactual conscious that leaves the follower void of the LORD. Only His Majesty can successfully unite spirituality with academia, thus enabling the disciple to view the world objectively without shying away from any of the facts. Ratiocination makes us understand that a man whose records were audited and exonerated, cannot then be debased.

Logic allows you to decipher the policies of a ruler who spent his own money on state projects and donated his personal property to build the infrastructure as keeping the people's best interest in mind. A sound analysis enables us to come to the conclusion that the Bible is written in parables because it is not possible to defy the laws of nature. His Majesty was perfect in all that he did and everything that took place during his reign justifies his divinity. This is the only gospel that will not betray your intelligence by offering an illogical spiritual ideology. Haile Sellassie The First is the absolute truth, in him is the fullness of light, all the ways of the LORD are righteous and from him comes true wisdom.

"Look not every man on his own things, but every man also on things of others. Let this mind be in you, which was also in Christ Jesus" (Philippians 2:4-5).

"And let the peace of God rule in your hearts, to the which also you are called in one body; and be ye thankful. Let the word of Christ dwell in you richly in all wisdom; teaching and admonishing one another in psalms and hymns and spiritual songs, singing with grace in your hearts to the Lord. But he that does wrong shall receive for the wrong which he has done: and there is no respect of persons" (Colossians 3:15-17, 24).

"But we see Jesus, who was made a little lower than the angels for the suffering of death, crowned with glory and honor; that he by the grace of God should taste death for every man. For it became him, for whom are all things, and by whom are all things, in bringing many sons unto glory, to make the captain of their salvation perfect through sufferings. For both he that sanctifies and they who are sanctified are all of one: for which cause he is not ashamed to call them brethren, Saying, I will declare your name unto my brethren, in the midst of the church will I sing praise unto thee. And again, I will put my trust in him. And again, Behold I and the children which God has given me. Forasmuch then as the children are partakers of flesh and blood, he also himself likewise took part of the same: that through death he might destroy him that had the power of death, that is, the devil; And deliver them, who through fear of death were all their lifetime subject to bondage. For verily he took not on him the nature of angels; but he took on him the seed of Abraham. Wherefore in all things it behoved him to be made like unto his brethren, that he might be a merciful and faithful high priest in things pertaining to God, to make reconciliation for the sins of the people" (Hebrew 2:9-17).

If you search for the LORD then you shall find him because he is not far from any of us.[17] We should therefore analyze the various religions of the world to find that there is only one King of Kings and Lord of Lords who established a government on earth. Emperor Haile Sellassie The First is our salvation, he demonstrated the guiding principles that will save humanity. Jesus said to worship His Majesty because only through him can you see God. Christ has the victory over death and the false doctrines of the devil because he follows the Word of Emperor Haile Sellassie The First. The world must admonish the divinity of His Majesty so that peace may reign and the corrupt principles which debase humanity will be nullified. Spirituality is the driving force behind all policies and actions, if it is corrupt then there can never be a beneficial outcome. We have noticed that there are some groups who use their religion to try to justify casting down other people. In the name of God they kill, oppress, and persecute the multitudes because they have the wrong outlook on life. Their actions are a clear demonstration that they are not of God and lack the proper understanding of spiritual matters. They claim to follow the Most Benevolent Creator, yet they abuse those who are not of their faith and deprive them of their basic human rights; as if these are the tenants or the example of our Heavenly Father. It is for this reason that the LORD sent his messenger Jesus Christ to teach the people that Haile Sellassie The First is the Almighty. If the world would adopt the policies of His Majesty then our current problems would quickly dissipate.

"For this is thankworthy, if a man for conscience toward God endure grief, suffering wrongfully. For what glory is it, if, when you be buffeted for your faults, you shall take it patiently? But if, when you do well, and suffer for it, you take it patiently, this is acceptable with God" (1 Peter 2:19-20).

"The Spirit of the Lord GOD is upon me; because the LORD has anointed me to preach good tidings unto the meek; he has sent me to bind up the brokenhearted, to proclaim liberty to the captives, and the opening of the prison to them that are bound; To proclaim the acceptable year of the LORD, and the day of vengeance of our God; to comfort all that mourn; To appoint unto them that mourn in Zion, to given unto them beauty for ashes, the oil of joy for mourning, the garment of praise for the spirit of heaviness; that they might be called trees of righteousness, the planting of the LORD, that he might be glorified" (Isaiah 61:1-3).

---

[17] Acts 17:27

"And he was seen many days of them which came up with him from Galilee to Jerusalem, who are witnesses unto the people. And we declare unto you glad tidings, how that the promise which was made unto the fathers, God has fulfilled the same unto us their children, in that he has raised up Jesus again; as it is also written in the second psalm, Thou art my Son, this day have I begotten thee" (Acts 13:31-33).

We know that the Son of God has risen and he has given us an understanding so that we may know that Emperor Haile Sellassie The First is the Almighty Father. The honest principles of salvation have been dictated by His Majesty, it is now up to us to uphold his high tenants. Racism and ethnocentricity are false because the idea that one set of people are chosen from birth to be better than everyone else is an absurd interpretation of the Bible that will only build strife due to its blatant unfair and vile premise. So whereas, the real Israelites go unrecognized because the world does not admonish Emperor Haile Sellassie The First, our reproach is not ethical as history can best attest to the saving grace of His Majesty. Yet the Jews in the Middle East, who claim to be of Zion, have caused tremendous afflictions through wars, oppression, monetary coercion, and deceit; but are held in high regard as somehow being the Israel of God. Our birthright is a spiritual adoption open to anyone who loves the LORD, for we have been born again to give praise unto the blessed and only Potentate, the King of Glory Emperor Haile Sellassie The First. Christ has comforted all that mourn in preaching the acceptable gospel of Yahweh that will free the world from perdition and strife.

"That you may with one mind and one mouth glorify God, even the Father of our Lord Jesus Christ. Wherefore receive ye one another, as Christ also received us, to the glory of God. Now I say that Jesus Christ was a minister of the circumcision for the truth of God, to confirm the promises made unto the fathers: And that the Gentiles might glorify God for his mercy; as it is written, For this cause I will confess to thee among the Gentiles, and sing unto your name. And again he said, Rejoice, ye Gentiles, with his people" (Romans 15:6-11).

"Therefore we ought to give the more earnest heed to the things which we have heard, lest at any time we should let them slip. For if the word spoken by angels was stedfast, and every transgression and disobedience received a just recompense of reward; How shall we escape, if we neglect so great salvation; which at the first began to be spoken by the Lord, and was confirmed unto us by them that heard him" (Hebrews 2:1-4).

"That their hearts might be comforted, being knit together in love, and unto all riches of the full assurance of understanding, to the acknowledgment of the mystery of God, and of the Father, and of Christ; In whom are hid all the treasures of wisdom and knowledge. And this I say, lest any man should beguile you with enticing word. For though I be absent in the flesh, yet am I with you in the spirit, joying and beholding your order, and the stedfastness of your faith in Christ. As you have therefore received Christ Jesus the Lord, so walk in him: Rooted and built up in him, and established in the faith, as you have been taught, abounding therein with thanksgiving. Beware lest any man spoil you through philosophy and vain deceit, after the tradition of men, after the rudiments of the world, and not after Christ. For in him dwells all the fullness of the Godhead bodily. And you are complete in him, which is the head of all principality and power" (Colossians 2:2-10).

It is not possible to know the truth unless you acknowledge the mystery which is that Emperor Haile Sellassie The First is the Almighty; this is the gospel of Christ. As there is only one God, there is room for only one faith so it is important for the devotee to understand the parables correctly so that you may become one with the LORD. The religious world is void of salvation because they look into space for an invisible sky djinni; but the children of Israel worship the King of Zion. We know the Creator because we have proof of his existence, the scriptures have promised us evidence to justify our beliefs and to prove our point. Before His Majesty was manifest in the flesh, the world could only hypothesize about theology but now speculation has been replaced with revelation. We must accept Emperor Haile Sellassie The First for he is the truth and there is none else.

"Therefore, seeing we have this ministry, as we have received mercy, we faint not; But have renounced the hidden things of dishonesty, not walking in craftiness, nor handling the word of God deceitfully; but, by manifestation of the truth, commending ourselves to every man's conscience in the sight of God. But if our gospel be hid, it is hid to them that are lost: In whom the god of this world has blinded the minds of them which believe not, lest the light of the glorious gospel of Christ, who is the image of God, should shine unto them" (2 Corinthians 4:1-4).

"Then Paul stood in the midst of Mars' hill, and said, Ye men of Athens, I perceive that in all things you are too superstitious. For as I passed by, and beheld your devotions, I found an altar with this inscription, TO THE UNKNOWN GOD. Whom therefore ye ignorantly worship, him declare I unto you. God that made the world

and all things therein, seeing that he is Lord of heaven and earth, dwells not in temples made with hands; Neither is worshipped with men's hands, as though he needed any thing, seeing he gives to all life, and breath, and all things; And has made of one blood all nations of men for to dwell on all the face of the earth, and has determined the times before appointed, and the bounds of their habitation; That they should seek the Lord, if haply they might feel after him, and find him, though he be not far from every one of us" (Acts 17:22-27).

His Majesty said, "Spiritual power is the eternal guide, in this life and the life after,"[18] therefore we know that the flesh profits nothing. We must realize that there is a living soul encapsulated in our bodies that passes on after our natural anatomy perishes. Therefore it would be incorrect to judge the divine distinction of Emperor Haile Sellassie The First based upon his corpse when the spirit is life. If we think that the Godhead is based upon him being physically immortal, then that would be incorrect because it defies the laws of nature which the LORD established; which is why His Majesty said, "In this world there lives no man, however prudent or zealous, who can escape death."[19] To believe that anyone who walked the earth can escape dying only means that you have the wrong outlook on life; the body is not eternal only the soul. With the right perspective we have been made to understand that the Spirit of Haile Sellassie The First is that of the Supreme Being who is omniscient and omnipotent; we worship his essence not the anatomy. Of course God is eternal and it is written that he would appear on earth so that we are not left on our own to debate his existence; he has proven his actuality through his own embodiment. For he is the Almighty before we have seen his face and he is the same after the body passes away; he always was and always will be the LORD. Everyone that was born shall die, the real question is how will we live; Haile Sellassie The First said, "Man is mortal, each one of Us here will, one day, face his Maker and answer for his actions."[20] The world beyond is a topic that only the Creator can discuss, but we can see how the righteous judgment of the Almighty is non evasive both in this life and the life after.

"First, I thank my God through Jesus Christ for you all, that your faith is spoken of throughout the whole world. For God is my witness, whom I serve with my spirit

---

[18] The Selected Speeches of Haile Selassie I, page 631
[19] Talbot, David Abner, Haile Selassie I Silver Jubilee, page 11
[20] The Selected Speeches of Haile Selassie I, page 416

in the gospel of his Son, that without ceasing I make mention of you always in my prayers" (Romans 1:8-9).

"For our exhortation was not of deceit, nor of uncleanness, nor in guile: But as we were allowed of God to be put in trust with the gospel, even so we speak; not as pleasing men, but God, which tries our hearts. For neither at any time used we flattering words, as you know, nor a cloke of covetousness; God is witness" (1 Thessalonians 2:3-6).

"For I am not ashamed of the gospel of Christ: for it is the power of God unto salvation to every one that believes; to the Jew first, and also to the Greek. For therein is the righteousness of God revealed from faith to faith: as it is written, The just shall live by faith. For the wrath of God is revealed from heaven against all ungodliness and unrighteousness of men, who hold the truth in unrighteousness; Because that which may be known of God is manifest in them; for God has showed it unto them. For the invisible things of him from the creation of the world are clearly seen, being understood by the things that are made, even his eternal power and Godhead; so that they are without excuse" (Romans 1:16-20).

There once was a time when man could only make an educated guess about the nature of the LORD; but the times of this ignorance have passed because Emperor Haile Sellassie The First has revealed that he is God. Before he appeared on earth, the people had no choice but to look into the sky and speculate on his divinity. Back then His Majesty was able to hear everybody's prayers and he still is because the Creator is eternal. The spirit realm cannot be considered to be supernatural because whatever parameters the LORD has established are the guidelines for which the entire universe is subject unto; it is only when we suppose that it is possible to deviate from the standard protocol that apocryphal traditions are set up. The Most High is infinite, he sees and knows everything, but the ethereal dimension does not impede upon our earthly sphere. Therefore we should not think that a ghost can interfere in our everyday lives or that our actions have been predestined for us. It is written how things will be because God is omniscient, he knows what we will do but he is not making us do it; we have been granted free will to decide our fate. We preach only that which we have learned from Emperor Haile Sellassie The First, our gospel is without subtlety because we do not craft together precepts which are unfounded or incorrect. It is important to be wise for we have studied His Majesty who was, is, and always will be, the greatest of all scholars.

The Fifth Letter

His Majesty sent a mighty one, which is our brother Jesus Christ, to save Israel, the people of God. The Bible says that Jesus will save us for he is the Prophet, the Savior of the world. Give glory to His Majesty through his Son Jesus Christ our Lord and Savior, the Ethiopian, native son of the Highest, Emperor Haile Sellassie The First, God of all ages.

"For Moses truly said unto the fathers, A prophet shall the Lord your God raise up unto you of your brethren, like unto me; him shall you hear in all things whatsoever he shall say unto you. And it shall come to pass, that every soul, which will not hear that prophet, shall be destroyed from among the people. Yea, and all the prophets from Samuel and those that follow after, as many as have spoken, have likewise foretold of these days. You are the children of the prophets, and of the covenant which God made with our fathers, saying unto Abraham, And in thy seed shall all the kindreds of the earth be blessed. Unto you first God, having raised up his Son Jesus, sent him to bless you, in turning away every one of you from his iniquities" (Acts 3:22-26).

"My covenant was with him of life and peace; and I gave them to him for the fear wherewith he feared me, and was afraid before my name. The law of truth was in his mouth, and iniquity was not found in his lips: he walked with me in peace and equity, and did turn many away from iniquity" (Malachi 2:5-6).

The world is blessed through Jesus Christ because his testimony is the truth about God. Only through the Son can we understand the mystery of the Father to know that Emperor Haile Sellassie The First is the Almighty. The only way to receive the gift of life in knowing God is by accepting the gospel of the LORD's messenger. The world has not obtained this level of salvation for if they did then they would be able to see the Most High as promised. To believe that Jesus was on earth around 7 AD goes against his purpose and prophecy. The deliverance of the Prophet is for us to accept the manifestation of God in the flesh. From that time until now, the only concept that people have of the Father is through paintings and sculptures which are banned in the Bible as being sacrilegious. That indicates that the interpretation which states that

Christ came thousands of years ago cannot be true according to the Bible. The principles of righteousness are to be established by the Son of God, even if people do not follow them, these edicts would at least be known after Jesus Christ has come. The evidence of the Messiah on earth is found in his testimony because the knowledge which he brings is unparalleled. As the world lay void in not being able to identify the Almighty Father, this is a clear indication that the prophecy was not fulfilled in antiquity.

"Wherefore, holy brethren, partakers of the heavenly calling, consider the Apostle and High Priest of our profession, Christ Jesus" (Hebrew 3:1).

"For the priest's lips should keep knowledge, and they should seek the law at his mouth: for he is the messenger of the LORD of hosts" (Malachi 2:7).

"But you shall be named the Priests of the LORD: men shall call you the Ministers of our God: you shall eat the riches of the Gentiles, and in their glory shall you boast yourselves" (Isaiah 61:6).

There is a high honor that comes with being chosen by God, it is important that the children of Israel live up to their calling. The first step is spiritual, you must ground yourself in the proper understanding of the LORD; which is to know that Emperor Haile Sellassie The First is the Almighty. After your heart has been made sure of the testimony of Christ, the next act is physical by putting his principles into action. As a person matures in the faith and corrects their unsavory ways which do not coincide with the purpose of His Majesty our leader, the distinct traits of Israel will be manifest for all people to respect and emulate. It is not acceptable to say that you are of God yet indulge in bad behavior. We have found that in the Middle East there is a set of people who label themselves as being Jewish yet they bolster the biggest homosexual celebration in the world and persecute other people who do not share their beliefs. It is written, "He that says to the wicked, You are righteous; him shall the people curse, the nations shall hate him" (Proverbs 24:24). The challenge of identifying the children of Israel has always been a question surrounding Ethiopia and Jerusalem. If we consider the horn of Africa, we would find an Emperor who was perfect in all his doings, bearing the name and the character of the Almighty upon the throne of David. Also if we study world history, we would know that from the ancient beginnings, the Ethiopian highlands were referred to as Punt, which means God's Land; and even the notion of going into the sky to meet the Lord derives from a depiction of Ethiopia with its mainland situated on top of vast elevated mountaintops that appear to reach into the clouds.

"Let every one of us please his neighbor for his good to edification. For even Christ pleased not himself; but, as it is written, The reproaches of them that reproached you fell on me. For whatsoever things were written aforetime were written for our learning, that we through patience and comfort of the scriptures might have hope. Now the God of patience and consolation grant you to be likeminded one toward another according to Christ Jesus: That you may with one mind and mouth glorify God, even the Father of our Lord Jesus Christ. Wherefore receive ye one another, as Christ also received us, to the glory of God. Now I say that Jesus Christ was a minister of the circumcision for the truth of God, to confirm the promises made unto the fathers" (Romans 15:2-8).

"Him has God exalted with his right hand to be a Prince and a Savior, for to give repentance to Israel, and forgiveness of sins" (Acts 5:31).

"I am the good shepherd: the good shepherd gives his life for the sheep. But he that is a hireling, and not the shepherd, whose own the sheep are not, sees the wolf coming, and leaves the sheep, and flees: and the wolf catches them, and scatters the sheep. The hireling flees, because he is a hireling, and cares not for the sheep. I am the good shepherd, and know my sheep, and am known of mine. As the Father knows me, even so know I the Father: and I lay down my life for the sheep. And other sheep I have, which are not of this fold: them also I must bring, and they shall hear my voice; and there shall be one fold, and one shepherd. Therefore does my Father love me, because I lay down my life, that I might take it again. No man takes it from me, but I lay it down of myself. I have power to lay it down, and I have power to take it again. This commandment have I received of my Father. There was a division therefore again among the Jews for these sayings. And many of them said, He has a devil, and is mad; why hear ye him? Others said, These are not the words of him that has a devil. Can a devil open the eyes of the blind" (John 10:11-21).

The real people of God are those who accept the testimony of Jesus Christ that Emperor Haile Sellassie The First is the Almighty. Men can label themselves to be anything but according to the Bible there are certain conditions which you would have to adhere to in order to be accepted by the LORD. It is therefore necessary that our faith be established to please God and not man.

Jesus is the Prophet of His Majesty, he preached the true message of salvation; everyone who loves the LORD will accept his gospel. It is not acceptable to make up your own interpretation of God to suite your perspective; everyone must adhere to the tenants of Christ. The reality is that the truth about the Most High must challenge our beliefs because none of us is perfect. Therefore we must be ready to question ourselves as the improper elements that we maintain will be condemned when we learn about the Almighty. That is why Jesus was rejected by those who loved their traditions more than the truth; his message is the determining factor that either justifies or else damns a person in the sight of God. If you make an honest assessment of your faith and realize that your customs do not coincide with reason and love then it would be impossible to find favor with the LORD. At that point it would be necessary to repent which is to renounce our unpleasant customs and ideologies. We all have the opportunity to be saved through Christ but we must accept correction because everyone has fallen short of the glory of Emperor Haile Sellassie The First. Let us remain true to the principles of salvation so that we may obtain favor from the Most High Jah Rastafari.

"And Jesus answered him, saying, It is written, That man shall not live by bread alone, but by every word of God. And the devil, taking him up into a high mountain, showed unto him all the kingdoms of the world in a moment of time. And the devil said unto him, All this power will I give you, and the glory of them: for that is delivered unto me; and to whomsoever I will, I give it. If you therefore will worship me, all shall be yours. And Jesus answered and said unto him, Get thee behind me, Satan: for it is written, You shall worship the Lord thy God, and him only shall you serve. And he brought him to Jerusalem, and set him on a pinnacle of the temple, and said unto him, If you be the Son of God, cast yourself down from here: for it is written, He shall give his angels charge over you, to keep you: And in their hands they shall bear you up, lest at any time you dash your foot against a stone. And Jesus answering said unto him, It is said, You shall not tempt the Lord thy God. And when the devil had ended all the temptation, he departed from him for a season. And Jesus returned in the power of the Spirit into Galilee: and there went out a fame of him through all the region round about. And he taught in their synagogues, being glorified of all. And he came to Nazareth, where he had been brought up: and, as his custom was, he went into the synagogue on the Sabbath day, and stood up for to read. And there was delivered unto him the book of the prophet Elias. And when he had opened the book, he found the place where it was written, The Spirit of the Lord is upon me, because he has anointed me to preach the gospel to the poor; he has sent

me to heal the brokenhearted, to preach deliverance to the captives, and recovering of sight to the blind, to set at liberty them that are bruised, To preach the acceptable year of the Lord. And he closed the book, and he gave it again to the minister, and sat down. And the eyes of all them that were in the synagogue were fastened on him. And he began to say unto them, This day is this scripture fulfilled in your ears" (Luke 4:11-21).

"The burden of Egypt. Behold, the LORD rides upon a swift cloud, and shall come into Egypt: and the idols of Egypt shall be moved at his presence, and the heart of Egypt shall melt in the midst of it. And I will set the Egyptians against the Egyptians: and they shall fight every one against his brother, and every one against his neighbor; city against city, and kingdom against kingdom. And the spirit of Egypt shall fail in the midst thereof; and I will destroy the counsel thereof: and they shall seek to the idols, and to the charmers, and to them that have familiar spirits, and to the wizards. And the Egyptians will I give over into the hand of a cruel lord; and a fierce king shall rule over them, says the Lord, the LORD of hosts. And the waters shall fail from the sea, and the river shall be wasted and dried up. And they shall turn the rivers far away; and the brooks of defence shall be emptied and dried up: the reeds and flags shall wither. The paper reeds by the brooks, by the mouth of the brooks, and every thing sown by the brooks, shall wither, be driven away, and be no more. The fishers also shall mourn, and all they that cast angle into the brooks shall lament, and they that spread nets upon the waters shall languish. Moreover they that work in fine flax, and they that weave networks, shall be confounded. And they shall be broken in the purposes thereof, all that make sluices and ponds for fish. Surely the princes of Zoan are fools, the counsel of the wise counsellors of Pharaoh is become brutish: how say ye unto Pharaoh, I am the son of the wise, the son of ancient kings? Where are they? where are your wise men? and let them tell thee now, and let them know what the LORD of hosts has purposed upon Egypt. The princes of Zoan are become fools, the princes of Noph are deceived; they have also seduced Egypt, even they that are the stay of the tribes thereof. The LORD has mingled a perverse spirit in the midst thereof: and they have caused Egypt to error in every work thereof, as a drunken man staggers in his vomit. Neither shall there be any work for Egypt, which the head or tail, branch or rush, may do. In that day shall Egypt be like unto women: and it shall be afraid and fear because of the shaking of the hand of the LORD of hosts, which he shaketh over it. And the land of Judah shall be a terror unto Egypt, every one that maketh mention thereof shall be afraid in himself, because of the counsel of the LORD of hosts, which he has determined against it. In that day shall five cities in the land of Egypt speak the language of

Canaan, and swear to the LORD of hosts; one shall be called, The city of destruction. In that day shall there be an altar to the LORD in the midst of the land of Egypt, and a pillar at the border thereof to the LORD. And it shall be for a sign and for a witness unto the LORD of hosts in the land of Egypt: for they shall cry unto the LORD because of the oppressors, and he shall send them a savior, and a great one, and he shall deliver them. And the LORD shall be known to Egypt, and the Egyptians shall know the LORD in that day, and shall do sacrifice and oblation; yea, they shall vow a vow unto the LORD, and perform it. And the LORD shall smite Egypt: he shall smite and heal it: and they shall return even to the LORD, and he shall be intreated of them, and shall heal them. In that day shall there be a highway out of Egypt to Assyria, and the Assyrian shall come into Egypt, and the Egyptian into Assyria, and the Egyptians shall serve with the Assyrians. In that day shall Israel be the third with Egypt and with Assyria, even a blessing in the midst of the land: Whom the LORD of hosts shall bless, saying, Blessed be Egypt my people, and Assyria the work of my hands, and Israel mine inheritance. In the year that Tartan came unto Ashdod, (when Sargon the king of Assyria sent him,) and fought against Ashdod, and took it; At the same time spake the LORD by Isaiah the son of Amoz, saying, Go and loose the sackcloth from off your loins, and put off your shoe from your foot. And he did so, walking naked and barefoot. And the LORD said, Like as my servant Isaiah has walked naked and barefoot three years for a sign and wonder upon Egypt and upon Ethiopia; So shall the king of Assyria lead away the Egyptians prisoners, and the Ethiopians captives, young and old, naked and barefoot, even with their buttocks uncovered, to the shame of Egypt. And they shall be afraid and ashamed of Ethiopia their expectation, and of Egypt their glory. And the inhabitant of this isle shall say in that day, Behold, such is our expectation, whither we flee for help to be delivered from the king of Assyria: and how shall we escape" (Isaiah Chapters 19 & 20).

It is written, my people are destroyed from lack of knowledge[21] because their misguided outlook on life makes them corrupt. The scriptures have warned us that the deceiver will present a false interpretation of the scriptures that does not coincide with logic or truth. We therefore need to be mindful not to be taken by clever prose and to study the end result of these religious teachings. If they offer you a pie in the sky or a perspective that neglects your intrinsic nature and intellect then it is not of God. We have to safeguard our humanity and maximize our potential; there is no other real

---

[21] Hosea 4:6

translation of salvation. The doctrine of Christ is the only way to know the truth, Jesus taught us as one who had authority because he understands the parables. His testimony is that Haile Sellassie The First is the Almighty God and history can best attest to the fact that the world would be a much better place if the people did not turn their backs on the Emperor. Jesus accepts the divinity of His Majesty and this makes him one with God. All of the descriptions of Christ indicate that he is a preacher not a political sovereign. There is only one Potentate and that is Emperor Haile Sellassie The First, it does not correlate with nature or reality for a father and his son to be the same entity. Christ is described with the titles of the Lord because he works for God's kingdom, he represents His Majesty; therefore when you see Jesus you see the Father because he does not speak about himself but Emperor Haile Sellassie The First. The parables of the Bible have a logical bearing, the Word offers concrete salvation because the scriptures are meant to save the soul of the devotee for which there is no fluff or illusion that can supersede our redemption.

"I will raise them up a Prophet from among their brethren, like unto thee, and will put my words in his mouth; and he shall speak unto them all that I shall command him" (Deuteronomy 18:18).

"And as Moses lifted up the serpent in the wilderness, even so must the Son of man be lifted up: That whosoever believes in him should not perish, but have eternal life. For God so loved the world, that he gave his only begotten Son, that whosoever believes in him should not perish, but have everlasting life. For God sent not his Son into the world to condemn the world; but that the world through him might be saved" (John 3:14-17).

"For he whom God has sent speaks the words of God: for God gives not the Spirit by measure unto him" (John 3:34).

God has delivered a Prophet unto us because throughout the world, people offer incorrect interpretations of the scriptures; their understanding of the Lord is false. If the Almighty loves humanity, he would make a way for us to obtain real salvation; so that our spiritual rituals may have a significant meaning and not just be a ceremonial expose which only pleases men. The Rastafarians openly declare that Emperor Haile Sellassie The First is the Almighty but then shy away from any religious categorization due to the depth of this issue. The notion of His Majesty being Christ in his kingly character is wrong as well as the popular reference that Revelation 5:5 is referring to Haile Sellassie The First. Just as the entire Bible indicates, God rose up a Prophet to preach the true message of salvation for which the rest of the world was unaware of. The descriptions of the Lamb in the book of Revelation portray a man who stood before the Throne of God and was found worthy to take the book out of the hand of the Almighty. This fascinating image outlines the fact that the Father and the Son are two different people; it also demonstrates which one of them is God the King. Only one person understands the mysteries that is why Jesus Christ is the way, the truth, and the light into heaven; he is the only one whose testimony about Rastafari coincided with the principles of the Emperor and the Bible. The religious leaders now have to sell their riches by forsaking their status and false ideologies; only in this way can they learn the true knowledge of the LORD, to then be found worthy of their position.

"I am come a light into the world, that whosoever believes on me should not abide in darkness. And if any man hear my words, and believe not, I judge him not: for I came not to judge the world, but to save the world. He that rejects me, and receives not my words, has one that judges him: the word that I have spoken, the same shall judge him in the last day. For I have not spoken of myself; but the Father which sent me, he gave me a commandment what I should say, and what I should speak. And I know that his commandment is life everlasting: whatsoever I speak therefore, even as the Father said unto me, so I speak" (John 12:46-50).

"And the spirit of the LORD shall rest upon him, the spirit of wisdom and understanding, the spirit of counsel and might, the spirit of knowledge and of the fear of the LORD" (Isaiah 11:2).

"The hand of the LORD was upon me, and carried me out in the spirit of the LORD, and set me down in the midst of the valley which was full of bones, And caused me to pass by them round about: and, behold, there were very many in the open valley; and, lo, they were very dry. And he said unto me, Son of man, can these bones live? And I answered, O Lord GOD, thou knowest. Again he said unto me, Prophesy upon these bones, and say unto them, O ye dry bones, hear the word of the LORD. Thus saith the Lord GOD unto these bones; Behold, I will cause breath to enter into you, and you shall live: And I will lay sinews upon you, and will bring up flesh upon you, and cover you with skin, and put breath in you, and you shall live; and you shall know that I am the LORD. So I prophesied as I was commanded: and as

I prophesied, there was a noise, and behold a shaking, and the bones came together, bone to his bone. And when I beheld, lo, the sinews and the flesh came up upon them, and the skin covered them above: but there was no breath in them. Then said he unto me, Prophesy unto the wind, prophesy, son of man, and say to the wind, Thus saith the Lord GOD; Come from the four winds, O breath, and breathe upon these slain, that they may live. So I prophesied as he commanded me, and the breath came into them, and they lived, and stood up upon their feet, an exceeding great army. Then he said unto me, Son of man, these bones are the whole house of Israel: behold, they say, Our bones are dried, and our hope is lost: we are cut off for our parts. Therefore prophesy and say unto them, Thus saith the Lord GOD; Behold, O my people, I will open your graves, and cause you to come up out of your graves, and bring you into the land of Israel" (Ezekiel 37:1-12).

The Bible describes the gospel of Christ as being life eternal because he preaches the true message of salvation which gives his disciples the correct understanding of God. This does not make you physically immortal, it makes you sanctioned by the LORD which allows you to be able to discern the righteous principles of heaven. The Father commanded the Son to preach the Word unto the dry bones of Israel, as this will cause breath to enter into their lungs, and shall raise them out of their graves. As the prophecy states that Christ was sent to speak unto the people, the dead implies a facet undone, this is when you do not know the truth about the Most High. But if you accept the gospel of the only begotten Son of God, then you shall inherit everlasting life, which is to know that Emperor Haile Sellassie The First is the Almighty. The Bible clearly states that Christ created men in the spiritual sense,[22] by teaching you the truth about God; you are made in the image of the LORD when you know who is the Father and accept his divinity. If you interpret these scriptures to be literal then this invokes an enchantment where human beings live forever in the flesh and the monotheistic deity is multiple entities. Our salvation must be real therefore we will avoid all false mythological ideologies.

"Verily, verily, I say unto you, the hour is coming, and now is, when the dead shall hear the voice of the Son of God: and they that hear shall live. Marvel not at this: for the hour is coming, in the which all that are in the graves shall hear his voice" (John 5:25 & 28).

---

[22] Ephesians 3:9

"For this is good and acceptable in the sight of God our Savior; Who will have all men to be saved, and to come unto the knowledge of the truth. For there is one God, and one mediator between God and men, the man Christ Jesus; Who gave himself a ransom for all, to be testified in due time. Whereunto I am ordained a preacher, and an apostle, (I speak the truth in Christ, and lie not;) a teacher of the Gentiles in faith and verity" (1 Timothy 2:3-7).

"As every man has received the gift, even so minister the same one to another, as good stewards of the manifold grace of God. If any man speak, let him speak as the oracles of God; if any man minister, let him do it as of the ability which God gives: that God in all things may be glorified through Jesus Christ, to whom be praise and dominion forever and ever. Amen" (1 Peter 4:10-11).

Iyesus Kristos was sent to teach the people the truth about the LORD because there was no man on earth who knew the correct interpretation of the scriptures. It is evident that they lack exactitude because they employ unreal ideologies, such as the supernatural, to explain the parables of the Bible. The miracles of Christ are allegories, what makes the Son of God so special is not that he is a great wizard but that his theological acumen is so stunningly prudent. When it says that he walked on water this means that his wisdom was above that of the world; his gospel was greater than all others. To understand the real significance of the Messiah would let anyone know that Jesus did not come in antiquity because the people still hold onto pagan ideas and do not know who God is. Of course everyone will not have the truth but those who claim to follow Christ should, or at least a remnant would, yet we have found all of them lacking. The paintings of Jesus that were approved by Rome, depict a fair skinned lad who came on earth around 7 AD. These are all fake because there was no mechanism to capture an accurate portrait of any individual during that time, in fact we know that the famous images of many subsequent prominent individuals such as Christopher Columbus and William Shakespeare are all alloyed for this same reason. That is why the Bible said do not put your trust in idols, deceitful works of art that mislead the congregant. The churches do not have the proper religious standpoint because they preach an irrational dogma and live an immoral life. If they knew who Jesus was, then they would know that Emperor Haile Sellassie The First is God; and if they accepted His Majesty then they would adopt his principles.

"If you abide in me, and my words abide in you, you shall ask what you will, and it shall be done unto you. Herein is my Father glorified, that you bear much fruit; so shall you be my disciples. As the Father has loved me, so have I loved you: continue ye in my love. If you keep my commandments, you shall abide in my love; even as I have kept my Father's commandments, and abide in his love. These things have I spoken unto you, that my joy might remain in you, and that your joy might be full. This is my commandment, That you love one another, as I have loved you. Greater love has no man than this, that a man lay down his life for his friends. You are my friends, if you do whatsoever I command you. Henceforth I call you not servants; for the servant knows not what his lord does: but I have called you friends; for all things that I have heard of my Father I have made known unto you. You have not chosen me, but I have chosen you, and ordained you, that you should go and bring forth fruit, and that your fruit should remain: that whatsoever you shall ask of the Father in my name, he may give it to you" (John 15:7-16).

"Grace be unto you, and peace, from God our Father, and from the Lord Jesus Christ. I thank my God always on your behalf, for the grace of God which is given you by Jesus Christ; That in every thing you are enriched by him, in all utterance, and in all knowledge; Even as the testimony of Christ was confirmed in you: So that you come behind in no gift; waiting for the coming of our Lord Jesus Christ: Who shall also confirm you unto the end, that you may be blameless in the day of our Lord Jesus Christ. God is faithful, by whom you were called unto the fellowship of his Son Jesus Christ our Lord. Now I beseech you, brethren, by the name of our Lord Jesus Christ, that you all speak the same thing, and that there be no divisions among you; but that you be perfectly joined together in the same mind and in the same judgment" (1 Corinthians 1:3-10).

"Endeavoring to keep the unity of the Spirit in the bond of peace. There is one body, and one Spirit, even as you are called in one hope of your calling; One Lord, one faith, one baptism, One God and Father of all, who is above all, and through all, and in you all. But unto every one of us is given grace according to the measure of the gift of Christ. Wherefore he said, When he ascended up on high, he led captivity captive, and gave gifts unto men. (Now that he ascended, what is it but that he also descended first into the lower parts of the earth? He that descended is the same also that ascended up far above all heavens, that he might fill all things.) And he gave some, apostles; and some, prophets; and some, evangelists; and some, pastors and teachers; For the perfecting of the saints, for the work of the ministry, for the edifying of the body of Christ: Till we all come in the unity

of the faith, and of the knowledge of the Son of God, unto a perfect man, unto the measure of the stature of the fullness of Christ: That we henceforth be no more children, tossed to and fro, and carried about with every wind of doctrine, by the sleight of men, and cunning craftiness whereby they lie in wait to deceive; But speaking the truth in love, may grow up into him in all things, which is the head, even Christ: From whom the whole body fitly joined together and compacted by that which every joint supplies, according to the effectual working in the measure of every part, makes increase of the body unto the edifying of itself in love. This I say therefore, and testify in the Lord, that you henceforth walk not as other Gentiles walk, in the vanity of their mind, Having the understanding darkened, being alienated from the life of God through the ignorance that is in them, because of the blindness of their heart: Who being past feeling have given themselves over unto lasciviousness, to work all uncleanness with greediness. But you have not so learned Christ; If so be that you have heard him, and have been taught by him, as the truth is in Jesus" (Ephesians 4:3-21).

The essence of monotheism means that there is only one truth and everyone on earth must adhere to it. It is not possible to have different interpretations about the same Creator and all of them be accurate, especially when God declared his position and sent his Prophet to affirm the gospel. The scriptures have directed us to follow Jesus Christ because he is the door into heaven, anyone who does not adhere to his testimony does not know the truth. The inaccurate explanations of the Bible leads to the corruption of the soul and the adaptation of unethical policies; that is why the main cause of war is religion. In order for the world to be liberated from the distorted principles that destroy humanity it is necessary for everyone to put their faith in God Emperor Haile Sellassie The First. His Majesty said, "We cannot impose our views by force. We have only the power of moral persuasion. This is our strength - and a great strength - if we will but use it."[23] It is important to note that the major religions grew in number because they violently imposed their beliefs upon people, whereas, the truth about Rastafari, shall win over the world by the wisdom of its counsel. Let HIM be Praised.

"I charge thee before God, and the Lord Jesus Christ, and the elect angels, that you observe these things without preferring one before another, doing nothing by partiality" (1 Timothy 5:21).

---

[23] The Selected Speeches of Haile Selassie I, page 271

"And he that searches the hearts knows what is the mind of the Spirit, because he makes intercession for the saints according to the will of God. And we know that all things work together for good to them that love God, to them who are the called according to his purpose. For whom he did foreknow, he also did predestinate to be conformed to the image of his Son, that he might be the firstborn among many brethren. Moreover, whom he did predestinate, them he also called: and whom he called, them he also justified: and whom he justified, them he also glorified. What shall we then say to these things? If God be for us, who can be against us? He that spared not his own Son, but delivered him up for us all, how shall he not with him also freely give us all things? Who shall lay any thing to the charge of God's elect? It is God that justifieth. Who is he that condemns? It is Christ that died, yea rather, that is risen again, who is even at the right hand of God, who also makes intercession for us. Who shall separate us from the love of Christ? Shall tribulation, or distress, or persecution, or famine, or nakedness, or peril, or sword? As it is written, For your sake we are killed all the day long; we are accounted as sheep for the slaughter. Nay, in all these things we are more than conquerors through him that loved us. For I am persuaded, that neither death, nor life, nor angels, nor principalities, nor powers, nor things present, nor things to come, Nor height, nor depth, nor any creature, shall be able to separate us from the love of God, which is in Christ Jesus our Lord" (Romans 8:27-39).

"Let as many servants as are under the yoke count their own masters worthy of all honor, that the name of God and his doctrine be not blasphemed. And they that have believing masters, let them not despise them, because they are brethren; but rather do them service, because they are faithful and beloved, partakers of the benefit. These things teach and exhort. If any man teach otherwise, and consent not to wholesome words, even the words of our Lord Jesus Christ, and to the doctrine which is according to godliness; He is proud, knowing nothing, but doting about questions and strifes of words, whereof comes envy, strife, railings, evil surmisings" (1 Timothy 6:1-4).

Faith is a personal sentiment, it is a vocation meant to please the LORD, offered from a person's own free will; it is not theater to gratify your family and friends. If anyone chooses to study religion objectively, it would be impossible to deny the divinity of Emperor Haile Sellassie The First. He is the first and the last King of Kings and Lord of Lords; the Bible says that God will not give his glory to another. Yet we have found that people do not approach the LORD honestly and for that reason they live immoral lives and do not accept the gospel of Jesus Christ. Our spiritual brothers are without excuse as to why they do not follow God; there is even double dealing within the Rastafarian camps which shall not go unpunished. The mission and goals of Emperor Haile Sellassie The First has nothing to do with smoking ganja, growing dreadlocks, singing reggae music, and holding fast to ancient customs. So how did we get to the point where our people are following customs that have nothing to do with the real purpose of their faith; the answer is the same among all religions. These traditions were set up by men for their own benefit, they never was sincere with God. That is why Jesus Christ is so important, he was the first person who did the LORD's will and not his own. Everyone must be honest with themselves and repent from their vain traditions that do not glorify the true King. The only genuine measure to determine if you really love God is found within your faith and deeds; you must accept the fullness of Emperor Haile Sellassie The First.

"You therefore, my son, be strong in the grace that is in Christ Jesus. And the things that you have heard of me among many witnesses, the same commit thou to faithful men, who shall be able to teach others also. You therefore endure hardness, as a good solider of Jesus Christ. No man that wars entangles himself with the affairs of this life; that he may please him who has chosen him to be a solider" (2 Timothy 2:1-4).

"Remember them which have the rule over you, who have spoken unto you the word of God: whose faith follow, considering the end of their conversation. Jesus Christ the same yesterday, and today, and forever. Be not carried about with divers and strange doctrines: for it is a good thing that the heart be established with grace; not with meats, which have not profited them that have been occupied therein" (Hebrew 13:7-9).

"Now the God of peace, that brought again from the dead our Lord Jesus, that great shepherd of the sheep, through the blood of the everlasting covenant, Make you perfect in every good work to do his will, working in you that which is wellpleasing in his sight, through Jesus Christ; to whom be glory forever and ever. Amen. And I beseech you, brethren, suffer the word of exhortation: for I have written a letter unto you in few words" (Hebrew 13:20-22).

It is written that Christ and his disciples were not of this world because they did not place the concerns of society above the will of God. It did not matter if they had the approval of their family and friends to be a Rastafarian; they did this because the only thing that was important to them was the message of salvation and its true interpretation. We know that the proper spiritual discernment is not present throughout the entire globe; therefore we do not seek to be sanctioned by men. The healing of the nations is for everyone to know that Emperor Haile Sellassie The First is the Almighty Creator; the gospel of Jesus Christ permits us to understand who God is. We must denounce the false understanding of the parables which leaves the parishioners ignorant of the essence of the LORD. The redemption of Christ brings us to God who alone can save us and teach us righteousness. It is therefore extremely important that we understand who the Son of God is. Many people know that the Roman painting of the white Jesus is false, so they in turn picture him as a black man; but this also is not pleasing. Replacing one false image with another is not liberation, especially when the same improper doctrine that advocates magic, consubstantiality, and iconography, is still in place misleading the congregation. We must lose our lives to gain it, meaning that we need to let go of all the false concepts that we have been accustomed to; so that we can understand the real gospel of Jesus Christ which is to know that Emperor Haile Sellassie The First is the Almighty Father.

"Blessed is the man that endures temptation: for when he is tried, he shall receive the crown of life, which the Lord has promised to them that love him" (James 1:12).

"But with the precious blood of Christ, as of a lamb without blemish and without spot: Who verily was foreordained before the foundation of the world, but was manifest in these last times for you, Who by him do believe in God, that raised him up from the dead, and gave him glory; that your faith and hope might be in God" (1 Peter 1:19-21).

"And who is he that will harm you, if you be followers of that which is good? But and if you suffer for righteousness' sake, happy are you: and be not afraid of their terror, neither be troubled; But sanctify the Lord God in your hearts: and be ready always to give an answer to every man that asks you a reason of the hope that is in you, with meekness and fear: Having a good conscience; that, whereas they speak evil of you, as of evildoers, they may be ashamed that falsely accuse your good conversation in Christ. For it is better, if the will of God be so, that you suffer for well doing, than for evil doing. For Christ also has once suffered for sins, the just for the unjust, that he might bring us to God, being put to death in the flesh, but quickened by the Spirit: By which also he went and preached unto the

spirits in prison; Which sometime were disobedient, when once the longsuffering of God waited in the days of Noah, while the ark was a preparing, wherein few, that is, eight souls were saved by water. The like figure whereunto even baptism does also now save us (not the putting away of the filth of the flesh, but the answer of a good conscience toward God,) by the resurrection of Jesus Christ: Who is gone into heaven, and is on the right hand of God; angels and authorities and powers being made subject unto him" (1 Peter 3:13-22).

The gospel of Christ is intended for all people because it is the sole means of gaining the proper understanding of God. We should not think that Rastafari is restricted to the Caribbean community, or to any other label because the LORD has no limitations. There is only one God, so whether you are black or white, rich or poor, young or old; regardless of your nationality, or any other human condition, we all come from the same Creator. Therefore the branding of Emperor Haile Sellassie The First has to target everyone; regardless of any man made segmentation. When the Rastafari movement is packaged as being a West Indian, reggae music, ganja smoking, dreadlock association, this limits the perspective and the reach of the operation. For those people who have a different culture, it becomes hard for them to accept the divinity of His Majesty when it is identified according to these constrained aspects. Oftentimes the perception is that if you are a Rastafarian then you must remit these customs or else you are not real; this leads some people to try to speak in a Jamaican accent or to mimic other traits of the Caribbean culture in an effort to be accepted. Even though these traditions have nothing to do with the Emperor of Ethiopia and cannot justify your faith; the Rastafari brand therefore has to be amended so that people view Haile Sellassie The First according to his genius. We need to establish a culture that coincides with His Majesty's mission; which would be along the lines of education, morality, politics, religion, global unity, and progress. If the Emperor's universal principles were highlighted then many more people would accept his divinity and the world would be saved.

"And beside this, giving all diligence, add to your faith virtue; and to virtue, knowledge; And to knowledge, temperance; and to temperance, patience; and to patience, godliness; And to godliness, brotherly kindness; and to brotherly kindness, charity. For if these things be in you, and abound, they make you that you shall neither be barren nor unfruitful in the knowledge of our Lord Jesus Christ" (2 Peter 1:5-8).

"Wherefore henceforth know we no man after the flesh: yea, though we have known Christ after the flesh, yet now henceforth know we him no more. Therefore if any man be in Christ, he is a new creature: old things are passed away; behold, all things are become new. And all things are of God, who has reconciled us to himself by Jesus Christ, and has given us the ministry of reconciliation; To wit, that God was in Christ, reconciling, the world unto himself, not imputing their trespasses unto them; and has committed unto us the word of reconciliation" (2 Corinthians 5:16-19).

"For we are not as many, which corrupt the word of God: but as of sincerity, but as of God, in the sight of God speak we in Christ" (2 Corinthians 2:17).

The world needs the correct definition of God and Christ in order for there to be peace and salvation. All of the religious books praise the LORD as the saving grace for all of humanity to follow; this was not in vain. But it is easy to assume, when you have the wrong perspective of the Creator, that the prophecies have not been fulfilled and that God is not present. When people wait for a magical presence in the clouds or believe in ideas that are entirely untrue, it is then impossible to accept God or to understand how he has helped humanity. The churches must accept the real message of the Bible, which is to know that Jesus Christ was a Prophet of the LORD; the Son is not the same element as the Father. There are many who corrupt the Word of God and offer an interpretation that defies logic and our intrinsic nature; these philosophies will be put to shame by the true ministry. In order to save the world this can only be done with definitive knowledge according to the scriptures. Jesus Christ is described as the teacher of the Word, only through him can we get to know God, that is why he is the express image of the LORD. If I obey and enlighten you on Emperor Haile Sellassie The First, then when you see me, you will see His Majesty (we are as God), because I am leading you to him. That is the order of the Bible, the significance of the Messiah is not that he is the Almighty but that he guides you to him.

"For to their power, I bear record, yea, and beyond their power they were willing of themselves; Praying us with much entreaty that we would receive the gift, and take upon us the fellowship of the ministering to the saints. And this they did, not as we hoped, but first gave their own selves to the Lord, and unto us by the will of God" (2 Corinthians 8:3-5).

"Grace be to you, and peace, from God the Father, and from our Lord Jesus Christ, Who gave himself for our sins, that he might deliver us from this present evil world, according to the will of God and our Father: To whom be glory forever and ever. Amen. I marvel that you are so soon removed from him that called you into the grace of Christ unto another gospel: Which is not another; but there be some that trouble you, and would pervert the gospel of Christ. But though we, or an angel from heaven, preach any other gospel unto you than that which we have preached unto you, let him be accursed. As we said before, so say I now again, If any man preach any other gospel unto you than that ye have received, let him be accursed. For do I now persuade men, or God? Or do I seek to please men? For if I yet pleased men, I should not be the servant of Christ. But I certify you, brethren, that the gospel which was preached of me is not after man. For I neither received it of man, neither was I taught it, but by the revelation of Jesus Christ" (Galatians 1:3-12).

"I am crucified with Christ: nevertheless I live; yet not I, but Christ lives in me: and the life which I now live in the flesh I live by the faith of the Son of God, who loved me, and gave himself for me. I do not frustrate the grace of God: for if righteousness come by the law, then Christ is dead in vain" (Galatians 2:20-21).

The LORD tries the hearts of men, it is therefore possible to deceive human kind through insincere inclinations but no one can fool God. To offer an interpretation that dreadlocks displays your dedication to Emperor Haile Sellassie The First cannot be considered an accurate assessment of service. His Majesty instructed us in true judgment as well as he demonstrated worthwhile acts of devotion; if anyone seeks to establish a watered-down version of Rastafari then this shall be abolished. The Nazarite vow in Numbers chapter 6 is not referring to your literal hairdo as this would turn the gospel into cosmetology. 1 Corinthians 11 explains that the head of every man is Christ and this is the devotion that we must not do away with. If their definition of spiritual matters is not in line with the meaningful purpose of Emperor Haile Sellassie The First or in conjunction with the message of the Bible, then it was devised by men for their own benefit. What we seek is the true meaning of the scriptures so that we may be approved by the LORD; for everything else is superficial. It does not matter what type of hairstyle a person has, our conversation must be more intelligent, we have to establish a more salient approach to determining who is true to His Majesty. The gospel has beckoned us to render our hearts and not our garments, therefore by their works they shall be known.

"Which things are an allegory: for these are the two covenants, the one from the mount Sinai, which genders to bondage, which is Agar. For this Agar is mount Sinai in Arabia, and answers to Jerusalem which now is, and is in bondage with her children" (Galatians 5:24-25).

"Blessed be the God and Father of our Lord Jesus Christ, who has blessed us with all spiritual blessings in heavenly places in Christ" (Ephesians 1:3).

"Peace be to the brethren, and love with faith, from God the Father and the Lord Jesus Christ. Grace be with all them that love our Lord Jesus Christ in sincerity. Amen" (Ephesians 6:23-24).

"And that every tongue should confess that Jesus Christ is Lord, to the glory of God the Father. Wherefore, my beloved, as you have always obeyed, not as in my presence only, but now much more in my absence, work out your own salvation with fear and trembling" (Philippians 2:11-12).

It must be understood that the Bible is written in parables, if this were not true then why would there be a mediator between God and man? We would not need a teacher to explain what the scriptures mean if it were not all allegories. But the scriptures said that no one understands the book[24] because the real definition is not according to the standard prose. If Jesus literally walked on water then how could anyone not comprehend it? Has not the vast majority of religious denominations taken the miracles as being actual events thereby making Christ, Moses, and the other Prophets into wizards? It does not make sense to categorize the popular accepted religious sentiments as being true if it is written that they all fall short of the glory. It is therefore counterfactual and naive not to understand that the Bible is figurative; as the literal interpretation of the Bible goes against the order of the universe and the message of salvation. Christ was sent because the people do not understand the parables, they have a carnal theological outlook. Their wrong point of view has led to numerous atrocities done in the name of the LORD, such as war, oppression, slavery, racism, etc. The end result of this type of philosophy, which advocates a plebeian translation of the scriptures, has and always will be corruption because it is not true. In order for the promises of peace and redemption to be fulfilled, the world has to understand and accept the correct interpretation of the Bible

---

[24] Jeremiah 4:20-29

which holds that Emperor Haile Sellassie The First is the Almighty God and Father of Jesus Christ.

"That the God of our Lord Jesus Christ, the Father of glory, may give unto you the spirit of wisdom and revelation in the knowledge of him: The eyes of your understanding being enlightened; that you may know what is the hope of his calling, and what the riches of the glory of his inheritance in the saints, And what is the exceeding greatness of his power to us-ward who believe, according to the working of his mighty power, Which he wrought in Christ, when he raised him from the dead, and set him at his own right hand in the heavenly places" (Ephesians 1:17-20).

"Concerning zeal, persecuting the church; touching the righteousness which is in the law, blameless. But what things were gain to me, those I counted loss for Christ. Yea doubtless, and I count all things but loss for the excellency of the knowledge of Christ Jesus my Lord: for whom I have suffered the loss of all things, and do count them but dung, that I may win Christ, And be found in him, not having mine own righteousness, which is of the law, but that which is through the faith of Christ, the righteousness which is of God by faith" (Philippians 3:6-9).

"Wherein in time past you walked according to the course of this world, according to the prince of the power of the air, the spirit that now works in the children of disobedience: Among whom also we all had our conversation in times past in the lusts of our flesh, fulfilling the desires of the flesh and of the mind; and were by nature the children of wrath, even as others. But God, who is rich in mercy, for his great love wherewith he loved us, Even when we were dead in sins, has quickened us together with Christ, (by grace ye are saved;) And has raised us up together, and made us sit together in heavenly places in Christ Jesus: That in the ages to come he might show the exceeding riches of his grace, in his kindness toward us, through Christ Jesus. For by grace are you saved through faith; and that not of yourselves: it is the gift of God: Not of works, lest any man should boast" (Ephesians 2:2-9).

At one point we listened to the serpent and accepted a dogma which lacks logic and evidence because we did not know what was the real translation. Under this cloak, we read the Bible as a history book that chronicled miraculous events that transpired in ancient times. We was told to believe that fire literally rained out of the sky, that a father and his son are the same entity, that a woman became pregnant from her piety, that someone gathered two of every type of living creature onto a ship and keep them all alive for forty days, that it is possible to physically die and come back to life, and live eternally in the flesh etc. When your perception has been corrupted, then you cannot view the LORD in the proper light nor order your life in the correct way. That's why people commit evil acts in God's name and feel as if they are doing the right thing. They pray to the Creator and ask for inappropriate things such as money, relations, children, or some other materialistic asset. But we know that the true reverence of the LORD is based upon spiritual matters. God was manifest in the flesh to teach us how to better our lives, if we want to improve our lot then we must put his principles into practice. His Majesty instructed us in the right path so that we would implement his policies therefore we cannot expect for God to do in our lives that which we must do for ourselves or that a supernatural force will magically solve our problems. Everyone has the freewill to either work or be lazy, to do good or evil, to shoot for the stars or shoot the hooch; so let us not blame the LORD for the conditions which humanity has constructed by their own craft or seek for him to manipulate any situation that is our responsibility to resolve. When we seek material benefits from God or expect for him to do our job for us, this indicates that we are incompetent and indolent.

"And now come I to thee; and these things I speak in the world, that they might have my joy fulfilled in themselves. I have given them your word; and the world has hated them, because they are not of the world, even as I am not of the world. I pray not that you should take them out of the world, but that you should keep them from the evil. They are not of the world, even as I am not of the world. Sanctify them through your truth: your word is truth. As you have sent me into the world, even so have I also sent them into the world" (John 17:13-18).

"Now I tell you before it come, that, when it is come to pass, you may believe that I am he. Verily, verily, I say unto you, He that receives whomsoever I send receives me; and he that receives me, receives him that sent me" (John 13:19-20).

"These things I command you, that you love one another. If the world hate you, you know that it hated me before it hated you. If you were of the world, the world would love his own: but because you are not of the world, therefore the world hates you. Remember the word that I said unto you, The servant is not greater than his lord. If they have persecuted me, they will also persecute you; if they have kept my sayings, they will keep yours also. But all these things will they do unto you for my name's sake, because they know not him that sent me" (John 15:17-21).

The literal translation of the Bible stems from the fact that the churches do not know who God is; they are therefore helpless when it comes to deciphering the parables correctly. If anyone chooses to analyze the scriptures objectively they would conclude that these miracles have to be allegories or else the scriptures are a lie. Most scholars are atheists because when you reach a certain level of understanding you will not accept nonsense. The churches are preventing great talent from entering into the ministry due to their dishonest position and as the dissemination of knowledge continues to increase, people will become more intelligent and understand that there is no way possible to interpret the Bible literally. It is absurd to think that the miracles are actual events, no matter how hard anyone prays, there is no way for these deeds to play out in real life. Christ is not of this world because the beliefs which people hold are completely inaccurate. We therefore have been commanded not to mingle with them, not to intermarry; which means never to accept their backwards philosophy. In order to identify who is a false Christ, we need to analyze the validity of their message in conjunction with the descriptions of the Prophet. There are many people waiting for the second coming of Jesus but because they have been taught to look for a supernatural event in the sky, they will never be able to identify the actual revelation. It is written that there are few who find the path to deliverance, so the question we should ask ourselves is not whether the doctrine you hear is popular but rather if it is true.

"Therefore, seeing we have this ministry, as we have received mercy, we faint not; but have renounced the hidden things of dishonesty, not walking in craftiness, nor handling the word of God deceitfully; but, by manifestation of the truth, commending ourselves to every man's conscience in the sight of God. But if our gospel be hid, it is hid to them that are lost; in whom the god of this world has blinded the minds of them which believe not, lest the light of the glorious gospel of Christ, who is the image of God, should shine unto them. For we preach not ourselves, but Christ Jesus the Lord; and ourselves your servants for Jesus' sake. For God, who commanded the light to shine out of darkness, has shined in our hearts, to give the light of the knowledge of the glory of God in the face of Jesus Christ. But we have this treasure in earthen vessels, that the excellency of the power may be of God, and not of us. We are troubled on every side, yet not distressed; we are perplexed, but not in despair; Persecuted, but not forsaken; cast down, but not destroyed; Always bearing about in the body the dying of the Lord Jesus, that the life also of Jesus might be made manifest in our body. For we which live are always delivered unto death for Jesus sake, that the life also of Jesus might be made manifest in our mortal flesh. So then

death works in us, but life in you. We having the same spirit of faith, according as it is written, I believed, and therefore have I spoken; we also believe, and therefore speak; Knowing that he which raised up the Lord Jesus shall raise up us also by Jesus, and shall present us with you. For all things are for your sakes, that the abundant grace might through the thanksgiving of many redound to the glory of God" (2 Corinthians 4:1-15).

"For though I would desire to glory, I shall not be a fool; for I will say the truth: but now I forbear, lest any man should think of me above that which he sees me to be, or that he hears of me. And lest I should be exalted above measure through the abundance of the revelations, there was given to me a thorn in the flesh, the messenger of Satan buffet me, lest I should be exalted above measure" (2 Corinthians 12:6-7).

Jesus Christ is the Savior because he has revealed the true God unto us: Emperor Haile Sellassie The First. We are not ashamed of the gospel, despite the condemnation that we receive from society. Death works in us because we are rejected, yet he which raised up Jesus shall also raise us up, because that which we preach is correct. According to the Bible, to die means to be refused,[25] therefore men may hold the opinion that we are wrong, but in the sight of God we are justified. So despite their vain attempts, it is not possible to destroy Christ because his doctrine is factual, no one can disprove the divinity of His Majesty. Our teachings hold true to biblical prophecy, the order of the universe, and the instructions of Emperor Haile Sellassie The First. Let us worship the LORD through his Son, and through us, the children of God: Blessed be Jah Rastafari.

The Sixth Letter

Why do the people say that Jesus Christ is God? That is wrong, the Bible says that Jesus is the Prophet, a Minister, a Teacher, the Master of the Scriptures, our Lord the High Priest, the Creator of True Theology. Christ is identified as the one who built the temple of God, the one who preached the coming of the Lord in Spirit and in Truth. It is through Christ that we Praise our King the Almighty Father: Emperor Haile Sellassie The First.

---

[25] 1 Corinthians 4:9-10

"The words of Agur the son of Jakeh, even the prophecy: the man spoke unto Ithiel, even unto Ithiel and Ucal, Surely I am more brutish than any man, and have not the understanding of a man. I neither learned wisdom, nor have the knowledge of the holy. Who has ascended up into heaven, or descended? Who has gathered the wind in his fists? Who has bound the waters in a garment? Who has established all the ends of the earth? What is his name, and what is his son's name, if you can tell" (Proverbs 30:1-4).

"You judge after the flesh; I judge no man. And yet if I judge, my judgment is true: for I am not alone, but I and the Father that sent me. It is also written in your law, that the testimony of two men is true. I am one that bear witness of myself, and the Father that sent me bears witness of me" (John 7:15-18).

"And God said, Let us make man in our image, after our likeness: and let them have dominion over the fish of the sea, and over the fowl of the air, and over the cattle, and over all the earth, and over every creeping thing that creeps upon the earth" (Genesis 1:26).

The Bible describes God and Jesus Christ as being two different people, therefore we must know who is the Father and who is the Son. If they were both the same entity then why would the scriptures ask us to identify separate terms for each? Is it prudent to name a single substance with conflicting designations? The Bible says that God and Christ are two men, there is no logical explanation to decipher how they could possibly be the same entity. Jesus is the Prophet of the LORD, he preaches the true message of salvation, he is one with the Father because his gospel is the real canon of the Almighty. Through Christ we are made whole because if we accept his testimony then we will be able to understand God and his operation; we are made in his image when we adhere to his principles. If we choose not to acknowledge the true declaration of the LORD then we are not "men" according to the Bible, which means that we do not follow God. It is not acceptable to make up your own philosophy to suite your needs, in this we would only be pleasing ourselves; not the Almighty. There is no such thing as "everyone must find their own truth" because there is only one truth for everyone. The various conflicting religious agendas has led to numerous wars and atrocities in the past, if we do not learn from history then it shall only repeat itself. People have interpreted the Bible to be a book that has asked them to kill and enslave others because they do not understand what they are reading. We must get everyone to accept the true gospel because only the real message of God can allow humanity to legitimately liberate itself from corruption. It also needs to be understood that only the correct interpretation of the scriptures contains the power to accomplish these goals.

"I will raise them up a Prophet from among their brethren, like unto thee, and will put my words in his mouth; and he shall speak unto them all that I shall command him. And it shall come to pass, that whosoever will not listen unto my words which he shall speak in my name, I will require it of him" (Deuteronomy 18:18-19).

"But those things, which God before had showed by the mouth of all his prophets, that Christ should suffer, he has so fulfilled. Repent ye therefore, and be converted, that your sins may be blotted out, when the times of refreshing shall come from the prescience of the Lord; And he shall send Jesus Christ, which before was preached unto you: Whom the heavens must receive until the times of restitution of all things, which God has spoken by the mouth of all his holy prophets since the world began. For Moses truly said unto the fathers, A prophet shall the Lord your God raise up unto you of your brethren, like unto me; him shall you hear in all things whatsoever he shall say unto you. And it shall come to pass, that every soul, which will not hear that prophet, shall be destroyed from among the people. Yea, and all the prophets from Samuel and those that follow after, as many as have spoken, have likewise foretold of these days. You are the children of the prophets, and of the covenant which God made with our fathers, saying unto Abraham, And in your seed shall all the kindreds of the earth be blessed. Unto you first God, having raised up his Son Jesus, sent him to bless you, in turning away every one of you from his iniquities" (Acts 3:18-26).

"Now the birth of Jesus Christ was on this wise: When as his mother Mary was espoused to Joseph, before they came together, she was found with child of the Holy Ghost. Then Joseph her husband, being a just man, and not willing to make her a public example, was minded to put her away privately. But while he thought on these things, behold, the angel of the Lord appeared unto him in a dream, saying, Joseph, thou son of David, fear not to take unto you Mary your wife: for that which is conceived in her is of the Holy Ghost. And she shall bring forth a son, and you shall call his name JESUS: for he shall save his people from their sins. Now all this was done, that it might be fulfilled which was spoken of the Lord by the prophet, saying, Behold, a virgin shall be with child, and shall bring forth a son, and they shall call his name Emmanuel, which being interpreted is, God with us" (Matthew 1:18-23).

The fulfillment of biblical prophecy is the most substantial evidence of the presence of God and it is only through the revelation that we can interpret the scriptures correctly. Emperor Haile Sellassie The First has declared that we must rid ourselves of superstition and ignorance, therefore we should no longer believe that supernatural occurrences are possible. It is only with the proper perspective that we would be able to determine that certain references, such as the Virgin Mary, are symbolic and not literal events. As we accept and implement the teaching of His Majesty, this will naturally lead us to a new outlook and greater understanding of the Bible. The Roman Emperor Constantine convened the council of Nicaea in 325 AD and established the current Christian cannon that Jesus is God, because they believe that Christ is consubstantial with the Father, thus adorning the pagan concept of superstition. Their interpretation was deemed the most suitable at the time but now that the promises have come to pass, we know that they did not have the correct understanding of the Word. The Son of God is described as the Prophet of the LORD, in order to avoid contradicting ourselves in the Bible and not to betray our intellect, it is necessary that we accept the true definition of Christ that has been given to us through the scriptures. Jesus has declared unto us that Emperor Haile Sellassie The First is the Almighty, he was not arrogant in exalting himself.

"He that comes from above is above all: he that is of the earth is earthly, and speaks of the earth: he that comes from heaven is above all. And what he has seen and heard, that he testifies; and no man receives his testimony. He that has received his testimony has set to his seal that God is true. For he whom God has sent speaks the words of God: for God gives not the Spirit by measure unto him" (John 3:31-34).

"And John bare record, saying, I saw the Spirit descending from heaven like a dove, and it abode upon him. And I knew him not: but he that sent me to baptize with water, the same said unto me, Upon whom you shall see the Spirit descending, and remaining on him, the same is he which baptizes with the Holy Ghost. And I saw, and bare record that this is the Son of God" (John 1:32-34).

"Peace I leave with you, my peace I give unto you: not as the world gives, give I unto you. Let not your heart be troubled, neither let it be afraid. You have heard how I said unto you, I go away, and come again unto you, If you loved me, you would rejoice, because I said, I go unto my Father: for my Father is greater than I" (John 14:27-28).

God and Jesus cannot be the same entity because it is written that the Father is greater than the Son. Christ has given us the true testimony of heaven that Emperor Haile Sellassie The First is the Almighty; thus we have set to our seal that God is true because we are able to see him. This may be scary for some people to think about and to accept new ideas but the only way to achieve progress is to venture into unchartered waters and challenge yourself. The ancient canon of the council of Nicaea was successful in establishing organized religion and bringing order to the Roman Empire but the question of teaching the truth about the LORD was not decreed. The Arian controversy, during that time, was causing tremendous turmoil and prompted these ecumenical conferences to take place in order to prevent their society from falling apart. The main reason why Constantine called these meetings was to preserve his nation, not to establish the true teachings of God; although the popular affirmation is to believe that it was an ecclesiastical convention. Many pagan concepts were adopted into Christianity, traditions surrounding Christmas, Easter, Lammas, etc., because the true teachings of the Lord was not the priority; they had no problem incorporating false tenants into their law, as long as it would subjugate the people under their rule. Arius argued that Jesus was the literal Son of God, that the Father created him first of all origins, and that there was a time when Christ did not exist because he was made after God. There will always be some tremendous challenges whenever someone tries to interpret the scriptures naturally because that is a flawed position. No one can validate what transpired during the formation of the universe because the scriptures are describing symbolic implications about the Father and the Son. Christ is the Prophet of the LORD, the one who teaches us the truth about God; we must learn how to apply these chronicles into real terms.

"Say ye of him, whom the Father has sanctified, and sent into the world, You blaspheme; because I said, I am the Son of God? If I do not the works of my Father, believe me not. But if I do, though you believe not me, believe the works: that you may know, and believe, that the Father is in me, and I in him" (John 10:36-38).

"And, behold, you shall conceive in your womb, and bring forth a son, and shall call his name JESUS. He shall be great, and shall be called the Son of the Highest; and the Lord God shall give unto him the throne of his father David" (Luke 1:31-32).

"The beginning of the gospel of Jesus Christ, the Son of God; As it is written in the prophets, Behold, I send my messenger before your face, which shall prepare thy way before thee" (Mark 1:1-2).

We must be able to interpret the entire Bible without contradiction, only then can we honestly say that what we believe in is true. If you think that Jesus is God, then that conflicts with the scriptures which state that he is the messenger of the LORD, the Son of the Highest. The only way to analyze all of the scriptures in conjunction with each other, is to interpret Christ as the Prophet, we can see the Father through him because he teaches us the truth about the Almighty; Jesus is not God. The term Prophet is currently used very loosely but it is a designation solely reserved for the Messiah. Just because a person is a great musician like Bob Marley or a great orator like Barack Obama, does not make them a Prophet; the correct manner in which to use this epithet should strictly be referenced when referring to Jesus. It is also wrong for someone to proclaim themselves to be Christ or a messenger of the LORD because the scriptures have prophesied that God will declare who is his only begotten Son. The Father bears witness of his devotee through the Bible, which means that the real seer will be confirmed by the descriptions and the prophecies of the scriptures. Anyone who is referred to as being a Prophet, first and foremost, must have full command of the Word to teach the people that Emperor Haile Sellassie The First is the Almighty. If we find that they hold certain beliefs which are false or harmful then it cannot be concluded that they are the express image of the LORD, as there is nothing incorrect about God.

"In the beginning was the Word, and the Word was with God, and the Word was God. The same was in the beginning with God. All things were made by him; and without him was not any thing made that was made. In him was life; and the life was the light of men. And the light shines in darkness; and the darkness comprehends it not" (John 1:1-5).

"But when the fullness of the time was come, God sent forth his Son, made of a woman, made under the law, To redeem them that were under the law, that we might receive the adoption of sons. And because you are sons, God has sent forth the Spirit of his Son into your hearts, crying, Abba, Father. Wherefore you are no more a servant, but a son; and if a son, then an heir of God through Christ. Howbeit then, when you knew not God, you did service unto them which by nature are no gods. But now, after you have known God, or rather are known of God, how turn you again

to the weak and beggarly elements, whereunto you desire again to be in bondage"
(Galatians 4:4-9).

"There is therefore now no condemnation to them which are in Christ Jesus, who
walk not after the flesh, but after the Spirit. For the law of the Spirit of life in Christ
Jesus has made me free from the law of sin and death. For what the law could not
do, in that it was weak through the flesh, God sending his own Son in the likeness
of sinful flesh, and for sin, condemned sin in the flesh: That the righteousness of the
law might be fulfilled in us, who walk not after the flesh, but after the Spirit. For
they that are after the flesh do mind the things of the flesh; but they that are after the
Spirit, the things of the Spirit. For to be carnally minded is death: but to be spiritu-
ally minded is life and peace. Because the carnal mind is enmity against God: for it
is not subject to the law of God, neither indeed can be. So then they that are in the
flesh cannot please God. But you are not in the flesh, but in the Spirit, if so be that the
Spirit of God dwell in you. Now if any man have not the Spirit of Christ, he is none
of his. And if Christ be in you, the body is dead because of sin; but the Spirit is life
because of righteousness. But if the Spirit of him that raised up Jesus from the dead
dwell in you, he that raised up Christ from the dead shall also quicken your mortal
bodies by his Spirit that dwells in you. Therefore, brethren, we are debtors, not to
the flesh, to live after the flesh. For if you live after the flesh, you shall die: but if you
through the Spirit do mortify the deeds of the body, you shall live. For as many as are
led by the Spirit of God, they are the sons of God. For you have not received the spirit
of bondage again to fear; but you have received the Spirit of adoption, whereby we
cry, Abba, Father. The Spirit itself bears witness with our spirit, that we are the chil-
dren of God: And if children, then heirs; heirs of God, and joint-heirs with Christ;
if so be that we suffer with him, that we may be also glorified together. For I reckon
that the sufferings of this present time are not worthy to be compared with the glory
which shall be revealed in us. For the earnest expectation of the creature waits for
the manifestation of the sons of God. For the creature was made subject to vanity,
not willingly, but by reason of him who has subjected the same in hope. Because the
creature itself also shall be delivered from the bondage of corruption into the glori-
ous liberty of the children of God" (Romans 8:1-21).

Jesus Christ is a minister who has preached the correct interpretation of the
scriptures, which has enabled us to understand the fullness of God. If you do
not accept his gospel then you will never be saved in knowing the true definition of righteousness; which has been exemplified by Emperor Haile Sellassie
The First. Just as with the Bible, you must have the proper perspective on His

Majesty in order to fathom his speeches, actions, and mission. Christ is the only one who can give you this vision, allowing you to approach and apply these topics correctly. We are made whole by the legitimate gospel of the Lord, which gives sight to the blind and life to the dead. Before Jesus came, we misinterpreted the parables and could not justify the divinity of Emperor Haile Sellassie The First; that made us dead, blind, and lame. But now we have full command of the scriptures, through Christ, and receive the spirit of adoption, whereby we cry, Abba Father; because we know that His Majesty is the Most High. The sons of God are those who have accepted the testimony of Jesus that Emperor Haile Sellassie The First is the Almighty. We now can reject the sinful dogmas, common in the world, that wreak havoc on earth by putting into play toxic policies that destroy our progress and happiness. Only when we stop putting our trust in carnal ideologies, such as the supernatural or idolatry, can we destroy evil and associate ourselves with the fellowship of angels who know God and glorify him in spirit and in truth. The people cannot see the Almighty because they have rejected His Majesty; but according to the Bible, if they have not the revelation then they are not following the gospel of Christ. The purpose of the Messiah is to save those who are sold under sin, which are those who do not know that Emperor Haile Sellassie The First is the Almighty; by Jesus we have become partakers of the promises and come before the throne of salvation giving glory and honor unto him who is worthy to be praised: King Rastafari.

"For I am not ashamed of the gospel of Christ: for it is the power of God unto salvation to every one that believes; to the Jew first, and also to the Greek" (Romans 1:16).

"Grace be to you, and peace, from God our Father, and from the Lord Jesus Christ. Blessed be the God and Father of our Lord Jesus Christ, who has blessed us with all spiritual blessings in heavenly places in Christ: According as he has chosen us in him before the foundation of the world, that we should be holy and without blame before him in love: Having predestinated us unto the adoption of children by Jesus Christ to himself, according to the good pleasure of his will, To the praise of the glory of his grace, wherein he has made us accepted in the beloved. In whom we have redemption through his blood, the forgiveness of sins, according to the riches of his grace; Wherein he has abounded toward us in all wisdom and prudence; Having made known unto us the mystery of his will, according to his good pleasure which he has purposed in himself: That in the dispensation of the fullness of times he might gather together in one all things in Christ, both which are in heaven, and which are

on earth; even in him: In whom also we have obtained an inheritance, being predestinated according to the purpose of him who works all things after the counsel of his own will: That we should be to the praise of his glory, who first trusted in Christ. In whom you also trusted, after that you heard the word of truth, the gospel of your salvation: in whom also, after that you believed, you were sealed with that holy Spirit of promise" (Ephesians 1:2-13).

"And you are witnesses of these things. And, behold, I send the promise of my Father upon you: but tarry ye in the city of Jerusalem, until you be endued with power from on high" (Luke 24:48-49).

Our testimony is not based upon an assumption about the interpretation of the Bible, we preach the fulfillment of prophecy. We are eye witnesses of the manifestation, that is how we know what is the proper context of the Father and Son. When you know who is God and Christ then you can correctly decipher their roles according to the scriptures. Before Emperor Haile Sellassie The First was crowned King of Kings and Lord of Lords on November 2, 1930, everything related to theology was based upon guesswork and superstition, but now that God has revealed himself, we can follow his philosophy which will allow us to read the Bible correctly. We are emboldened by the gospel of Christ because we preach a doctrine without spot or blemish. That is why it is written that Jesus was born from the Virgin Mary, this symbolizes that his testimony came from God and not man; it is pure. We have witnessed how the false pastors of the world are zealous in attaining as much followers as they can, and by them getting their message out, people assimilate to that which is popular; even if it is wrong. It is therefore our responsibility to spread the Word to the four corners of the earth because there are people everywhere who pray to God seeking for his mercy; we must give them the opportunity to be saved because it will not come from the Roman edict. In this pursuit we need not be timid, as all things work in favor of those who do the will of the LORD; our conscious is free from condemnation because everything we say is supported by facts and logic. This is the gospel of salvation, the end result of following Emperor Haile Sellassie The First will make the world into a much better place; how can any good hearted individual go against this agenda?

"God, who at sundry times and in divers manners spoke in time past unto the fathers by the prophets, Has in these last days spoken unto us by his Son, whom he has appointed heir of all things, by whom also he made the worlds; Who being the

brightness of his glory, and the express image of his person, and upholding all things by the word of his power, when he had by himself purged our sins, sat down on the right hand of the Majesty on high" (Hebrew 1:1-3).

"Now of the things which we have spoken this is the sum: We have such a high priest, who is set on the right hand of the throne of the Majesty in the heavens" (Hebrew 8:1).

"Let us therefore fear, lest, a promise being left us of entering into his rest, any of you should seem to come short of it. For unto us was the gospel preached, as well as unto them: but the word preached did not profit them, not being mixed with faith in them that heard it. For we which have believed do enter into rest, as he said, As I have sworn in my wrath, if they shall enter into my rest: although the works were finished from the foundation of the world. For he spoke in a certain place of the seventh day on this wise, And God did rest the seventh day from all his works. And in this place again, If they shall enter into my rest. Seeing therefore it remains that some must enter therein, and they to whom it was first preached entered not in because of unbelief: Again, he limited a certain day, saying in David, Today, after so long a time; as it is said, Today if you will hear his voice, harden not your hearts. For if Jesus had given them rest, then would he not afterward have spoken of another day. There remains therefore a rest to the people of God. For he that is entered into his rest, he also has ceased from his own works, as God did from his. Let us labor therefore to enter into that rest, lest any man fall after the same example of unbelief. For the word of God is quick, and powerful, and sharper than any two edged sword, piercing even to the dividing asunder of soul and spirit, and of the joints and marrow, and is a discerner of the thoughts and intents of the heart. Neither is there any creature that is not manifest in his sight: but all things are naked and opened unto the eyes of him with whom we have to do. Seeing then that we have a great high priest, that is passed into the heavens, Jesus the Son of God, let us hold fast our profession. For we have not a high priest which can not be touched with the feeling of our infirmities; but was in all points tempted like as we are, yet without sin. Let us therefore come boldly unto the throne of grace, that we may obtain mercy, and find grace to help in time of need" (Hebrew 4:1-16).

"Wherefore, seeing we also are compassed about with so great a cloud of witnesses, let us lay aside every weight, and the sin which does so easily beset us, and let us run with patience the race that is set before us, Looking unto Jesus the author and finisher of our faith; who for the joy that was set before him endured the cross, despising the shame, and is set down at the right hand of the throne of God. For consider him that endured such contradiction of sinners against himself, lest ye be wearied and faint in your minds. You have not yet resisted unto blood, striving against sin. And you have forgotten the exhortation which speaks unto you as unto children, My son, despise not thou the chastening of the Lord, nor faint when you are rebuked of him: For whom the Lord loves he chastises, and scourges every son whom he receives. If you endure chastisement, God deals with you as with sons; for what son is he whom the father chastises not? But if you be without chastisement, whereof all are partakers, then are you bastards, and not sons. Furthermore, we have had fathers of our flesh which corrected us, and we gave them reverence: shall we not much rather be in subjection unto the Father of spirits, and live? For they verily for a few days chastened us after their own pleasure; but he for our profit, that we might be partakers of his holiness. Now no chastening for the present seems to be joyous, but grievous: nevertheless afterward it yields the peaceable fruit of righteousness unto them which are exercised thereby. Wherefore lift up the hands which hang down, and the feeble knees; And make straight paths for your feet, lest that which is lame be turned out of the way: but let it rather be healed. Follow after peace with all men, and holiness, without which no man shall see the Lord: Looking diligently lest any man fail of the grace of God; lest any root of bitterness springing up trouble you, and thereby many be defiled; Lest there be any fornicator, or profane person, as Esau, who for one morsel of meat sold his birthright. For you know how that afterward, when he would have inherited the blessing, he was rejected: for he found no place of repentance, though he sought if carefully with tears. For you are not come unto the mount that might be touched, and that burned with fire, nor unto blackness, and darkness, and tempest, And the sound of a trumpet, and the voice of words; which voice they that heard entreated that the word should not be spoken to them any more: (For they could not endure that which was commanded, And if so much as a beast touch the mountain, it shall be stoned, or thrust through with a dart: And so terrible was the sight, that Moses said, I exceedingly fear and quake) But you are come unto mount Sion, and unto the city of the living God, the heavenly Jerusalem, and to an innumerable company of angels, To the general assembly and church of the first born, which are written in heaven, and to God the Judge of all, and to the spirits of just men made perfect, And to Jesus the mediator of the new covenant, and to the blood of sprinkling, that speaks better things than that of Abel" (Hebrew 12:1-24).

The gospel of Christ is the standard of righteousness, it is the contrast between good and evil. Those who are of God will accept his message, while the offspring of Satan will reject him. The truth is compelling, it is not something which anyone can deny unless they are lying or delusional. Your conscious will recognize the power of God, although what we display for people to see is oftentimes different from how we feel, those who are sincere in their relationships with the LORD shall accept his Word. Jesus sits at the right hand of God because the Father and the Son are two different people. To conclude based off of these descriptions that they are consubstantial is a grossly illogical assessment. We must explain the parables based upon precepts that are actually conceivable and coherent. It is not possible to receive the salvation of the Lord without being reproved; as knowledge is infinite no one should be so high-minded as to believe that they have received all the education that they would ever need. If we choose not to learn more and correct those elements which have been proven false and useless, then we will never progress. God was manifest in the flesh to instruct the world in the right way, so that we can live a better life, he furthermore sent forth Jesus Christ to put us in remembrance of the teachings of Emperor Haile Sellassie The First. Our faith is the greatest of all dogmas because it is the Word of God, we are justified in the spirit which is through undeniable evidence and acumen. Therefore as some may pretend that our testimony has no bearings, we all shall witness as this gospel conquers the earth. Praise ye the LORD Emperor Haile Sellassie The First through his Son and Savior Jesus Christ, and through us, the children of the Most High.

The Seventh Letter

Let us Praise the Only True and Living God, Emperor Haile Sellassie The First of Ethiopia. Greetings to my brethrens and sistrens and to the little ones that are in the Faith. Blessed love to all, in the name of the One and Only God, Emperor Haile Sellassie The First of Ethiopia, and peace in the name of Our Lord, Our Teacher, Jesus Christ, the Son of the Highest, Elohim Sabbath, Haile Sellassie The First, the Great and Holy One of Israel. I, Kenyatta Felix (Primus St. Croix), an Apostle of Jesus Christ, by the Commandment of Haile Sellassie The First Our Savior, unto you all my fellow brethrens and sistrens in the Faith of Christ. The Word of Haile Sellassie The First, is that God raised up Christ and made him sit down on his right hand side, in 1930, the acceptable year of the Lord as it is written in The Holy Bible. His Majesty glorified Christ, for Jesus upholds everything by the gospel and his Word is the power of God. The doctrine of Jesus, the Son of Haile Sellassie The First, is the manifestation of prophecy.

To everyone in the faith; grace, mercy, and peace from God, Our Father, Emperor Haile Sellassie The First. I am bound to thank His Majesty for all my fellow brethrens and sistrens who accept Christ, in you the faith grows exceedingly. It is wonderful to know that we are bound together in one body, which is Christ, gathering together in perfect love to praise the Father of Christ, Haile Sellassie The First, on the Sabbath Day. I am separate from you in the flesh but in the spirit we are one through the Word because we all carry the cross of Christ and suffer for the glorification of His Majesty. The Bible, in 1 Timothy 4:10 says, that we suffer reproach, because we trust in the living God Emperor Haile Sellassie The First; just as our brethrens Jesus Christ and Paul suffered reproach the same remains true with us today. I truly love you all in Christ with the blessed union that His Majesty established with us on November 2, 1930. Let the whole world bear witness that the gospel of Christ is to glorify Emperor Haile Sellassie The First on the Sabbath Day. These are the true praises of God: that the Son has declared his Father's name to the church. Haile Sellassie The First has not given us the spirit of fear but of power and truth. Therefore we have a sound mind and are not ashamed of the testimony of Jesus Christ because we know that God was manifested in the flesh. We are ministers like Christ preaching the Word of Haile Sellassie The First to the world according to the dispensation of God, for the people to know that His Majesty is the Alpha and Omega, the maker of all mankind. Haile Sellassie The First has fulfilled the Word of God; even the mystery which has been hidden from all generations, but now is made manifest to his saints. God chooses who he would to know the doctrine, which is Christ, purging our sins, to present every man and woman perfect in the gospel to praise Emperor Haile Sellassie The First.

Grace be to you all, and peace from God, Our Father, Emperor Haile Sellassie The First and from the Lord Jesus Christ, the Son of the Most High Jah Rastafari. Blessed be the God and Father of our Lord Jesus Christ, who has blessed us with all spiritual blessings in heaven according to his mercy. His Majesty has chosen us before the foundation of the world, that we should be holy and without blame before him on the Sabbath Day; having predestinated us unto the adoption of children by Jesus Christ according to the good pleasure of his will. We in St. Lucia thank Haile Sellassie The First for you, always making mention of you all in our prayers, remembering without ceasing your work of faith and patience of hope in our Lord Jesus Christ, the Son of Haile Sellassie The First. Brothers and sisters, we were elected by The Almighty to become followers of Jesus Christ, having received the Word in much affliction, yet joyful in the Holy Ghost, to praise His Majesty on the Sabbath Day. Now if the spirit of Haile Sellassie The First dwell in you, then he shall quicken your mortal bodies through grace. Therefore brethren, we are debtors but not to the flesh, for if we live after the flesh we shall die in vain, but if we through the spirit mortify the deeds of the body, then we shall inherit eternal life through Christ. The spirit of Haile Sellassie The First is to fulfill his Ten Commandments, and we are the sons and daughters of His Majesty, for we have not received the spirit of bondage to fear, but we have received the spirit of adoption whereby we cry Abba Father, Emperor Haile Sellassie The First Liveth. The spirit itself bears witness with our spirit that we are the children of God, and if children then heirs of salvation, if we suffer with him so that we may also be glorified together with Christ on the Sabbath Day. The sufferings of this present time are not worthy to be compared with the glory that shall be revealed in us who Praise Haile Sellassie The First.

I, Kenyatta Felix (Primus St. Croix), wish you all peace and happiness in the name of Emperor Haile Sellassie The First. Blessed love in the name of God, may the spirit of Christ be with you always. Amen.

The Eighth Letter

Greetings to all the beloved of Christ, blessed be the Almighty God Emperor Haile Sellassie The First, who has made it possible for us to communicate his message. It is a blessing to know the true gospel of Christ Yesus, we must strengthen the bond we hold together in the grace of His Majesty. Here in St. Lucia, people are living the same way as those in America. Everyone has neglected the commandments of His Majesty but we must remain faithful. I pray for the day that we will celebrate the holy day together again as one through the body of Christ, only remain steadfast in the law of His Majesty. For this is the love of God, that we keep his commandments. We all are brothers and sisters if we do the will of our Father who is in Heaven Ethiopia. Hebrews 2:11 says that both he, Yesus, and us that are sanctified are all of One: Haile Sellassie The First. That is why he, Yesus, was not ashamed to call us his brethrens in the spirit, it says for this reason I, Yesus, will manifest your name, Haile Sellassie The First, to my brethren in the church, and will praise the Emperor on the Sabbath Day. His Majesty made this day for us and told us to be glad in it. In John 17:11,

Yesus says to keep them, those that you have given me, that they may be one as we are one. Saint Paul, the servant of His Majesty, said in Romans 15:6 that with one mind and one mouth let us glorify God, the Father of our Lord Yesus Christos, whose dwelling is on high, Emperor Haile Sellassie The First. Praise Jah Rastafari for the great book that has all the knowledge about him, has been fulfilled before all the nations. The eyes of the blind shall be opened and the ears of the deaf shall be unlocked through Christ Yesus.

If we say that we are God's children then we must keep the Sabbath Day Holy. His Majesty said that the Bible is the refuge and rallying point for all humanity, in it man will find the necessary guidance for their future actions. If you read the Bible as Haile Sellassie The First told us to do, then you will know the truth, Yesus the Son also read it and that is how he knew that His Majesty is the Eternal God who rested on the Seventh Day. Hebrews 4:4 says, for he spoke in a certain place of the seventh day on this wise, and God Emperor Haile Sellassie The First, did rest the seventh day from all his works. That scripture is found in the Bible that His Majesty said contains the solution to our present difficulties. Hebrews 4:10 says that he who enters into his rest, has also ceased from his own works as God Haile Sellassie The First rested from his. Ezekiel 20:12 says, moreover also I gave them my Sabbaths, the Seventh Day belongs to His Majesty, it is a sign between me and them, that they might know that Emperor Haile Sellassie The First does sanctify them, because he has sanctified the seventh day from creation. Yesus the Christ was there with him, the Bible teaches us that we have such a high priest at the right hand of the Majesty on high. Let us not make the same mistakes as our forefathers and not hallow the Sabbath. Through faith we are able to inherit the promises of salvation kept hidden from the foundation of the world from those who were disobedient to his Word. Ezekiel 20:20 says to hallow the Sabbath Day, it shall be a sign between God and us, that we may know that Jah Rastafari is the true God who rested on November 2, 1930, in Zion Ethiopia. Deuteronomy 5:12 says to keep the Sabbath Day holy, to sanctify it as the LORD Haile Sellassie The First, has commanded you. In His Majesty's Bible speech, he said that his advice to all is to fulfill the ten commandments. Deuteronomy 4:13 says that he declared unto you his covenant, which he commanded you to perform, even the ten commandments, and he wrote them upon two tables of stone, which is the old and the new testament. Yesus Christos, the Son of Haile Sellassie The First, says in John 15:9 and 10, as the Father has loved me, so have I loved you: continue in my love. If you keep my commandments, you shall abide in my love. 1 John 5:3 says for this is the love of His Majesty, that we keep his commandments: and his commandments are not grievous. Luke 4:16 says that it was the custom of our brethren Christ Yesus to enter into the synagogues on the Sabbath Day. We have to maintain the integrity of our Father Haile Sellassie The First, and his Son Yesus Christos by following the ordinances which he has instructed us to emulate. Ecclesiastes 12:13 says, let us hear the conclusion of the whole matter: fear God Emperor Haile Sellassie The First and keep his commandments: for this is the whole duty of man. In Psalm 111:10 it says that the fear of the LORD is the beginning of wisdom: a good understanding have all they that keep his commandments. He will be praised from sun up to sun down, from Sabbath to Sabbath, world without end. The Bible says that God gave us this commandment to save us in Psalm 71:3, also read Isaiah 48, Isaiah 56, Isaiah 58, Isaiah 66 and Hebrews 4. His Majesty loved us by revealing that he is the Eternal God on November 2, 1930, the Sabbath Day.

Now when we go to church, it is not the building that can save but the ordinances we follow which either give life or death; therefore we must do what the Bible instructed us. Colossians 1:24 says, I now rejoice in my sufferings for you and fill up in my flesh what is lacking in the afflictions of Christ, for the sake of his body, which is the church. Hebrews 2:11 and 12 says, for both he who sanctifies and those who are being sanctified are one, for which reason Yesus is not ashamed to call them brethren, saying, "I will declare your name to my brethren; in the midst of the assembly will I sing praises unto you." Ephesians 3:21 says, to Haile Sellassie The First be glory in the Church by Yesus Christos to all generations, forever and ever: Amen. Hebrews 3:6 says that Christ as a son over his own house, whose house we are if we hold fast the confidence and the rejoicing of the hope firm unto the end. Therefore going to the temple on the Sabbath Day is the holy custom but the love of God is to believe in him who sanctified the seventh day on November 2, 1930: Emperor Haile Sellassie The First. Whosoever believes the gospel shall have life everlasting, Christ commanded us to keep His Majesty's law which is the faith and the commandments. If we love God we must believe in him, for he magnified and sanctified himself before the eyes of all the nations when he was crowned King of Kings and Lord of Lords. We will never forsake this holy covenant as the world does, they want us to become like the heathen and neglect the spirit, which is the Word. But we will die for Christ sake and suffer for the fulfillment of the gospel and overcome the evil. His Majesty told us to fulfill the ten commandments, that is not a small thing brethren, this is serious. The Bible says that some of us will have the name of God Emperor Haile Sellassie The First on our lips but in our heart he is far away. What that means is if we are not obeying his laws then our faith in him is not sincere. Rastafari is the Sabbath Day, to keep it holy is to follow his instructions and ordinances. Hebrews 10:23-27 says let us hold fast the confession of our hope without wavering, for he who promised us is faithful. And let us consider one another in order to stir up love and good works, not forsaking the assembling of ourselves together, as is the manner of some, but exhorting one another and so much the more as you see the day approaching. For if we sin willfully after we have received the knowledge of the truth, there no longer remains sacrifice for sins. Fear God Emperor Haile Sellassie The First, through his Son the mediator Yesus Christos.

The Ninth Letter

Perfect love in the name of the Almighty Jah Rastafari and grace through our brethren Jesus who has enabled us to come into the full understanding of the Lord. I tried my best to leave you all with the words of His Majesty, the gospel of Christ, so that you may know the goodness of the Most High Emperor Haile Sellassie The First. We must get the message out to everyone in the world so that our fellowmen that have not had the chance to hear the good news may come into the full assurance of the Lord. It is our hope that the gospel will be received by our loved ones and it is important for us to continue in what we have been predestined to fulfill. His Majesty has chosen us for His purpose, just as He choose Jesus Christ to preach the Word to every creature. I know that the world knows us not because they do not accept Haile Sellassie The First but His Majesty commanded us to study the Bible and we will find the truth. We have to show the people the revelation, what we have been made to know in the Bible that Haile Sellassie The First of Ethiopia is the Almighty God. The people must understand that the message of Jesus Christ is about his Father, not himself, what he preached was the gospel of salvation for all generations to follow. His Majesty alone is God, the world cannot be saved unless they believe in Him. We must keep the commandments of the Lord and the testimony of Jesus Christ that Haile Sellassie The First is the Almighty; the heavens smile upon those who follow the Bible.

I keep all of you in my prayers, everyone who fulfills the law of His Majesty, so that we all may be one in the spirit of Christ, worshipping Emperor Haile Sellassie The First on the Sabbath Day as our brother Jesus did. He also instructed us to preach the gospel to all the nations so that they may know that His Majesty is the Father of Christ. All of us here in St. Lucia are hoping that you maintain fellowship on the Sabbath, as Haile Sellassie The First, the

Creator of the heavens and earth, commanded us because that is the love of Jah Rastafari. Our conversation has to be according to the Word of God, just as Paul also told us. We must be knowledgable in the Bible so that we can teach our fellowmen who have not heard the good news, the gospel of salvation, which is the revelation of God on earth, when His Majesty was crowned King of Kings and Lord of Lords. Hebrews 4:16 says that we shall come before the throne of grace boldly and in Isaiah 66:23 it says, and it shall come to pass that from one new moon to another and from one Sabbath to another, all flesh shall come to worship before the LORD. So brethrens that is what Ethiopia has lost but we have found the Emperor by grace. We should not let go of the faith because only Haile Sellassie The First can save the world. Jesus never turned away from His Majesty and neither can we. The love of Christ is for us to believe in him who sits upon the Throne of Heaven Ethiopia, the Bible teaches us to love one another as the Father loves us, this means to believe in Haile Sellassie The First; this is the true Christian faith. Jesus is the Son of God, which means that he is the Prophet of Haile Sellassie The First. Christ shed his blood for us to be saved by grace, which is the gospel, for he kept us in the name of his Father. Read Acts 13:22-38, Acts 20:24-38, 1 Corinthians 1:3-10, 2 Corinthians 4:1-15, 1 Peter 2:1-25; read these important gospels my beloved brethrens, share them with others as well. His Majesty guide and keep you safe through Christ his mediator. May the Lord shine his face upon you all, blessed love from me Brother Kenyatta (Primus St. Croix).

The Tenth Letter

We will begin with scriptures to strengthen us in the Spirit:

"Give ear, O my people, to my law: incline your ears to the words of my mouth. I will open my mouth in a parable: I will utter dark sayings of old: Which we have heard and known, and our fathers have told us. We will not hide them from their children, showing to the generation to come the praises of the LORD, and his strength, and his wonderful works that he hath done. For he established a testimony in Jacob, and appointed a law in Israel, which he commanded our fathers, that they should make them known to their children: That the generation to come might know them, even the children which should be born; who should arise and declare them to their children" (Psalm 78:1-7).

"That it might be fulfilled which was spoken by the prophet, saying, I will open my mouth in parables; I will utter things which have been kept secret from the foundation of the world" (Matthew 13:35).

"Now to him that is of power to establish you according to my gospel, and the preaching of Jesus Christ, according to the revelation of the mystery, which was kept secret since the world began, But now is made manifest, and by the scriptures of the prophets, according to the commandment of the everlasting God, made known to all nations for the obedience of faith: To God only wise, be glory through Jesus Christ forever. Amen" (Romans 16:25-27).

The fact that Emperor Haile Sellassie The First is the Almighty is the great mystery of godliness that has been kept secret since the world began. People have been looking for a sign from the LORD since the dawn of humanity. This pursuit has led many worshippers to invent stories and circumstances where they claim to have been touched by the hand of God or to have witnessed some supernatural phenomena as a means to justify their belief in the higher power. But no longer do we have to lie in God's name to prove his existence or to demonstrate that we are approved of the LORD. His Majesty has revealed himself to be the Holy Creator through his Prophet Jesus Christ; we bear witness to the fact that the promises have come to pass. People can now learn the true edicts and ways of the Almighty, instead of associating God with false tenants such as idolatry or paranormal activity. The last days signify the end of deception and only the legitimate gospel of God has the power to disprove and destroy all the false entities that abound.

"Jesus answered them, and said, My doctrine is not mine, but his that sent me. If any man will do his will, he shall know of the doctrine, whether it be of God, or whether I speak of myself" (John 7:16-17).

"The high priest then asked Jesus of his disciples, and of his doctrine. Jesus answered him, I spoke openly to the world; I always taught in the synagogue, and in the temple, where the Jews always resort, and in secret have I said nothing. Why ask thou me? ask them which heard me what I said unto them: behold they know what I said." (John 18:19-21).

"Pilate therefore said unto him, Are you a king then? Jesus answered, You say that I am a king. To this end was I born, and for this cause came I into the world, that

I should bear witness unto the truth. Everyone that is of the truth hears my voice" (*John 18:37*).

We all have the freedom to decide whether or not we will believe in God; the deciding factor will be if we accept the gospel of Christ. No one else understood the parables of the Bible, Jesus taught us as one having authority and not as the common preachers of the world. The Messiah is the lawful teacher of theology because he has full command of the scriptures. The Bible states that if you knew the doctrine you would know whether he speaks of himself or of God. Those who think that he was self-centered are mistaken, as well as, any attempt to try to explain the consubstantial concept will prove to be a failed cause. There is no correlation between Jesus being described as having a superior and distinguished doctrine, as he is called the "Light of the World," yet explaining his gospel using incoherent and inconceivable terms such as the supernatural and idolatry. There is no logical conclusion to validate accepting the notion that a Father and his Son are both the same quantity. We adhere to a higher and more intelligent meditation, which designates God and Christ as being two separate people, the same way that nature and the scriptures prescribed for them. Jesus is the high priest of the LORD, he preached that Emperor Haile Sellassie The First is the Almighty, as it is written, he kept us in the name of the Father. If we reject his message, then we shall never witness the promises of the Bible being made manifest. Let us worship His Majesty through his Son, the compulsory mediator between God and man, Jesus Christ the firstborn minister of Ethiopia Mt. Zion.

"And from Jesus Christ, who is the faithful witness and the first begotten of the dead, and the prince of the kings of the earth. Unto him that loved us, and washed us from our sins in his own blood, And has made us kings and priests unto God and his Father; to him be glory and dominion forever and ever. Amen" (*Revelation 1:5-6*).

"And they sung a new song, saying, Thou are worthy to take the book, and to open the seals thereof: for you was slain, and have redeemed us to God by your blood out of every kindred, and tongue, and people, and nation; And have made us unto our God kings and priests: and we shall reign on the earth" (*Revelation 5:9-10*).

"If you put the brethren in remembrance of these things, you shall be a good minister of Jesus Christ, nourished up in the words of faith and of good doctrine, which you have attained. But refuse profane and old wives' fables, and exercise yourself

rather in godliness. For bodily exercise profits little: but godliness is profitable unto all things, having promise of the life that now is, and of that which is to come. This is a faithful saying and worthy of all acceptation. For therefore we both labor and suffer reproach, because we trust in the living God, who is the Savior of all men, especially of those that believe" (1 Timothy 4:6-10).

The gospel of Christ has allowed us, who accept his Word, to be regarded as kings and priests before the Most High God. Our designation is a complimentary adoration meant to symbolize the prestige of the message which we preach. This title is neither for us to seek exhortation or a testament to our personal traits; for we are saved by the grace and mercy of Emperor Haile Sellassie The First. As Jesus submitted unto His Majesty and became one with the Father inside the kingdom of heaven, so do we acquiesce and likewise obtain the honor of being sovereign over the gospel. Christ was the King of the Jews which means the leader of God's people or the head of anyone who is committed unto the LORD. The disciples have received the power to become one of the sons of God which is why it is written that they have also risen as kings. Anyone that believes his testimony has set to his seal that God is true because you would be able to see the Creator Emperor Haile Sellassie The First. His Majesty is the blessed and only Potentate, Christ and his followers are one with the Father, which gives them the designation of being a crowned head because they have found favor with the Supreme Being. The heavenly realm is that of the King of Kings and Lords of Lords, those who worship the Most High in spirit and in truth, enter into this kingdom by accepting the divinity of the Emperor. Therefore the designation of us being labeled as monarchs is honorary because none of us are political rulers, it is this principle that has been enforced when describing Jesus, who in reality was a carpenter and a preacher, but was honored and risen by the Almighty to be regarded as a king because his message was true. This same scenario has been put forth when admonishing the apostles, who are rewarded with the equivalent citation as Christ, as they have been given the power to raise the dead and cure the blind; just as Jesus did.

"You have heard how I said unto you, I go away and come again unto you. If you loved me, you would rejoice, because I said, I go unto the Father: for my Father is greater than me. And now I have told you before it come to pass that when it is come to pass, you might believe" (John 14:28-29).

"Then Simon Peter answered him, Lord, to whom shall we go? you have the words of eternal life. And we believe and are sure that you are the very Christ, the Son of the living God" (John 6:68-69).

"For I have not spoken of myself; but the Father which sent me, he gave me a commandment, what I should say, and what I should speak. And I know that his commandment is life everlasting: whatsoever I speak therefore, even as the Father said unto me, so I speak" (John 12:49-50).

The second coming of Christ is described as being a glorious and significant event because this is when the mystery of God will be fulfilled; when all the speculation and questions pertaining to the LORD will finally be answered. It is written that we shall see God and it is through the revelation that our third eye is opened; which means that our awareness is heightened. As we learn the truth about the Almighty, which is to know that Emperor Haile Sellassie The First is the Creator, we then must abdicate from our previous understanding which could never bring us before the Throne of grace. The first man is our first comprehension of God, which has proven to be false, the second man is the Lord from heaven, that is the legitimate gospel of the Almighty; saving all those who believe. It is written that Jesus must come again because our first understanding of Jesus was not the true Jesus, therefore we need a new Christ to come, which is in fact the original Christ. This signifies that we never received the promises of salvation, although we claim that we was saved and follow Jesus; we was actually deficient in the entire postulate. The world needs the correct understanding of theology, only then can we enter the kingdom of heaven and become one with the Majesty on High. As we learn and adopt the principles of Emperor Haile Sellassie The First, we would be raising our standards and attaining mercy from the LORD Almighty. We are comforted in knowing that our doctrine was not built upon a hypothesis but historical facts, that is why Christ said that the Comforter shall come after his resurrection. We lift up the Son of man by putting on the whole armor of God thereby empowering ourselves to combat the deceit which the devil uses to corrupt the world. As we increase in understanding by taking the time to learn about Emperor Haile Sellassie The First, reading about him and cross referencing the divergent viewpoints on him, we will then be able to comprehend the truth which no form of doctrine could ever overcome. Our comfort is knowing the LORD, which only Jesus can teach you, but it is not something that you can fully grasp overnight; this requires diligent study. It takes time to understand and master the parables, when you have increased to the point that you are fully established in righteousness, then nothing can separate you from the love of God Emperor Haile Sellassie The First. At that point you would have attained the legitimate doctrine of Christ therefore being fully grounded in the true faith of the Almighty. His Majesty is the Highest of all High, let him be praised.

"The word which God sent unto the children of Israel, preaching peace by Jesus Christ: (he is Lord of all:) That word, I say, you know was published throughout all Judaea, and began from Galilee, after the baptism which John preached; How God anointed Jesus of Nazareth with the Holy Ghost and with power: who went around doing good, and healing all that were oppressed of the devil; for God was with him" (Acts 10:36-38).

"Therefore if any man be in Christ, he is a new creature: old things have passed away; behold all things are become new. And all things are of God, who has reconciled us to himself by Jesus Christ, and has given to us the ministry of reconciliation; To wit, that God was in Christ, reconciling the world unto himself, not imputing their trespasses unto them; and has committed unto us the word of reconciliation" (2 Corinthians 5:17-19).

"For verily he took not on him the nature of angels; but he took on him the seed of Abraham. Wherefore in all things it behoved him to be made like unto his brethren, that he might be a merciful and faithful high priest in things pertaining to God, to make reconciliation for the sins of the people" (Hebrews 2:16-17).

"And one of the scribes came, and having heard them reasoning together, and perceiving that he had answered them well, asked him, Which is the first commandment of all? And Jesus answered him, The first of all the commandments is Hear O Israel; the Lord our God is one Lord: And you shall love the Lord your God with all your heart, and with all your soul, and with all your mind, and with all your strength: this is the first commandment. And the second is like namely this, You shall love your neighbor as yourself. There are no other commandments greater than these. And the scribe said unto him, Well, Master, you have spoken the truth: for there is one God; and there is none other but he" (Mark 12:28-32).

Jesus Christ the Son of Haile Sellassie The First has told us the truth, that there is only one God and he has declared who is that person; the Supreme Being. Through the administration of the gospel we have come to know that Emperor Haile Sellassie The First of Ethiopia is the Almighty God. It is him who Jesus testified of and it was through the scriptures that Christ understood the truth about God the Father. "Now I say that Jesus Christ was a minister of the circumcision for the truth of God, to confirm the promises made unto the fathers: And that the Gentiles might glorify God for his mercy; as it is written, For this cause I will confess to thee among the Gentiles and sing unto thy name" (Romans 15:8-9). What is written about Christ describes his personality and purpose, we must accept him according to what the Bible says. Jesus is the Prophet of His Majesty, he is the messenger of a better covenant; which signifies that his gospel is greater than what is found in the world because his testimony is based upon facts not superstition and mythology.

"And behold, one came and said unto him, Good Master, what good thing shall I do that I may have eternal life? And he said unto him, Why callest thou me good? there is none good but one, that is God: but if you will enter into life, keep the commandments" (Matthew 19:16-17).

"In the beginning God created the heaven and the earth. And the earth was without form and void; and darkness was upon the face of the deep. And the Spirit of God moved upon the face of the waters. And God said, Let there be light: and there was light" (Genesis 1:1-3).

"Teach me to do your will; for you are my God: thy spirit is good; lead me into the land of uprightness" (Psalm 143:10).

The idea that Jesus Christ is God does not come from the Bible but from people who misinterpret the Word because they do not understand the parables. It is written that darkness covers the earth because they have not the true canon. This analogy is typically used to describe the creation of the universe that took place billions of years ago or as a condemnation of the immorality and corruption that plague the earth. Very few will understand the correct context of this parable which is that the peoples spiritual perspective is flawed and even less will be able to recognize their position in relation to this analogy. When it comes to the topic of God, everyone wants to believe that they are on the good side, no matter how wicked or sinful they are. As a result the scriptures which condemn the evil on earth, no one draws any connections to it, as if the people that these verses are speaking about do not exist. The illustration of the entire earth being void and dark is referring to everyone, if you cannot understand what constitutes an apocryphal viewpoint then you would be in danger of believing in those ordinances. If you are not able to see God, the King of Glory in the flesh, then you do not have the gospel of Jesus Christ. The Son has subscribed all praise unto the Father Emperor Haile Sellassie The First, for he alone is worthy to be praised. If anyone has not this message then they are void of the promises of salvation, that indicates all human beings: past, present, and future.

"How beautiful upon the mountains are the feet of him that brings good tidings, that publishes peace; that brings good tidings of good, that publishes salvation; that says unto Zion, Thy God reigneth!" (Isaiah 52:7).

"How much more shall the blood of Christ, who through the eternal Spirit offered himself without spot to God, purge your conscience from dead works to serve the living God? And for this cause he is the mediator of the new testament, that by means of death, for the redemption of the transgressions that were under the first testament, they which are called might receive the promise of eternal inheritance" (Hebrews 9:14-15).

"And he said unto them, This is my blood of the new testament, which is shed for many. Verily I say unto you, I will drink no more of the fruit of the vine, until that day that I drink it new in the kingdom of God" (Mark 14:24-25).

The distinguishing trait of Christ is his gospel which teaches you who God is without lowering your intelligence quotient. This unique endeavor is something that only the chosen Prophet of the LORD can fulfill, no one else can explain the scriptures correctly; the Bible has confirmed these circumstances. Everyone needs to realize that the only way to speak with authority about the manifestation of God is to worship Emperor Haile Sellassie The First. His Majesty is the only King of Kings and Lord of Lords, so whereas there may be some people who want to subscribe this christen to a fictional entity or debate the validity of our claim, we are justified through proven and numerous historical records which all confirm that Haile Sellassie The First alone bears the titles of God. You cannot be coherent in the Bible unless you confess the revelation and abide by the high standard of the LORD. As ministers of the Word, we represent the doctrine that we preach, for if the messenger was separate from the message then the purpose of following the gospel is void. Gandhi said, "We must be the change we wish to see in the world." The notion of do as I say but not as I do nullifies the purpose of saying anything at all. If you expect another person to live according to the principles that you disregard then you have given them a good reason not to take you seriously because no matter how sound your advice is, it must not be that important if you do not follow it. We must emulate the exemplary character and perfect ideal of His Majesty, because the Emperor achieved all of his accomplishments through natural feats to lead by example so that everyone can do what he did. The revelation of God has proven to provide real deliverance, not because we were whisked away into the sky, but rather because we have been instructed in the true path of righteousness. From this testimony, we can transform our planet into a fair and happy medium for all people to enjoy and progress if we would only mirror the ways of Emperor Haile Sellassie The First.

"The first shall say to Zion, Behold, behold them: and I will give to Jerusalem one that brings good tidings" (Isaiah 41:27).

"And Jesus returned in the power of the Spirit into Galilee: and there went out a fame of him through all the region round about. And he taught in their synagogues, being glorified of all. And he came to Nazareth, where he had been brought up: and as his custom was, he went into the synagogue on the Sabbath day, and stood up for to read. And there was delivered unto him the book of the prophet Esaias. And when he had opened the book, he found the place where it was written, The Spirit of the Lord is upon me, because he has anointed me to preach the gospel to the poor; he has sent me to heal the brokenhearted, to preach deliverance to the captives, and recovering of sight to the blind, to set at liberty them that are bruised, To preach the acceptable year of the Lord. And he closed the book, and he gave it again to the minister, and sat down. And the eyes of all them that were in the synagogue were fastened on him. And he began to say unto them, This day is this scripture fulfilled in your ears" (Luke 4:14-21).

"Verily, verily, I say unto you, He that hears my word and believes on him that sent me, has everlasting life, and shall not come into condemnation; but is passed from death unto life" (John 5:24).

It is necessary for the whole world to hear the true gospel of Christ that Emperor Haile Sellassie The First is the Almighty Father. His Majesty has fulfilled his part in accomplishing all that has been prophesied concerning the coming of the LORD. Yet only with the correct interpretation of the Bible would you be able to understand that the revelation has come to pass; that is why the Prophet Jesus was sent. Humanity as a whole has demonstrated that they cannot attain the proper theological standpoint on their own; either due to a lack of knowledge or discipline. This was especially true before Emperor Haile Sellassie The First revealed his face on earth and sadly this was also the case after His Majesty established his kingdom in Ethiopia. With the Almighty Creator right before their eyes, the world treated him like he was an ordinary man, they neglected him, and fought against him; although everything he stood for was righteous and he was seeking to make the world a better place for all people. Notwithstanding, God continued to show mercy on us by sending his Prophet after he completed his own work, because his desire is for everyone to be saved; even if we are our own worst enemies in dismissing the LORD who alone can offer salvation. Christ provided further instruction as to why it is so important to follow His Majesty and he explained the correlation between the Bible and the Emperor. It must be understood that Haile Sellassie The First was not going to preach himself therefore the people had to understand diplomacy and theology in order to comprehend and appreciate His Majesty's mission. Because no one could fathom the full scope of his reign, Jesus was sent to give the people the correct perspective on the actions and speeches of Haile Sellassie The First. It was not conducive for everyone to make up whatever they wanted to think about the Emperor because this did not produce the desired results. The Bible has therefore declared that all men must go through Jesus Christ to know the truth about the Father, he is the door into heaven, for he alone understood the parables which provides the people with the proper outlook necessary to save humanity.

"And this is life eternal, that they might know thee the only true God, and Jesus Christ, who you have sent. I have glorified thee on earth: I have finished the work which you gave me to do. And now, O Father, glorify thou me with thine own self with the glory which I had with thee before the world was. I have manifested thy name unto the men which you gave me out of the world: thine they were, and you gave them to me; and they have kept your word. Now they have known that all things whatsoever you have given me are of thee. For I have given unto them the words which you gave me; and they have received them, and have known surely that I came out from thee, and they have believed that you did send me. I pray for them: I pray not for the world, but for them which you have given me, for they are yours.

And all mine are yours, and yours are mine; and I am glorified in them. And now I am no more in the world, but these are in the world, and I come to you. Holy Father, keep through your own name those who you have given me, that they may be one, as we are" (John 17:3-11).

"How shall we escape, if we neglect so great salvation; which at the first began to be spoken by the Lord, and was confirmed unto us by them that heard him; God also bearing them witness, both with signs and wonders, and with divers miracles, and gifts of the Holy Ghost according to his own will" (Hebrews 2:3-4).

"That confirms the word of his servant, and performs the counsel of his messengers; that says to Jerusalem, You shall be inhabited; and to the cities of Judah, You shall be built, and I will raise up the decayed place thereof" (Isaiah 44:26).

Jesus declared the name of the Father unto his disciples, which means that he explained through the Bible how Emperor Haile Sellassie The First is the Almighty. The scriptures indicate that God will establish his kingdom on earth and he will send his Prophet to teach the world how the prophecies have been fulfilled. This describes two different individuals, the Father and the Son, each having a unique person, purpose, and identity. Because humanity never understood the message of the Bible, they have corrupted the Word by devising various incorrect interpretations of theology; that will confuse any astute observer. A major challenge which has hindered world progress has been accepting the notion that the Almighty Creator will appear on earth but the entire message of the scriptures indicates that he will be made manifest, as well as the fact that it is very hard to prove that God exists if you cannot see him. Christ understood the full scope of the Bible, what he preached opposed the common and popular doctrines of the world; that is why he was vilified. He said to repent because the kingdom of heaven is at hand, God revealed himself in the flesh, all of the scriptures have foretold of this great event. Jesus accepted the message of salvation and was able to see God thereby proving the existence of the LORD with awesome clarity and acumen because he worshipped His Majesty. This tangible justification can only be substantiated by believing in Emperor Haile Sellassie The First. Theology, just like any subject, can only be explained properly by a competent pundit; the Bible has indicated that this teacher is the Messiah. The correct reading of the scriptures says that God and his Son are two separate individuals, one is the Almighty and the other is his Prophet. Only through the revelation can our faith be validated, we must have evidence of that which we believe in, to prove to ourselves as well as to others, that what we hold is true.

"But as God is true, our word toward you was not yes and no. For the Son of God, Jesus Christ, who was preached among you by us, even by me and Silvanus and Timotheus, was not yes and no, but in him was yes. For all the promises of God in him are yes, and in him Amen, unto the glory of God by us. Now he which establishes us with you in Christ, and has anointed us, is God. Who has also sealed us, and given the earnest of the Spirit in our hearts" (2 Corinthians 1:18-22).

"Now he that has wrought us for the selfsame thing is God, who also has given unto us the earnest of the Spirit" (2 Corinthians 5:5).

"That you may with one mind and one mouth glorify God, even the Father of our Lord Jesus Christ. Wherefore receive ye one another, as Christ also received us to the glory of God. Now I say that Jesus Christ was a minister of the circumcision for the truth of God, to confirm the promises made unto the fathers: And that the Gentiles might glorify God for his mercy; as it is written, For this cause I will confess to thee among the Gentiles and sing unto your name" (Romans 15:6-9).

If we are serious about following God then we must investigate our faith to make sure that what we believe in is actually true. This requires an objective analysis of our beliefs and only those who are sincere in their relationship with the LORD will be honest with themselves. It is written that those with ears shall hear because the message of Christ is prepared for the true seekers of God. If a person has evil intentions or is unfamiliar with the gospel, then they will oppose the true sayings of the Almighty out of enmity or ignorance. Most people are innocent as far as deciphering contention, that is why it has to be stressed that just because someone else rejects something does not necessarily mean that it is wrong. There is no way to know why someone is opposing a particular opinion, they could be sincere in their argument or they could be trying to deceive people. You cannot let society give you your opinion, especially when we are discussing the revelation of God. Everyone has their own heart and mentality, which only the Creator can examine to determine who is real or not. The results of this test is made manifest in either their acceptance or denial of Emperor Haile Sellassie The First. We also know that many are called but few are chosen, therefore the real gospel of Jesus is not a doctrine which has been received by the masses.

The question should not be if it is mainstream but rather if it makes sense. If we judge the validity of religion based upon popularity then we are putting our trust in man rather than God. People are imperfect creatures who always must strive to improve themselves because we all make mistakes. It therefore is a very precarious position to leave it in their hands to resolve the salvation of our souls; this actually is a decision that each individual must make on their own.

"In that hour Jesus rejoiced in spirit and said, I thank thee, O Father, Lord of heaven and earth, that you have hid these things from the wise and prudent, and have revealed them unto babes: even so, Father; for so it seemed good in your sight" (Luke 10:21).

"Wherefore, holy brethren, partakers of the heavenly calling, consider the Apostle and High Priest of our profession, Christ Jesus; Who was faithful to him that appointed him, as also Moses was faithful in all his house" (Hebrews 3:1-2).

"The LORD possessed me in the beginning of his way, before his works of old. I was set up from everlasting, from the beginning, or ever the earth was. When there were no depths, I was brought forth; when there were no fountains abounding with water. Before the mountains were settled, before the hills was I brought forth: While as yet he had not made the earth, nor the fields, nor the highest part of the dust of the world. When he prepared the heavens, I was there: when he set a compass upon the face of the depth: When he established the clouds above: when he strengthened the fountains of the deep: When he gave to the sea his decree, that the waters should not pass his commandment: when he appointed the foundations of the earth: Then I was by him, as one brought up with him: and I was daily his delight, rejoicing always before him; Rejoicing in the habitable part of his earth; and my delights were with the sons of men" (Proverbs 8:22-31).

Jesus is a minister who has declared unto us that Haile Sellassie The First is the Almighty. He is the first person to fully understand the Bible and properly explain the theological position of His Majesty in conjunction with the Emperor's speeches and actions. The prophecies have designated the founder of the gospel which deciphers the scriptures correctly as Christ, therefore if we claim that this person came during ancient times then his teachings should be known to us by now. But if we adhere to illogical, incoherent, superstitious, and blasphemous edicts then we should not dishonor God or his Prophet by associating our ignorance with the message of life. When we are referring to false doctrines, we are not talking about traditions which are unpopular or censored, we are alluding to ideas which betray knowledge and neglect our intrinsic nature. It is a great tragedy to say that Jesus has come, yet not to be able to show who God is, or to explain the Bible without clarity, revelation, or rationale. If this is the case, then what exactly is the purpose or significance of Christ, why is he regarded as being so great and compulsory, if his followers have no knowledge? It is written that he revealed unto his disciples who the Father is and gave them the same power that he has, so shouldn't we know God and have a certain level of dexterity in the scriptures? These questions have led the churches to commit another grave error in seeking to explain that Jesus is the father because this idea is not supported by any verse or prophecy. If you think that you have received the gospel of Christ then certain key elements you must understand according to the Bible; first, you have to know who God is and who is his Prophet; you have to be able to identify these two individuals. Furthermore, you must be able to understand and explain the entire context of the holy books in conjunction with each other, without contradiction and without illusion; for the true gospel is a superior doctrine. This does not mean that everyone will be able to quote the entire Bible, but it does affirm that all those with the message of salvation must be able to save themselves and others.

"Wherefore laying aside all malice, and all guile, and hypocrisies, and envies, and all evil speakings, As newborn babes, desire the sincere milk of the word, that you may grow thereby: If so be you have tasted that the Lord is gracious. To whom coming, as unto a living stone, disallowed indeed of men, but chosen of God and precious, You also as lively stones, are built up a spiritual house, a holy priesthood to offer up spiritual sacrifices, acceptable to God by Jesus Christ. Wherefore also it is contained in the scripture, Behold I lay in Sion a chief corner stone, elect, precious: and he that believes on him shall not be confounded. Unto you therefore which believe he is precious: but unto them which be disobedient, the stone which the builders disallowed, the same is made the head of the corner, And a stone of stumbling and a rock of offense, even to them which stumble at the word, being disobedient: whereunto also they were appointed. But you are a chosen generation, a royal priesthood, a holy nation, a peculiar people; that you should show forth the praises of him who has called you out of darkness into his marvelous light: Which in time past were not a people, but are now the people of God: which had not obtained mercy, but now have obtained mercy" (1 Peter 2:1-10).

"That you may walk worthy of the Lord unto all pleasing, being fruitful in every good work, and increasing in the knowledge of God; strengthened with all might, according to his glorious power, unto all patience and longsuffering with joyfulness; Giving thanks unto the Father, which has made us meet to be partakers of the inheritance of the saints in light" (Colossians 1:10-12).

We have to be honest with ourselves and admit when something is wrong. If we are following traditions that are not positive, then we should not try to justify them or present it as something other than what it really is. If we believe in an illogical ideology then we should not deceive ourselves into thinking that it can somehow be true. The various religions in the world hold that supernatural episodes are real, that they are a sign from the LORD; this then leads their supporters to invent fables about peculiar situations that never really happened. They have to lie to try to justify their belief because what they follow is false. The supernatural is not a realistic, scientific, or legitimate theory; it is an unadulterated sham. Anyone who understands the world and accepts reality would be able to come to this conclusion quite naturally. If we want to please God, we must do that which is reasonable and positive. It only serves the traditions of men to follow unnatural and unreasonable edits that clearly are false. Christ was rejected because his message was true, the masses did not accept him because they wanted to continue following a dishonest scheme. This depiction was never meant to be associated with fabled events that supposably took place thousands of years ago. The Bible is a living document designed in a unique format so that any reader can relate to the stories. No matter what era you live in, you have to be able to tell that the scriptures are describing events that are happening in your time period. If we did that, then we would know that God has forewarned us not to follow the world because they are corrupt and sacrilegious. The next step after this would be to question everything and reject that which is false and backwards. Yet the spiritual guides do not encourage you to do any critical thinking because what they want you to follow is incorrect. They portray Jesus as a remote magical figurehead who appeared during ancient times, which creates a disconnection between the trials of Christ and our own tribulations. Instead of realizing that the afflictions of the Son of God are the same burdens that we bear, many people have been misled to think that the story of Christ took place way before their time. In this they prevent themselves from accepting the promise of seeing God and torpedo their ability to understand the Bible. The only way to avoid this dilemma is to put your trust in God and not men.

"Blessed be God, even the Father of our Lord Jesus Christ, the Father of mercies, and the God of all comfort; Who comforts us in all our tribulation, that we may be able to comfort them which are in any trouble, by the comfort wherewith we ourselves are comforted of God. For as the sufferings of Christ abound in us, so our consolation also abounds by Christ. And whether we be afflicted, it is for your consolation and salvation, which is effectual in the enduring of the same sufferings which we also suffer: or whether we be comforted, it is for your consolation and salvation. And our hope of you is stedfast, knowing that as you are partakers of the sufferings, so shall you be also of the consolation. For we would not brethren, have you ignorant of our trouble which came to us in Asia, that we were pressed out of measure above strength, insomuch that we despaired even of life: But we had the sentence of death in ourselves, that we should not trust in ourselves, but in God which raises the dead: Who delivered us from so great a death, and does deliver: in whom we trust that he will yet deliver us; You also helping together by prayer for us, that for the gift bestowed upon us by the means of many persons thanks may be given by many on our behalf" (2 Corinthians 1:3-10).

"O magnify the LORD with me, and let us exalt his name together" (Psalm 34:3).

"Praise ye the LORD. O give thanks unto the LORD; for he is good: for his mercy endures forever. Who can utter the mighty acts of the LORD? who can show forth all his praise? Blessed are they that keep judgment and he that does righteousness at all times. Remember me, O LORD, with the favor that you bear unto your people: O visit me with your salvation; That I may see the good of your chosen, that I may rejoice in the gladness of your nation, that I may glory with your inheritance" (Psalm 106:1-5).

Through the gospel of Iyesus Kristos we are able to see and know the Father of Creation Emperor Haile Sellassie The First. The world crucified and rejected the message of Christ because they did not want to repent from their delusive convictions and accept the true word that His Majesty is God. We are not ignorant to believe that if they classified our Master as Beelzebub, a false teacher, that they would accept us who follow his teachings. We therefore are prepared for both the ridicule and the praise that come along with being an active Christian; one who glorifies Emperor Haile Sellassie The First, the Father of Jesus Christ. Our message is the message of the Bible: God was manifest in the flesh, justified in the spirit, the King of Glory, Governor of the nations, hallowed be thy name, his name is One. But the time is evil, therefore many people reject that which is good and try to write His Majesty off as being a tyrant; they are unable to accept the right thing because they are too corrupt and ignorant. All of this has been foretold in the Bible, that they would try to change the glory of the incorruptible God into the image of a corruptible man, and for this cause God gave them over to the uncleanness of their own wicked hearts to believe a lie and to dishonor themselves.[26] The prophecies of the scriptures have come to pass, for we witness how the true Savior, Emperor Haile Sellassie The First, is rejected; people would rather look to the sky for a sign from heaven. They think that the Lord's glory and presence is witnessed through wonders in the environment, such as a panoramic sunset, a majestic mountain range, an aurora, the metamorphosis of a butterfly, etc., but while all of these occurrences are quite spectacular, none of them should be considered heavenly or godly. Christ was directing us to his Father because only the Almighty can offer deliverance. We need to put our trust in His Majesty because all other deities, doctrines, and phenomena are ultimately vain and unprofitable in regard to being divine episodes. People are looking for God in all the wrong places because they have been indoctrinated with bogus religious tenants. Only Jesus can explain theology properly, that is why despite the fight that we receive, we remain steadfast because we understand that all of our criticism is baseless and benighted. Eternal life is the everlasting gospel of Iyesus Kristos, which is to know that Emperor Haile Sellassie The First is the Almighty; this message shall stand the test of time.

"It is a good thing to give thanks unto the LORD, to sing praises unto thy name, O Most High: To show forth thy lovingkindness in the morning, and your faithfulness every night, Upon an instrument of ten strings, and upon the psaltery; upon the harp with a solemn sound. For thou LORD, has made me glad through your work: I will triumph in the works of your hands" (Psalm 92:1-4).

"Now thanks be unto God, which always causes us to triumph in Christ, and makes manifest the savior of his knowledge by us in every place. For we are not as many which corrupt the word of God: but as of sincerity, but as of God in the sight of God speak we in Christ" (2 Corinthians 2:14&17).

"Only let your conversation be as it becomes the gospel of Christ: that whether I come and see you, or else be absent, I may hear of your affairs, that you stand fast in

---

[26] Romans 1

one spirit, with one mind striving together for the faith of the gospel; And in nothing terrified by your adversaries: which is to them an evident token of perdition, but to you of salvation and that of God" (Philippians 1:27-28).

To know the true and living God Emperor Haile Sellassie The First, enlightens you with the wisdom to overcome your challenges and live life more abundantly; this knowledge, when applied, provides you with a resolute inner peace in being successful and righteous. By studying the life and the policies of His Majesty, we would notice that he went through the same human struggles that we are faced with, this was done to teach us how we should conduct ourselves. It is possible to change the world for the better and to achieve greatness without sacrificing your dignity or morality. Emperor Haile Sellassie The First has demonstrated this capability under much more strenuous and provocative circumstances than our own plight, there is therefore no excuse for any sort of folly or underachievement. We must follow the Almighty who sits upon the Throne of Zion. Jesus is his minister, who accurately preached the divinity of the Father; he told us that we ought to do as His Majesty has done. The Bible indicates that Christ is on the right hand side of the LORD,[27] which means that he is the Prophet of God, sent to teach people the true meaning of theism as his testimony and deeds are acceptable before the Holy Creator. If we neglect this great deliverance and follow the ways of the heathen, their interpretation would have you believe that the Father and Son are somehow both the same entity. Therefore the Almighty who sits on the Throne, is also Jesus on the right hand side of the LORD; so God is standing next to God. That is a phantasmal portrayal, a completely illogical premise, which imagines that two people share the same soul. This would also make Christ a mediator of himself because he would be the Father for whom he said to worship; which then contradicts the Bible because it is written that Jesus did not speak of himself.[28] Furthermore this absurd premise implies that there are two gods, the Father and the Son, who are one in essence and dual in embodiment. Although the crooked ways are abundant, we will not follow or accept a false and senseless gospel. The heathens resort to violence and intimidation to implement their religion because they cannot persuade people to accept that which is unintelligible. But we put our trust in the true and living God Emperor Haile Sellassie The First and shall not fear the devices of man. The message that we preach is

---

[27] Psalm 110
[28] John 12:49

the true sayings of Christ and whoever is offended by our doctrine is contrary to the LORD. Our focus is upon completing the works which His Majesty has called upon us to do, not to compromise with immoral and misguided people who are not of God.

"But we are bound to give thanks always to God for you, brethren beloved of the Lord, because God has from the beginning chosen you to salvation through sanctification of the Spirit and belief of the truth: Whereunto he called you by our gospel, to the obtaining of the glory of our Lord Jesus Christ. Therefore brethren, stand fast, and hold the traditions which you have been taught, whether by word, or our epistle. Now our Lord Jesus Christ himself, and God, even our Father, which has loved us, and has given us everlasting consolation and good hope through grace, Comfort your hearts and establish you in every good word and work" (2 Thessalonians 2:13-17).

"Now to him that is of power to establish you according to my gospel, and the preaching of Jesus Christ, according to the revelation of the mystery, which was kept secret since the world began, But now is made manifest, and by the scriptures of the prophets, according to the commandment of the everlasting God, made known to all nations for the obedience of faith. To God only wise, be glory through Jesus Christ forever. Amen" (Romans 16:25-27).

"And to know the love of Christ, which passes knowledge, that you might be filled with all the fulness of God. Now unto him that is able to do exceeding abundantly above all that we ask or think, according to the power that works in us, Unto him be glory in the church by Christ Jesus throughout all ages, world without end. Amen" (Ephesians 3:19-21).

It is written that Christ was born from a virgin which means that his blood (gospel) is pure and trustworthy. The true testimony of the Messiah is coherent and factual. All the superstitious and illogical ideologies present throughout the world have to be condemned or else people might regard it as the message of Iyesus Kristos. It is difficult to identify the correct interpretation of the scriptures because the devil works behind a veil of deceit to appear as an angel of light. But we are guided by wisdom, for we denounce that which is unnatural and incoherent. If you are searching for the truth, then you must pursue the factual and rational approach. This is how we know that two people cannot be the same entity, Christ declared that his Father Emperor Haile Sellassie The First alone is God. Now there is a popular notion which states that the

Almighty is invisible in heaven and cannot be seen but he manifest himself on earth by lowering himself in taking on the nature of a man in the person of Jesus Messiah; who would then be God the Son. If anyone accepts this theory then they have not only contradicted themselves but they have also betrayed the message of the Bible because it states in Isaiah 9 that the "Everlasting Father" will establish his kingdom on earth. There is not one verse in the scriptures that will repudiate your logic if you had the correct interpretation of the prophecy. It is written that both God and his Prophet will appear before humanity to fulfill the promises of salvation. If the spiritual guides understood the mystery, they would know that the covenant is for the Creator to reveal himself before the eyes of all the nations and to also send forth his Son into the world to teach the proper meaning of the parables. There are many people who have not this confirmation and are still searching for the truth. Those who are sincere in their relationship with the LORD are guided by knowledge not superstition, they accept facts not fables. This pursuit will lead you before the King of Glory and to the full assurances of redemption which is Emperor Haile Sellassie The First; God in the flesh.

"Make a joyful noise unto the LORD, all ye lands. Serve the LORD with gladness: come before his presence with singing. Know ye that the LORD he is God: it is he that has made us and not we ourselves; we are his people, and the sheep of his pasture. Enter into his gates with thanksgiving, and into his courts with praise: be thankful unto him and bless his name. For the LORD is good; his mercy is everlasting; and his truth endures to all generations" (Psalm 100:1-5).

"And he answered and said unto them, Have you not read, that he which made them at the beginning made them male and female" (Matthew 19:4).

"O give thanks unto the LORD; for he is good: for his mercy endures forever" (Psalm 118:29).

If people have the wrong concept about God then they would never be able to understand the meaning of life or create fair and humane living conditions for everyone to enjoy. The psychological effect of teaching the multitudes that they are born sinners entices the general public to do the wrong thing because subconsciously the message relayed is that we are innately bad. This will create a society where evil is more abundant than good, and that is what is present in every community where this theory is accepted. The truth about

Adam and Eve is not what is represented by the blind guides who teach a literal and misguided translation of the Bible. Male and female were made to be one because the woman represents the church or your spiritual sense, Eve was then corrupted by the serpent because humanity follows a doctrine contrary to the Word of God. The theory that the Lord condemned us all, before we was born, due to the original sin of our ancient ancestors is false and unfair; people could only be judged impartially based upon their own actions. The devil entices us all on a daily basis to deny His Majesty and to follow an inaccurate ideology which would result in a miserable existence. Therefore everyone is faced with the temptation of Adam and Eve, the choice to follow God or Baal is referring to our present tribulations, not an ancient fable that supposably transpired millions of years ago. The first Adam represents those who follow the wrong spiritual concepts, while the second Adam depicts those who follow Jesus. Christ was sent to teach people about the Father so that humanity may finally be saved in knowing the true and living God Emperor Haile Sellassie The First; no one knew the truth before the Messiah preached his message. The correct depiction of Iyesus Kristos is that of a priest, the Prophet of the Almighty King; every verse and saying in the scriptures confirms this fact. To misinterpret the Bible to state that Jesus is God, who was killed as a human sacrifice to himself, so that he could save us through his hemoglobin, is an erroneous interpretation meant to spread ignorance and keep the people fearful and unrighteous. We have to break the mental chains of the devil and follow the principles of Emperor Haile Sellassie The First so that we may have the proper understanding of the Bible and live a healthy life. That cannot happen under a mythological and superstitious dogma because those types of doctrines ground you in ignorance which then develops a wayward character.

"Give ear, O ye heavens, and I will speak; and hear, O earth, the words of my mouth. My doctrine shall drop as the rain, my speech shall distil as the dew, as the small rain upon the tender herb, and as the showers upon the grass: Because I will publish the name of the LORD: ascribe ye greatness unto our God. He is the Rock, his work is perfect: for all his ways are judgment: a God of truth and without iniquity, just and right is he" (Deuteronomy 32:1-4).

"I will lift up my eyes unto the hills, from whence cometh my help. My help comes from the LORD, which made heaven and earth" (Psalm 121:1-2).

"O LORD of hosts, God of Israel, that dwells between the cherubims, you are God, even you alone, of all the kingdoms of the earth, you have made heaven and earth" (Isaiah 37:16).

The Almighty is described as being pious and holy, infinite in wisdom and mercy. These traits would have to be manifest in his actions or else these accolades would be hollow and meaningless. Only a coward accepts that which is wrong without searching for solace. The religious world believes in a definition of God that does not match their interpretation but they never question if what they follow is valid because they have become comfortable in their sin. If they knew how to interpret the Bible they would understand what it means by God is good and would not associate him with certain crude behavior; they would search for the greater and correct meaning of the scriptures. Jesus was not killed as a human sacrifice to himself, it is not holy or pious to shed blood and murder people; we cannot associate the true Creator with pagan practices like that of the Aztec traditions of Tezcatilpoca. Hemoglobin does not wash away sin, the Lord is not pleased with the sacrifice any human being or animal as an act of devotion; these rituals are repulsive and backwards. There is a much greater meaning to the Bible that offers verifiable salvation through the proper interpretation of the parables. The blood of Jesus is his gospel and if you would accept his testimony, that Emperor Haile Sellassie The First is the Most High, then you will be clean from sin because you would have the true message of the Bible. Human sacrifice does not exercise wisdom or righteousness in any way, it is totally blasphemous to associate God with these types of deeds. But these blind spiritual guides hold onto a literal and supernatural translation of the scriptures despite its blatant illegitimacy and flawed design; they debase the glory of the Father by depicting his adoration in this manner. No one will ever know the truth unless you can think objectively about your faith and reject that which does not make sense.

"But Christ being come a high priest of good things to come, by a greater and more perfect tabernacle, not made with hands, that is to say, not of this building; Neither by the blood of goats and calves, but by his own blood he entered in once into the holy place, having obtained eternal redemption for us. For if the blood of bulls and of goats, and the ashes of a heifer sprinkling the unclean, sanctifieth to the purifying of the flesh: How much more shall the blood of Christ, who through the eternal Spirit offered himself without spot to God, purge your conscience from dead works to serve the living God" (Hebrews 9:11-14).

"And I saw another angel fly in the midst of heaven, having the everlasting gospel to preach unto them that dwell on the earth, and to every nation, and kindred, and tongue, and people. Saying with a loud voice, Fear God, and give glory to him; for the hour of his judgment is come: and worship him that made heaven, and earth, and the sea, and the fountains of waters" (Revelation 14:6-7).

"Happy is he that has the God of Jacob for his help, whose hope is in the LORD his God: which made heaven and earth, the sea and all that therein is: which keeps truth forever" (Psalm 146:5-6).

Jesus is the honorable minister of the Most High with a testimony greater than that of man. He is the Son of God because he preaches the true sayings of the Lord, whereas everyone else speculates and hypothesizes about what they think the Bible means. Christ is the authority on theology because he accepts God Emperor Haile Sellassie The First and adheres to the message of the Father. The blood of bullocks and other animals represents the base gospels of the world which are all void of truth. They say that their interpretation is valid, that they have the right religion, yet they lack evidence and coherency in the scriptures. To believe in the supernatural, human sacrifice, idolatry, etc., only reveals their shame and ignorance. To explain the Almighty according to shallow definitions like "God is God" or "God is the only true God;" demonstrates that they have no knowledge because this clarifies nothing. The blood of Christ represents a gospel which gives a valid explanation of the Bible, one which does not contradict itself and reveals the Almighty unto those who believe the testimony. That is why his message has been classified as being greater than anything else found in the world, an acceptable offering that cleanses you from sin. Jesus taught his disciples that Emperor Haile Sellassie The First is God the Father, this is the only edict that can save.

"O come, let us sing unto the LORD: let us make a joyful noise to the rock of our salvation. Let us come before his presence with thanksgiving, and make a joyful noise unto him with psalms. For the LORD is a great God, and a great King above all gods. In his hand are the deep places of the earth: the strength of the hills is his also. The sea is his, and he made it: and his hands formed the dry land. O come, let us worship and bow down: let us kneel before the LORD our maker. For he is our God; and we are the people of his pasture, and the sheep of his hand. Today if you will hear his voice" (Psalm 95:1-7).

"O taste and see that the LORD is good: blessed is the man that trusts in him" (Psalm 34:8).

"O God, you are my God, early will I seek thee: my soul thirsts for you, my flesh longs for you in a dry and thirsty land, where no water is; To see your power and your glory, so as I have seen thee in the sanctuary. Because thy lovingkindness is better than life, my lips shall praise thee. Thus will I bless thee while I live: I will lift up my hands in your name. My soul shall be satisfied as with marrow and fatness; and my mouth shall praise thee with joyful lips" (Psalm 63:1-5).

What sets Christ apart is the revelation, everyone depicts the Lord as being invisible or an idol, but the Son of God actually divulges the Father. If we are active Christians then we would inherit the promises of salvation and have our blindness cured, making us able to see God Emperor Haile Sellassie The First. The Almighty is described as a great King above all gods, in a land where no water (truth) is, blessed is the man that trusts in him. Christ was crucified because they rejected his message, they did not accept the Father despite the fact that His Majesty is the King of Kings and Lord of Lords. Many people have imagined the Creator to be a certain way, whether that be a certain color or height or facet, and because it is impossible for one being to look the same according to everyones different opinion, we therefore should not trust in our imagination. But that is what has happened and as a result they reject the Almighty Emperor Haile Sellassie The First because he does not comply with their descriptions of what they dreamed the Creator to be; although he fulfilled the prophecy of the Lord. The notion that the mystery could be revealed through an alternate outline separate from their wool-gatherings has not been considered, they all feel as if they have the correct interpretation; even if what they believe in is not logical. The Bible gave us fair warning not to fall into this trap like the rich man who does not want to sell his riches because that faith which he professes is so dear to him that he cannot let it go even when it has been proven wrong and the true transla-tion has been revealed. We must repent for the kingdom of God is at hand: Emperor Haile Sellassie The First is the Almighty.

"The heavens are yours, the earth also is yours: as for the world and the fulness thereof, you have founded them. The north and the south you have created them: Tabor and Hermon shall rejoice in your name. You have a mighty arm: strong is your hand, and high is your right hand. Justice and judgment are the habitation *of your throne: mercy and truth shall go before your face. Blessed is the people that know the joyful sound: they shall walk, O LORD, in the light of your countenance. In your name shall they rejoice all the day: and in your righteousness shall they be exalted. For you are the glory of their strength: and in your favor our horn shall be exalted. For the LORD is our defense; and the Holy One of Israel is our king"* (Psalm 89:11-18).

"Praise ye the LORD. Sing unto the LORD a new song, and his praise in the congregation of saints. Let Israel rejoice in him that made him: let the children of Zion be joyful in their King" (Psalm 149:1-2).

"And have put on the new man, which is renewed in knowledge after the image of him that created him" (Colossians 3:10).

We are fortunate to be born during a time when we can learn about Emperor Haile Sellassie The First. The beginning in the Bible marks the moment when humanity can learn the truth about the LORD, this took place on November 2, 1930, in Ethiopia. In his name shall we rejoice throughout the day, for God is our defense and the glory of our strength, let the children of Zion be joyful in their King. The old philosophies of the world, that were alloyed before His Majesty manifest the truth, were all contrived on guesswork. But now we can learn the real interpretation of the scriptures if we would adopt the principles of the Emperor; the new testament signifies the new man. The Bible has appealed for us to accept the gospel of Christ so that we can comprehend the truth about the LORD. If we did this then we would know that the way we used to think about God was false; people believe that the Creator is a supernatural being who is invisible and communicates with us telepathically. This theory has reduced the Almighty into an abstract entity because you cannot see him, you have to meditate and invent the discourse that you are having with him. But is this form of devotion really obeying the Word of God or is this trusting your own conscience? If anyones superego was cultivated and astute to the point where they could listen to their inner voice to solve their problems then that would mean that they are God. There would be no purpose in looking to the Most High, if all of our answers were found within our conscience; we could just look to ourselves. It is also an almost schizophrenic and childish approach to think that the Lord communicates with us like a clairvoyant. Should we be hearing voices in our heads or pretending that we have an imaginary friend named Jesus who is invisible walking with us and talking to us? The time has come for us to sing a new song unto the Almighty, one of truth and revelation so that our fidelity is acceptable before God as we comply with his divinity. This form of exaltation only comes from worshipping Emperor Haile Sellassie The First.

"This I say therefore, and testify in the Lord, that you henceforth walk not as other Gentiles walk, in the vanity of their mind, Having the understanding darkened, being alienated from the life of God through the ignorance that is in them, because of the blindness of their heart: Who being past feeling have given themselves over unto lasciviousness, to work all uncleanness with greediness. But you have not so learned Christ; If so be that you have heard him, and have been taught by him, as the truth is in Jesus: That you put off concerning the former conversation the old man, which is corrupt according to the deceitful lusts; And be renewed in the spirit of your mind; And that you put on the new man, which after God is created in righteousness and true holiness" (Ephesians 4:17-24).

"God is gone up with a shout, the LORD with the sound of a trumpet. Sing praises to God, sing praises: sing praises unto our King, sing praises. For God is the King of all the earth: sing ye praises with understanding. God reigneth over the heathen: God sits upon the throne of his holiness" (Psalm 47:5-8).

"And he that shall swear by heaven, swears by the throne of God, and by him that sitteth thereon" (Matthew 23:22).

There is a real meaning to the Bible, all of the events described in the scriptures will be fulfilled but it will not transpire in the way that people imagine it to be because they all have the wrong interpretation of the parables. When you take the holy book literally you nullify the purpose of the mediator because the only reason a teacher would be needed to explain non-figurative stories is if everyone in the world was illiterate. How could anyone not understand what these spiritual accounts mean if they occurred exactly as you read them; what exactly would be the mystery? But this is what has happened, people think that they know the Almighty when they say terms such as, "there is no God except for God;" which has reduced the Creator into a word, instead of acknowledging the being that this noun is referring to. Reading the Bible and saying a prayer to the LORD does not mean that you know who is the entity that you worship. You must be able to identify the Almighty by seeing him and explaining how he is God. As it is written, sing praises unto our King, for God is the King of all the earth, sing praises with understanding. And he that shall swear by heaven, swears by the throne of God, and by him that sits thereon. These are not the descriptions of a lexeme but rather a living organism, until you know who that individual is that the scriptures proclaim, there is no way to honestly conclude that you know the LORD. It is only when you accept the divinity of Emperor Haile Sellassie The First that you can say that you know the Almighty; because he is God and there is none else.

"Therefore seeing we have this ministry, as we have received mercy, we faint not; But have renounced the hidden things of dishonesty, not walking in craftiness, nor handling the word of God deceitfully; but by manifestation of the truth commending ourselves to every man's conscience in the sight of God. But if our gospel be hid, it is hid to them that are lost: In whom the god of this world hath blinded the minds of them which believe not, lest the light of the glorious gospel of Christ, who is the image of God, should shine unto them. For we preach not ourselves, but Christ Jesus the Lord; and ourselves your servants for Jesus' sake. For God, who commanded the light to shine out of darkness, hath shined in our hearts, to give the light of the knowledge of the glory of God in the face of Jesus Christ. But we have this treasure in earthen vessels, that the excellency of the power may be of God, and not of us. We are troubled on every side, yet not distressed; we are perplexed, but not in despair; Persecuted, but not forsaken; cast down, but not destroyed; Always bearing about in the body the dying of the Lord Jesus, that the life also of Jesus might be made manifest in our body. For we which live are always delivered unto death for Jesus' sake, that the life also of Jesus might be made manifest in our mortal flesh. So then death worketh in us, but life in you. We having the same spirit of faith, according as it is written, I believed, and therefore have I spoken; we also believe, and therefore speak; Knowing that he which raised up the Lord Jesus shall raise up us also by Jesus, and shall present us with you. For all things are for your sakes, that the abundant grace might through the thanksgiving of many redound to the glory of God" (2 Corinthians 4:1-15).

"But we all, with open face beholding as in a glass the glory of the Lord, are changed into the same image from glory to glory, even as by the Spirit of the Lord" (2 Corinthians 3:12).

"O give thanks unto the LORD; call upon his name: make known his deeds among the people. Sing unto him, sing psalms unto him: talk ye of all his wondrous works.

Glory ye in his holy name: let the heart of them rejoice that seek the LORD. Seek the LORD, and his strength: seek his face evermore" (Psalm 105:1-4).

The revelation of the kingdom of heaven is a covenant made at the beginning of time that God would not permit humanity to destroy itself. Haile Sellassie The First was manifest during a time when the weapons of warfare were industrialized making it possible to annihilate all forms of life relatively quickly and easily; the Emperor stood up as the voice of reason to object to this end. He furthermore sent forth his Son (the Prophet) to preach deliverance so that people may know that His Majesty is God. The only way to conclude that you adhere to the gospel of Christ is if you know the Father. This means that you must be able to see the King of Kings and Lord of Lords, not just articulate that you know the Almighty. Everyone who thinks that they follow Jesus has to live up to this standard if they want to be considered true Christians; you must receive that which the Messiah has promised you. The story of Christ is an ancient prophecy, depicted in various forms from the ancient of days. If you believe that Jesus already came on earth then you must address the most important aspect of his gospel and reveal the evidence of the LORD. Just because the tale of Christ is composed in the new testament does not mean that it was fulfilled while it was written. It has been foretold what Jesus would do in the old testament,[29] the promises of the Son of God were known before the Bible was written.[30] There is nothing new about reading the account of the Prophet of the Lord, the only thing that would be unique is if we received that which he promised us; which is to see and know the Father. No one can accurately conclude that they are following the gospel of Christ until they worship Emperor Haile Sellassie The First; he is the sole manifestation of the King of Kings and Lord of Lords on earth. Let him be praised.

"One thing have I desired of the LORD, that will I seek after; that I may dwell in the house of the LORD all the days of my life, to behold the beauty of the LORD, and to inquire in his temple" (Psalm 27:4).

"Behold, bless ye the LORD, all ye servants of the LORD, which by night stand in the house of the LORD. Lift up your hands in the sanctuary, and bless the LORD. The LORD that made heaven and earth bless thee out of Zion" (Psalm 134:1-3).

---

[29] Isaiah 53
[30] The Egyptian Book of the Dead

"His foundation is in the holy mountains. The LORD loveth the gates of Zion more than all the dwellings of Jacob. Glorious things are spoken of thee, O city of God. Selah. I will make mention of Rahab and Babylon to them that know me: behold Philistia, and Tyre, with Ethiopia; this man was born there. And of Zion it shall be said, This and that man was born in her: and the highest himself shall establish her" (Psalm 87:1-5).

Due to the wrong perception of spiritual matters, when people think about seeing God they believe that this could only happen when they physically die. As a result they view the establishment of the LORD's kingdom on earth as an event that will end humanity. What has been neglected are the spiritual connotations of the prophecy because the Bible is written in parables. We must lose our lives to gain it, which means to abandon the old (wrong) way that we think about God because it is preventing us from accepting the truth. If we are waiting for a supernatural event to transpire that will move the earth and halt civilization, then that will never happen. The manifestation of God in the flesh is referring to Emperor Haile Sellassie The First. But in order for people to understand and accept the divinity of His Majesty, the old way of thinking (which signifies the old world) must be abolished. A new world (a new doctrine) will have to be created because the previous interpretations never could reveal who God is; therefore they could not offer salvation. But now that providence has come, the facts have been manifest to all, Emperor Haile Sellassie The First is the King of Kings and Lord of Lords, blessed is the man who puts his trust in the Most High. Only from His Majesty can we learn the correct interpretation of the scriptures and be saved.

"God is known in her palaces for a refuge. For, lo, the kings were assembled, they passed by together. They saw it, and so they marvelled; they were troubled, and hasted away. Fear took hold upon them there, and pain, as of a woman in travail. Thou breakest the ships of Tarshish with an east wind. As we have heard, so have we seen in the city of the LORD of hosts, in the city of our God: God will establish it forever. Selah. We have thought of thy lovingkindness, O God, in the midst of thy temple. According to thy name, O God, so is thy praise unto the ends of the earth: thy right hand is full of righteousness. Let mount Zion rejoice, let the daughters of Judah be glad, because of thy judgments. Walk about Zion, and go round about her: tell the towers thereof. Mark ye well her bulwarks, consider her palaces; that ye may tell it to the generation following. For this God is our God forever and ever: he will be our guide even unto death" (Psalm 48:3-14).

"The LORD shall increase you more and more, you and your children. Ye are blessed of the LORD which made heaven and earth" (Psalm 115:14-15).

"For thus saith the LORD that created the heavens; God himself that formed the earth and made it; he hath established it, he created it not in vain, he formed it to be inhabited: I am the LORD; and there is none else. I have not spoken in secret, in a dark place of the earth: I said not unto the seed of Jacob, Seek ye me in vain: I the LORD speak righteousness, I declare things that are right" (Isaiah 45:18-19).

God is our refuge, he will help us in our time of need but we should not solely be looking to him when we are in trouble or need something. If our relationship with the Almighty was sincere then we would be in prayer when times are both good and bad. Those who seek him with their whole heart will not have any problem accepting the gospel of Jesus Christ. The entire Bible explains that Emperor Haile Sellassie The First is God but only through the spirit, which is the correct interpretation, would you be able to understand the scriptures. People take the parables literally or carnally which misconstrues the Word and leads to a tainted spiritual outlook where they ask the Lord for inappropriate things. His Majesty is aware of our wants and needs but his holy realm should be revered with godly worship and piety. The Bible is strictly referring to spiritual matters, it is not talking about corporeal punishment, hairstyles, material gains, or sexual immorality, etc. We must look to the Almighty for everything in life but there is an honest approach and an unscrupulous method in seeking his blessings. If there is anyone who forgets about the Lord when times are going good but remembers him when their luck has changed; then this is not a sincere relationship with God. If we are praying for material advancement then we have not understood the direction and purpose of the Bible which is to give us the proper spiritual outlook; we should be praying for his guidance because from his teachings we would know how to attain that which we desire. And if we do not receive the material rewards that we hope for, that does not mean that His Majesty has neglected us. It is comely to approach Emperor Haile Sellassie The First according to the pattern that has been outlined in the scriptures, which is with praise and reverence. The Lord is aware of all that we are going through and all that we need, but our purpose should be to focus on the salvation of our souls and our prayers should emulate the holy example found throughout the scriptures. That is why it is written seek ye first the kingdom of God and all things shall be added unto you.[31]

"Praise ye the LORD. Praise ye the LORD from the heavens: praise him in the heights. Praise ye him, all his angels: praise ye him, all his hosts. Praise ye him, sun and moon: praise him, all ye stars of light. Praise him, ye heavens of heavens, and ye waters that be above the heavens. Let them praise the name of the LORD: for he commanded, and they were created. He hath also established them forever and ever: he hath made a decree which shall not pass. Praise the LORD from the earth, ye dragons, and all deeps: Fire, and hail; snow, and vapor; stormy wind fulfilling his word: Mountains, and all hills; fruitful trees, and all cedars: Beasts, and all cattle; creeping things, and flying fowl: Kings of the earth, and all people; princes, and all judges of the earth: Both young men, and maidens; old men, and children: Let them praise the name of the LORD: for his name alone is excellent; his glory is above the earth and heaven. He also exalteth the horn of his people, the praise of all his saints; even of the children of Israel, a people near unto him. Praise ye the LORD" (Psalm 148:1-14).

"Now I say that Jesus Christ was a minister of the circumcision for the truth of God, to confirm the promises made unto the fathers: And that the Gentiles might glorify God for his mercy; as it is written, For this cause I will confess to thee among the Gentiles, and sing unto thy name. And again he saith, Rejoice, ye Gentiles, with his people. And again, Praise the Lord, all ye Gentiles; and laud him, all ye people" (Romans 15:8-11).

"O praise the LORD, all ye nations: praise him, all ye people. For his merciful kindness is great toward us: and the truth of the LORD endureth forever. Praise ye the LORD" (Psalm 117:1-2).

The message of the Bible is for us to accept and praise God. If the world submitted unto the Word they would know that Emperor Haile Sellassie The First is the Almighty. The scriptures describe the Lord as being a Great King, who will establish his government on earth, the Highest was born in Ethiopia and his name is One. If we followed the prophecy then we would be reading the Bible to understand who God is, not to obtain a supernatural blessing that will reap material benefits. The scriptures do not refer to secular matters or any bizarre phenomena, it is focused upon spiritual affairs in its entirety. Therefore just

---

[31] Luke 12:31

because someone wins a competition or makes a lot of money does not mean that God has blessed them. It is in our power to strive and achieve these benchmarks with or without the gospel of Jesus Christ. There are many atheists and agnostics who have become rich and successful due to their work ethic. Obtaining material opulence has nothing to do with your faith because there also are plenty of believers who are poor and destitute. Mankind has created the political conditions which determine the opportunities which some people have and others do not, irrespective of their talent and ability. This is an unfair system therefore it would be completely false to associate the higher your standard of living with the blessings of God. It should also be recognized that a lot of rich people became that way through unscrupulous and immoral behavior therefore if we are seeking to be like them, then we would be following the wrong example. To win the Lord's favor we must submit unto him, this is the message of the Prophets and the supplication of the Bible. If we first focus upon perfecting our spiritual sense then we would have the right values to deal with our secular issues properly. That is why the Bible is entreating us to praise God because when we adhere to righteous principles, this will create positive results in every aspect of our life; whether that be with our family, job, friends, leaders, etc. Emperor Haile Sellassie The First is the only one who can instruct humanity in the true teachings of salvation; that is why we must put our trust in him.

"And again, when he bringeth in the firstbegotten into the world, he saith, And let all the angels of God worship him" (Hebrews 1:6).

"And a voice came out of the throne, saying, Praise our God, all ye his servants, and ye that fear him, both small and great. And I heard as it were the voice of a great multitude, and as the voice of many waters, and as the voice of mighty thunderings, saying, Alleluia: for the Lord God omnipotent reigneth. Let us be glad and rejoice, and give honor to him: for the marriage of the Lamb is come, and his wife hath made herself ready. And to her was granted that she should be arrayed in fine linen, clean and white: for the fine linen is the righteousness of saints. And he saith unto me, Write, Blessed are they which are called unto the marriage supper of the Lamb. And he saith unto me, These are the true sayings of God. And I fell at his feet to worship him. And he said unto me, See thou do it not: I am thy fellowservant, and of thy brethren that have the testimony of Jesus: worship God: for the testimony of Jesus is the spirit of prophecy" (Revelation 19:5-10).

"Wherefore he is able also to save them to the uttermost that come unto God by him, seeing he ever liveth to make intercession for them. For such a high priest became us, who is holy, harmless, undefiled, separate from sinners, and made higher than the heavens" (Hebrews 7:25-26).

The common perception of the second coming of Jesus has people looking for a supernatural event in the sky where God will show his face from on top of a cloud. They believe that Christ first appeared thousands of years ago in the Middle East, physically died and was resurrected three days later to hover into the biosphere and remain there until he emerges again, in the same body, during the last days. These zealots will be searching for the marks of his crucifixion to confirm that it is him, so either they are under the impression that he does not age or they are waiting for someone who will look over three thousand years old. Either way this opinion of the Messiah is completely inaccurate and will not manifest; there will never be sound proof of any supernatural phenomena because it doesn't exist. Because the people are looking for the wrong sign they will not recognize the true coming of the Lord. Emperor Haile Sellassie The First admonished the world to be wise when he said, "Knowledge is a treasure that must be grasped and which none can confiscate, it is a diamond without price which prevents the breaking of heaven's decrees and preserves one from the path of destruction. Knowledge allows you to inherit the Kingdom of God, which the mind of man cannot conceive; and is a counselor in time of adversity. So may God grant you to attain a wisdom and knowledge such as I have described."[32] When people have the proper outlook on life they will be able to comprehend the difference between fact and fiction; which would lead to the rejection of fallacies and the declaration of accuracies. Jesus preached a testimony which does not break heaven's decrees, it affirms them, therefore we cannot seek to oppose the laws of nature by believing in supernatural theories because this leads to destruction and illusion. The saving grace of the Almighty is confirmed through truth, piety, and vision; upon this foundation the gospel of Christ shall stand and save all those who follow his Word: Blessed be Jah Rastafari.

"And Jesus, which is called Justus, who are of the circumcision. These only are my fellowworkers unto the kingdom of God, which have been a comfort unto me" (Colossians 4:11).

---

[32] Haile Selassie I, when he was Regent Ras Tafari Makonnen, opening speech on May 2, 1925, to inaugurate the Tafari Makonnen School

"And when they were come to him, he said unto them, Ye know, from the first day that I came into Asia, after what manner I have been with you at all seasons, Serving the Lord with all humility of mind, and with many tears, and temptations, which befell me by the lying in wait of the Jews: And how I kept back nothing that was profitable unto you, but have shewed you, and have taught you publicly, and from house to house, Testifying both to the Jews, and also to the Greeks, repentance toward God, and faith toward our Lord Jesus Christ. And now, behold, I go bound in the spirit unto Jerusalem, not knowing the things that shall befall me there: Save that the Holy Ghost witnesseth in every city, saying that bonds and afflictions abide me. But none of these things move me, neither count I my life dear unto myself, so that I might finish my course with joy, and the ministry, which I have received of the Lord Jesus, to testify the gospel of the grace of God. And now, behold, I know that ye all, among whom I have gone preaching the kingdom of God, shall see my face no more. Wherefore I take you to record this day, that I am pure from the blood of all men. For I have not shunned to declare unto you all the counsel of God" (Acts 20:18-27).

"Now after that John was put in prison, Jesus came into Galilee, preaching the gospel of the kingdom of God, And saying, The time is fulfilled, and the kingdom of God is at hand: repent ye, and believe the gospel" (Mark 1:14-15).

The Bible is speaking about spiritual matters, its purpose is to lead you to God. If you follow the descriptions of the Lord that have been depicted in the scriptures, you will find the fulfillment in Emperor Haile Sellassie The First. The prophecy directs you to the Almighty and from him we learn about all the different aspects of life and how to handle them properly. It is important to understand this order because if we confuse this pattern then people would not know where to look to and receive the legitimate tenants of salvation. For example, if you read the Bible for guidance on how to solve your secular issues, then you would have a literal translation of the scriptures which is not going to offer you any palpable solutions because this leads to superstition. His Majesty is the one who has articulated the teachings and demonstrated the character on how to master your environment; but he is not going to instruct you on how he is God. Therefore, once again, the Bible chronicles who the Creator is and from the LORD we learn the righteous principles of life. The Father also sent his Son to testify about God because he is not going to preach himself, this is the true holy example that everyone must follow if you love the Lord; we cannot speak about ourselves. If your works are true, then your name shall be written in the book of life and others shall testify of your deeds but if your intentions are to win the world and please man, then you will be shut out from the kingdom. Only those who live for God and seek to do his will, shall be exalted in heaven; not those who indulge in self glorification. The right values is a vital asset because it determines your success and happiness; therefore we should know where to find true guidance. People will only function according to their original God-intended design when they accept and adopt the morals and ethics of Emperor Haile Sellassie The First. This is our challenge because everything in our lives revolves around our values, such as our personality, actions, ambitions, etc., and unless we emulate the high character of His Majesty, we will never produce a pleasant outcome.

"One generation shall praise thy works to another, and shall declare thy mighty acts. I will speak of the glorious honor of thy majesty, and of thy wondrous works. And men shall speak of the might of thy terrible acts: and I will declare thy greatness. They shall abundantly utter the memory of thy great goodness, and shall sing of thy righteousness. The LORD is gracious, and full of compassion; slow to anger, and of great mercy. The LORD is good to all: and his tender mercies are over all his works. All thy works shall praise thee, O LORD; and thy saints shall bless thee. They shall speak of the glory of thy kingdom, and talk of thy power; To make known to the sons of men his mighty acts, and the glorious majesty of his kingdom. Thy kingdom is an everlasting kingdom, and thy dominion endureth throughout all generations. The LORD upholdeth all that fall, and raiseth up all those that be bowed down. The eyes of all wait upon thee; and thou givest them their meat in due season. Thou openest thine hand, and satisfiest the desire of every living thing. The LORD is righteous in all his ways, and holy in all his works" (Psalm 145:4-17).

"But as we were allowed of God to be put in trust with the gospel, even so we speak; not as pleasing men, but God, which trieth our hearts. For neither at any time used we flattering words, as ye know, nor a cloke of covetousness; God is witness: Nor of men sought we glory, neither of you, nor yet of others, when we might have been burdensome, as the apostles of Christ. But we were gentle among you, even as a nurse cherisheth her children: So being affectionately desirous of you, we were willing to have imparted unto you, not the gospel of God only, but also our own souls, because ye were dear unto us. For ye remember, brethren, our labour and travail: for labouring night and day, because we would not be chargeable unto any of you, we preached unto you the gospel of God. Ye are witnesses, and God also, how holily and justly and unblameably we behaved ourselves among you that believe: As ye know how we exhorted and comforted and charged every one of you, as a father doth his children,

That ye would walk worthy of God, who hath called you unto his kingdom and glory. For this cause also thank we God without ceasing, because, when ye received the word of God which ye heard of us, ye received it not as the word of men, but as it is in truth, the word of God, which effectually worketh also in you that believe" (1 Thessalonians 2:4-13).

"For the word of the LORD is right; and all his works are done in truth. He loveth righteousness and judgment: the earth is full of the goodness of the LORD. By the word of the LORD were the heavens made; and all the host of them by the breath of his mouth. He gathereth the waters of the sea together as a heap: he layeth up the depth in storehouses. Let all the earth fear the LORD: let all the inhabitants of the world stand in awe of him. For he spake, and it was done; he commanded, and it stood fast. The LORD bringeth the counsel of the heathen to nought: he maketh the devices of the people of none effect. The counsel of the LORD standeth forever, the thoughts of his heart to all generations. Blessed is the nation whose God is the LORD; and the people whom he hath chosen for his own inheritance. The LORD looketh from heaven; he beholdeth all the sons of men. From the place of his habitation he looketh upon all the inhabitants of the earth. He fashioneth their hearts alike; he considereth all their works. There is no king saved by the multitude of a host: a mighty man is not delivered by much strength. A horse is a vain thing for safety: neither shall he deliver any by his great strength. Behold, the eye of the LORD is upon them that fear him, upon them that hope in his mercy; To deliver their soul from death, and to keep them alive in famine. Our soul waiteth for the LORD: he is our help and our shield. For our heart shall rejoice in him, because we have trusted in his holy name" (Psalm 33:4-21).

If we pick out what scriptures we accept and reject others that do not fit into our interpretation or tradition then we can rest assured that what we believe in is false. It is only when you receive the entire Bible without contradiction that you will know that your understanding is correct. Also if you are engaged in a religious debate and try to debunk the verses that someone else quoted with your own biblical references, then it is not the person that you have opposed but the scriptures that they recited. If you reject any part of the Word then your position is not of God. We must be able to offer the correct interpretation, considering all the holy verses, while giving a logical spiritual explanation that has no discrepancies. Only Jesus Christ can present this point of view, if we accept his testimony then we would be able to preach the gospel truthfully. The correct paradigm of the

Bible affirms that God is the Supreme Potentate, Creator of the Universe and Jesus Christ is his Holy Son, the Master Prophet of Theology; the LORD and his messenger are two different people with separate souls and personalities. If anyone does not accept or understand this pattern then they would never be able to explain the parables of the Bible properly. When you read the scriptures, the only interpretation that will make sense is to translate God as the Most High King of Glory and Jesus Christ as his preacher, the mediator between God and man. Although the prophecies have already been fulfilled, no one will be able to recognize it without the correct outlook on spiritual matters. Therefore wisdom is the principle thing, so make sure that with everything you get, you acquire some understanding.[33]

"Thou shalt not take the name of the LORD thy God in vain; for the LORD will not hold him guiltless that taketh his name in vain. Remember the Sabbath day, to keep it holy" (Exodus 20:7-8).

"Let them praise thy great and terrible name; for it is holy" (Psalm 99:3).

"My mouth shall speak the praise of the LORD: and let all flesh bless his holy name forever and ever" (Psalm 145:21).

"Praise waiteth for thee, O God, in Sion: and unto thee shall the vow be performed. O thou that hearest prayer, unto thee shall all flesh come" (Psalm 65:1-2).

Theology is a very important subject that must be taken seriously. We should not become comfortable with following a religious tradition that has been passed down to us if it takes on a fallacious nature. Everyone must make sure that what they follow is valid and trustworthy because only through God can we save our souls. The purpose of salvation is for us to create a better world for everyone to enjoy. Our objective is not to live for the afterlife but to work here on earth for the betterment of society. That is why God Emperor Haile Sellassie The First established his kingdom in Ethiopia, for the world to take notice and follow his wise counsel to further humanity. During this modern technological age where new inventions have unlocked vast possibilities, it must be recognized that our standard of living should have dramatically improved. But ungodly men who have no morals or ethics will never handle their

---

[33] Proverbs 4:7

responsibility in a righteous manner and produce the changes that will uplift all of mankind; even when it is in their power to do so. It is up to those people with a pure heart to develop their spiritual attributes by searching through the Bible for the truth and accept God. Because it is only from him who the scriptures describe as being the Savior that we can learn the true principles of righteousness that will transform this world into a better place. Some people lie down and accept whatever is given to them regardless of the injustice or circumstances. They don't think that anything can be done to make things better because they have been indoctrinated and intimidated. But you also have people like Dietrich Bonhoeffer who studied the Bible and realized that you must act here on earth to oppose evil, even if it means that you are killed for it. If we interpreted the scriptures correctly we would know that a magical supernatural event orchestrated by the Almighty is not going to solve our problems; we must object to unfair treatment in order for things to get better. As one generation succeeds another, our quality of life should steadily improve but this will only happen if people seek for and demand for righteousness to prevail. Everyone must examine their conscience and conduct to determine where they land in this equation; are you a pacifist or an activist?

"And when thou prayest, thou shalt not be as the hypocrites are: for they love to pray standing in the synagogues and in the corners of the streets, that they may be seen of men. Verily I say unto you, They have their reward. But thou, when thou prayest, enter into thy closet, and when thou hast shut thy door, pray to thy Father which is in secret; and thy Father which seeth in secret shall reward thee openly. But when ye pray, use not vain repetitions, as the heathen do: for they think that they shall be heard for their much speaking. Be not ye therefore like unto them: for your Father knoweth what things ye have need of, before ye ask him. After this manner therefore pray ye: Our Father which art in heaven, Hallowed be thy name. Thy kingdom come. Thy will be done in earth, as it is in heaven. Give us this day our daily bread. And forgive us our debts, as we forgive our debtors. And lead us not into temptation, but deliver us from evil: For thine is the kingdom, and the power, and the glory, forever. Amen" (Matthew 6:5-13).

"Then the people rejoiced, for that they offered willingly, because with perfect heart they offered willingly to the LORD: and David the king also rejoiced with great joy. Wherefore David blessed the LORD before all the congregation: and David said, Blessed be thou, LORD God of Israel our father, forever and ever. Thine, O LORD, is the greatness, and the power, and the glory, and the victory, and the majesty: for

all that is in the heaven and in the earth is thine; thine is the kingdom, O LORD, thou art exalted as head above all. Both riches and honour come of thee, and thou reignest over all; and in thine hand is power and might; and in thine hand it is to make great, and to give strength unto all. Now therefore, our God, we thank thee, and praise thy glorious name" (1 Chronicles 29:9-13).

"Keep the Sabbath day to sanctify it, as the LORD thy God hath commanded thee. Six days thou shalt labour, and do all thy work: But the seventh day is the Sabbath of the LORD thy God: in it thou shalt not do any work, thou, nor thy son, nor thy daughter, nor thy manservant, nor thy maidservant, nor thine ox, nor thine ass, nor any of thy cattle, nor thy stranger that is within thy gates; that thy manservant and thy maidservant may rest as well as thou. And remember that thou wast a servant in the land of Egypt, and that the LORD thy God brought thee out thence through a mighty hand and by a stretched out arm: therefore the LORD thy God commanded thee to keep the Sabbath day" (Deuteronomy 5:12-15).

The Bible describes God as our Father, hallowed be thy name, thine is the kingdom and the power forever, thou are exalted as head above all. Emperor Haile Sellassie The First was courted by leaders from around the world for advise on how to solve important political matters because they recognized the wisdom he displayed in overcoming his own challenges. Furthermore, His Majesty went to the United Nations and instructed all the nations on what they must do to ensure the survival and prosperity of humanity. Every description of the Almighty coincides with the actions of Emperor Haile Sellassie The First. We must submit unto the LORD and accept his divinity, this is how we observe the Sabbath and win favor with the Most High. Those who want to please the Almighty will recognize that the Bible is talking about His Majesty, whereas those who seek to be respected by men will follow popular traditions that are not affirmed in the scriptures. The gospel of Christ is an undeniable testimony, those who cannot receive our message have a corrupt spirit. Now, when we refer to the spirit, we are not speaking about a supernatural mystical force, we are talking about your understanding. There is no such thing as obeah, sorcery, or witchcraft, these ideas are used to mentally cripple people into becoming docile and fearful; they are afraid of a phenomenon that does not exist. But the times of this ignorance have past, we now must learn how the world really operates so that we can develop a healthy and accurate outlook on life.

"There remaineth therefore a rest to the people of God. For he that is entered into his rest, he also hath ceased from his own works, as God did from his" (Hebrews 4:9-10).

"The LORD is good to all: and his tender mercies are over all his works. All thy works shall praise thee, O LORD; and thy saints shall bless thee. They shall speak of the glory of thy kingdom, and talk of thy power; To make known to the sons of men his mighty acts, and the glorious majesty of his kingdom. Thy kingdom is an everlasting kingdom, and thy dominion endureth throughout all generations. The LORD upholdeth all that fall, and raiseth up all those that be bowed down. The eyes of all wait upon thee; and thou givest them their meat in due season. Thou openest thine hand, and satisfiest the desire of every living thing. The LORD is righteous in all his ways, and holy in all his works. The LORD is nigh unto all them that call upon him, to all that call upon him in truth. He will fulfill the desire of them that fear him: he also will hear their cry, and will save them. The LORD preserveth all them that love him: but all the wicked will he destroy. My mouth shall speak the praise of the LORD: and let all flesh bless his holy name forever and ever" (Psalm 145:9-21).

"In the beginning God created the heaven and the earth" (Genesis 1:1).

God was manifest on earth to teach the world the truth so that humanity can thrive and prosper. We know that no one is perfect, except for the LORD, therefore the ultimate solution to our problems could not be conjured up by man. Therefore we should look to the Almighty for guidance instead of following the popular myths that abound on earth which have no validity. Emperor Haile Sellassie The First taught us to be realistic and determined in our approach to reaching our goals and overcoming the tribulations of life. Our success is determined by our work ethic and our resolve; for as they say, God helps those who help themselves. This means that you reap what you sow, the man who goes the extra mile cannot be denied his gain. Do we then conclude that only those who work hard are the chosen people, of course not, but regardless of your spiritual awareness, we will only be compensated based upon our efforts. If we attribute our circumstances, achievements, or failures, to anything other than our own acumen and resolve then we have deceived ourselves. To blame other forces for your conditions is to be irresponsible and delusional. Your lot is created based upon your deeds, there are not ghosts in the biosphere who alter reality. We must approach life according to the laws of creation that the Almighty established in the beginning. Emperor Haile Sellassie The First accomplished everything by normal means and vouched for the legitimacy of the laws of nature which no one can alter.

"Thus the heavens and the earth were finished, and all the host of them. And on the seventh day God ended his work which he had made; and he rested on the seventh day from all his work which he had made. And God blessed the seventh day, and sanctified it: because that in it he had rested from all his work which God created and made" (Genesis 2:1-3).

"Let us therefore fear, lest, a promise being left us of entering into his rest, any of you should seem to come short of it. For unto us was the gospel preached, as well as unto them: but the word preached did not profit them, not being mixed with faith in them that heard it. For we which have believed do enter into rest, as he said, As I have sworn in my wrath, if they shall enter into my rest: although the works were finished from the foundation of the world. For he spake in a certain place of the seventh day on this wise, And God did rest the seventh day from all his works. And in this place again, If they shall enter into my rest. Seeing therefore it remaineth that some must enter therein, and they to whom it was first preached entered not in because of unbelief" (Hebrews 4:1-6).

"I beseech you therefore, brethren, by the mercies of God, that ye present your bodies a living sacrifice, holy, acceptable unto God, which is your reasonable service. And be not conformed to this world: but be ye transformed by the renewing of your mind, that ye may prove what is that good, and acceptable, and perfect, will of God" (Romans 12:1-2).

To observe the Sabbath means to praise the true and living God Emperor Haile Sellassie The First. The seventh day has nothing to do with the calendar because the days of the week cannot save anybody. We therefore should not place any significance upon when you worship because what really matters is who you worship. A person who follows the wrong principles and venerates a false deity is not a Sabbatarian no matter what time they hold service. To enter into the rest of the LORD is a holy convocation, those who observe this keystone adhere to the Word of God; which means that they follow the true principles of heaven. All of the idolatrous and pagan beliefs which deceive and defile humanity are classified as worship on the wrong day: they follow the wrong elements. For example, the idea that demonic spirits are able to overtake your body and control your soul against your free will is incorrect. Yet people have been made to believe that ghosts have the power to cause physical harm to you without there being any solid proof to support this theory; only stories, myths, and speculation. If someone consumes poison or intakes a harmful powder or elixir, this cannot be used to support the idea of zombies or the supernatural. It is a scientific theorem that certain solutions can kill you, cripple you, slow your heart rate, blind you, etc., so this does not validate the existence of alchemy. These misguided sects who believe that demons and supernatural entities exist, have failed to realize that the very grounds that they use to demonstrate their faith actually causes a colossal contradiction within their principles because they follow a very rational and logical conduit to administer their "spells." They formulate toxins, in the same way that a scientist makes viruses in a lab, then they give it to their victim, which causes an injury or worse. That is a rational form of sabotage but to pray for someone to fail will not unleash a swarm of banshees who have the power to harm people. Tangible and honest proof to legitimize the idea of superstition has not and will not ever be produced because it is an unreal concept. Emperor Haile Sellassie The First opposed this point of view and challenged us to think clearly and become educated. Those who wish to observe the Sabbath and be saved must accept the Word of God and follow that which His Majesty has instructed us in.

"Forasmuch then as Christ hath suffered for us in the flesh, arm yourselves likewise with the same mind: for he that hath suffered in the flesh hath ceased from sin; That he no longer should live the rest of his time in the flesh to the lusts of men, but to the will of God. For the time past of our life may suffice us to have wrought the will of the Gentiles, when we walked in lasciviousness, lusts, excess of wine, revellings, banquetings, and abominable idolatries: Wherein they think it strange that ye run not with them to the same excess of riot, speaking evil of you: Who shall give account to him that is ready to judge the quick and the dead. For this cause was the gospel preached also to them that are dead, that they might be judged according to men in the flesh, but live according to God in the spirit. But the end of all things is at hand: be ye therefore sober, and watch unto prayer. And above all things have fervent charity among yourselves: for charity shall cover the multitude of sins. Use hospitality one to another without grudging. As every man hath received the gift, even so minister the same one to another, as good stewards of the manifold grace of God. If any man speak, let him speak as the oracles of God; if any man minister, let him do it as of the ability which God giveth: that God in all things may be glorified through Jesus Christ, to whom be praise and dominion forever and ever. Amen. Beloved, think it

not strange concerning the fiery trial which is to try you, as though some strange thing happened unto you: But rejoice, inasmuch as ye are partakers of Christ's sufferings; that, when his glory shall be revealed, ye may be glad also with exceeding joy. If ye be reproached for the name of Christ, happy are ye; for the spirit of glory and of God resteth upon you: on their part he is evil spoken of, but on your part he is glorified. But let none of you suffer as a murderer, or as a thief, or as an evildoer, or as a busybody in other men's matters. Yet if any man suffer as a Christian, let him not be ashamed; but let him glorify God on this behalf. For the time is come that judgment must begin at the house of God: and if it first begin at us, what shall the end be of them that obey not the gospel of God? And if the righteous scarcely be saved, where shall the ungodly and the sinner appear? Wherefore let them that suffer according to the will of God commit the keeping of their souls to him in well doing, as unto a faithful Creator" (1 Peter 4:1-19).

"Blessed be the God and Father of our Lord Jesus Christ, who hath blessed us with all spiritual blessings in heavenly places in Christ: According as he hath chosen us in him before the foundation of the world, that we should be holy and without blame before him in love: Having predestinated us unto the adoption of children by Jesus Christ to himself, according to the good pleasure of his will, To the praise of the glory of his grace, wherein he hath made us accepted in the beloved. In whom we have redemption through his blood, the forgiveness of sins, according to the riches of his grace; Wherein he hath abounded toward us in all wisdom and prudence" (Ephesians 1:3-8).

"For God hath not given us the spirit of fear; but of power, and of love, and of a sound mind. Be not thou therefore ashamed of the testimony of our Lord, nor of me his prisoner: but be thou partaker of the afflictions of the gospel according to the power of God; Who hath saved us, and called us with a holy calling, not according to our works, but according to his own purpose and grace, which was given us in Christ Jesus before the world began" (2 Timothy 1:7-9).

The Holy Spirit is the correct outlook of ecclesiastical affairs which only comes from following the teachings of His Majesty. Ever since his Coronation on November 2, 1930, Emperor Haile Sellassie The First was worshipped as God incarnate because he is the King of Kings and Lord of Lords. There were many people who accepted the revelation because they understood the significance of these titles but there also were a lot of naysayers who denied His Majesty's divinity because they imagined that the prophecy would be fulfilled in a different way.

When Emperor Haile Sellassie The First walked the earth from 1892 to 1975, the Rastafarians were making quite an impact upon the world stage as Bob Marley was extremely popular through his music, as well as, His Majesty was the most famous celebrity of the 20th Century. But the scriptures in the Bible that describe the LORD as being the great King of all the earth, did not resonate with those people who believe in necromancy and superstition. They characterized the Emperor as being a "regular man" because he never displayed or advocated any form of magic. Their literal and carnal interpretation of the parables (miracles) has led them to look for signs and wonders that do not exist. These false institutions, such as the Catholic Church, invent supernatural experiences to deceive the world; keeping them blind to the truth. As long as people believe in magic, they will never know God and will never be intelligent enough to produce the lasting effects to redeem humanity. His Majesty was fighting against this cruel deterrent by instructing everyone to educate themselves and to accept the message of the Bible. When both science and the scriptures agree, you will gain the correct perception, which will in turn, allow you to understand that Emperor Haile Sellassie The First is the Almighty.

"But, beloved, remember ye the words which were spoken before of the apostles of our Lord Jesus Christ; how that they told you there should be mockers in the last time, who should walk after their own ungodly lusts. These be they who separate themselves, sensual, having not the Spirit. But ye, beloved, building up yourselves on your most holy faith, praying in the Holy Ghost, Keep yourselves in the love of God, looking for the mercy of our Lord Jesus Christ unto eternal life. And of some have compassion, making a difference: and others save with fear, pulling them out of the fire; hating even the garment spotted by the flesh. Now unto him that is able to keep you from falling, and to present you faultless before the prescence of his glory with exceeding joy, To the only wise God our Savior, be glory and majesty, dominon and power, both now and forever. Amen" (Jude 1:17-25).

"O clap your hands, all ye people; shout unto God with the voice of triumph. For the LORD most high is terrible; he is a great King over all the earth. He shall subdue the people under us, and the nations under our feet. He shall choose our inheritance for us, the excellency of Jacob whom he loved. Selah. God is gone up with a shout, the LORD with the sound of a trumpet. Sing praises to God, sing praises: sing praises unto our King, sing praises. For God is the King of all the earth: sing ye praises with understanding. God reigneth over the heathen: God sitteth upon the throne of his holiness" (Psalm 47:1-8).

"That ye may with one mind and one mouth glorify God, even the Father of our Lord Jesus Christ. Wherefore receive ye one another, as Christ also received us to the glory of God. Now I say that Jesus Christ was a minister of the circumcision for the truth of God, to confirm the promises made unto the fathers" (Romans 15:6-8).

There are many false doctrines in the world, that is why it is written that broad is the way that leads to destruction. Christ is thee minister of God, he was sent because no one in the world was following the truth. We have witnessed how those who do not know His Majesty follow carnal precepts, as well as, the people who call upon his name also do not regard his principles. The Rastafarians have rejected the teachings of Emperor Haile Sellassie The First by regarding His Majesty as a supernatural entity which results in a false deification. The notion of amending the laws of nature is essentially anti-God because this theory seeks to defy the order which the Almighty created in the beginning. Haile Sellassie The First has said that he was created the same as everyone else but certain elders deny that the Emperor died in 1975; they claim that he is physically immortal, currently living in Ethiopia as a priest named Abba Quiddus. But the LORD did not create us to be indissoluble and there is a speech where His Majesty said that he is mortal; which means that he will die. He that comes unto God must believe that he is God,[34] therefore anyone who accepts the divinity of Emperor Haile Sellassie The First must adhere to his principles. It would be better to come in your own name, if you have no intention of adopting His Majesty's tenants, than to take the Lord's name in vain, by seeming to represent something that you do not accept. If you go against that which the Emperor has advocated then why worship him; this type of devotion categorizes Rastafari along with idolatry because it is all worthless and vain. It is written in the Bible that the flesh profits nothing because his divinity is not upheld according to his anatomy; he is justified in the spirit. We therefore should look upon things which are eternal, and that is the message of salvation which His Majesty has accorded unto us. Let us be obedient to his Word so that we may acquire wisdom and save our souls.

"Give unto the LORD, O ye mighty, give unto the LORD glory and strength. Give unto the LORD the glory due unto his name; worship the LORD in the beauty of holiness. The voice of the LORD is upon the waters: the God of glory thundereth: the LORD is upon many waters. The voice of the LORD is powerful; the voice of the

---

[34] Hebrews 11:6

LORD is full of majesty. The voice of the LORD breaketh the cedars; yea, the LORD breaketh the cedars of Lebanon. He maketh them also to skip like a calf; Lebanon and Sirion like a young unicorn. The voice of the LORD divideth the flames of fire. The voice of the LORD shaketh the wilderness; the LORD shaketh the wilderness of Kadesh. The voice of the LORD maketh the hinds to calve, and discovereth the forests: and in his temple doth every one speak of his glory. The LORD sitteth upon the flood; yea, the LORD sitteth King forever" (Psalm 29:1-10).

"The voice of joy, and the voice of gladness, the voice of the bridegroom, and the voice of the bride, the voice of them that shall say, Praise the LORD of hosts: for the LORD is good; for his mercy endureth forever: and of them that shall bring the sacrifice of praise into the house of the LORD. For I will cause to return the captivity of the land, as at the first, saith the LORD" (Jeremiah 33:11).

"My days are like a shadow that declineth; and I am withered like grass. But thou, O LORD, shalt endure forever; and thy remembrance unto all generations. Thou shalt arise, and have mercy upon Zion: for the time to favor her, yea, the set time, is come. For thy servants take pleasure in her stones, and favor the dust thereof. So the heathen shall fear the name of the LORD, and all the kings of the earth thy glory. When the LORD shall build up Zion, he shall appear in his glory. He will regard the prayer of the destitute, and not despise their prayer. This shall be written for the generation to come: and the people which shall be created shall praise the LORD" (Psalm 102:11-18).

The LORD will not hold him guiltless who takes his name in vain, Christ was sent for this reason, to cast down the false imagination of the Pharisees and scribes (the blind leaders of the world). Spirituality is a very important topic because all the problems in the world stem from neglecting the laws of God; he is called the Savior because only the Almighty can lead us along a path of everlasting peace and equality. Haile Sellassie The First has both demonstrated and articulated the essential tenants for liberation, furthermore Jesus reaffirmed his Father's covenant; the heavens have declared his righteousness. We have been made aware that His Majesty is God, so if we choose to neglect him then we have decided upon an inevitable doom. It is not a coincidence that the Emperor's name, deeds, and character are all perfectly aligned with biblical prophecy. The LORD will not give his glory to another, he is the first and the last; therefore when we see someone fulfilling what has been foretold, then that is the person who it is referring to. An impostor cannot actualize the Bible, anyone can claim to be Christ or God; but only the actions of the chosen one will correlate with what is written in the scriptures. The Most High has actually made it fairly simple for us to identify him, in this regard, because it states that he alone will come according to this pattern; his descriptions are written in the holy books. We therefore need to cast aside our own understanding of spiritual matters and accept that which Emperor Haile Sellassie The First has instructed us in his speeches, interviews, and writings. There is a vast library of information from His Majesty, detailing the solutions to all issues and everything that he revealed was true; all we have to do is follow him. It could only be pride or ignorance that would prevent a person from accepting a perfect explanation; let us ensure that we do not end up in this stock, we have to emulate the life of Emperor Haile Sellassie The First.

"Let them give glory unto the LORD, and declare his praise in the islands" (Isaiah 42:12).

"Ye are my witnesses, saith the LORD, and my servant whom I have chosen: that ye may know and believe me, and understand that I am he: before me there was no God formed, neither shall there be after me. I, even I, am the LORD; and beside me there is no savior. I have declared, and have saved, and I have shewed, when there was no strange god among you: therefore ye are my witnesses, saith the LORD, that I am God. Yea, before the day was I am he; and there is none that can deliver out of my hand: I will work, and who shall let it? Thus saith the LORD, your redeemer, the Holy One of Israel; For your sake I have sent to Babylon, and have brought down all their nobles, and the Chaldeans, whose cry is in the ships. I am the LORD, your Holy One, the creator of Israel, your King. Thus saith the LORD, which maketh a way in the sea, and a path in the mighty waters; Which bringeth forth the chariot and horse, the army and the power; they shall lie down together, they shall not rise: they are extinct, they are quenched as tow. Remember ye not the former things, neither consider the things of old. Behold, I will do a new thing; now it shall spring forth; shall ye not know it? I will even make a way in the wilderness, and rivers in the desert. The beast of the field shall honor me, the dragons and the owls: because I give waters in the wilderness, and rivers in the desert, to give drink to my people, my chosen. This people have I formed for myself; they shall shew forth my praise" (Isaiah 43:10-21).

"Bow down thine ear, O LORD, hear me: for I am poor and needy. Preserve my soul; for I am holy: O thou my God, save thy servant that trusteth in thee. Be merciful

unto me, O Lord: for I cry unto thee daily. Rejoice the soul of thy servant: for unto thee, O Lord, do I lift up my soul. For thou, Lord, art good, and ready to forgive; and plenteous in mercy unto all them that call upon thee. Give ear, O LORD, unto my prayer; and attend to the voice of my supplications. In the day of my trouble I will call upon thee: for thou wilt answer me. Among the gods there is none like unto thee, O Lord; neither are there any works like unto thy works. All nations whom thou hast made shall come and worship before thee, O Lord; and shall glorify thy name. For thou art great, and doest wondrous things: thou art God alone. Teach me thy way, O LORD; I will walk in thy truth: unite my heart to fear thy name. I will praise thee, O Lord my God, with all my heart: and I will glorify thy name forevermore" (Psalm 86:1-12).*

If people do not read the Bible then they will never know the descriptions of God; which would then make it impossible to recognize him. You will not be able to accept the LORD at his coming if your perception of the prophecy does not correlate with what is written in the scriptures. The only way to know if you have the truth is to validate your beliefs by reading the Bible to see if what you follow is the actual message portrayed in the scriptures. It is written that the LORD is our King, he has declared and saved and shown, when there was no strange god among you, therefore we are his witnesses. From these depictions we must realize that God is the only one who can fulfill the prophecy, as well as, the interpretation that the Almighty is invisible only means that they do not accept him. If they do not believe in Emperor Haile Sellassie The First, then they have negated the message of the Bible. If His Majesty or anyone else is able to fulfill the Bible without being the real person that it is referring to, then that not only contradicts the Bible, it makes the holy book useless and vain because the descriptions and message in it cannot be trusted to lead us to the right conclusion. Yet we know that it is true, Emperor Haile Sellassie The First is the King of Kings and Lord of Lords, and we will worship him as God because it is written that the man with these titles is the Most High. We accept the Bible and its great message of salvation, that is why we praise His Majesty.

"I am the LORD, and there is none else, there is no God beside me: I girded thee, though thou hast not known me: That they may know from the rising of the sun, and from the west, that there is none beside me. I am the LORD, and there is none else" (Isaiah 45:5-6).

"That the residue of men might seek after the Lord, and all the Gentiles, upon whom my name is called, saith the Lord, who doeth all these things" (Acts 15:17).

"But Peter and John answered and said unto them, Whether it be right in the sight of God to hearken unto you more than unto God, judge ye. For we cannot but speak the things which we have seen and heard. So when they had further threatened them, they let them go, finding nothing how they might punish them, because of the people: for all men glorified God for that which was done. For the man was above forty years old, on whom this miracle of healing was shewed. And being let go, they went to their own company, and reported all that the chief priests and elders had said unto them. And when they heard that, they lifted up their voice to God with one accord, and said, Lord, thou art God, which hast made heaven, and earth, and the sea, and all that in them is: Who by the mouth of thy servant David hast said, Why did the heathen rage, and the people imagine vain things? The kings of the earth stood up, and the rulers were gathered together against the Lord, and against his Christ. For of a truth against thy holy child Jesus, whom thou hast anointed, both Herod, and Pontius Pilate, with the Gentiles, and the people of Israel, were gathered together, For to do whatsoever thy hand and thy counsel determined before to be done. And now, Lord, behold their threatenings: and grant unto thy servants, that with all boldness they may speak thy word, By stretching forth thine hand to heal; and that signs and wonders may be done by the name of thy holy child Jesus. And when they had prayed, the place was shaken where they were assembled together; and they were all filled with the Holy Ghost, and they spake the word of God with boldness" (Acts 4:19-31).

The only person who can fulfill the prophecy of the Bible is the one that it is referring to. When it says that there is no God besides me, that means there will never be another revelation to accomplish what was foretold. One sign shall be given, the LORD will establish his kingdom on earth and it will be up to us to accept him or else decide upon bedlam. Emperor Haile Sellassie The First is the Savior, all of his actions are in accordance with the promises; it is written that he shall reveal himself before the eyes of many nations.[35] His Majesty arose to give guidance on the vital affairs that will produce far-reaching gratifying results in this world, but it is up to us to follow his teachings so that this end may be accomplished. The LORD had to come in the flesh because there is no other logical way for him to teach us anything, but he will not

---

[35] Ezekiel 38:23

force us to follow him as we all have free will. Now, if humanity, based upon their own initiatives, already understood and implemented the principles of righteousness then there would be no need for a Savior but the earth was void of truth. For if we say that we have no sin, then we deceive ourselves, and the truth is not in us; therefore no man should feel as if they are above correction.[36] The Emperor has said that he is not Jesus Christ which does not mean that he denied being the Almighty. If we search the scriptures we will find that the Son of God is described as being the holy child of the LORD. This should then lead us to question whether it makes sense to conclude that parents and their children are the same entity; because according to the laws of this universe it does not. His Majesty has beckoned us to approach life and spirituality, rationally and intelligently, which is the true message of the Bible, but who is following these tenants? Instead of believing a supernatural myth that depicts a Father and his Son as the same being, let us put our trust into that which makes sense, into that which Haile Sellassie The First has instructed, which is the same message of the Bible; God and Christ cannot both be God if there is only one God. Mathematically, scientifically, realistically, holistically, scripturally, etc., it is completely absurd to think that two different people are the same entity, yet people have become accustomed to this backwards concept and have eventually accepted it; without ever doing a serious inquiry to determine if this is an accurate position. Anyone who chooses to study will find that the Bible does not label Jesus as God, therefore His Majesty was actually proclaiming his divinity and seeking to correct the traditions of the church by denying that he is Christ. He has instructed us according to the proper interpretation of the scriptures, free from all superstition and deceit, so that we may know that he is the Almighty: Emperor Haile Sellassie The First.

"For what if some did not believe? shall their unbelief make the faith of God without effect? God forbid: yea, let God be true, but every man a liar; as it is written, That thou mightest be justified in thy sayings, and mightest overcome when thou art judged" (Romans 3:3-4).

"We know that whosoever is born of God sinneth not; but he that is begotten of God keepeth himself, and that wicked one toucheth him not. And we know that we are of God, and the whole world lies in wickedness. And we know that the Son of God is come, and hath given us an understanding, that we may know him that is true,

---

[36] 1 John 1:8-10

and we are in him that is true, even in his Son Jesus Christ. This is the true God, and eternal life. Little children, keep yourselves from idols. Amen" (1 John 5:18-21).

"This I say therefore, and testify in the Lord, that ye henceforth walk not as other Gentiles walk, in the vanity of their mind, Having the understanding darkened, being alienated from the life of God through the ignorance that is in them, because of the blindness of their heart: Who being past feeling have given themselves over unto lasciviousness, to work all uncleanness with greediness. But ye have not so learned Christ; If so be that ye have heard him, and have been taught by him, as the truth is in Jesus: That ye put off concerning the former conversation the old man, which is corrupt according to the deceitful lusts; And be renewed in the spirit of your mind; And that ye put on the new man, which after God is created in righteousness and true holiness. Wherefore putting away lying, speak every man truth with his neighbor: for we are members one of another" (Ephesians 4:17-25).

Although the scriptures are clear that God is the first and the last, many people will not put their trust in Emperor Haile Sellassie The First chalking up his deeds as mere coincidences in regard to biblical prophecy. In analyzing this position we find that not only is it counterintuitive to the covenant, it also acknowledges the fact that His Majesty has fulfilled the Bible; albeit with a feeble attempt to downplay it. There is no logical argument to disprove the divinity of Haile Sellassie The First, those who fight against the LORD have done so in defiance of reason and righteousness. That is why, for the most part, the Emperor is ignored with no valid scholarship ever being done to justify his ostracism. If everyone in the world rejects His Majesty, then the world shall erode into decadence but the truth regarding his person shall remain the same. The Bible promised us eternal life, that is the unconditional truth which shall stand from generation to generation; the gospel of Christ. Only the Son of God interpreted the scriptures alongside the speeches of His Majesty coherently and without contradiction. To deny a message that makes perfect sense only demonstrates that some people want evil to prosper; but this end shall never be accomplished. We know that our testimony is irrefutable, which is why we have written this book, to record the foundation of the gospel for anyone to study and prove for themselves. We are not afraid of having our statements investigated, in fact we invite you to do so. That which we preach is pure and undefiled, we have to safeguard the doctrine against the false and illogical precepts of the devil. Emperor Haile Sellassie The First is God the Father of Jesus Christ, the King of Kings and Lord of Lords; if you choose to investigate these claims you will find that His Majesty bears these titles. We know that the supernatural is a false concept therefore we reject the idea that a Father and his Son are the same personage. You cannot refute our testimony with a valid premise; that which we preach is the gospel of salvation, this shall stand forever. Nothing can overcome the Kingdom of God; His Majesty is the Almighty.

"And this is life eternal, that they might know thee the only true God, and Jesus Christ, whom thou hast sent. I have glorified thee on the earth: I have finished the work which thou gavest me to do. And now, O Father, glorify thou me with thine own self with the glory which I had with thee before the world was. I have manifested thy name unto the men which thou gavest me out of the world: thine they were, and thou gavest them me; and they have kept thy word. Now they have known that all things whatsoever thou hast given me are of thee. For I have given unto them the words which thou gavest me; and they have received them, and have known surely that I came out from thee, and they have believed that thou didst send me. I pray for them: I pray not for the world, but for them which thou hast given me; for they are thine. And all mine are thine, and thine are mine; and I am glorified in them. And now I am no more in the world, but these are in the world, and I come to thee. Holy Father, keep through thine own name those whom thou hast given me, that they may be one, as we are. While I was with them in the world, I kept them in thy name: those that thou gavest me I have kept, and none of them is lost, but the son of perdition; that the scripture might be fulfilled. And now come I to thee; and these things I speak in the world, that they might have my joy fulfilled in themselves. I have given them thy word; and the world hath hated them, because they are not of the world, even as I am not of the world. I pray not that thou shouldest take them out of the world, but that thou shouldest keep them from the evil. They are not of the world, even as I am not of the world. Sanctify them through thy truth: thy word is truth. As thou hast sent me into the world, even so have I also sent them into the world. And for their sakes I sanctify myself, that they also might be sanctified through the truth. Neither pray I for these alone, but for them also which shall believe on me through their word; That they all may be one; as thou, Father, art in me, and I in thee, that they also may be one in us: that the world may believe that thou hast sent me. And the glory which thou gavest me I have given them; that they may be one, even as we are one: I in them, and thou in me, that they may be made perfect in one; and that the world may know that thou hast sent me, and hast loved them, as thou hast loved me. Father, I will that they also, whom thou hast given me, be with me where I am; that they may behold my glory, which thou hast given me: for thou lovedst me before

the foundation of the world. O righteous Father, the world hath not known thee: but I have known thee, and these have known that thou hast sent me. And I have declared unto them thy name, and will declare it: that the love wherewith thou hast loved me may be in them, and I in them" (John 17:3-26).

"If ye then be risen with Christ, seek those things which are above, where Christ sitteth on the right hand of God. Set your affection on things above, not on things on the earth. For ye are dead, and your life is hid with Christ in God. When Christ, who is our life, shall appear, then shall ye also appear with him in glory" (Colossians 3:1-4).

"And he said, Therefore said I unto you, that no man can come unto me, except it were given unto him of my Father" (John 6:65).

It is expedient to search for the truth, to determine the lawful and logical interpretation of the scriptures rather than accepting an improbable proposition. Iyesus Kristos said that he is praying for all of us to become one with the Father, just as he is one with the Almighty. Now there are many blind guides who do not consider the full scope of the gospel and single in on the verse "Jesus is one with God" to mean that he is the Most High. But the Bible gives us an intelligent explanation of these verses because we all are to attain this same level as Christ by being one with the Father; this means for us to praise the LORD in spirit and in truth. In order to do this, we must acknowledge that Emperor Haile Sellassie The First is the Supreme Being. Jesus is unique in the sense that he is the only one who can show you God; that is what makes him significant and prompted the Jews to seek to kill him. The philosophies of men are littered with pagan ideas and unsound concepts, one of the most popular theories out there is the notion that God is invisible. When someone comes along and challenges our beliefs, we naturally become defensive but if there is not a good answer to combat this rebuttal, we can either acquiesce or become irate. We read in the Bible how Christ was teaching everyone the new testament and the Jews sought to challenge him because his doctrine objected to their traditions. However they was not able to prove him wrong so they then sought to kill him without reason. This prophecy has been made manifest in these last days as His Majesty is rejected in defiance of what is written in the scriptures. Jesus showed us who God is, that is how we know that Emperor Haile Sellassie The First is true. This gospel is backed up by the entire Bible but as it is written, they hate us without a cause.

"It is written in the prophets, And they shall be all taught of God. Every man therefore that hath heard, and hath learned of the Father, cometh unto me. Not that any man hath seen the Father, save he which is of God, he hath seen the Father" (John 6:45-46).

"For this is good and acceptable in the sight of God our Savior; Who will have all men to be saved, and to come unto the knowledge of the truth. For there is one God, and one mediator between God and men, the man Christ Jesus" (1 Timothy 2:3-5).

"I charge you by the Lord that this epistle be read unto all the holy brethren" (1 Thessalonians 5:27).

Those who are of God will hear his words, which are they who accept the revelation of Emperor Haile Sellassie The First. We follow the Bible as it has led us to the throne of salvation and before him who is true. From His Majesty we learn what righteousness really means, for he has taught us by his deeds and edicts. If we adopt his principles then the spirit of the LORD rests upon us but if we lean upon our own understanding then the truth is not in us. The children of God will humble themselves and repent from their false teachings which do not coincide with the principles of the Emperor. This is the key factor in being one with the Father, you must denounce your understanding and follow the teachings of Haile Sellassie The First. Jesus was the first person to do this, the world neglected His Majesty's instructions despite the validity and dexterity of his message. As a result, we have only multiplied our problems and search for a solution that we already rejected. The time has come to break the cycle of confusion, humanity is lost in a sea of corruption and vanity. Our only hope to rid the world of this affliction is to worship Emperor Haile Sellassie The First in spirit and in truth.

The Eleventh Letter

The Bible, Quran, and the Bhagavad-Gita all say that Emperor Haile Sellassie The First is the Almighty God; the message throughout the sacred books is identical, the gospel is one and the same, that is the mystery of the day of Pentecost (Acts 2): the people were amazed and confounded, because every man heard them speak in his own language (religion). Jesus Christ, the Prophet of Allah, gave us the understanding to know that there is one God, therefore one revelation shall fulfill all prophecies; Emperor Haile Sellassie The First has accomplished this fete. His Majesty said, "Hence, if anybody says that differences exist between Moslems and Christians, that person is an enemy of Ethiopia,"[37] this means that we must think on a higher level and understand the similarities found throughout all the religions. The meek shall inherit all the spiritual denominations on earth for we preach a universal doctrine and fulfill the true meaning of these various divisions; we are the real Christians, Muslims, Buddhists, Hindus, Rastafarians, etc. The prayers of the Jews and Gentiles are both heard by the same God, when we acknowledge the person who is Supreme to creation, then we have accomplished the real meaning of all faiths.

"And put thy trust in Him Who lives and dies not; and celebrate his praise; and enough is He to be acquainted with the faults of His servants; He Who created the heavens and the earth and all that is between, in six days, and is firmly established on the Throne (of Authority): Allah Most Gracious: ask thou, then, about Him one well informed" (Sura 25:58-58).

"Realizing this, he becomes attached to the Supreme Personality of Godhead and surrenders to Him. At such a time one can understand that Lord Sri Krsna's mercy is everything, that He is the cause of all causes, and that this material manifestation is not independent from Him" (Gita 7:19).

"Your kingdom is an everlasting kingdom and your dominion endures throughout all generations. The LORD is faithful to all his promises and loving toward all he has made" (Psalm 145:13).

The scriptures describe the Almighty as a Great King who manifest himself on earth to save humanity from their own perniciousness. Reading these descriptions in the various texts indicates that Emperor Haile Sellassie The First is him to whom it appertains. God cannot die for he is not validated by his skin for sanctity, he is justified in the Spirit. This has led many people to believe that the LORD has no face or body but that is not the message being conveyed. The promise is for the kingdom of God to stand throughout all generations, therefore the truth about the Almighty must be clear and defiant; which is accomplished through manifestation not fish stories.

---

[37] Eritrea Hails Her Sovereign, page 50

"Everyone upon the earth will perish, And there will remain the Face of your Lord, Owner of Majesty and Honor. So which of the favors of your Lord would you deny" (Sura 55:26-28).

"The Absolute Truth is the Personality of Godhead, Sri Krsna, and this is confirmed in every step. In this verse, in particular, it is stressed that the Absolute Truth is a person [...] These authorities leave no doubt that the Absolute Truth is the Supreme Person, the cause of all causes [...] There is no truth superior to that Supreme Person, because He is the supermost. He is smaller than the smallest, and He is greater than the greatest" (Gita 7:7).

"And there shall be no more curse: but the throne of God and of the Lamb shall be in it; and his servants shall serve him: And they shall see his face; and his name shall be in their foreheads" (Revelation 22:4).

All of the holy books relay the same message that the Almighty Creator is a person whose face we can see; if we follow his solemn course. Those who deny this testimony have betrayed their own canon. You cannot cherry pick what scriptures you want to admonish, you must acknowledge the entire declaration if you want to know the truth. We give credence to the full doctrine and can interpret all the scriptures without any contradiction for all things work in our favor. We accept the gospel of Christ and thereby have come to know the King of Glory: Emperor Haile Sellassie The First.

"He is Allah, other than whom there is no deity, The King, the Pure, the Perfection, the Bestower of Faith, the Overseer, the Exalted in Might, the Compeller, the Superior. Exalted is Allah above whatever they associate with Him" (Sura 59:23).

"It is said that one can neither see, hear, understand nor perceive the Supreme Lord, Krsna, by material senses. But if one is engaged in loving transcendental service to the Lord from the beginning, then one can see the Lord by revelation" (Gita 11:4).

"Now to the King eternal, immortal, invisible, the only wise God, be honor and glory forever and ever. Amen" (1 Timothy 1:17).

God is invisible to those who have no faith and adhere to a corrupt dogma, but those who seek his face shall find him. Only the LORD can fulfill the prophecy, his glory cannot be subscribed to an impostor. Emperor

Haile Sellassie The First actualized everything that has ever been attributed to the Creator. It is written that he is a Holy King, who is manifest right before our eyes but the only way to know that he is God, is to understand the prophecy. When you understand all of his descriptions, then you will have to conclude that His Majesty is the Almighty because he accomplished everything.

"Whatever is in the heavens and on earth - let it declare the Praises and Glory of Allah: for He is the Exalted in Might, the Wise. To Him belongs the kingship of the heavens and the earth: It is He Who gives Life and Death; and He has Power over all things. He is the First and the Last, the Evident and the Immanent: and He has full knowledge of all things. He it is Who created the heavens and the earth in Six Days, and is moreover firmly established on the Throne (of Authority). He knows what enters within the earth and what comes forth out of it, what comes down from heaven and what mounts up to it. And He is with you wheresoever ye may be. And Allah sees well all that ye do. To Him belongs the kingship of the heavens and the earth: and all affairs are referred back to Allah" (Sura 57:1-5).

"It was spoken by the Lord when He was present personally on this planet for the guidance of mankind" (Gita 1:1).

"For the kingdom of God is not in word, but in power" (1 Corinthians 4:20).

The sacramental verses describe God and his disposition so that we will recognize him and revere him when he appears before mankind. This ancient caveat has been passed down from generation to generation and adopted by various civilizations according to their own interpretation of the prophecy. By reading all the sacred books we will recognize corresponding themes that are found within every religion; this in turn makes one to know what is apocryphal as it would not correspond with the overall resolution. Some people may attempt to create a tradition that suites their own desires and point of view but the Word of God cannot be expunged by the false edicts of man. We have been promised to see the Almighty in actual terms, not in a dream or the hereafter, but in real life. This is how we know that the reign of Emperor Haile Sellassie The First is the fulfillment of prophecy, it is not a coincidence that he accomplished everything according to the presages of the LORD.

"He it is Who created the heavens and the earth in six Days - and His Throne was over the waters - that He might try you, which of you is best in conduct. But if thou wert to say to them, 'Ye shall indeed be raised up after death,' the Unbelievers would be sure to say, 'This is nothing but obvious sorcery'" (Sura 11:7).

"In the Bhagavad-gita, in plain and simple language, it is stated that Sri Krsna is the Supreme Personality of Godhead. There is none equal to or greater than Him. He is mentioned as the father of Brahma, the original father of all human beings. In fact, Sri Krsna is said to be not only the father of Brahma but also the father of all species of life. He is the root of the impersonal Brahman and Paramatma; the Supersoul in every entity is His plenary portion. He is the fountainhead of everything, and everyone is advised to surrender unto His lotus feet. Despite all these clear statements, they deride the personality of the Supreme Lord and consider Him merely another human being. They do not know that the blessed form of human life is designed after the eternal and transcendental feature of the Supreme Lord" (Gita 7:15).

"And I saw a great white throne and him that sat on it, from whose face the earth and the heaven fled away; and there was found no place for them" (Revelation 20:11).

These ancient heralds have forecasted the turn of events that will transpire, not for us to become lost in the vanity of the world but to safeguard our salvation so that we can recognize the LORD at his coming. It is written that although he is the Almighty Creator of heaven and earth, people will look upon him as a regular man. Although he is the Highest himself, people will not accept him in spite of his perfection. Emperor Haile Sellassie The First is the only one who fits these descriptions yet the masses have not acknowledged the revelation. The scriptures were written for this purpose, to tell us who God is so that we will accept him when he appears, but many have failed in this aspect despite having a sure confirmation of events. Those who are blessed will rise from the dead mentality that prevents people from knowing the LORD, into the beauty of heaven which makes one to know the Father. Let us take heed and worship His Majesty, for he is God and there is none else.

"And it was not [possible] for this Qur'an to be produced by other than Allah, but [it is] a confirmation of what was before it and a detailed explanation of the [former] Scripture, about which there is no doubt, from the Lord of the worlds. Or do they say [about the Prophet], 'He invented it?' Say, 'Then bring forth a surah like it and call

upon [for assistance] whomever you can besides Allah, if you should be truthful'"
(Sura 10:37-38).

"Now, as far as Arjuna is concerned, he says that his illusion is over. This means that Arjuna no longer think so of Krsna as a mere human being, as a friend of his, but as the source of everything. Arjuna is very enlightened and is glad that he has such a great friend as Krsna, but now he is thinking that although he may accept Krsna as the source of everything, others may not" *(Gita 11:1).*

"Then the word of the LORD came unto me, saying, Before I formed thee in the belly I knew thee; and before thou camest forth out of the womb I sanctified thee, and I ordained thee a prophet unto the nations. Then said I, Ah, Lord GOD! behold, I cannot speak: for I am a child. But the LORD said unto me, Say not, I am a child: for thou shalt go to all that I shall send thee, and whatsoever I command thee thou shalt speak. Be not afraid of their faces: for I am with thee to deliver thee, saith the LORD. Then the LORD put forth his hand, and touched my mouth. And the LORD said unto me, Behold, I have put my words in thy mouth. See, I have this day set thee over the nations and over the kingdoms, to root out, and to pull down, and to destroy, and to throw down, to build, and to plant" *(Jeremiah 1:4-10).*

One of the corresponding themes found within all the holy books states that God sent forth his Prophet to preach his Word so that humanity may know the truth. Any other interpretation is not coherent with the prophecy, as we find this same analogy put forth in the works of Moses, Joshua, David, Jesus, Muhammad, Arjuna, etc., and all other authoritative texts. To break from this plan, creates a contradiction which the LORD did not intend; the messenger is described as a pious man who was chosen by the Father to lead the people unto salvation. God is not the author of confusion, his instructions are clear and accurate, but mankind with wicked intentions have misconstrued the scriptures to promote their own self interests to thrust the world into darkness. If every epistle reads that the Almighty will send forth a messenger, how do we then come to the conclusion that the Son of God is also the Father, when it is written that Jesus Christ is a Prophet? If all of the sacred writings indicate that the LORD will appear on earth, how can we then say that he is invisible? If we limit our scope then we have hindered our prospect of attaining the truth, but this should not be our undertaking if we want to know the Almighty.

"O mankind! there hath come to you a direction from your Lord and a healing for the (diseases) in your hearts - and for those who believe, a guidance and a Mercy" (Sura 10:57).

"This universal form is not possible to be seen by any ordinary man. Krsna must give one the power to see it" (Gita 11:5).

"No man hath seen God at any time; the only begotten Son, which is in the bosom of the Father, he hath declared him" (John 1:18).

To understand that Emperor Haile Sellassie The First is God means that you can interpret the scriptures according to the correct format. This gift comes from accepting the gospel of Christ, for his message is the full authority on spiritual matters. The Word was given unto the Prophet to offer the world salvation, for he preaches the true message of the LORD, he declares him who is All Powerful. To neglect his testimony only means that you will never attain the summit of righteousness, but his account will stand forever because it is infallible. We therefore are in agreement with all the original undiluted Vedas which uniformly declare that the Almighty is a Great King who will establish his Kingdom on earth. This ancient unmodifiable doctrine has been fulfilled by Emperor Haile Sellassie The First of Ethiopia on November 2, 1930, when he was crowned King of Kings and Lord of Lords; the highest of all titles.

"Allah is He Who raised the heavens without any pillars that ye can see; is firmly established on the throne (of authority); He has subjected the sun and the moon (to his Law)! Each one runs (its course) for a term appointed. He doth regulate all affairs, explaining the signs in detail, that ye may believe with certainty in the meeting with your Lord" (Sura 13:2).

"But you cannot see Me with your present eyes. Therefore I give you divine eyes. Behold My mystic opulence" (Gita 11:8).

"Therefore said they unto him, How were thine eyes opened? He answered and said, A man that is called Jesus made clay, and anointed mine eyes, and said unto me, Go to the pool of Siloam, and wash: and I went and washed, and I received sight" (John 9:10-11).

The blind receiving sight is a metaphor which denotes a spiritual awakening. Christ has opened our eyes through the gospel which provides us with the proper interpretation of the scriptures so that we may know the Father. The promise of all the sacred writing is that we will see the Most High, that is why Jesus preached that Emperor Haile Sellassie The First is the Almighty. All the other would be sages did not comprehend the parables and could not reveal the mystery of God. The Messiah is special in this aspect and necessary because only through him can we acquire the correct solemn perspective that would allow our faith to actually correspond with the message of the scriptures by worshipping the LORD incarnate: Emperor Haile Sellassie The First.

"The day We shall gather the righteous to (Allah) Most Gracious, like a band presented before a king for honors" (Sura 19:85).

"For in the future there would be so many impostors who would pose themselves as incarnations of God. The people, therefore, should be careful; one who claims to be Krsna should be prepared to show his universal form to confirm his claim to the people" (Gita 11:3).

"Thus will I magnify myself, and sanctify myself; and I will be known in the eyes of many nations, and they shall know that I am the LORD" (Ezekiel 38:23).

It is fairly easy for anyone to say that they are God, that is why everyone should know that His Majesty never stated that he is the Almighty through words but in deeds. Emperor Haile Sellassie The First did something that only the Creator could do and that is to sit upon the Throne of David with the titles of the Most High. As it is written, he will not give his glory unto another, so the person who accomplishes this feat will be the first and the last to do so. There are many impostors who proclaim to be the one yet their descriptions do not match what is written in the holy books. Only His Majesty corresponds with the entire representation of God recorded in all of the holy books because he is the truth.

"And call not, besides Allah, on another god. There is no god but He. Everything will be destroyed except His Face. His is the judgement, and to Him you will be returned" (Sura 28:88).

"Sanjaya said: O King, having spoken thus, the Supreme Lord of all mystic power, the Personality of Godhead, displayed His universal form to Arjuna" (Gita 11:9).

"For though there be that are called gods, whether in heaven or in earth, (as there be gods many, and lords many,) But to us there is but one God, the Father, of whom are all things, and we in him; and one Lord Jesus Christ, by whom are all things, and we by him" (1 Corinthians 8:5-6).

The divinity of Emperor Haile Sellassie The First shall stand forever because this gospel is founded upon facts not opinions. We can study history and confirm that His Majesty was crowned King of Kings and Lord of Lords. So whereas others may claim that we are heretics, our faith is validated by the scriptures. It is fairly easy to call someone a false teacher, for they labeled Jesus Christ the same. Yet proving what is right and wrong requires a higher skill set than mere rhetorical theater. We have showcased our evidence for anyone to study why we worship Emperor Haile Sellassie The First. This gospel shall consume and eliminate all other brands of spirituality because there could only be one truth, as there is only one Savior. In order to be justified in your faith you would have to praise His Majesty, for he alone is God.

"And [remember] when I inspired to the disciples, 'Believe in Me and in My messenger Jesus.' They said, 'We have believed, so bear witness that indeed we are Muslims [in submission to Allah].' [And remember] when the disciples said, 'O Jesus, Son of Mary, can your Lord send down to us a table [spread with food] from the heaven?' [Jesus] said, 'Fear Allah, if you should be believers.' They said, 'We wish to eat from it and let our hearts be reassured and to know that thou hast indeed told us the truth and be among its witnesses.' Said Jesus, the son of Mary, 'O Allah, our Lord, send down to us a table [spread with food] from the heaven to be for us a festival for the first of us and the last of us and a sign from You. And provide for us, and You are the best of providers.' Allah said, 'Indeed, I will send it down to you, but whoever disbelieves afterwards from among you - then indeed will I punish him with a punishment by which I have not punished anyone among the worlds.' And behold! Allah will say: 'O Jesus the son of Mary! Didst thou say unto men, worship me and my mother as gods in derogation of Allah?' He will say: 'Glory to Thee! never could I say what I had no right (to say). Had I said such a thing, thou wouldst indeed have known it. Thou knowest what is in my heart, Thou I know not what is in Thine. For Thou knowest in full all that is hidden. I said nothing to them except what You commanded me - to worship Allah, my Lord and your Lord. And I was a witness over

them as long as I was among them; but when You took me up, You were the Observer over them, and You are, over all things, Witness'" (Sura 5:111-117).

"The Lord wants to explain the above-mentioned system of knowledge because Arjuna is Krsna's confidential devotee and friend" (Gita 7:20).

"Jesus cried and said, He that believeth on me, believeth not on me, but on him that sent me. And he that seeth me seeth him that sent me. I am come a light into the world, that whosoever believeth on me should not abide in darkness. And if any man hear my words, and believe not, I judge him not: for I came not to judge the world, but to save the world. He that rejecteth me, and receiveth not my words, hath one that judgeth him: the word that I have spoken, the same shall judge him in the last day. For I have not spoken of myself; but the Father which sent me, he gave me a commandment, what I should say, and what I should speak. And I know that his commandment is life everlasting: whatsoever I speak therefore, even as the Father said unto me, so I speak" (John 12:44-50).

"So Arjuna conquered both sleep and ignorance because of his friendship with Krsna. As a great devotee of Krsna, he could not forget Krsna even for a moment, because that is the nature of a devotee" (Gita 1:24).

"Giving thanks unto the Father, which hath made us meet to be partakers of the inheritance of the saints in light: Who hath delivered us from the power of darkness, and hath translated us into the kingdom of his dear Son: In whom we have redemption through his blood, even the forgiveness of sins: Who is the image of the invisible God, the firstborn of every creature: For by him were all things created, that are in heaven, and that are in earth, visible and invisible, whether they be thrones, or dominions, or principalities, or powers: all things were created by him, and for him: And he is before all things, and by him all things consist. And he is the head of the body, the church: who is the beginning, the firstborn from the dead; that in all things he might have the preeminence. For it pleased the Father that in him should all fulness dwell; And, having made peace through the blood of his cross, by him to reconcile all things unto himself; by him, I say, whether they be things in earth, or things in heaven" (Colossians 1:12-20).

It is a false proclamation to call Jesus, the Almighty, because all of the scriptures state that he is the Son of God. This classification of being a progeny denotes that he is the messenger who preaches the true Word, he reveals who the Father is. Christ was not speaking about himself during his sermons, this is clearly stated throughout the prophecies but certain churches with dubious intentions have deceived the world into accepting a fake supernatural interpretation of the texts to make the child of God also the progenitor. This edict which declares Jesus to be the Almighty, does not come from the scriptures, it has been concocted by men who cherry picked certain verses to portray a certain image that is in clear defiance of the entire presentment. When Christ was made God by the Roman ecumenical councils, this combined paganism with Christianity and was thus effective in mitigating the empire; let us not confuse this with theology. The full representation of Jesus, found within all the books, declares him to be a Prophet, a devotee, one who obeys the commandments of the LORD. It is written that if you believe in Christ, then you believe not in him, but in the Father who sent him, because it is the procreator who holds significance; Christ is only important because he leads us to God. Therefore worshipping Jesus is idolatry because he is not the Almighty, he is a preacher who was chosen by the Most High to carry out a specific mission. In this way he found favor with the LORD because he fulfilled the works that he was instructed to perform; he taught the gospel the way it was intended to be instilled. Christ is the express image of the invisible God because through him we can see and know the LORD, this was an order for everyone to fulfill yet only the Messiah accomplished. In analyzing the full context of the holy books it would be entirely counterfactual and contradictory to come to the conclusion that the bairn is the Almighty when it is desired for us all to rise to the level of Christ. The eminence of the Most High cannot be shared with anyone or else he could not be categorized as the Highest.

"On the Day We will say to Hell, 'Have you been filled?' and it will say, 'Are there some more, And Paradise will be brought near to the righteous, not far,' [It will be said], 'This is what was promised for you - for every one who turned (to Allah) in sincere repentance, who kept (His Law), Who feared (Allah) Most Gracious Unseen, and brought a heart turned in devotion (to Him): Enter ye therein in Peace and Security; this is a Day of Eternal Life! There will be for them therein all that they wish - and more besides in Our Presence'" (Sura 50:30-35).

"The last class of duskrti are those of demonic principles. This class is openly atheistic. Some of them argue that the Supreme Lord can never descend upon this material world, but they are unable to give any tangible reason as to why not" (Gita 7:15).

"Because that which may be known of God is manifest in them; for God hath shewed it unto them. For the invisible things of him from the creation of the world are clearly seen, being understood by the things that are made, even his eternal power and Godhead; so that they are without excuse: Because that, when they knew God, they glorified him not as God, neither were thankful; but became vain in their imaginations, and their foolish heart was darkened. Professing themselves to be wise, they became fools, And changed the glory of the uncorruptible God into an image made like to corruptible man, and to birds, and fourfooted beasts, and creeping things. Wherefore God also gave them up to uncleanness through the lusts of their own hearts, to dishonour their own bodies between themselves: Who changed the truth of God into a lie, and worshipped and served the creature more than the Creator, who is blessed forever. Amen" (Romans 1:19-25).

If God can create the universe and make man in his own image then why is it considered impossible for him to manifest in the flesh and appear on earth? It is in clear defiance of his ability to believe that he cannot accomplish this objective as well as contradictory to his purpose. When he constructed the entire cosmos, did he forget to actualize his own existence? Why would he generate mass and anatomies for other beings but not for himself? The Almighty is not a ruler who is contrary to his own edicts, this is also how we know that the supernatural is an insubstantial theory, when the Ten Commandments were given to the children of Israel, these were laws that God himself followed. The LORD rested on the seventh day and instructed us to observe the Sabbath, we are to be holy as he is holy. People cannot see the Creator because they do not believe in Emperor Haile Sellassie The First, it is not because God is far from us or that he has no materialness, it is because they have no faith in him. Even the concept of "Amen" derives from the Egyptian deity "Amun," who was the King of Gods and always characterized as "A man." This is a universal theme, found throughout all the holy books, which promises those who seek him shall find him. His Majesty has appeared on earth to accomplish this end.

"Bear, then with patience, all that they say, and celebrate the praises of thy Lord, before the rising of the sun and before (its) setting" (Sura 50:39).

"The Lord wants to explain the above-mentioned system of knowledge because Arjuna is Krsna's confidential devotee and friend" (Gita 7:20).

"For God hath not given us the spirit of fear; but of power, and of love, and of a sound mind. Be not thou therefore ashamed of the testimony of our Lord, nor of me his prisoner: but be thou partaker of the afflictions of the gospel according to the power of God; Who hath saved us, and called us with a holy calling, not according to our works, but according to his own purpose and grace, which was given us in Christ Jesus before the world began, But is now made manifest by the appearing of our Savior Jesus Christ, who hath abolished death, and hath brought life and immortality to light through the gospel: Whereunto I am appointed a preacher, and an apostle, and a teacher of the Gentiles. For the which cause I also suffer these things: nevertheless I am not ashamed: for I know whom I have believed, and am persuaded that he is able to keep that which I have committed unto him against that day. Hold fast the form of sound words, which thou hast heard of me, in faith and love which is in Christ Jesus" (2 Timothy 1:7-13).

We are not ashamed to worship Emperor Haile Sellassie The First, although some people may say that we have gone astray, we know that our faith is valid and justified throughout all the scriptures. Our aim is to win the world but we do not please the world, we must gain men without conforming to their ways; Jesus was a friend of God not man. The fight against our religion is subjugated by knowledge as the truth is on our side, there is not an argument or report which can discredit the divinity of Emperor Haile Sellassie The First. Understanding the gospel and knowing His Majesty's nature will develop your confidence and character to respond to the skeptics with a perfect answer that will quell all their disputing and eventually turn the hearts of those who are sincere in their inquiries to you. This is the power of Christ, he imparted us with an irreproachable gospel that will shatter all that is contrary.

"Verily this is the word of a most honorable Messenger, Endued with Power, with rank before the Lord of the Throne, With authority there, (and) faithful to his trust. And (O people!) your companion is not one possessed; And without doubt he saw him in the clear horizon. Neither doth he withhold grudgingly a knowledge of the Unseen. Nor is it the word of an evil spirit accursed. When whither go ye? Verily this is no less than a Message to (all) the Worlds: (With profit) to whoever among you wills to go straight: But ye shall not will except as Allah wills - the Cherisher of the Worlds" (Sura 81:19-29).

"Therefore, only Lord Krsna, or His bona fide representative the spiritual master, can release the conditioned soul. Without such superior help, one cannot be freed from the bondage of material nature" (Gita 7:14).

"For this is good and acceptable in the sight of God our Savior; Who will have all men to be saved, and to come unto the knowledge of the truth. For there is one God, and one mediator between God and men, the man Christ Jesus" (1 Timothy 2:3-5).

Christ is the man who brings us before the Throne of God, for his gospel is the absolute truth concerning theology. We will know that the Messiah has risen by the dexterity of his message because only he preaches the Word correctly. The popular postulates do not have the power to unify the entire world underneath one God because they do not acknowledge the similitude found amongst all the various religions. What has happened is Jews attack Muslims because they feel that their deity is better, Christians go against Animists and look down upon their traditions, and this cycle goes on and on throughout the world. But spirituality was never intended to cause discord and strife between man, its true purpose is the opposite, to unify humanity and create a better world for everyone to enjoy. This has not been the case when nearly all of the wars fought on earth have been over religion. This demonstrates that the people do not know God neither do they comprehend their own system of beliefs. Jesus therefore was sent to teach people the correct demonstration of faith which will unify all denominations. Emperor Haile Sellassie The First expressed these sentiments and Christ followed him, which is how he was endued with the power to walk on water (subdue the earth).

"Blessed be He in Whose hands is Dominion; and He over all things hath Power; He Who created Death and Life, that He may try which of you is best in deed: and He is the Exalted in Might, Oft-Forgiving; He Who created the seven heavens one above another: No want of proportion wilt thou see in the Creation of (Allah) Most Gracious. So turn thy vision again: seest thou any flaw? Again turn thy vision a second time: (thy) vision will come back to thee dull and discomfited, in a state worn out" (Sura 67:1-4).

"Even though Arjuna was a personal friend of Krsna and the most advanced of learned men, it was still not possible for him to know everything about Krsna" (Gita 11:6).

"I give thee charge in the sight of God, who quickeneth all things, and before Christ Jesus, who before Pontius Pilate witnessed a good confession; That thou keep this commandment without spot, unrebukeable, until the appearing of our Lord Jesus Christ: Which in his times he shall shew, who is the blessed and only Potentate, the King of kings, and Lord of lords; Who only hath immortality, dwelling in the light which no man can approach unto; whom no man hath seen, nor can see: to whom be honor and power everlasting. Amen" (1 Timothy 6:13-16).

God is on a stratum which no man is even remotely close to reaching; he created the universe. Therefore to associate anyone or anything with the Almighty only means that the signification of him being the Most High, has not resonated. It is written that he cannot be seen because there is no one who can be compared to him. None of the angels in heaven, neither his Son or any of the Prophets are equal in nature to the LORD; God is greater than everyone. He alone possess the power to be omniscient, omnipotent, and omnipresent; he is Supreme over all entities. The idea of Christ or anyone else being equivalent with the Almighty is grossly inaccurate and cannot be considered sound doctrine. The scriptures do not support this position as it would be a clear contradiction to associate another man as being equal with God and then to label God as the Supreme Being. If he is the Most High than everyone else is lower than him, he cannot be considered analogous with anyone. If we are not able to grasp the full scope of the discourse then we would remain oblivious to the true interpretation of the scriptures.

"Whatever is in the heavens and whatever is on the earth is exalting Allah, The King, the Pure, the Exalted in Might, the Wise" (Sura 62:1).

"Krsna is the Supreme Person, father of religion" (Gita 7:3).

"For the LORD is a great God, and a great King above all gods. In his hand are the deep places of the earth: the strength of the hills is his also. The sea is his, and he made it: and his hands formed the dry land. O come, let us worship and bow down: let us kneel before the LORD our maker" (Psalm 95:3-6).

The message found throughout all the sacred texts indicates that we are to praise the King of Heaven for he alone is God. We know that Haile Sellassie The First is the blessed and only Potentate who the scriptures are referring to, for he is the King of Kings and Lord of Lords. A great calamity is taking place on earth because humanity regards His Majesty as being a regular man and they associate themselves as being tantamount with the Emperor. All of this, in clear defiance of Haile Sellassie's most excellent character, superior intellect, and impeccable morality. When you make someone equal with God, you void out the significance and mighty works of the LORD. It therefore does not matter that he is holy and righteous because anyone can consider themselves to be reciprocal with the Father even though they have not displayed the same eminence. This then makes righteousness vain because there would be no reason to follow the great example of God if those who have not his character and discipline are considered to be identical with him. Even Jesus said, why do you call me good, there is only one good and that is God; he confessed on various instances that the Father is greater than him. To make someone equivalent with the Most High is a ploy to nullify piety because only from the Almighty will we get the perfect example of righteousness. It is written that he dwells in an unapproachable light because there is no one like him, so if we say that there is, we lie and do not adhere to the gospel of salvation. The original concept of the trinity never stated that Jesus Christ is part of the Godhead,[38] the churches have bastardized the Word because there is a conspiracy to oppose Emperor Haile Sellassie The First so that evil will prosper. But we know that this design shall fail, the prophecy shall play out and all those who oppose His Majesty will be put to shame; as it is written.

"Or have they a god other than Allah? Exalted is Allah far above the things they associate with Him! Were they to see a piece of the sky falling (on them), they would (only) say: 'Clouds gathered in heaps'" (Sura 52:43-44).

"Others on the battlefield could not see this form, because Krsna gave the vision only to Arjuna" (Gita 11:13).

"Not that any man hath seen the Father, save he which is of God, he hath seen the Father" (John 6:46).

People regard Emperor Haile Sellassie The First as being a regular man because they do not understand the prophecies written throughout the scriptures. Although His Majesty fits the descriptions of God perfectly, they deceive themselves into rejecting that which is quite obvious. They are looking

---

[38] 1 John 5:7

for a supernatural occurrence to transpire but if they cannot accept Emperor Haile Sellassie The First based upon the mighty works that he has already displayed, then even if he would make the sky fall on them, they would still deny his divinity. Everything that we hope for has been fulfilled by His Majesty. The only people who do not feel this way are those who are not of God. Christ has given us the true gospel so that we may know the Almighty Father: Blessed be Jah Rastafari.

"And (Jesus) shall be a Sign (for the coming of) the Hour (of Judgment): therefore have no doubt about the (Hour), but follow ye Me: this is a Straight Way. Let not the Evil One hinder you: for he is to you an enemy avowed. When Jesus came with Clear Signs, he said: 'Now have I come to you with Wisdom, and in order to make clear to you some of the (points) on which ye dispute: therefore fear Allah and obey me. For Allah, He is my Lord and your Lord: so worship ye Him: this is the Straight Way.' But sects from among themselves fell into disagreement: then woe to the wrong-doers, from the Penalty of a Grievous Day" (Sura 43:61-65).

"One will find in the Bhagavad-gita all that is contained in other scriptures" (Gita 1:1).

"Neither is there salvation in any other: for there is none other name under heaven given among men, whereby we must be saved" (Acts 4:12).

There is no conformity found throughout the holy books if we seek to argue that Jesus Christ is God. The role of the Messiah is that of a messenger, if we interpret his gospel in any other way then we have created an alien tradition which does not fit properly within the context of any scripture. Even if we create a vacuum where our traditions did not have to be justified, we would still only be deceiving ourselves if we follow a doctrine based upon superstition; for that which is incorrect shall always remain so in spite of anyones objections to the contrary. It is written that Moses is a Prophet - he is not God, Muhammad is a Prophet - he is not God, Arjuna is a Prophet - he is not God, Jesus is a Prophet - and he is God?!? Where is the coherency within this postulate? The messenger does not speak of himself, he complies with and completes an operation for God; he is a friend to the LORD because he does the will of the Father. If we understood the role of Christ it would be impossible to come to the conclusion that Jesus is the Almighty. All of the books define the Prophet as a pious person who was chosen by God to preach the message of salvation. To break from this line of reasoning is not supported in the scriptures.

"A revelation from Him Who created the earth and the heavens on high. (Allah) Most Gracious is firmly established on the throne (of authority). To Him belongs what is in the heavens and on earth, and all between them, and all beneath the soil. If thou pronounce the word aloud, (it is no matter): for verily He knoweth what is secret and what is yet more hidden. Allah! there is no god but He! To Him belong the most Beautiful Names. Has the story of Moses reached thee? Behold, he saw a fire: So he said to his family, 'Tarry ye; I perceive a fire; perhaps I can bring you some burning brand therefrom, or find some guidance at the fire.' But when he came to the fire, a voice was heard: 'O Moses! Verily I am thy Lord! therefore (in My presence) put off thy shoes: thou art in the sacred valley Tuwa. I have chosen thee: listen, then, to the inspiration (sent to thee). Verily, I am Allah: There is no god but I: So serve thou Me (only), and establish regular prayer for celebrating My praise'" (Sura 20:4-14).

"Those who are actually interested in understanding the Supreme Personality of Godhead, Krsna, and who follow in the footsteps of Arjuna should understand that Krsna not only theoretically presented Himself as the Supreme, but actually revealed Himself as the Supreme" (Gita 11:8).

"And ye said, Behold the LORD our God has showed us his glory and his greatness, and we have heard his voice out of the midst of the fire: we have seen this day that God does talk with man, and he lives" (Deuteronomy 5:24).

That which is written concerning the invisible God refers to people's disbelief or his eminence; not to his embodiment. They cannot see him because they have no faith in him or the scriptures are referring to his supremacy. But it was always intended for us to know who the LORD is because the sacred texts describe him so that we would recognize him when he appears on earth. The measure of salvation is defined by those who accept God incarnate, Emperor Haile Sellassie The First; for he is the judgement. Only through him can we understand the holy books and unite the world underneath the one God. There is no other gospel whereby we can be saved; Jesus Christ kept us in the name of his Father: Emperor Haile Sellassie The First.

"Exalted is the Lord of the heavens and the earth, Lord of the Throne, above what they describe [of him]" (Sura 43:82).

"The Supreme Lord Krsna has senses and a body like the ordinary man" (Gita 11:43).

"And the LORD shall be king over all the earth: in that day shall there be one LORD and his name one" (Zechariah 14:9).

The revelation of God on earth is subscribed to take place on the Throne of David and Emperor Haile Sellassie The First is the last of the Solomonic Kings. Therefore if we do not believe in him then we would have neglected the herald that fulfills all the descriptions of the Almighty and there will be no other sign that aligns with biblical prophecy. There are certain factions who seek to restore the Ethiopian monarchy but His Majesty has already completed everything that they are searching for. The purpose of the Solomonic Dynasty was for God to establish his kingdom on earth and that end has been accomplished. To be legally considered the Emperor of Ethiopia, the indigenous leaders must concede to your authority as well as the Tewahedo Church must approve of your sovereignty, the most common way that this is done is through a Coronation. If these two provisions are not met it would be no different from me calling myself the head of state, there is no credibility. Therefore when the Provisional Military Administrative Committee (Derg) proclaimed Asfa Wossen as the king of Ethiopia it was an illegitimate succession because Haile Sellassie The First never signed an abdication nor did he renounce his rights. Asfa Wossen himself considered all the acts of the Derg as being illegal and refused to acknowledge any of the titles conferred upon him by this terroristic regime. But when he finally did accept sovereign dominion in April 1989, this honor was conferred upon him by a small Ethiopian community in London, and not by the native rulers of the land or the Tewahedo Church. Haile Sellassie The First is the last legitimate Solomonic Monarch, if we put our trust in him then we would find everything that we are looking for.

"Say, 'I seek refuge in the Lord of mankind, The King of mankind, The God of mankind, From the mischief of the Whisperer (of Evil), who withdraws (after his whisper), Who whispers [evil] into the hearts of mankind, Among Jinns and among men'" (Sura 146:1-6).

"No one can understand how Krsnha the Supreme LORD comes to earth in physical form and executed common activities as an ordinary human being" (Gita 10:2).

"And in the days of these kings shall the God of heaven set up a kingdom, which shall never be destroyed: and the kingdom shall not be left to other people, but it shall break in pieces and consume all these kingdoms, and it shall stand forever" (Daniel 2:44).

The rank of Lord is an aristocratic title for a noble commander but when the scriptures refer to "The Lord" it is referring to the Creator of the Universe; these premises are however interrelated. In order for our faith to be justified we must learn the reality of God and abdicate from fictional dogmas; we need to see God as a present sovereign on this planet. The prophecy of the LORD establishing his Kingdom on earth is a promise that has been fulfilled so it is imperative to make the correct correlation between the presage and the proclamation to accept the revelation. Ethiopia is the oldest aristocracy on earth but it is sometimes mentioned that the title of Lord is not an official appellation of the Imperial government. This could only be applied in linguistics since Lord is an English word that does not come from Ethiopia; there is however a status equivalent in their society which is Ras. If we cannot understand corresponding terms then someone may think that Spanish people do not believe in God because they say Dios or that Arabic people do not believe in God because they refer to him as Allah but translators are utilized to avoid such a benighted fiasco. Speaking in the name of other gods does not mean talking in a different language, people are guilty of this when they call upon other deities besides the Supreme Potentate. Ethiopia does not use the word King either but everyone acknowledges their monarchy because of the correspondent designation of Negus. Lord in the British Isles is a general title for a prince or a feudal superior. Before the Hanoverian succession, before the use of "prince" became settled practice, royal sons were styled the Lord Forename. Traditionally Lords were landholders with considerable wealth who were responsible for ruling a part of the country under the Crown. This honor was normally given to people who performed an exemplary service for England; for those with authority, control, or power over others; a master, chief, or ruler. There are five ranks of the British peerage to designate a Lord: Duke, Marquess, Earl, Viscount and Baron; in order of prominence from the greatest to the least. In Ethiopia, Ras is the most senior title below that of Negus and has customarily been bestowed on the greatest leaders of the Empire. The person known as "Ras" is equivalent to Commander, Generalissimo, or Duke; the governor of a province, it is a noble title, literally meaning "head." Emperor Haile Sellassie The First issued this rank very sparingly. If you analyze the definitions for Ras and Lord you will find absolutely no difference between these two appellations. Ras is the rank below that of King and Lord is a general title for a prince. Ras is bestowed upon the greatest leaders of Ethiopia and Lord is normally given to those who have performed an exemplary service for England. A Ras is a governor of a province and a Lord was a landholder responsible for ruling a part of the country. Ras is equivalent to Duke, and a Duke is the highest rank of a Lord. They mean exactly the same thing, the only difference is in linguistics which we cannot expect the entire world to speak the same dialect. And this is all in hindsight of the fact that various publications have already defined Ras as Lord and attributed Lord to be an appellation of Tafari Makonnen. His Majesty cannot be denied, Emperor Haile Sellassie The First is emphatically the King of Kings and Lord of Lords. All of the books and all of the prophecies perfectly align with His reign because He alone is the Almighty, the Highest Himself, God in the flesh, the Savior of humanity. Let Him be praised.

The Twelfth Letter

"The word which God sent unto the children of Israel, preaching peace by Jesus Christ: he is Lord of all" (Acts 10:36).

"How shall we escape, if we neglect so great salvation; which at the first began to be spoken by the Lord, and was confirmed unto us by them that heard him; God also bearing them witness, both with signs and wonders, and with divers miracles, and gifts of the Holy Ghost, according to his will" (Hebrews 2:3-4).

"Ye are witnesses, and God also, how holily and justly and unblameably we behaved ourselves among you that believe; As you know how we exhorted and comforted and charged every one of you, as a father does his children, That you would walk worthy of God, who has called you unto his kingdom and glory. For this cause also thank we God, who has called you unto his kingdom and glory" (1 Thessalonians 2:10-13).

As God the Almighty has given us His Spirit, we the children must speak as He spoke because He has declared the truth about Himself. There are no mixed messages in God's Word, He is who the Bible says He is; Emperor Haile Sellassie The First is the Almighty. The characteristics of God are written in His Word, so when you read the Bible you can see God through His Word, for He Himself is the Word in action and in doing as the Word has said about His character, He reigned as a King and Governor over the world; His Name is One. Through the revelation we understand that what we see is the absolute truth and it will always stand as such throughout all eternity, so that the future generations in their time will also come into the fullness of the Lord's grace. Now, in all our doings as men one thing must remain paramount in our life and that is to seek God, to know Him, and to have a relationship with Him; for He made us and not we ourselves. If the Bible says that He sits in between the cherubims, He has Christ at His right hand side, He is clothed in Majesty, His vesture is dipped in blood, He wears the helmet of salvation, the crown of glory, He is a Great God and a great King above all gods, in His hand are the deep places of the earth, He shall be King over all the earth, the Governor of nations; then we must believe in Him who the Bible is talking about. All of this information is written about Him in His Word, so that we can find Him, if we seek after Him for He is not far from us; by Him we move and have our Being. Praise ye the Lord, Emperor Haile Sellassie The First of Ethiopia, He is the Highest who alone fulfilled all the prophecies pertaining to the Almighty.

All of us have to speak the truth to one another because His Majesty is the true and living God, in Revelation 11:15-17 it explains the full exposition that God will make Himself known to mankind, the scriptures have come to pass for He has revealed Himself. The Bible says before the day was, it was Him; there was no God formed before Him, neither shall there be after Him. God was manifest in the flesh, He has declared who He is, and the Most High is Emperor Haile Sellassie The First of Ethiopia Holy Mount Zion. He that was invisible has made Himself visible so that we may know Him who is true and His holy Prophet Jesus Christ. Blessed be Jah Rastafari Emperor Haile Sellassie The First, He alone is worthy to be Praised.

Conclusion

Renew your spirit through Christ. In the past you did not keep the commandments but now we have to repent and cleanse our spirit. The judgment of God is against all sinners and against all ungodliness. Do not let men deceive you, he that does not believe in Christ has the wrath of God abiding upon him forever. But if we are renewed, we should speak and walk as a new person who will follow after righteousness and holiness. For God is the record and we do everything through Christ. We renew ourselves to praise His Majesty on the seventh day in his blessed and sanctified name: Haile Sellassie The First. The wicked reject Christ and crucify him but we who accept Christ must do those things which please God. Now as we receive the Holy Spirit, to keep God's commandments, we have to be active in works and faith. Do not be slothful because in such the Lord takes no pleasure. Those who overcome will know the truth in Christ, that Emperor Haile Sellassie The First is the living God. He has established Zion and sent his Prophet into the world to preach what is acceptable. Prophecy has been fulfilled in modern times not thousands of years ago; that old Roman philosophy will leave us without any comprehension of the true meaning of the Bible. Idols have always been banned in the scriptures therefore the truth about God cannot be made by men. The Old Testament represents those blind philosophies that leave us void of the Lord. The New Testament is the truth in Christ; God manifest in the flesh for all to see.

Haile Sellassie The First sanctified the Sabbath day on November 2, 1930, by declaring and proving to be the King of Kings and Lord of Lords. His plan cannot be changed and God requires that we are knowledgeable of his commandments. Those who believe in his name become immune to the poisons of the earth. It becomes impossible to deceive them with worldly doctrines. If you worship Haile Sellassie The First then you have life. In Romans 8 it says that there is no condemnation to them who are in Christ. God's house has many mansions, meaning that anyone whose faith is sincere will be accepted into the Lord's kingdom; therefore we should not let the gentiles vex our spirits with their cavilings. "For what have I to do to judge them that are without? Do not you judge them that are within" (1 Corinthians 5:12). We are ministers, according to the dispensation of God which is given for the fulfillment of prophecy. Even the mystery that has been hidden from all ages but now is made manifest to his saints (Colossians 1:25-26). So that their hearts might be comforted, being knit together in love, unto all riches of the full assurance of understanding, to the acknowledgement of God: Emperor Haile Sellassie The First. In whom all the treasures of wisdom and knowledge are hid. And this I say, lest any man should beguile you with enticing words (Colossians 2:2-4). We have been chosen before the foundation of the world, that we should be holy and without blame before God. He has predestinated us unto the adoption of children by Jesus, to himself, according to the good pleasure of his will. Therefore we have redemption through the blood of Christ, the forgiveness of sins, according to the riches of his grace (Ephesians 1). The Son of God came to teach us that Emperor Haile Sellassie The First is the Almighty Creator; that you might be rooted and grounded in the truth because the whole family of heaven is named after him. Everlasting destruction is upon them who doubt God and his Prophet. The saints will bring vengeance and judgment; they got this authority from Haile Sellassie The First. What shall we then say to these things? If God is for us, who can be against us? (Romans 8:31).

Through the love of righteousness we do the Lord's work. His calling is for the advancement of humanity. David was chosen because of his heart, the Lord looked past his seven brothers who were all physically able but lacked wisdom. David had the same will and intentions of the Lord and was blessed because of his spirit. Therefore those who are clean escape those who live in error based upon their principals. Haile Sellassie The First did his work to be remembered and emulated by the future generations. He revealed his sanctified name on November 2, 1930. The dragon denies the truth and seeks to confuse the world. But we know that we are of God and have overcome the wicked. "We declare unto you good tidings, how that the promise which was made unto the fathers, God has fulfilled the same unto us their children" (Acts

13:32-33). "For which cause we faint not; for our light affliction, which is for a moment, worketh for us a far more exceeding and eternal weight of glory. We look not at the things which are seen, but at the things which are not seen. For the things which are seen are temporal, but the things which are not seen are eternal" (2 Corinthians 4:16-18). "Both he that sanctifieth and they who are sanctified are all one: for which cause he (Christ) is not ashamed to call them brethren" (Hebrews 2:11). Behold, Jesus and the children whom the Lord has given are for signs and wonders in Israel (Isaiah 8:18).

"Now the Spirit speaketh expressly, that in the latter times some shall depart from the faith, giving heed to seducing spirits and doctrines of devils. Speaking lies in hypocrisy, having their conscience seared with a hot iron. Forbidding to marry, and commanded to abstain from meats, which God has created to be received with thanksgiving by them who believe and know the truth. Exercise yourself rather in godliness and refuse profane and old wives fables. For bodily exercise profiteth little: but godliness is profitable unto all things. This is a faithful saying and worthy of all acceptance. Therefore we both labor and suffer reproach, because we trust in the living God, who is the Savior of all men, specially of those who believe. These things command and teach. Let no man despise you, but be thou an example to the believers, in word, in conversation, in charity, in spirit, in faith, in purity. Give attendance to reading and exhortation. Neglect not the gift that is in you, which was given to thee by prophecy, with the laying on of the hands of the presbytery. Meditate on these things and give yourself wholly to them. Take heed unto thyself, and unto the doctrine, continue in them, for in doing this you shall both save yourself, and those who hear you" (1 Timothy 4).

Bibliography

Byrne, Robert: *1,911 Best Things Anybody Ever Said*. Ballantine Books, 1988

Cornwell, John: *Hitler's Pope - The Secret History of Pius XII*. Viking, 1999

De Bono, Emilio: *La Preparazione E Le Prime Operazioni*. Instituto Nazionale Fascista di Cultura, Rome, 1937

Del Boca, Angelo: *The Negus -The Life and Death of the Last King of Kings*. Arcada Books, Ethiopia, 2012

Douglass, Frederick: *Narrative of the Life of Frederick Douglass an American Slave*. Public Domain, USA, 1845

Elia, A.R.: *Opening Round - The Tournament*. Mulebox Books, 2006

Eritrea Hails Her Sovereign. Imperial Ethiopian Government Press and Information Department, Ethiopia, 1952

Erlich, Haggai: *Alliance and Alienation - Ethiopia and Israel in the days of Haile Selassie*. Red Sea Press, USA, 2014

Fernand Rey, Sir Charles: *The Real Abyssinia*. Seeley Service & Co., University of Michigan, 1935

The Holy Bible. King James Version

Howell, Leonard P.: *The Promised Key.* Headstart Printing & Publishing Co. Ltd

Important Utterances of H.I.M. Emperor Haile Selassie I. Imperial Ethiopian Ministry of Information, Ethiopia, 1972

Leeman, Dr. Bernard: *The Ark of the Covenant - Evidence Supporting the Ethiopian Traditions.* Queen of Sheba University, 2010

Mack, Douglas R.A.: *From Babylon to Rastafari.* Research Associates School Times Publications & Frontline Distribution International Inc., 1999

Murrell, Nathaniel Samuel: *Afro-Caribbean Religions: An Introduction to Their Historical, Cultural, and Sacred Traditions.* Temple University Press, 2009, http://books.google.com/books?id=9h5KDRfZ-JgC&pg=PA305&lp-g=PA305&dq=italian+journalist+nyabinghi&source=bl&ots=O-4QTWDX1Ms&sig=NM7SCdoSME9yZbu_yfMULN-i2y-c&hl=en&sa=X&ei=orD4UMe0OYLe8ASDvoCoAw&sqi=2&ved=0C-C0Q6AEwAA#v=onepage&q=italian%20journalist%20 nyabinghi&f=false

The Noble Quran. Sahih International and Yusuf Ali Translation

Princess Asfa Yilma: *Haile Selassie: Emperor of Ethiopia.* One Drop Books, USA, 2002

Sarvepalli Radhakrishnan: *Foreign Affairs Record,* Volumes 11-12 (1965-1966). India Ministry of External Affairs, India

The Selected Speeches of His Imperial Majesty Haile Selassie I. Imperial Ethiopian Ministry of Information, Ethiopia, 1972

Simpson, James B.: *Simpson's Contemporary Quotations Revised Edition - Most Notable Quotes From 1950 to the Present.* William Morrow, 1997

Swami Prabhupada, A.C. Bhaktivedanta: *Bhagavad-Gita As It Is*, Second Edition. The Bhakitivedanta Book Trust International Inc., 2006

Tafia, Bairu: *The Coptic Encyclopedia*, Volume 4. Macmillan, 1991 http://ccdl.libraries.claremont.edu/cdm/singleitem/collection/cce/id/950/rec/1

Talbot, David Abner: *Contemporary Ethiopia*. Philosophical Library, 1952

Talbot, David Abner: *Haile Selassie I Silver Jubilee*. W.P. Van Stockum, 1955

The Wisdom of Rastafari. Forgotten Books, 2007 http://www.aren.org/prison/documents/african/16/16.pdf

Internet Sources

Biography on Atse Haile Selassie I http://www.ethiopianreview.com/content/6695

Biography on Emperor Haile Selassie I http://www.spokeo.com/Haile+Selassie+I+1

The Brooklyn DA, News Releases 2001 http://www.brooklynda.org/News/press_releases%202001.htm

The Bryan H. Roberts Gallery, March 2001 http://robertsgallery.com

Catholic League President William Donohue, October 11, 2000 http://www.catholicleague.org/justice-denied-in-brooklyn-church-vandal-case/

The Coronation of Haile Selassie I http://rastaites.com/HIM/coronation.html

CNS Commentary from the Free Congress Foundation, October 13, 2000, Nicholas Sanches

Eisenhower, Dwight D., Toasts of the President and Emperor Haile Selassie of Ethiopia, May 26, 1954, http://www.presidency.ucsb.edu/ws/?pid=9902.

Ethiopia fact file
http://news.bbc.co.uk/2/hi/programmes/this_world/3359367.stm

Haile Selassie, el polemico redentor de Sion
http://www.almamater.cu/sitio%20nuevo/paginas/voces/2010/marzo/selassie.html

Haile Selassie I Interview with Dr. Oswald Hoffman, December 25, 1968
http://en.wikisource.org/wiki/Haile_Selassie_Christmas_Interview_with_Dr._Oswald_Hoffman

Historic Papal Apology
http://www.sacredheart.edu/pages/12654_pope_john_paul_ii_asks_for_forgiveness_march_12_2000_.cfm

History of the Nyabinghi
http://www.suppressedhistories.net/articles/nyabingi/bagirwa.html

Lyndon B. Johnson, Remarks of Welcome at the White House to Haile Selassie I Emperor of Ethiopia, February 13, 1967
http://www.presidency.ucsb.edu/ws/index.php?pid=28572

The Plain Truth, December 1973
http://www.ababajanhoy.com/mag/Plain_Truth.pdf

Religious Affiliation of History's 100 Most Influential People
http://www.adherents.com/adh_influ.html

The Rise of a Movement
http://www.ghanaweb.com/GhanaHomePage/election2008/artikel.php?ID=91028

Speech delivered by Mr. Nelson Mandela at the launch of Mindset Network, July 16, 2003, http://db.nelsonmandela.org/speeches/pub_view.asp?pg=item&ItemID=NMS909&txtstr=education%20is%20the%20most%20 powerful

Newspapers & Periodicals

Boca Raton News. June 18, 1972, USA

Canarsie Courier. December 13, 2001, USA
http://m.canarsiecourier.com/news/2001-12-13/TopStories/008.html

Catholic League. October 11, 2000, USA

Catholic World News. May 18, 2000

The Chicago Tribune. Haile Selassie I Interview with Oriana Fallaci, June 24, 1973, USA

Evening Post. Volume CXXI Issue 2, January 3, 1936, New Zealand
http://paperspast.natlib.govt.nz/cgi-bin/
paperspast?a=d&d=EP19360103.2.77

Jamaica Gleaner. When Selassie talked about his Faith, December 16, 2003, Jamaica, http://jamaica-gleaner.com/gleaner/20031216/mind/
mind2.html

Los Angeles Times. World Report, February 9, 1993, USA
http://pqasb.pqarchiver.com/latimes/doc/281894226.
html?FMT=ABS&FMTS=ABS%3AFT&type=current&date=Feb+09%2C+1993&author=STANLEY+MEISLER&pub=Los+Angeles+-
Times+&edition&startpage&desc

New York Daily News. March 17, 2000, USA
http://articles.nydailynews.com/2000-03-17/
news/18129930_1_virgin-mary-vandal-churches

New York Daily News. March 27, 2000, USA
  http://articles.nydailynews.com/2000-03-27/
  news/18136201_1_statues-virgin-mary-restoration

New York Daily News. May 18, 2000, USA

New York Post. September 6, 2000, USA

New York Times. November 3, 1930, USA

New York Times. May 18, 2000, USA

New York Times. May 27, 2000, USA

New York Times. October 2, 2000, USA

Time Magazine. The Lion is Freed, September 8, 1975, USA

The Voice. Volume 114 No. 8,729, St. Lucia

The Voice of Ethiopia. Haile Selassie I Interview with the Editor, April 5,
  1948, Ethiopia

The Vancouver Sun. September 7, 1935, Canada

Yoga Journal. July-August 1983 Issue No. 51, USA

Video & Film

Demissie, Yemane I.: *Twilight Revelations: Episodes in the Life & Times of
  Emperor Haile Selassie.* Right Hand Pictures, 2009

Haile Selassie I Interview on Meet the Press. October 1963
  http://www.youtube.com/watch?v=7J4lgxXpe80

Prince Ermias Sahle-Selassie discussion at the Library of Congress. December 9, 2010, http://youtu.be/syw-Z6aH5tc

Teferra, Tikher: *His Imperial Majesty Emperor Haile Selassie I Man of the Millennium.* 4th Avenue Films, 2007